DOING
PHILOSOPHY
HISTORICALLY

Frontiers of Philosophy

Peter H. Hare, Series Editor

Advisory Board

DOING
PHILOSOPHY
HISTORICALLY

edited by Peter H. Hare

PROMETHEUS BOOKS
Buffalo, New York

Published 1988 by Prometheus Books
700 East Amherst Street, Buffalo, New York 14215
Copyright © 1988 Department of Philosophy
State University of New York at Buffalo

Library of Congress Cataloging-in-Publication Data

Doing philosophy historically.

  (Frontiers of philosophy)
  Bibliography: p.
  Includes index.
  1. Philosophy—History. 2. History—Philosophy.
I. Hare, Peter H. II. Series.
B29.D62   1988   109   87-32812
ISBN 0-87975-426-5

Printed in the United States of America

Acknowledgments

The conference whose proceedings compose this volume was funded by the National Endowment for the Humanities, the Marvin Farber Memorial Fund, the SUNY Conversations in the Disciplines, the SUNY/Buffalo Conferences in the Disciplines, and Department of Philosophy. Once again the Farber Fund provided the basis on which to seek additional conference funds, and in this case we were notably successful in doing so. Such generous support is much appreciated.

Next I wish to express appreciation to those who helped in the planning of the program. Richard Rorty gave a crucial piece of advice at an early stage. Jorge J. E. Gracia and Kenneth Barber aided at every stage of the planning, including selection of the papers.

I am grateful to those who ably chaired the sessions: Kah Kyung Cho, Richard H. Cox, Lee Dryden, Newton Garver, Rodolph Gasché, Carolyn Korsmeyer, Richard R. LaCroix, Kenneth Lucey, Peter Manicas, Herbert J. Nelson, and Lynn E. Rose. They also did much informally to contribute to discussion throughout the conference. My thanks also go to Timothy Madigan for organizing a Nietzschean entertainment that gave the conference a unique flavor.

Charlotte Hamilton was largely responsible for our success in obtaining funds. She was also indispensable at every stage, including the occasion of the conference itself, in making the myriad practical arrangements needed for a successful conference. Without her efforts it would have been a very different conference, if it had taken place at all.

As they have done with any activity of the Buffalo Philosophy Department for many years, Marie Fleischauer and Judith Wagner provided secretarial assistance unstintingly.

Contents

PART III. DESCARTES

PART IV. KANT

PART V. HEGEL

PART VI. THE SCOTTISH COMMONSENSE TRADITION

Introduction

Peter H. Hare

1

Although every decade of this century has seen both the development of original philosophical ideas and significant work in the history of philosophy, between roughly World War II and 1980 there were many English-speaking philosophers who were outspoken in expressing the view that philosophers, if they are to make progress in solving problems and thereby achieving knowledge, must practice philosophy independently of the *history of* philosophy. These philosophers (usually labeled "analytic") were seldom so rash as to claim that the history of philosophy has no value whatsoever; they conceded that the history of philosophy has *historical* value as part of the history of culture. They even conceded that the history of philosophy has philosophical value of a pedagogical sort; students, they allowed, can develop their powers of philosophical analysis by exercising them on dead philosophers—by dissecting philosophical cadavers, as it were. Philosophical analysts also recognized that the same writer could on some occasions practice original philosophical analysis and on other occasions write the history of ideas. But, in their understanding of the independence of doing original philosophy from writing the history of philosophy, they denied the possibility of simultaneously and responsibly engaging in these two activities in the same work.

The purism of the analysts was matched by the purism of some historically minded philosophers. While the analysts were insisting that works of original philosophy should not be contaminated by history, some historians of philosophy were insisting that works in the history of philosophy should not be contaminated by attempts to solve philosophical problems, by "presentism." From their historicist perspective, these philosophical historians charged the analysts with writing anachronistic history, when the analysts deigned to write history at all.

What must be noticed is that the analysts and the historicists agreed that a philosopher cannot at once make a contribution to the solution of current philosophical problems and a contribution to the history of thought. However, the conference whose proceedings compose this volume was organized in the belief that an increasing number of philosophers are coming to recognize that "doing philosophy historically" is possible, that the purism of both the analysts and the historicists is misguided. Those who share the rejection of such purism have widely differing views of how historical philosophy should be practiced, and it is hoped that some of the most important of those views are exhibited and discussed in the papers that follow.

2

For a number of reasons, Jonathan Bennett was invited to be the subject of the opening session of the conference. Bennett's work is among the most controversial and influential in the genre that was the focus of the conference; he is often cited by historicists as a practitioner of anachronistic history of philosophy, as someone who distorts earlier philosophy by examining it through the lens of analytic philosophy. Yet Bennett is an analytic philosopher who throughout his career has taken exceptional pains in writing about major figures in modern philosophy; history of philosophy is, for him, not merely a pedagogical sideline. Since the chief aim of the conference was to give doing philosophy historically a more thorough and fair hearing than it has been given hitherto, it seemed appropriate to begin by discussing a recent book by a philosopher whose work provocatively raises the relevant metaphilosophical issues.

By discussing Bennett's *A Study of Spinoza's Ethics,* Daniel Garber reflects on why and how the history of philosophy is important to the enterprise of arriving at philosophical truth. Bennett, Garber suggests, considers history to be a storehouse of materials useful in the search for philosophical knowledge. These materials include instructive mistakes as well as successful arguments and true positions. However, Bennett's view that the history of philosophy is valuable primarily as a means to the end of finding philosophical truth is an approach not without costs. After describing those costs, Garber assures us that he considers Bennett's approach to be, on balance, a valuable one.

Garber suggests, however, that an approach in which a philosopher's work is understood in terms of its historical context is also of value. If one believes, as Bennett does, that a greater yield of philosophical truth usually accompanies greater historical accuracy in describing Spinoza's views, such "*historical* reconstruction" will sometimes produce results very like what Bennett's method produces. But Garber thinks it is important to understand that historical reconstruction, while not a method that should *replace* Bennett's, is one that can complement his by providing certain *philosophical* benefits that even Bennett's self-consciously philosophical approach does not provide. He argues that "disinterested history" is not only of value as cultural history but also indirectly aids our search for philosophical truth by making us aware of philosophical *questions* that Bennett's method is unlikely to uncover. Garber illustrates this point by describing the seventeenth-century conception of philosophy and its relation to science.

In his response, Bennett expresses enthusiasm for the view that the history of philosophy raises questions, but he cannot find genuine contrast between that view and his own since he has never taken himself to be exclusively concerned with answers. Bennett appears to find no serious fault with what Garber describes and practices as "disinterested history." Although the image of Spinoza's intellectual character that guides Bennett's reconstruction is different from Garber's, he does not consider his reconstruction to be more or less disinterested than Garber's. Perhaps methodologically all that divides Garber and Bennett is that Garber believes that more contextual detail is often useful in raising philosophical questions; Bennett seems to think that in delving into such contextual details one reaches a point of diminishing returns sooner than Garber supposes. Garber's disinterested history appears to be a form of doing philosophy historically that incorporates more contextual detail than some other forms; it may not be any more disinterested than Bennett's approach.

While Jonathan Rée expresses a preference for "a more contextual and antiquarian approach" than Bennett's, he recognizes that no simple contrast between "anachronism" and "historical fidelity" can be made. "[M]eticulous historical accuracy may distort a work . . . while reckless anachronism may uncover unsuspected depths."

In some detail, Rée contrasts his own rhetorical or "romantic" reading of Spinoza's *Ethics* with Bennett's treatment of it as a "hypothetico-deductive" system. He does not claim that Bennett's reading is "illegitimate or unilluminating" but that it involves some historical misrepresentations and does not invalidate the reading Rée favors. Despite his sympathy with historicists like Ayres, Rée is sympathetic also with doing philosophy historically: "'[H]istory or philosophy?' is a false dilemma." Rée's quarrel with Bennett is not with Bennett's doing philosophy historically but rather with his apparent presumption that there are not other equally legitimate ways (e.g., the romantic) of combining history and philosophy in discussing Spinoza's work.

In response, while Bennett assures Rée that he respects literary readings of Spinoza, he is not persuaded that his hypothetico-deductive reading misrepresents Spinoza in the respects Rée claims. He also will not concede that his reading is less exegetical than the readings of those whose goal is the understanding of an author's text in his own terms—an impossible goal in Bennett's view. Although Bennett readily admits that his interpretation is not exhaustive, he is not prepared to concede that his interpretation is anachronistic. Indeed, he thinks that he can give examples where partisans of a contextual approach get history wrong.

Bennett explains that when dealing with a genius one is likely to discover philosophical truths by finding out what the philosopher actually meant. To do so is to treat historical accuracy as an *instrumental* value. It appears that among those doing philosophy historically: (1) some consider philosophical illumination valuable primarily as a means to historical accuracy; (2) others consider historical accuracy valuable primarily as a means to philosophical illumination; and (3) still others consider both historical accuracy and philosophical illumination to have much of both intrinsic and instrumental value. Perhaps Rée can be identified with the first position, Bennett with the second, and Garber with the third. These forms of doing philosophy historically can be distinguished both from analytic purism and from purist historicism that considers the search for philosophical illumination to have negative, or at least negligible, instrumental value as a means to the intrinsic value of historical accuracy.

3

The remaining six sections of this volume are arranged in the chronological order of the subjects of the papers. Although some metaphilosophical analysis is included, the authors largely illustrate doing philosophy historically in various periods and traditions. The genre is best illuminated by a balance between specific examples and metaphilosophical analysis.

Daniel A. Dombrowski begins the section on ancient philosophy with a discussion of Richard Rorty's treatment of Plato. Dombrowski argues that in important respects Rorty's account of Plato is historically inaccurate, so seriously inaccurate that Plato appears as a villain in a book in which he should properly be one of the heroes. With some qualifications, Rorty considers Plato to be the founder of the foundationalist tradition that he wishes to replace by a conception of philosophy as edification. Dombrowski contends that philosophy as edification can be found not only in *Socrates;* there is, he says, much more edifying philosophy in Plato himself than Rorty allows.

Charles Griswold, in his commentary, after making some remarks on Rorty's conception of philosophy and its relation to its past, finds historical faults in both Rorty's and Dombrowski's versions of Plato. Although he shares Dombrowski's belief that Plato does not have the conception of philosophy supposed by Rorty, he finds problems with Dombrowski's use of the *Sophist* to establish that claim. Furthermore, he doubts that Rortyan philosophy can be found in either Plato or Socrates.

Next in the ancient philosophy section we have a paper by Jorgé J. E. Gracia that begins with the most sustained discussion of philosophical historiography in this volume. The arguments contained in that compact treatise cannot be summarized here. Suffice it to quote the propositions he defends: "(1) that philosophy and its history are not incompatible, (2) that the history of philosophy is not necessary for philosophy, although it is very useful for it, and (3) that philosophy is necessary for the history of philosophy."

It is interesting to note that, although this view of the relation between philosophy and its history contrasts clearly with such views as historicism and Hegelianism, it is not immediately clear how it provides a basis for choosing between the varying approaches of Garber, Rée, and Bennett, who are likely to accept all three of Gracia's propositions. Perhaps a clue can be found in what Gracia has to say about Veatch's work on Aristotle.

Contrary to Veatch's description of his own book, Gracia maintains that *Aristotle* is a work in the history of philosophy that makes some use of philosophy rather than being primarily a work of philosophy. He thinks that Veatch misunderstands the nature of his work because he has a mistaken notion of the history of philosophy, according to which interpretation and evaluation (i.e., philosophy) are excluded. Also, because of this mistaken notion, Veatch does not feel obliged to provide the historical detail that any convincing work in the history of philosophy must contain.

Consideration of Veatch's *Aristotle* is instructive for philosophical historiography despite Veatch's modest intention of popular pedagogy. Historicists are fond of using such books to discredit the genre of doing philosophy historically. Having criticized Veatch's history, they tell us that that is precisely what we can expect from those so misguided as to work in this genre.

Among the positions of Rée, Bennett, and Garber as I have described them, which, then, would Gracia choose? His criticism of Veatch suggests that he would side with Garber. He would consider both historical accuracy and philosophical illumination to have much of both intrinsic and instrumental value in doing philosophy historically.

Veatch, in response, agrees that to do philosophy historically well one must do well both one's history and one's philosophy and that doing one well involves doing the other well. However, he understands that Gracia also holds that ultimately historical judgments and philosophical judgments are the same. It is not clear on what remarks of Gracia he bases that claim. Veatch also surprisingly attributes to Gracia the view that, when doing philosophy historically, one makes philosophical judgments on the basis of historical evidence only.

Robert Turnbull presents the second commentary on Veatch's work. Although he expresses sympathy with Veatch's support for the commonsensical aspects of Aristotle's philosophy, he thinks that there are serious faults in Aristotle's ontology that Aristotelians like Veatch should recognize. The bulk of Turnbull's paper is a dense critique of Aristotle's use of what Turnbull calls "philosophical entities." Instead of commenting in detail on Veatch or discussing philosophical historiography, Turnbull gives us an extended example of doing philosophy historically. By presenting central elements of an analytic ontology in a critique of Aristotle, he shows us how philosophy is done historically in one branch of the analytic tradition.

In reply, Veatch expresses pleasure that Turnbull does not take exception to characterizing Aristotle's philosophy as commonsensical but is unhappy with Turnbull's finding fault with Aristotle's realistic metaphysics. Although Veatch agrees that Aristotle's science is outmoded, he is not convinced by Turnbull's arguments that Aristotle's ontology is outmoded also.

The last part of the section on ancient philosophy consists of a paper by Daniel W. Graham on anachronism in Aristotle together with commentary by Josiah B. Gould. Graham discusses what is perhaps the most celebrated and—for better or worse—the most influential piece of history of philosophy ever written: Aristotle's history of the Presocratics in Book A of the *Metaphysics*. Although the anachronism of this history is notorious, Graham provocatively argues that there are important senses in which anachronism in the history of philosophy is legitimate and, consequently, that Harold Cherniss and others are unjustified in being severely critical of Aristotle.

Graham suggests that Aristotle is writing "a schematic history" in which he is not trying to describe the thought of each Presocratic by itself but is showing how the thought of each "fits into a larger historical pattern," a pattern in the development of concepts of cause. In this genre of history of philosophy, Graham thinks, philosophers' intentions can be appropriately ignored and concepts can be anachronistically—but legitimately—applied.

Gould, after remarking that what Graham defends as cases of legitimate anachronism are not cases of anachronism at all, expresses concern about the relation between schematic history of philosophy and "get-it-right" history of philosophy. The former genre, he says, does not replace the latter; instead it presupposes that the latter has already been done, and Cherniss rightly holds that "get-it-right" history cannot be found in Aristotle. Unfortunately, Aristotle's history was often *taken* by subsequent historians as "get-it-right" history and as such had the pernicious influence Cherniss describes. Graham cannot, Gould tells us, reasonably use a rough match between Aristotle's accounts of these philosophers and modern accounts as justification for considering Aristotle's accounts accurate since modern accounts, Cherniss shows, were derived from Aristotle's.

Although Gould thinks Graham's rejection of Cherniss's critique of Aristotle is unjustified, he expresses sympathy for a genre of history of philosophy akin to Graham's schematic history. If not taken as a replacement for "get-it-right" history, this additional type can be valuable, Gould believes.

What is the relation between the schematic history of philosophy that Graham finds in Aristotle and the genre of doing philosophy historically? As Graham sometimes describes Aristotle's motivation, it does not appear that Aristotle was seeking *philosophical* illumination as well as historical illumination. If Aristotle wished merely to see his theory of causes as the end point of a rational pattern of development, he was not seeking philosophical as well as historical truth. On the other hand, if he sought additionally to improve his understanding of the nature of causation by criticizing his predecessors, Aristotle was not merely doing a distinctive sort of history of philosophy—he was doing philosophy as well as history of philosophy (i.e., doing philosophy historically). As I am using our title phrase, to count as doing philosophy historically, it is not enough that a history of philosophy require the use of philosophy. In my view, *any* history of philosophy that deserves to be taken seriously satisfies that condition.

4

In recent decades Descartes has attracted large numbers of practitioners of doing philosophy historically. Perhaps that can be explained partly by the fact that analytic philosophers skilled in mathematical logic and trained to respect the physical sciences expect to find much philosophical truth in the historical study of the work of someone who was a great mathematician and a distinguished physical scientist as well as the founder of modern philosophy.

In Part Three are three sets of two papers each on Descartes. In the first set Georges Dicker reconstructs Descartes's argument for mind-body dualism in order to show both its power and the limits of its implications. As Dicker interprets the argument, it satisfies the opponents of materialism by showing "the logical possibility of the mind's existing without the body, and its consequent nonidentity with the body," while disappointing the opponents of materialism by its failure to *"show that it is causally possible for conscious states to exist apart from physical states."*

Dicker has taken pains to read closely texts now centuries old, and the argument reconstructed and evaluated is directly relevant to today's philosophical problems. In the current search for a solution to the mind-body problem, the success or failure of Descartes's arguments make a difference.

While José Benardete in his commentary applauds the historical accuracy of Dicker's reconstruction of the argument and fully appreciates its contemporary relevance, he does not think it succeeds even partially in demonstrating the falsity of materialism.

In the second set of Descartes papers, Frederick P. Van De Pitte explains what he takes doing philosophy historically to be and gives an example of it by discussing the interpretation of Descartes's mathematical method and how it responded successfully to the problems of empiricism before the struggle between rationalism and empiricism was joined. Since we are still wrestling with the problems of empiricism, Descartes's view, Van De Pitte argues, can provide a solution to some of today's philosophical problems. We can get hold of this solution to a present philosophical problem, he claims, only if we can manage to recover the historically correct perspective from which to view Descartes's work. He describes how this is done. Interestingly, he believes that Descartes's contemporaries did not view his work in the appropriate perspective and consequently were not convinced by his argument. Historicists, of course, have always urged us to read a philosophical text from the perspective of well-informed contemporaries. Apparently, Van De Pitte wishes us somehow to be even more historical than the historicists have demanded. However, he thinks it often best not to attempt to give the full details of the context—"minimal reconstruction of the context is sometimes heuristically preferable to the very complex."

Although Richard A. Watson believes that the standard interpretation of Descartes is more correct than Van De Pitte's, in his commentary he focuses on Van De Pitte's methodological recommendations. He is puzzled by the fact that Van De Pitte does not follow his own recommendation to give "minimal reconstruction." Instead Van De Pitte takes pains to give the contextual details needed to explain how Descartes's contemporaries and subsequent philosophers came to misunderstand him.

In the final set of two papers on Descartes, a discussion of omnipotence and modality by Lilli Alanen is accompanied by a comment by George I. Mavrodes, It may appear that such a discussion can be philosophically as well as historically illuminating only to those who accept a theistic framework. Despite the constant references to God, the problems addressed concerning the nature of possibility and necessity do not depend on theological assumptions. As Alanen says, the solution of these problems that she attributes to Descartes "raises interesting and important questions concerning the nature and foundation of rationality and conceivability." Since this theory of modality is akin to the modern "conventionalist" or "linguistic" views, those views will be strengthened if Descartes's theory can be shown not to be incoherent or irrationalist, as Alanen argues. Mavrodes's contribution to the discussion is the proposal of "an anti-cartesian thesis." He hopes the critical examination of this thesis, in contrast to Descartes's alleged theory, will help illuminate the nature of modality as well as the question of what theory can be reasonably attributed to Descartes.

However, there are difficult questions of historical interpretation. Scholars of Descartes have given varying accounts of his theory of the creation of eternal truths. Alanen gives as much attention to defending her interpretation against those scholars who read the relevant texts differently as she gives to a consideration of the philosophical merits of what she takes to be Descartes's theory.

5

Like Descartes, Kant has received much recent attention from those working in the genre that is the focus of this volume. Part Four consists of three papers on varying aspects of Kant's epistemology/metaphysics.

John Biro argues that, contrary to what Strawson and other commentators suppose, Kant's notion of transcendental synthesis is not a philosophical embarrassment that was a consequence of an obsolete scientific framework. Transcendental synthesis can be understood, he thinks, in terms of recent neuroscience, and he offers historical evidence in correspondence that Kant was open to the possibility of such a link with neurophysiology, even if he did not see how the account could work in terms of the science of his day. If Biro's reasoning is even roughly right, it has important implications both historically and philosophically. Historically, we might come to understand Kant's philosophy as much less in conflict with physicalism than we had hitherto supposed. Philosophically, by coming to understand important respects in which neurophysiological accounts of cognitive processes are compatible with Kant's transcendental psychology, we might find the philosophical case for naturalism strengthened.

The second Kant paper also discusses transcendental psychology. David G. Stern gives an account of the numerous problems encountered when one tries to use Kant's apparatus to solve Kant's problem of understanding how knowledge of the world is possible. He argues that, if Kant retains his transcendental psychology, he is burdened with a discredited faculty psychology. However, if Kant jettisons his dubious psychology, he has other serious problems in making the remaining apparatus do the job. Unlike Biro, Stern does not believe that neuroscience can help and consequently does not reach conclusions that strengthen the case for naturalized epistemology.

In the final Kant paper James Van Cleve reconstructs and assesses an argument for monadism found in a little-studied appendix to the *Critique of Pure Reason*. Interestingly, it is an argument that Kant reconstructed from Leibniz in order to assess its implications for his own metaphysics; Van Cleve takes as material for his doing philosophy historically a piece of work in which Kant was engaging in the same genre.

To the usual problems of historical reconstruction are added difficult problems of logical reconstruction. Van Cleve finds it necessary to lay out the argument step-by-step for detailed examination. Just this sort of elaborate logical analysis of short passages in a large work is what historicists often dismiss as not to be taken seriously as history of philosophy. However, practitioners of doing philosophy historically consider that the presence of logical as well as historical complexities does not make the reconstruction any less legitimate as history, and in cases such as this one the difficulties are worth overcoming because fundamental issues in metaphysics are at stake.

6

Part Five is devoted to what is perhaps the most radical type of doing philosophy historically, a type not prevalent in the English-speaking world. Kenneth L. Schmitz offers an account of Hegel's conception of the relation between philosophy and its history. As he explains Hegel, philosophy is the unity of all philosophies; the history of philosophy is to be studied in the expectation that the totality of all philosophies will together make sense: "the history of philosophy is itself in some way *constitutive* of philosophy." This view of the history of philosophy as inseparable from philosophy must be distinguished from the more common views. Usually, as we have seen, it is thought that, while the history of philosophy can have much instrumental value in the discovery of philosophical truth, it is not, except in some trivial sense, necessary to all developments in philosophical knowledge; much less is the history of philosophy considered constitutive of philosophy.

James Lawler and Vladimir Shtinov in their commentary on Schmitz attempt to explain more fully Hegel's views on the relations between philosophy and history. Carefully considering the question of how to understand passages in which Hegel seems to consider philosophical logic as independent of, and presupposed by, the study of history, they use Hegel's criticism of Schelling as an illustration of how Hegel conceived of history as intrinsic to philosophy. The history of philosophy is seen as a series of negations of earlier positions, but each negated position contributes positively to all subsequent positions. Although they more than Schmitz wish to stress the role of negation in the Hegelian conception of philosophy in relation to its history, they recognize that "in the final Hegelian systematic conception . . . the negative tends to give way to the positive, and the historical yields to the logical."

7

Todd L. Adams and Phillip Cummins in Part Six discuss the treatment of the freedom and determinism issue in the Scottish commonsense tradition. Because a number of prominent contemporary philosophers have much in common with this tradition, it has increasingly attracted commentators who hope that by combining historical and philosophical analyses they can illuminate such perennial problems as those concerning agency.

As Adams explains, the commonsense philosophers, starting with Reid, tried to show that the concept of cause is not applicable to human action by showing that motives are not causes. Although Reid did not supply criteria to distinguish motives from causes, his successors interestingly discussed what those criteria might be. Adams finds Henry P. Tappan especially impressive on this point, and most of Adams's paper is a sympathetic exposition of the thought of that nineteenth-century American philosopher.

Adams rebuts some objections to Tappan's agency theory, but time limits did not permit extended argument for the theory. In his commentary Cummins, instead of attempting to contribute to the purely historical side of the discussion, tries to formulate the relevant arguments in more detail so that we can assess their plausibility more confidently. He concludes that Tappan's arguments fail to establish that motives are not causes and consequently are not good reasons to accept indeterminism.

8

The final section of the volume contains discussions of recent philosophy. Edward H. Madden and Gerald E. Myers consider Myers's just-published book on the American pragmatist William James. Frithjof Rodi and Rudolf Lüthe discuss recent historical philosophy in Germany.

Like Bennett's book on Spinoza discussed at the beginning of this volume, Myers's *William James, His Life and Thought,* is respected by many as a model of how to practice philosophy in the genre that is the focus of this collection. Although Madden makes it plain that he shares that assessment of Myers's book, before evaluating the work in detail he wishes to dissociate himself from the claim that this is the *only* appropriate way of writing the history of philosophy; he also values histories in which "the truth or falsity of past claims and systems is never at issue." This is an important point, which would likely be echoed by every contributor to this volume. There is no good reason to regard doing philosophy historically as having a monopoly on legitimacy in historical inquiry about past thought. In fact, Madden thinks that Myers felicitously blends the two approaches.

Since the book is a large one about a philosopher of impressive scope, it is necessary for Madden to be selective in his comments. On each issue chosen for discussion Madden raises questions either about the historical accuracy of Myers's description of James's views or about his estimate of the truth of those views, and often about both. This he does not with the intention of withdrawing his assessment of the book as a notable achievement, but with the aim of stimulating Myers (and others) to engage in further dialogue with James.

One of the several topics Myers discusses in his reply is James's intuitionism in ethics. In response to Madden's doubts about James's principle of negative utilitarianism being intuitive in character, Myers emphasizes that James had in mind an "undogmatic," "dynamic, forward-looking" intuition that is "communally tested." However, Myers readily admits that he is still unsure how far James's negative utilitarianism is defensible; his exchange with Madden on this question nicely illustrates the blending of questions of historical interpretation with questions of truth.

Unquestionably, from Hegel to the present there has been more doing philosophy historically and more philosophical historiography in Germany than anywhere else. Rodi and Lüthe are here able only to scratch the surface of this vast literature.

Building on the work of such influential thinkers as Dilthey and Gadamer, Rodi wishes to clarify the "articulative tension" between the language of the tradition in which a philosopher is working and the language needed to formulate new ideas. Tradition, he suggests, both supports original philosophizing by providing a conceptual framework in which new questions can be asked and hinders original philosophy by "the onesidedness of its concepts." Perhaps reflecting a tradition of dialectical method in Germany, Rodi views a combination of contrasting philosophical approaches as exhibiting "productive tension"; whereas Anglo-Saxon philosophers are often inclined to expect such combinations to produce incoherent and useless results.

Lüthe responds to those skeptical of the legitimacy of combinations of history and philosophy. Distinguishing between "productive assimilation," where the emphasis is on original philosophizing, and "objective reconstruction," where the emphasis is on historical accuracy for its own sake, he suggests that both approaches are legitimate, and their integration is legitimate as well.

9

Readers will be quick to recognize the gaps in this volume's coverage of the chosen topic. Few examples of moral philosophy and social/political philosophy are presented. Less glaring but still regrettable is the lack of examples in logic and philosophy of science, areas in which the genre has been thriving recently. Important periods (e.g., the medieval) have also been neglected, and it hardly needs to be said that non-Western philosophy has been ignored altogether. I can only plead that without fragmentation comprehensiveness was not feasible in a short conference on such a basic topic. However, it is hoped that the papers included, emphasizing metaphysics and epistemology, are sufficiently varied to be a more extensive exhibit and discussion of the genre than has been published previously. For too long have discussions of the genre been confined to hostile treatments buried in general treatises on philosophical historiography or in collections of work in the history of philosophy edited by scholars of a historicist persuasion. This volume is intended to stimulate readers to begin a careful and fair examination of a mode of philosophizing that has come to play a major role on the philosophical scene.

BIBLIOGRAPHY NOTE

Those wishing to read in recent philosophical historiography may find the following books and articles of interest:

Dauenhauer, Bernard P., ed. *At the Nexus of Philosophy and History.* Athens and London: The University of Georgia Press, 1987.

Galgan, Gerald. "What's Special about the History of Philosophy." *American Philosophical Quarterly* 24, no. 1 (1987).

Geldsetzer, Lutz. "Fragen der Hermeneutik der Philosophiegeschichtsschreibung." In *La Storiografia Filosofica e la sua Storia.* Padova: Antenore, 1982.

Graham, Daniel. "The Structure of Explanation in the History of Philosophy." *Metaphilosophy,* forthcoming.

Holland, A. J., ed. *Philosophy, Its History and Historiography.* Dordrecht: D. Reidel, 1985.

Kelley, Donald R. "Horizons of Intellectual History: Retrospect, Circumspect, Prospect." *Journal of the History of Ideas* 48, no. 1 (1987).

King, Preston, ed. *The History of Ideas: An Introduction to Method.* Totowa: Barnes & Noble, 1983.

Krämer, Hans. "Funktions—und Reflectionsmöglichkeiten de Philosophiehistorie. Vorschläge zu ihrer wissenschaftstheoretischen Ortsbestimmung." *Zeitschrift für allgemeine Wissenschaftstheorie* 16, no. 1 (1985).

Kristeller, Paul Oskar. "Philosophy and its Historiography." *Journal of Philosophy* 82, no. 11 (1985).

Kuklick, Bruce. "Studying the History of American Philosophy." *Transactions of the Charles S. Peirce Society: A Quarterly Journal in American Philosophy* 18, no. 1 (1982).

Mandelbaum, Maurice. *Philosophy, History, and the Sciences: Selected Critical Essays.* Baltimore: Johns Hopkins University Press, 1984.

Murphey, Murray G. "Toward an Historicist History of American Philosophy." *Transactions of the Charles S. Peirce Society: A Quarterly Journal in American Philosophy* 15, no. 1 (1979).

O'Hear, Anthony. "The History that is in Philosophy." *Inquiry* 28 (1985).

Philosophiques 1, no. 1 (April, 1974). Articles on the history of ideas and the history of philosophy.

Pitt, Joseph C., ed. *The Role of History in and for Philosophy.* Synthesis 67, no. 1 (1986).

Popkin, Richard H. "Philosophy and the History of Philosophy." *Journal of Philosophy* 82, no. 11 (1985).

Rée, Jonathan, Michael Ayers, and Adam Westoby. *Philosophy and its Past.* Hassocks, Sussex: The Harvester Press, 1978.

Rorty, Richard, J. B. Schneewind, and Quentin Skinner, eds. *Philosophy in History: Essays on the Historiography of Philosophy.* Cambridge: Cambridge University Press, 1984.

Sass, Hans-Martin. "Philosophische Positionen in der Philosophiegeschichtsschreibung. Ein Forschungsbereicht." *Deutsche Vierteljahresschrift für Literaturwissenschaft und Geistesgeschichte* 86, Heft 3 (1972).

Schmidt, Alfred. *History and Structure. An Essay on Hegelian-Marxist and Structuralist Theories of History.* Cambridge: MIT Press, 1981.

Shapiro, Gary. "Canons, Careers, and Campfollowers: Randall and the Historiography of Philosophy." *Transactions of the Charles S. Peirce Society: A Quarterly Journal in American Philosophy* 23, no. 1 (1987).

Thayer, H. S. "The Philosophy of History and the History of Philosophy: Some Reflections on the Thought of John Herman Randall, Jr. *Transactions of the Charles S. Peirce Society: A Quarterly Journal in American Philosophy* 23, no. 1 (1987).

The above was compiled by Craig Walton, the Editor, and other participants in the conference as a supplement to Walton's "Bibliography of the Historiography and Philosophy of the History of Philosophy," in *International Studies in Philosophy* 19, (1977).

Part One
Raising the Issues

Does History Have a Future?

Some Reflections on Bennett and Doing Philosophy Historically

Daniel Garber

The history of philosophy seems to play a very significant role in the actual practice of philosophy; historical figures come up again and again in the courses we had to take, both as undergraduates and as graduate students, and historical figures continue to come up again and again in the papers we read, the courses we teach, the conferences we attend. Philosophy seems to be a subject that is obsessed with its past, but it is more than just an obsession. Most of us here would agree that understanding the history of philosophy is somehow important to *doing* philosophy, that we are better philosophers for knowing the history of our subject. I think that this is true. As philosophers, we have an obligation to ourselves to reflect on this fact: *why* is history important to our enterprise, and *how* is history important to our enterprise?

This is what I would like to do in this short talk, make some observations about the ways in which history of philosophy can and does influence the practice of philosophy. I shall begin by discussing the view of history found in Jonathan Bennett's recent and already enormously influential book, *A Study of Spinoza's Ethics.* I have chosen to talk about that book in good part because it is, I think, the best representative of a certain genre of writing in the history of philosophy; Bennett nicely articulates a view of the history of philosophy that is widespread among writers on the subject, particularly those writing in English. Bennett's view, widely shared, is that history is important because studying historical figures can teach us philosophy; in the history of philosophy we have a storehouse of arguments and positions worth taking seriously as philosophy, worth discussing and debating in the same way the work of a very good contemporary philosopher is worth discussing and debating. I shall not really criticize Bennett's view of the matter. There is a sense in which he and the multitude of other philosophers and historians of philosophy who share his view are absolutely correct. But, I shall argue, Bennett makes use of only a portion of the riches that history has to offer. In the second part of this paper I shall try to sketch and illustrate a somewhat different conception of the use of history in philosophy that complements the conception Bennett offers.

HISTORY AS STOREHOUSE

I would like to begin my discussion by outlining what I take to be Jonathan Bennett's attitude toward history in his recent book, A Study of Spinoza's Ethics. My interest in the book will be largely metaphilosophical (or, perhaps, metahistorical); though I have some disagreements with Bennett on matters of substance, I shall do my best not to drag them in here and muddy the waters.

Early in the book, Bennett gives the reader ample indication of the nature of his interest in Spinoza. "I am not writing biography," he notes; "I want to understand the pages of the Ethics in a way that will let me learn philosophy from them."[1] A bit later in the book, Bennett indicates that his interest is "not with Spinoza's mental biography but with getting his help in discovering philosophical truth."[2] At the end of the book Bennett writes:

> The courtly deference which pretends that Spinoza is always or usually right, under some rescuing interpretation, is one thing; it is quite another to look to him, as I have throughout this book, as a teacher, one who can help us to see things which we might not have seen for ourselves. That is showing him a deeper respect, but also holding him to a more demanding standard.[3]

Bennett's interest here is clear: it is finding philosophical truth and avoiding philosophical falsehood that he is after, and the study of Spinoza is supposed to help us in this search. What he says about Spinoza presumably holds more generally for the study of other figures in the history of philosophy. So conceived, the history of philosophy is a kind of storehouse of positions and arguments, positions and arguments that we can use as guides or inspirations to the positions we should take, or illustrations of dead ends that we should avoid.

This last provision is important. The point is not that Spinoza (or any other historical figure) will simply hand us philosophical truth on a platter, arguments or positions that we can immediately adopt without change. Bennett's Spinoza often makes mistakes, and bad ones; hardly an argument in the Ethics can stand without some correction. Yet we can learn from Spinoza even when he is wrong (or, at least we *usually* can; Bennett seems unsure about whether anything can be learned from the mistakes Spinoza makes when discussing the immortality of the mind).[4] Bennett writes:

> I do say that Spinoza's total naturalistic program fails at both ends and in the middle; as though he undertook to build a sturdy mansion all out of wood, and achieved only a rickety shack using bricks, as well as wood. But his attempt was a work of genius; and a thorough, candid study of it can be wonderfully instructive. The failures have at least as much to teach as the successes, if one attends not only to *where* Spinoza fails but *why*.[5]

Bennett completes the thought a few pages later:

> I spoke of how much we can learn from Spinoza's successes and, especially, his failures. It is his minimalism that makes his work so instructive. If you set a mechanical genius to build an automobile engine out of a Meccano set, you won't get a working engine from him, but as you watch him fail you will learn a lot about automobile engines.[6]

(In giving these quotations I don't mean to imply that they are transparently intelligible or true on their face, but I would like to postpone those questions for the moment.)

What does the history of philosophy look like from Bennett's point of view? We begin by trying to reconstruct the arguments the philosopher we are studying gave, trying to follow the train of thought he followed. But our ultimate goal is philosophical truth, and it is with that in mind that we must approach our reconstruction; we must carefully examine the truth of the premises, the validity of the inferential steps, and with a cold and unsentimental eye, judge the truth or falsity of the conclusion and the adequacy of the means by which the conclusion was reached. If appropriate, we might make *some* attempt to patch up the argument, adding new premises, substituting better premises for worse, trying a new path to the conclusion in question, or whatever. This is, I think, a fair representation of what Bennett is doing in the Spinoza book.

All of this is interesting and, in an important sense, valuable activity. But if we are to follow Bennett and hold that the history of philosophy is valuable primarily insofar as it helps us to find philosophical truth, in some more or less direct sense, then there are certain consequences we must accept.

First of all, if we insist on philosophical truth as the *only* motivation for studying history, then a great deal of the history of philosophy may turn out to be marginal to the philosopher. Bennett would agree that few historical figures have any large store of doctrines or arguments that we would now consider live candidates for truth or even approximate truth. There are those who study Aristotle or Saint Thomas, Kant or Marx, because they think that at least some of what they wrote is close to being true, and because they believe that attention to their writings can help lead us directly to insights we would not otherwise have. But how many study Descartes or Leibniz or Spinoza for this reason? The noble attempts of the past, one might argue, are instructive in their *failures*. But while failures *can* be instructive, a few can go a long way. The student architect can learn to fit the building to the available materials and know the strengths and weaknesses of both from the building that collapsed. But one learns to design successful buildings by studying *successful* buildings, not just failures. Having had a deprived childhood, I'm not sure I know exactly what a Meccano set is, but if it is what I think it is, I doubt that I could learn much about automobile engines by watching someone try to build one from a Meccano set, no matter how talented one might be. Similarly, the philosopher must learn to recognize a bad argument and must be trained to avoid the mistakes people make. This is only a small portion of one's philosophical education, which, I think, should focus on positions and arguments that people think are live candidates for the truth, at least insofar as one is being trained to seek philosophical truth. Bennett may overestimate what we can learn directly from failed arguments and programs. Insofar as the great majority of historical arguments, positions, and programs are failures when judged against the high standard of philosophical truth (as we see it), the study of the history of philosophy may have less to contribute to philosophy than Bennett seems to think, and less than we historians would like.

There is another feature of Bennett's position worth drawing out. Bennett's position has the danger of distorting the history of philosophy. First of all, insofar as we regard history of philosophy as contributing to the discovery of philosophical truth, we are led to emphasize those portions of a philosopher's work that speak to our interests, that address our conception of where philosophical truth is to be found, leaving other aspects of the work aside, thereby mutilating what may be a unified and systematic point of view. Bennett has *not* done any such thing to Spinoza, but one can call to mind the numerous commentaries on Descartes and anthologies of his writing that barely mention his work in mathematics, physics, or biology; the accounts of Pascal that focus on the wager argument without indicating its larger context; books like Anthony Kenny's little book *Aquinas,* in the Past Masters series, or John Mackie's *Problems from Locke,* which quite self-consciously use standards of contemporary relevance to choose what to discuss and what to ignore. In each case, the focus on philosophical *truth* distorts our *historical* understanding of the figure and his position. But there is another way in which historical distortions may enter. If our interest is philosophical truth, then the point of the historical enterprise is to capture whatever philosophical truth or interesting philosophical falsehood there may be in some philosopher's writings. What this has often meant in practice is what has been dubbed *rational reconstruction,* taking the argument or position as given and making sense of it in terms that make sense of it to our philosophical sensibilities, whether or not the reformulation captures anything the philosopher himself would have acknowledged. Examples of this include Bernard Williams's reconstruction of the argument of Decartes's *Meditations* using modern epistemological concepts, or Benson Mates's reconstruction of Leibniz's doctrine of possible worlds using contemporary modal logic. Bennett is tempted in this direction as well. In a passage, part of which we have already quoted, he writes:

> I want to understand the pages of the *Ethics* in a way that will let me learn philosophy from them. For that, I need to consider what Spinoza had in mind, for readings of the text which are faithful to his intentions are likely to teach me more than ones which are not—or so I believe, as I think him to be a great philosopher. And one can be helped to discover his intentions by knowing what he had been reading, whose problems he had been challenged by, and so on. But this delving into backgrounds is subject to a law of diminishing returns: while some fact about Maimonides or Averroes might provide the key to an obscure passage in Spinoza, we are more likely to get his text straight by wrestling with it directly, given just a fair grasp of his immediate background. I am sure to make mistakes because of my inattention to Spinoza's philosophical ancestry; but I will pay that price for the benefits which accrue from putting most of one's energies into philosophically interrogating Spinoza's own text.[7]

Indeed, many benefits come from directly interrogating a historical text, leaving aside nice worries about historical context, but there is a danger of misunderstanding. (In Bennett's Spinoza book this comes out most clearly in his discussion of space and his attribution of a "field metaphysic" to Spinoza in chapter 4, a lovely philosophical position, but one that I do not think occurred to Spinoza.)

This may sound like a criticism of the approach Bennett takes to history, but I assure him, it is not. If our only goal is philosophical truth, then history of philosophy may turn out to be marginal, if not altogether expendable; if our goal is simply philosophical truth, we must face up to the facts in an unsentimental way. And, if our goal is philosophical truth, then historical veracity can have only an instrumental value at best; it is of value only insofar as it helps us attain our principal goal. The point of interpretation, on this view, is to make the philosophy breathe, to make it available to us, and historical veracity is important only insofar as it serves this end.

In calling for us to focus on the truth and falsity of Spinoza's claims, the adequacy and inadequacies of his arguments, Bennett is implicitly contrasting the approach that he takes with other more disinterestedly historical and, in one sense, less philosophical approaches that one might take to the material. In one place Bennett contrasts his approach with that of "intellectual biography," with "mental biography" in another, and with that "which pretends that Spinoza is always or usually right, under some rescuing interpretation" in a third passage.[8] Now, it seems to me that the disinterested historian shouldn't always assume that Spinoza is *right*. But insofar as we agree with Bennett that Spinoza was "a great philosopher," we should at very least subscribe to the working hypothesis that what Spinoza is up to is *sensible*, the sort of thing that a smart person might believe in a particular historical context, given what he had learned, what others around him believed, the assumptions taken for granted, and so on. (This is just a special case of what has been called the principle of charity or, in variant, the principle of humanity in the theory of interpretation in the philosophy of language.) This is not to say that we should not expect to find lapses of reasoning and judgment, even when the whole context is open to us, or that this kind of historical inquiry will clear up all of our puzzlements. It is important to remember that Spinoza, for example, was a puzzle to his contemporaries as well, and they had more access to his context than any of us can ever hope to have. In its way, this kind of rationality is no less demanding a standard to hold Spinoza to than philosophical truth is.

Unlike philosophical truth, which judges Spinoza by what is true, or by what we have come to think is true, this standard is *internal*. The alternative to the sort of history Bennett advocates is a *historical reconstruction* of Spinoza's views, the attempt to understand Spinoza's positions and arguments in terms that he or a well-informed contemporary of his may have understood. It involves coming to understand what Spinoza or a contemporary of his would have considered unproblematic background beliefs, what they would have had trouble with, and in the light of that and other similar contexts, coming to understand what Spinoza's conception of his project was, how he thought he had established the conclusions he had reached, and what he thought was important about those conclusions, all under the assumption that, by and large, Spinoza's project is the work of a smart person working within a particular historical context. This sort of investigation is not biography of any sort, neither intellectual nor mental; it is, quite simply, the history of philosophical ideas.

In practice, the kind of history I was sketching *may* come out looking very little different from the history Bennett prefers. As Bennett has pointed out, if it is the lessons of history for philosophical truth that interest us, then the lessons are likely to be more interesting the closer we come to a genuine representation of Spinoza's (or whomever's) thought. The only conspicuous difference may be the relative lack of judgments of truth and falsity in the sort of disinterested history I propose. If our interest is in historical reconstruction, the question of the ultimate truth or falsity of the doctrines is simply not at issue; the only thing that is important is whether or not our account has made the beliefs intelligible. Sometimes this will call for a judgment that *on his own terms*, some premise or inference a philosopher uses may not be available to him, properly speaking. If we are interested in historical reconstruction, then, for example, the falsity of a premise then universally accepted is not a relevant part of the story.

Bennett would certainly have to agree that there is a real project here, whether or not he himself is interested in carrying it out. I think that he would also have to agree that there is no reason why one must choose one conception of the history of philosophy over the other. While in practice a single scholar may find it difficult to pull off both sorts of history at the same time, within the confines of a single essay or book, they are not competing programs in the sense in which, say, deontological programs for ethics compete with teleological programs. One can find the history of philosophy richer for having both approaches represented in the literature, one can find both interesting and never be put into the position of having to choose one over the other. In this sense the two approaches to history of philosophy are complementary rather than competing.

A question remains, a central question. On Bennett's view, the history of philosophy is important to philosophy in an obvious way; on his conception, history of philosophy actually contributes to the unearthing of philosophical truths. Now, as I noted, the sort of disinterested historical reconstruction I have sketched can *contribute* to Bennett's enterprise, but taken by itself, does it have any philosophical interest at all? Leaving aside the question of the philosophical truth it may help to uncover, is the purely historical study of philosophical ideas of more than antiquarian interest? Is there any reason for philosophers *qua* philosophers to take an interest in such disinterested history?

IN DEFENSE OF DISINTERESTED HISTORY

In arguing for the philosophical significance of disinterested history, I would like to proceed historically and begin with a consideration of the views of a philosopher whose opinion on the matter is in many ways attractive to me. The philosopher I have in mind here is Descartes. As Bennett proposes we learn from Spinoza, I propose that there is much we can learn from Descartes.

Descartes may seem at first glance an odd character to turn to in this connection. Descartes was conspicuously unsympathetic to the study of books, old or new. In the *Discourse*, Descartes wrote:

> [A]s soon as I was old enough to emerge from the control of my teachers, I entirely abandoned the study of letters. Resolving to seek no knowledge other than that which could be found in myself or else in the great book of the world, I spent the rest of my youth in traveling. . . . For it seemed to me that much more truth could be found in the reasoning which a man makes concerning matters that concern him than in those which some scholar makes in his study about speculative matters. For the consequences of the former will soon punish the man if he judges wrongly, whereas the latter have no practical consequences and no importance for the scholar except that perhaps the further they are from common sense the more pride he will take in them, since he will have had to use so much more skill and ingenuity in trying to render them plausible.[9]

This attitude also comes out nicely in a letter from 1638. Unfortunately, the recipient of the letter is unknown, as is the book Descartes is commenting on in the letter, but his point is clear:

> [The author's] plan of collecting into a single book all that is useful in every other book would be a very good one if it were practicable; but I think that it is not. It is often very difficult to judge accurately what others have written, and to draw the good out of them without taking the bad too. Moreover, the particular truths which are scattered in books are so detached and so independent of each other, that I think one would need more talent and energy to assemble them into a well-proportioned and ordered collection . . . than to make up such a collection out of one's own discoveries. I do not mean that one should neglect other people's discoveries when one encounters useful ones; but I do not think one should spend the greater part of one's time in collecting them. If a man were capable of finding the foundation of the sciences, he would be wrong to waste his life in finding scraps of knowledge hidden in the corners of libraries; and if he was no good for anything else but that, he would not be capable of choosing and ordering what he found.[10]

Descartes does not mince words here. If it is truth we are after, books will not help us to find it. He does not seem to think that we can learn much from other people's mistakes, unlike Bennett; mistakes just engender other mistakes. The truths we find in books are so rare and so scattered that anyone who has the ability to recognize them and seek them out would be better off simply looking for them on his own, directly, without the help of these paper-and-ink teachers. If it is philosophical truth you are after, Descartes tells Bennett (and anyone else who will listen), then don't look to the philosophers of the past. (It is somewhat disquieting to the historian when one of his or her subjects talks back in such a rude way.)

Descartes, in general, has little truck with scholarship, with the study of the past, but Descartes was not altogether dismissive of history. Though he thought it inappropriate to look for philosophical truth in history, he did not think that reading the authors of the past is *altogether* without value. In the *Discourse* he wrote:

> I knew . . . that reading good books is like having a conversation with the most distinguished men of past ages—indeed, a rehearsed conversation in which these authors reveal to us only the best of their thoughts.[11]

This conversation is valuable to us for an interesting reason. According to Descartes:

> [C]onversing with those of past centuries is much the same as traveling. It is good to know something of the customs of various peoples, so that we may judge our own more soundly and not think that everything contrary to our own ways is irrational, as those who have seen nothing of the world ordinarily do.[12]

Through such experience in books and in the world Descartes claims that he learned that there are "many things which, although seeming very extravagant and ridiculous to us, are nevertheless commonly accepted and approved in other great nations; and so I learned not to believe too firmly anything of which I had been persuaded only by example and custom."[13]

The idea is an interesting one. We can learn from the past in something of the same way we can learn from travel. By traveling we can get a certain kind of perspective on our lives and the way we lead them, the things we do and the things we believe. We go to other countries, learn their languages, observe their customs, eat their foods (or, at least, observe the kinds of food they eat), discuss their beliefs about the world. This, Descartes thinks, can give us a certain perspective on our own lives. It can, among other things, free us of the belief that the way *we* see things is the way things *have* to be, that X is fit for human consumption but Y is not, that weeks must have seven days, that children must be raised by their own parents, etc. Descartes's point is not relativistic here; he would be among the last to say that anything goes. Even though we observe others eating a certain food we do not, we may still shun it and continue to hold the belief that it is unhealthy or improper for us to eat. Seeing what others do may at least get us to raise the question for ourselves *why* we have the beliefs and customs we do and, perhaps, lead us to see what is arbitrary and what is well grounded in our beliefs and behavior.

A similar case can be made with respect to the study of the past in general, and the study of past philosophy in particular, Descartes suggests. Many of the philosophical beliefs we now take for granted are not shared by figures in the past. By studying the past, taking the past seriously, we are led to reflect on our beliefs, in just the same way as we are led by travel to reflect upon our customs. Such reflection need not lead to a change in our beliefs. The fact that some past geographers thought the earth flat, or past physicists thought that there is such a thing as elemental fire that by its nature rises, these historical observations should not move us to give up our present conceptions of geography or combustion. Reflection on some of the things people have believed should at least cause us to ask ourselves *why* we believe the things we do, and *whether* our grounds are sufficient to support the explicit or implicit beliefs we have and assumptions we make.

Is such reflection important for us as philosophers? It does not *directly* contribute to the discovery of philosophical truth in the way in which discovering a good argument (or an interesting false one) in the work of a historical figure perhaps might, in the way in which Bennett conceives of history contributing to the practice of philosophy. The sort of contribution Descartes saw was of a different, and more subtle, though no less important kind. Historical investigation conceived in this alternative way gives us a kind of perspective on the beliefs we have and the assumptions we make. It helps us sort the good from the bad, the arbitrary from the well grounded, insofar as it challenges us to reflect on why we believe what we do. While it may not help lead us directly to new arguments and new philosophical truths, it leads us directly to something just as valuable: *philosophical questions.*

All of this is very abstract and cries out for some concrete examples, specific assumptions and beliefs we make that are illuminated by such historical reflection. Before I present such an example, I would like to continue a bit longer in this abstract vein.

Descartes has suggested a philosophical use for the history of philosophy different from the one Bennett suggests; the suggestion, as I have developed it, is that the history of philosophy can be important not because it leads to philosophical *truths,* but because it leads to philosophical *questions.* But what sort of history is relevant here? To learn from history in the way Descartes suggests we can involves trying to understand historical figures on *their own terms.* If I travel to Tokyo or Nairobi, look for what is familiar to me in the alien setting, and seek it out, I may acquire a nice camera cheaply, or learn one way *not* to make a pizza. I may indeed have a lovely vacation, but I will not learn what I might. Similarly, if what I am looking for in history is a guide to philosophical truth, if I look for things recognizable *to me* as interesting philosophical problems and promising (if possibly flawed) philosophical arguments, as

Bennett seems to suggest we should, then I may miss features of philosophy as it has been that might raise interesting questions about philosophy as it is. To learn from history in the way Descartes suggests, we should— we must, I think—undertake the kind of disinterested historical investigation I suggested earlier as an alternative to the sort to which Bennett's views lead him. If it is a historical *perspective* on our beliefs and assumptions we are interested in, then the truth or the falsity of past views is *simply irrelevant*. It matters not at all whether Descartes's or Aristotle's or Kant's views are true or false for this use of history. What is important is that we understand *what* their views were, and that we understand *how* it is that smart people could have *regarded* them as true. It is not their truth, much less their falsity, that causes us to reflect on our own beliefs; it is the fact that smart people took seriously views often very different from ours that is important here.

This, I think, answers the question posed at the end of the last section. The sort of disinterested historical reconstruction I proposed as a complement to Bennett's philosophically informed investigation of the history of philosophy *is* philosophically significant, a worthwhile activity for philosophers to engage in, though for a reason somewhat different from what Bennett suggests for his program. Bennett's history seeks philosophical truth, *answers* to philosophical questions; mine seeks the *questions themselves*.

RAISING QUESTIONS: SCIENCE AND PHILOSOPHY

I have been sketching out a way of doing philosophy historically, using a disinterested historical reconstruction of past thought as a way of raising important philosophical questions that might otherwise escape our notice. A brief example illustrates the approach I have been advocating.

Bennett makes an interesting statement in the course of his commentary on Spinoza. He writes: "Much of the *Ethics* is philosophical rather than scientific, i.e., is answerable to conceptual analysis rather than to empirical observation."[14] The claim is *not* central to Bennett's reading of Spinoza, and in raising questions about it I don't mean to cast doubt on Bennett's larger interpretation (though I do think that on at least one occasion it does lead him a bit astray). The quotation appeals to a certain widely held conception of philosophy: that it is an activity pretty largely distinct from scientific activity, and that philosophy makes use of conceptual analysis, whereas science makes use of observation and experience. This conception of philosophy and its relation to science is worth some historical examination.

We might begin by noting that in Spinoza's day, things were not so neatly partitioned. It is now generally recognized that the words "philosophy" and "science" didn't have distinct and separate meanings in the seventeenth century. While "philosophy" was sometimes used narrowly, in perhaps something of the way we use it now,[15] it was also used more broadly to include knowledge in general, including what we now call science, as in the title to Descartes's *Principia Philosophiae,* three-fourths of which is scientific by our standards. Similarly, while "science" was sometimes used as we do now,[16] it often took on a meaning derived from its Latin origin, *scientia,* knowledge. This, of course, is only a matter of terminology. The important question is not what things were called, but whether Spinoza and his contemporaries drew an interesting distinction between what *we* call philosophy and what *we* are inclined to call science; between a certain collection of foundational questions, investigated through argument and conceptual analysis, and a different set of questions about the natural world, investigated through observation and experience.

Here, I think we can say that while we can certainly find different questions studied by different thinkers using different modes of investigation, there is no radical distinction between what we call philosophical and what we call scientific.

It is quite widely known that arguments that are in general terms philosophical play a major role in seventeenth-century science. A nice example is the derivation Descartes gave for his laws of motion. Descartes started from two main premises. The first was an analysis of the "nature of time," which, Descartes claims, is "such that its parts are not mutually dependent," and from which he argued that God is required to keep everything in existence at every moment.[17] The second premise was that God is immutable by his nature and operates "in a manner that is always constant and immutable."[18] From these premises Descartes argued that a constant quantity of motion is maintained in the world, and that bodies in uniform rectilinear motion will tend to remain in uniform rectilinear motion.[19] These conclusions, conclusions that spring from Descartes's metaphysical foundations, were enormously influential on later seventeenth-century physicists. Though not altogether correct in detail, Descartes's conclusions constituted the first published statement of a conservation principle and the first clear version of what Newton was later to call the principle of inertia. When Newton presented his version of these laws in his *Principia* almost fifty years later, the metaphysical argument was gone. But it wasn't dead. Leibniz, Newton's great and greatly maligned contemporary, a physicist and mathematician whose only clear better was Newton himself, made free use of metaphysical arguments in his physics. Like Descartes, Leibniz chose to derive the laws of motion from God, though in a different way: from God the creator of the best (and so, most orderly) of all possible worlds, not God the moment-by-moment sustainer of all. God, Leibniz reasoned, would want to create the world in such a way that whatever power, whatever ability there is to do work in a complete cause, must be found intact in its full effect. Using this as his main premise, Leibniz established two of the main principles of classical mechanics, the law of conservation of what we call kinetic energy (mv^2, *vis viva*), and the conservation of what we call momentum (mv).[20]

These arguments establish what we would call scientific conclusions by way of what we would call philosophical premises. There are also instances in which what we would call (and Bennett has called) conceptual analysis taken more narrowly is used in the service of science. What I have in mind is Descartes's celebrated arguments for the identification of space and body, and his conclusion that there is no empty space, no vacuum. In one representative version, noted by Spinoza in his *Principles of Descartes' Philosophy*, quoted and discussed by Bennett in his commentary, the claim reads:

> Space and body do not really differ [because] body and extension do not really differ, and space and extension do not really differ. It involves a contradiction that there should be a vacuum [i.e.] extension without bodily substance.[21]

Bennett claims that this position is a purely philosophical one, and that neither Descartes nor, following him, Spinoza should confuse this with doing science. He writes: "[W]hen he [Descartes] says that there is no vacuum, he is not predicting what you will find if you ransack the physical universe. His point is a conceptual one."[22] Bennett furthermore regrets "that he words this possible philosophical truth so that it sounds like a scientific falsehood" and goes on to chastise Descartes and Spinoza for their occasional lapses into thinking that this philosophical argument has empirical consequences for physics.[23] Bennett is too charitable here, and in his charity, he misses the point of the argument, both in Descartes and in Spinoza. Descartes's point was *precisely* to establish that there is no vacuum in the physical world, and I know of no reason to believe that Spinoza read the argument any differently. Whether or not there is a philosophical truth in the claim, it was what we have come to recognize as a scientific falsehood that interested Descartes and his contemporaries; the denial of a vacuum not only in philosophy but also *in rerum natura* was an important feature of Cartesian physics, one that grounds Cartesian cosmology, the vortex theory of planetary motion.[24]

The examples so far are of cases in which philosophical argument, conceptual analysis, leads to what we would consider scientific conclusions. There are a few interesting and, to the modern mind, very strange instances in which seventeenth-century philosophers used empirical claims to support conclusions that we would consider philosophical. The case is strange, and I'm not entirely sure I have it right, but Leibniz seems to have taken such a position. Leibniz held (or, at least, he *often* held) that animals are genuine substances, corporeal substances. As substances, Leibniz argued, they cannot arise through natural means, nor can they perish by natural means. This is a conclusion Leibniz often establishes by pure philosophical argument; it is a conclusion of the celebrated predicate-in-notion argument of *Discourse on Metaphysics,* §8,[25] and, Leibniz sometimes argues, of the no-less-philosophical principle of continuity.[26] Leibniz also called on the exciting discoveries of microscopists like Leeuwenhoek and Malpighi for support. For example, he wrote to Queen Sophie Charlotte in May 1704 concerning an important consequence of his view of corporeal substance:

> Speaking with metaphysical rigor, there is neither generation nor death, but only the development and enfolding of the same animal. . . . Experience confirms these transformations in some animals, where nature herself has given us a small glimpse of what it hides elsewhere. Observations made by the most industrious observers also lead us to judge that the generation of animals is nothing but growth joined with transformation.[27]

Microscopic examiners are being called upon to support one of the basic propositions of Leibniz's metaphysics, the natural ungenerability and incorruptibility of substance.

If this strikes us as being a bit strange, stranger still is Henry More, who calls upon the world of ghosts and goblins as *empirical* support for his belief in the existence of incorporeal souls. In his *Immortality of the Soul* (1662 edition) More calls our attention to

> such extraordinary Effects as we cannot well imagine any natural, but must needs conceive some free or spontaneous Agent to be the Cause thereof, whereas yet it is clear that they are from neither Man nor Beast. Such are speakings, knockings, opening of doors when they were fast shut, . . . shapes of Men and several sorts of Brutes, that after speech and converse have suddenly disappeared.[28]

That there are such happenings is, for More if not for us, an empirical fact. For More these apparitions speak strongly in favor of souls distinct from body: "Those and like extraordinary Effects . . . seem to me to be an undeniable Argument that there be such things as *Spirits* or *Incorporeal Substances* in the world."[29] More may have been deluded in thinking that there are ghosts and obscure about how the phenomenon in question is supposed to support his conclusion, but he certainly seemed to think that the question of the existence of incorporeal substance, a metaphysical question par excellence, could be settled by a trip to a haunted house.

In this he was not alone. Hobbes, no advocate of immaterial substance, made a special point of denying the reality of ghosts as part of his case against incorporeal souls.[30] While he did not support the view More was pressing, Hobbes certainly seemed to think that empirical evidence was germane to the question.

Why are these historical observations interesting? For one, they do pertain to the proper interpretation of Spinoza and his contemporaries; they suggest that we should be careful about attributing *our* distinction between philosophy and science to earlier thinkers. There is a philosophical lesson to be learned as well. My point is *not* that we should look for philosophical truth in the sorts of arguments I was discussing; the laws of motion shouldn't be derived from God, nor should the question of the vacuum be settled by an appeal to our intuitions about space and extension. Nor do I think that metaphysical issues about the nature of substance can be settled by looking into microscopes, nor should we consider seriously the ontological status of ghosts and goblins. Much that was live in seventeenth-century thought is now dead, and I don't intend to revive it. The examples I have given do raise an interesting question: Why is it that *we* tend to see such a radical break between philosophy and science, and, more importantly, *should* we? The question can be raised directly, without the need for history, as Quine has done. But history brings the point home in an especially clear way: it shows us an assumption we take for granted by pointing out that it is not an assumption everyone makes.

CONCLUSION

Some years ago, an anthropologist friend told me something of what it is like to do field work. When one enters a new community, she said, it is all very alien, an alien language, alien customs, alien traditions. After a while things change; the language and customs become familiar, and one is inclined to think that the differences are only superficial, that the once-alien community is just like home. The final stage comes when the similarities and differences come into focus, when one recognizes what one's subjects share with us, while at the same time appreciating the genuine differences there are between them and us. The case is similar for the history of philosophy. We cannot ignore the ways in which past thinkers are involved in projects similar to ours, and the ways in which we can learn from what they have written, how it can contribute to our search for philosophical enlightenment. At the same time, we cannot ignore the ways in which they differ from us, the way in which their programs differ from ours, the way in which they ask different questions and make different assumptions. Both are important to a genuine historical understanding of the philosophical past, but just as importantly, we as philosophers can learn from both.

NOTES

1. Jonathan Bennett, *A Study of Spinoza's Ethics* (Indianapolis, Ind.: Hackett Publishing Company, 1984), p. 15.

2. Ibid., p. 35.

3. Ibid., p. 372.

4. Ibid., pp. 372, 357.

5. Ibid., p. 38.

6. Ibid., p. 41.

7. Ibid., pp. 15-16.

8. Ibid., pp. 15, 35, 372.

9. Descartes, *Discours de la methode*, I, in Charles Adam and Paul Tannery, eds., *Oeuvres de Descartes* (revised edition, Paris: J. Vrin, 1964-1976), 6:9-10; translated in John Cottingham, Robert Stoothoff, and Dugald Murdoch, eds. and trans., *The Philosophical Writings of Descartes* (Cambridge: Cambridge University Press, 1985), 1:115. Hereafter Adam and Tannery will be abbreviated "AT," followed by volume number in Roman numeral and page number in Arabic numeral; Cottingham, Stoothoff, and Murdoch will be abbreviated "CSM," with volume and page treated the same way.

10. AT II 346-47; translated in Anthony Kenny, ed. and trans., *Descartes: Philosophical Letters* (Minneapolis: University of Minnesota Press, 1970), pp. 59-60.

11. *Discours* I, AT VI 5; CSM I 113.

12. *Discours* I, AT VI 6; CSM I 113-14.

13. *Discours* I, AT VI 10; CSM I 115-16.

14. Bennett, *Spinoza*, p. 24.

15. See, e.g., *Discours* I, AT VI 6, 8-9; CSM I 113, 114-15.

16. See, e.g., the Preface to the French translation of the *Principia Philosophiae*, AT IXB 14, CSM I 186.

17. *Principia* I 21, AT VIIIA 13; CSM I 200.

18. *Principia* II 36, AT VIIIA 61; CSM I 240.

19. *Principia* II 36-39, AT VIIIA 61-65; CSM I 240-42.

20. For an account of Leibniz's work here, see, e.g., Martial Gueroult, *Leibniz: dynamique et metaphysique* (Paris: Aubier-Montaigne, 1967), chapter 3.

21. C. Gebhardt, ed., *Spinoza Opera* (Heidelberg: Carl Winter, 1925), 1:187-88, as paraphrased in Bennett, *Spinoza*, p. 100. Spinoza refers the reader here to Descartes's *Principia* II 17-18, AT VIIIA 49-50; CSM I 230-31.

22. Bennett, *Spinoza*, p. 101.

23. Ibid.

24. Descartes's view was that the present state of the world can be explained if we imagine an initial state of disorder, which sorts itself out into swirls of fluid by way of the laws of motion alone. These swirls of fluid, vortices, are what Descartes identifies with planetary systems, a sun at the center of each, and planets circling about the sun. Essential to this account is the assumption

that all motion produces circular motion, which Descartes derives from the doctrine of the plenum. It is because all space is full, he argues, that all motion must ultimately be circular, one hunk of material substance moving to make room for a given moving body, a third hunk moving to make room for the second, and so on until a final hunk moves to take the place left by the original moving body. In this way, Descartes's whole cosmology depends upon the denial of the vacuum. For the account of motion as circular, see *Principia* II 33 (AT VIIIA 58-59; CSM I 237–39) and for the derivation of the cosmos from an initial state, see *Principia* III 46ff. (AT VIIIA 100ff.; CSM I 256ff.).

25. See C. I. Gerhardt, ed., *Leibniz: Philosophische Schriften* (Berlin: Weidmannsche Buchhandlung, 1875-1890), 4:432-33, translated in Leroy Loemker, ed. and trans., *Leibniz: Philosophical Papers and Letters* (Dordrecht: D. Reidel, 1969), pp. 307-8. See also the letter to Arnauld, 28 November/8 December 1686, Gerhardt 2:76.

26. See Leibniz's letter to Queen Sophie Charlotte, 8 May 1704, Gerhardt 3:345.

27. Ibid. See the discussion of this and the references cited in Michel Serres, *Le systeme de Leibniz* (Paris: Presses Universitaires de France, 1968), 1:354ff.

28. Henry More, *The Immortality of the Soul*, p. 50, in *A Collection of Several Philosophical Writings of Dr Henry More* (London: William Morden, 1662).

29. Ibid.

30. Hobbes, *Leviathan*, chapter 46; cf. chapter 2.

History, Philosophy, and Interpretation

Some Reactions to Jonathan Bennett's *Study of Spinoza's Ethics*[1]

Jonathan Rée

Together with Socrates and Seneca, Spinoza is distinguished from most of the rest of the Great Dead Philosophers by an aura of saintliness. People get emotional about him. They fall in love with him, identify with him, worship him, and crave him to love them back. Attachment to one of the "three S's" (as you might say) has as much to do with abject discipleship as with rigorous scholarship. The doctrines are presumed true, even if their meaning is a mystery; and anyway, the focus of attention is not the doctrines, but the hero's style of life and death. Devotees are tormented by a fear—indeed, a certainty—that they are unworthy of their master. Dr. Nahum Fischelson, a meek philosopher stricken with poverty and age in a story by Isaac Bashevis Singer, speaks for all true Spinozists when he marries and falls in love. "Divine Spinoza, forgive me," he cries out loud to the midnight air of Market Street, Warsaw, "I have become a fool."[2]

The main point which the romantic Spinoza stands for is that we should strive to see the world *sub specie aeternitatis* ("from the point of view of eternity") rather than *sub specie durationis* ("from the point of view of duration"). The aesthetic values by reference to which he is celebrated are those of the sublime: terrible seas and skies, howling winds, torrential floods, waterfalls, volcanoes and jagged peaks, and the silent, strong figure of Spinoza looking on impassively, an inspiration to his awe-struck admirers.

German thought has been both delighted and disquieted by Spinoza's sublimity, by the "bright pure mind of Spinoza," as Jacobi saw it. The alluring horror of Spinoza, to Schelling, was that he could "strive . . . to drown in the infinity of the absolute object" and "work for his own annihilation." Even Hegel was disconcerted. "The grandeur of Spinoza's

44

manner of thought," he said, affords a glimpse of "Eastern thought" with its renunciation of "everything determinate and particular." His trade as a lens-grinder was "no arbitrary choice" either, since it was concerned with light, which "represents in the material sphere the absolute identity which forms the foundation of the Oriental view of things." His premature death from consumption, Hegel rather tastelessly adds, "was in harmony with his system of philosophy, according to which all particularity and individuality pass away in the one substance."[3]

The same romantic spirit of Spinoza has haunted English thought. The God of Spinoza was "an Ararat" to Coleridge in the 1790s, when he was trying to convince Wordsworth of the falsity of "the determinations which go to make the individual." George Eliot turned to writing novels when she realized that her attempts to translate Spinoza into English would not be sufficient for "making Spinoza accessible to a larger number." To Matthew Arnold, Spinoza had "something in him which can influence character, which is edifying." Spinoza's calm contemplation of a comfortless world would help transform the lower self into the higher, "freed from passions" so that we might "Through clouds of individual strife/ Draw homeward to the general life." In short, Spinoza was "a noble and lofty character," a character, indeed, *in the grand style.*"[4]

There was a time, I admit, when I fell under the lugubrious spell of this character; but nowadays I am more often tempted to think of him as an officious prig, whose selflessness is only a perverse form of self-regard—his calm a frozen frenzy of sadism, his disciplined style a pretentious pose. What a breath of fresh air when Nietzsche denounces Spinoza's philosophy: not love of wisdom, he says, but "love of *his own* wisdom." And what a relief to hear the celebrated "mathematical form in which Spinoza clad his philosophy" denounced as "Hokuspokus."[5] What a pleasure, too, to find Jonathan Bennett, a century later, patrolling the territories liberated by Nietzsche, and remorselessly flushing out the last refuges of romantic Spinozism. And yet, I hesitate: May there not be some life left in the old romantic idea of Spinoza?

HISTORY OR PHILOSOPHY?

For twenty years or more, Jonathan Bennett has waged an admirable and energetic campaign to get his fellow analytic philosophers to see that the study of the discipline's classics "can be one of the most rewarding and demanding of philosophical exercises," rather than, as they have tended to assume, "only a marginally useful activity which may be adequately conducted with the mind in neutral."[6]

But the considerable controversy which Bennett's work has stirred up has not been in the quarter against which his arguments were directed.

He has been criticized not for taking philosophy's past too seriously, but for failing to take it seriously enough. He has been accused of treating the Old Masters "unhistorically," applying "modern analytical techniques" to them as if unaware of the obvious anachronism involved.

The subtlest and most formidable of Bennett's critics is Michael Ayers, who has argued that Bennett's way of "reconstructing" the classics threatens to filter out every past doctrine which does not harmonize with today's orthodoxies. And if there is a difference between the modern philosopher's reconstruction of an old theory and the modern historian's version of it, then it is probably the latter which has the greater philosophical interest. Hence Bennett's brisk, modernizing manner may beguile him into losing out philosophically as well as historically. And the fact that Bennett's attentions have often led to the demolition rather than the preservation of the structures to which they are applied seems to some to give empirical support to Ayers's forebodings.[7]

My instinctive sympathies are with Ayers: I prefer a more contextual and antiquarian approach to philosophy's past than Bennett's. But I doubt whether the quarrel can be resolved by appeal to general principles of method. It is certainly a mistake to think of the historiography of philosophy as a kind of mixture of two separate substances, the philosophical and the historical, so that you can only increase the proportion of one by decreasing the proportion of the other. Bennett's work is intended, after all, to represent the historical facts about what the Great Dead Philosophers thought, and no one could object on principle to his using the conventions of modern philosophy for this purpose. You obviously cannot appreciate a philosophical thought without articulating it in a language which you understand; so, as Merleau-Ponty once said, "if ever a history needed our interpretation, it must be the history of philosophy."[8]

It may be useful to think of the interpretation of philosophies by analogy with the performing arts. This permits one to take a quite relaxed attitude to the variety of interpretations, without however implying that they are all of equal validity. In music, for example, some performances will be indefensible, but none can be perfect: it may be impossible to bring out the beauty of a musical phrase, for instance, without sacrificing the urgency of its rhythm; in that case a knowledge of different kinds of performance will enhance an appreciation of the work itself. Just as you could welcome Karajan's recordings of Strauss alongside Böhm's, or Strauss's own, so too, perhaps, you could embrace Bennett's Spinoza as well as Matthew Arnold's and, of course (if the analogy will stretch this far), Spinoza's.

The main value of the analogy is that it reveals the drastic inadequacy of the commonsense ideas of "anachronism" and "historical fidelity" in terms of which rival interpretations are customarily evaluated. When people debate the virtues of Bach keyboard music on a grand piano, or

Tosca set in Fascist Rome, and *Romeo and Juliet* in punk London, then the concept of authenticity turns out to be catastrophically paradoxical: a wilfully anachronistic production, by Wieland Wagner or Jonathan Miller, may reveal far more about a classic than a loyally traditional one by Zeffirelli or Peter Hall. In philosophy too, meticulous historical accuracy may distort a work, or obscure its author's intentions, while reckless anachronism may uncover unsuspected depths. "History *and* philosophy" may be a false hope; but equally, "history *or* philosophy" is a false dilemma.

THE STRUCTURE OF THE ETHICS

Alasdair MacIntyre says that Spinoza is "of all philosophers the one whose life has least apparent connection with his work."[9] Spinoza seems to have agreed, claiming that his circumstances are as irrelevant to philosophy as Euclid's are to geometry.[10] In the Preface to Part Three of the *Ethics,* Spinoza presents himself as a kind of generalized spirit of Euclid. "I shall consider human actions and appetites in exactly the same way as I would lines, planes, and bodies," he says. Of course, he expected his readers to be appalled at the recklessness of this attempt "to treat the vices and failings of men in geometrical form . . . and to explain by strict reasoning those matters which they see as totally irrational, and vain, absurd and repulsive." "*Sed mea haec est ratio,*" says Spinoza with melodramatic emphasis: "Yet such is indeed my plan" (3 Preface).

With devices of this kind, Spinoza manages to make the *Ethics* both personal and impersonal at the same time, both selfless and egocentric. The serene mask of the *species aeternitate* slips to reveal, as Nietzsche put it, an irascible *species Spinozae.*[11] The mechanism by which Spinoza produces this disconcerting and fascinating effect involves the phenomena which Wayne Booth has discussed under the celebrated rubric of "the implied author"—not the actual author, but a character, possibly fictional or even fantastic, whom one imagines as the writer or narrator of what one is reading.[12]

The friends who, after Spinoza's death, arranged the publication of the *Ethics* affirmed that a more-than-adequate picture of Spinoza's manner of life was revealed by his philosophical writings, scrupulously self-effacing as they are. Indeed, many of Spinoza's most enthusiastic advocates have reacted more to the personality which they believed they could trace in Spinoza's "style," than to the thoughts whose vehicle it was supposed to be. Goethe, for instance, marveled at "the boundless unselfishness which shone forth in every sentence." George Eliot felt that the "style" of Spinoza's writing gave the intriguing impression of "a person of great capacity who has led a solitary life" and who speaks "from his own soul." And Merleau-Ponty offers Spinoza as a paradigm of a writer whose "style" provides an "initial outline" of meaning, which can be understood only by "working your way into the manner in which the thought exists, and by reproducing the philosopher's tone and accent." The testimony of Yakov Bok in Bernard Malamud's *The Fixer* is the same; he responded to reading the *Ethics* "through the man rather than the work."

> I read through a few pages and kept on going as though there were a whirlwind at my back. As I say, I didn't understand every word but when you're dealing with such ideas you feel as though you were taking a witch's ride. After that I wasn't the same man. . . . What I think it means is that he was out to make a free man out of himself . . . by thinking things through and connecting everything up.[13]

It is striking that Bennett, in spite of his hostility to the romantic interpretation of Spinoza and his impatience with merely personal and literary approaches to philosophical works in general, begins his book with a chapter offering "a Character Sketch of the *Ethics*" followed by another on "the Cast of Spinoza's Mind." Despite its rigid theoreticist armor (the numbered definitions, propositions, proofs, and corollaries), the *Ethics* seems to have some of the qualities of a novel, even a memoir or a confession. It therefore faces its readers with a rhetorical and psychological question about its own structure: Who is speaking to whom in this work, or how is the implied reader meant to learn from the implied author? Bennett formulates the issue concisely. "What is supposed to be happening to us," he asks, "as we work our way through the *Ethics?*" (21). I shall now argue that the *Ethics* contains a bold though not unparadoxical answer to this question; that this answer is very different from Bennett's own; and that it restores a validity to the romantic interpretation of Spinoza—despite Bennett's withering skepticism.

Grades of Knowledge and the Rhetoric of the Ethics

Like many another philosophy book, the *Ethics* includes a philosophy of philosophical education, which provides readers with a kind of guide to help them use the book. Not unusually, the *Ethics* pictures its readers as occupying the middle portion of a ladder which stretches from the untutored multitudes beneath them to what one might call the book's implied philosopher up above. The book is a message from the top rung, addressed to those lower down.

In the *Ethics*, Spinoza repeatedly distinguishes between the lower grades of knowledge (*imaginatio*) and the higher (*intellectus*). But in a note devoted to the subject (2p40s2), he divides the scale into three: *imaginatio*, which contains universal notions, but only ones formed from random encounters with individual objects or from hearsay; *ratio*, which is constituted by "adequate ideas of the properties of things," but which cannot grasp the essence of any individual thing (cf. 2p37); and finally *scientia intuitiva*, which "proceeds from an adequate idea of the formal essence of certain attributes of God, to an adequate knowledge of the essences of things."

The laxity of Spinoza's exposition of the grades of knowledge is notorious, scandalous even. But it seems that he would have excused himself by claiming that the grades shade into one another, and by resorting to his favorite expression, *quatenus*, "in so far as." Transcendental terms such as *ens, res,* and *aliquid* ("being," "thing," "something") are lamentable confusions; the more they occupy our minds, the further we are from the highest form of knowledge. The same goes for universal or general terms such as "man," "dog," or "horse," which, insofar as they are not derived from an adequate idea of the essence of God, may apply to indefinitely many instances, or, for all we know, to none at all. It is only insofar as our mind contains ideas which have at least and at most one object (ideas, that is, of properties like extension, which are "common to all," and "equally in a part and in the whole," and, paradigmatically, of God or Nature) that it achieves its highest state and is able to see everything *sub specie aeternitatis*.

It seems clear that readers of the *Ethics* are meant to climb the ladder of knowledge until they acquire an adequate idea of God. But it is also clear that this plan confronted Spinoza with some intractable problems. In theory, the *Ethics* ought to contain nothing but the best kind of knowledge, presented purely from the point of view of eternity. But if it did, then the book would make sense only to readers whose minds were already at that level, and who therefore had nothing to gain from reading it. In practice, therefore, Spinoza was obliged to admit inadequate notions into the world of the *Ethics*, if only in order to argue them out of it again. To make matters worse, people with inadequate notions do not think alike: soldiers seeing a horse will associate it with war, for instance, but peasants will be led to think of ploughing (2p18s). So though he might wish he were a Euclid, inhabiting a world of pure forms, Spinoza actually had to be an Ovid, desperately trying to keep track of the indefinitely various metamorphoses of his readers' fallacious imaginations.

Spinoza's predicament, in short, was like that of politicians who need to negotiate with bodies whose existence they cannot afford to recognize. And ethics—the eponymous topic of his book—is, according to Spinoza, actually constituted by inadequate ideas. It is a tissue of superstitious fictions ("good, evil, virtue, sin, praise and blame, order and confusion, beauty and ugliness"), portraying a world where the gods are no less delirious (*delirare*) than ourselves (1 Appendix). *Ethics* deceives us into imagining ourselves as "an empire within an empire" (3 Preface) in which we exercise something called "free will" in our search for something called "good" and our flight from something called "evil." We foolishly imagine that at the end we will be judged by a transcendent God who will be benignly delighted by us, or jealously furious, as the case may be (4 Preface). In our vain confusion we find comfort in ridiculous philosophers peddling their inane definitions of humanity (featherless bipeds, risible or rational animals, etc. [2p40s1]) and their "fictitious" and "metaphysical" ideas of "faculties" (2p48s). Spinoza was certain that this ethical imagery was false; he had to take it seriously, though, because we are all "by nature inclined to embrace it" (1 Appendix).

Spinoza's need to enter into dialogue with what he must condemn as inferior grades of knowledge explains the fact that the *Ethics* is, as Gilles Deleuze puts it, "a simultaneous book, double-written."

> There is, first, the unbroken flood of definitions, propositions, proofs and corollaries unfolding the great speculative themes with all the rigor of the head; but then there is also the broken chain of scholia, a discontinuous volcanic line, a second version beneath the first, giving expression to all the rages of the heart, and to the practical theses of denunciation and liberation.[14]

These ungeometrical passages—the scholia, appendices, and prefaces—resemble "asides to the reader" in eighteenth-century novels. In them, Spinoza (or rather, the implied philosopher of the *Ethics*) enters into dialogue with inferior grades of knowledge (for instance, "*respondebis fortasse; . . . At instabunt*" [1 Appendix]), dealing with "general notions of the vulgar," "common sayings," and "objections" by the way (5p41s; 4 Preface; 2p49s). Though they constitute less than half of the *Ethics*, these passages usually receive the greater part of the attention of readers and commentators.

In Parts Four and Five of the *Ethics*, however, Spinoza's attempt to segregate the central truths from the peripheral commentaries ran into difficulties, as he permitted suspect and inadequate terms—particularly "good" and "evil"—to figure in the "geometrical" propositions themselves. "We have to retain them," he says, even though they "do not refer to anything positive in things themselves, and are merely modes of thought, or notions, which we form by comparing things to one another."

> In what follows, therefore, I shall understand by good what we certainly know is a means by which we may approach nearer and nearer to the exemplar of human nature which we place before ourselves. By bad, what

we certainly know prevents us from becoming like that exemplar. (4 Preface, trans. Bennett, 296, amended)

Bennett rightly observes that this passage is awkward, not to say incoherent, and suggests that it is also unnecessary, given that Spinoza has already offered an account of the meaning of "good" in terms of "feeling and desire." Bennett therefore suggests that Spinoza's reference to the "exemplar of human nature" is a relic of an earlier draft, which Spinoza carelessly forgot to remove when revising his copy (296).

That earlier account of the meaning of "good" occurs in a scholium and states that "we do not try for, will, want or desire anything because we judge it to be good; on the contrary, we judge something to be good because we try to get it, will it, want it, and desire it" (3p9s; cf. Bennett, 223). But this comment is not meant as a statement of what Spinoza understood by goodness, still less as a true definition of it. It is intended only as an explanation of a vulgar usage which arises, according to Spinoza, from the fact that "the mind is constituted both by adequate and by inadequate ideas" (3p9d). The later passage about "the exemplar of human nature," which Bennett understandably queries, is not therefore a functionless vestige of "earlier stages in Spinoza's thought," as Bennett supposes: it is a vital attempt on Spinoza's part to justify the fact that the propositions and proofs of Parts Four and Five make use of terms belonging to the "lower grades of knowledge."

Spinoza's predicament is particularly embarrassing in view of the fact that the vulgar notions through which he risks contaminating the species aeternitatis are, according to him, not really false at all, since "all ideas, insofar as they are related to God, are true" (2p32). But in that case, there could be no point in our reading the Ethics, or in his writing it. The idea that there are errors which have to be corrected would itself be an error if Spinoza were right; and it would be comic, to say the least, to see him earnestly and quixotically setting out to combat the error of believing in the reality of error.

Yet this seems to be exactly the task which the Ethics sets itself. It will attack believers in a transcendent God—but they "do not understand what they are saying" (1p15s). It will denounce people who suppose that human actions depend on the will—although they "have no idea" what their words may mean (2p35s). And it will demolish the illusions of those who hold that the mind controls the body—except that they "know not what they say" (3p2s). Since, on Spinoza's admission, there can be nothing "positive" separating us all from the highest grade of knowledge, it would seem better to admit that we are all there already, and that (to use Spinoza's example) we are no more in need of the intellectual refurbishment which Spinoza offers than "the man I heard shouting the other day that his hallway had flown into his neighbor's chicken" who,

Spinoza concedes, was not really mistaken, "since his mind seemed to me to be sufficiently clear" (2p47s).

The inevitable conclusion is that the Ethics is a structurally paradoxical work, and not ingenuously so. The doctrine of the grades of knowledge leading up to the species aeternitatis shows what the book is supposed to do to its readers; but sub specie aeternitatis, the doctrine is vacuous, since the grades all collapse into one. The Ethics is therefore comparable to Wittgenstein's Tractatus Logico-Philosophicus, which was of course given its pretentious name in honor of Spinoza. It uses ordinary words in order to state the important truth that ordinary words cannot be used to state important truths; and all it seems to teach us is, as Wittgenstein put it, "how little is achieved when these problems are solved."[15]

Jonathan Bennett has steered clear of these self-consciously sophisticated, artistic, or writerly aspects of Spinoza's work. And his book closes with a trenchantly negative chapter about the last twenty propositions of the Ethics—its literary climax and, for lovers of the romantic Spinoza, the best bit. In these pages, Spinoza develops the concept of "intuitive knowledge" in terms of "the intellectual love of God" and the eternity of the mind which is capable of it. Although Bennett admits to having "hated writing" his assessment of these propositions and to having had "scruples and fears about publishing it" (375), he does not mince his words. Earlier commentators may have derived "a sort of poetical glow" from these propositions, but Bennett finds only errors; and unlike those he has detected earlier in the Ethics, these errors are "not committed in the honorable service of a recognizably worthwhile philosophical project" (374). These pages are "a disaster" (357): "Spinoza is talking nonsense and there is no reason for us to put up with it" (373).

Spinoza's doctrine of the grades of knowledge gives an attractive answer to Bennett's question, "What is supposed to be happening to us as we work our way through the Ethics?" We are supposed to be acquiring intuitive knowledge, or in other words the "intellectual love of God." Bennett has, however, an alternative answer: that Spinoza intended his book to be read "as a hypothetico-deductive system," in the sense that it starts with general hypotheses and deduces particular consequences which may then be compared with empirical and conceptual data collected independently (20, 23-24). This has the advantage of enabling the Ethics to be treated like a basket of fortune cookies, rather than as a through-composed work of art whose elements can be interpreted only in terms of the rhetorical structure of the whole. I shall now test this "hypothetico-deductive" approach against the rhetorical one suggested by the doctrine of the grades of knowledge by considering Spinoza's treatment of personal identity and suicide.

Personal Identity and Suicide

According to the interpretation of the *Ethics* which has moved me and many other readers, its principal message is that the idea of an individual self is an illusion. The theme arises from Spinoza's view that the mind *is* (rather than *has*) its ideas, and that ideas can be pinpointed only in two ways. First, horizontally: they can be linked to other ideas. But these in turn, according to Spinoza, are also impersonal, constitutionally invulnerable to private take-overs; indeed their circuit is ultimately that of God or Nature as a whole, and "we are parts of a thinking being, whose thoughts—some in their entirety, some in fragments only— constitute our mind."[16] Or second, we can pinpoint ideas vertically, by relating them to the particular portion of matter to which they correspond; and then we can see that "the object of the idea which constitutes a human mind is the body" (2p13). But according to Spinoza, no portion of matter can be understood adequately in isolation from the rest, and "every body, insofar as it exists modified in a particular manner, must be considered as a part of the whole universe."[17]

It follows that as we educate ourselves in physics or metaphysics, our identity with a particular personal body gets dispersed. In the *Ethics*, the implications of this doctrine are left to the readers' imaginations; but they are spelled out in a letter, where Spinoza explains that if a father really loves his son, then his thought of the son is the same as the son's, and they are one and the same mind and one and the same body: "since the father, because of this union with his son, is a part of the said son, the soul of the father must necessarily participate in the ideal essence of the son."[18] And as one's comprehension grows to include larger and larger portions of the universe, so one's identity is gradually dissolved in God's; hence, the mind "is eternal insofar as it conceives things *sub specie aeternitatis*" (5p21s). But of course, this mind is no longer mine or anyone else's: the love of God is the end of the individual.

Suicide involves the idea of individual selfhood not once but three times, since it means that *you*, of *your own* volition, kill *yourself*. Spinoza's teaching about suicide is contained in a scholium to the *Ethics* (4p20s). Here he argues that a person can commit suicide only if driven by external forces, for example, when someone else "forces back the hand in which by chance he holds his sword"—which, of course, means that suicide would hardly be the right word in the first place. Within Spinoza's system, therefore, suicide seems to be impossible.

The conclusion can be derived with threefold certainty. In the first place, to the extent that one can, through inadequate ideas, abstract an individual body from its surroundings, one does so, according to Spinoza, by identifying it as the locus of a kind of life-force: a constantly renewed effort by a piece of matter to differentiate itself from its environment. But insofar as something destroyed itself or committed suicide, this would show that it had been a mistake to locate a life-force in it at the outset; it cannot ever have been a genuine individual.

Second, the so-called act of suicide could not be a free action. Even if, as Spinoza puts it, Seneca died in order "to avoid a greater evil by encountering a less," he would still be the victim of "external causes." For, according to Spinoza, free action is what issues from a mind constituted by adequate ideas, and these by definition do not have individual instances for their objects, or for that matter good and evil (2p40s1).

And third, insofar as the deed in question could be called voluntary, it would not really be a case of suicide. For, according to Spinoza, death may mean simply that a mind, insofar as it is individuated at all, leaves its old body behind.

> For there is no reason which requires me to say that a body cannot die unless it becomes a corpse: indeed experience seems to teach the contrary. For it sometimes happens that a man suffers such changes that it would be hard to say that he remains the same. For instance, there is a Spanish poet I have heard of who became ill; and when he recovered, he was so oblivious of his past that he did not believe that the tales and tragedies which he had written were his own. (4p39s)

Spinoza chooses, however, to abandon this topic "half way" (in medio), for fear of supplying "material for the superstitious to raise new questions about." But he must have known that few readers would fail to rise to that sort of bait and supply the missing half of the argument—which is, presumably, that insofar as your mental power increases, you leave your individual body behind, not necessarily as a corpse, but perhaps as the correlative of a mind less adequate than your own, which is soaring to an identity with "the common life" and eventually with God or Nature as a whole. It does not die, and therefore it cannot have committed suicide.

Bennett's reading of Spinoza's remarks about suicide is very different. He begins by ascribing to Spinoza a "substantive morality" based on "strong individual egoism"—the very reverse of the romantic opinion (231). He then notes that this leads, through a plausible deductive argument, to the conclusion that self-destruction is impossible; and "since the conclusion is false," he says, "the argument is faulty" (234). Among the faults he finds is Spinoza's refusal to countenance the possibility that a thing's definition might include its destruction or limited duration (235-36). Another is Spinoza's failure to recognize that an act of suicide like Seneca's may be voluntary, even if he would ideally have preferred to avoid it. After all, as Bennett says, if I want an orange but would prefer an apple, and Bennett eats the last of the apples, then when I eat the orange I am not doing so against my will or under compulsion (237).

Romantic Spinozists will easily duck these attacks. No definition of a thing, they will say, can include its eventual destruction. If it did, then the situation where the thing in question no longer existed would itself be included in the definition; therefore, the definition would turn out to be of the larger whole of which that thing was only a part or phase, and that larger whole would not have been destroyed.

And even if Seneca chose death the way I choose an orange, he would not have chosen freely, since individual apples and oranges belong only to the world of imagination, and we are free only insofar as we escape that world.

It is becoming clear that the argument between Bennett and the romantics concerning Spinoza's doctrine of suicide goes round in circles. Bennett will find that the romantic version is evading criticism only by losing contact with everything except its own fantastic world; it is forgetting about the data, in other words, which control the "hypothetico-deductive" way of reading the *Ethics*. Spinoza ought to admit, says Bennett, "that his doctrine of individual egoism is true only because of how he defines 'individual,' and that it may well be false when understood in terms of our normal concept of a single individual, person, or the like." After all, from Bennett's point of view, "we have a pretty secure grip on the idea of what constitutes a single human being" (251). But the romantics will reply that Spinoza's greatness lies in his attempt to rise above such normal concepts, and that if we allow him to, Spinoza will speak as eloquently as can be to anyone who fears—surely not quite without grounds—that it is not we that have "a pretty secure grip on the idea of what constitutes a human being," but rather the idea of personal identity which has a pretty secure grip on us.

Bennett would of course consider this vision of a transcendance of personal identity ridiculous as a philosophical theory, and also inaccurate as a representation of what Spinoza actually meant. The romantics, however, would argue that Spinoza meant to be interpreted as denying that any concept of personal identity really makes sense. But both Bennett and the romantics would expect that the issue between them could be definitely settled by proper discussion among competent historians of philosophy. It is this faith in the possibility of such positive results in the interpretation of philosophy which I want, in concluding, to challenge.

THE USES OF HISTORY

When I suggested that the interpretation of philosophy has something in common with the performing arts, I noticed that the comparison might lead to a very relaxed attitude to conflicts of interpretation. Even the creator's beliefs as to the correct interpretation of a work need have no sovereignty—neither Beethoven's wish that his piano sonatas should be played almost impossibly fast, for instance, nor Spinoza's that the Ethics be read as a work of theism. This attitude has an attractive allure of radical democracy too: just as Tom Paine contended "for the rights of the living, and against the manuscript assumed authority of the dead,"[19] so philosophers might claim a right to interpret their discipline's classics however they like and declare their independence from their tyrannical pasts, whether the reconstructed one offered by Bennett, or the authentic one proposed by Ayers.

In spite of its fashionable up-to-dateness, this endorsement of the limitless interpretability of philosophical works expresses an important truth: that no thoughts, least of all philosophical ones, can be definitively represented, since no system of representation is definitive; or conversely, that all thinkers, especially philosophical ones, can be aware that their thoughts might best be represented in ways that they cannot even imagine. This is why anachronistic interpretations, whether in art or in theory, can reveal aspects of a work which historically authentic interpretations may conceal. But it is crazy to conclude, as some contemporary critics do, that the act of interpretation has no real connection with works produced in the past, or that the idea of interpretative fidelity is illusory. On the contrary: it is the actual open-endedness of the inherited interpretanda which places an obligation of inventiveness on the modern interpreter.

It is for this reason that I disagree with Bennett's approach to Spinoza, without automatically embracing the piously authentic ones which he shuns. It is not that I find his skeptical, hypothetico-deductive reading of Spinoza illegitimate or unilluminating, but that I do not see that it invalidates the romantic alternative. It seems to me, in fact, that Bennett's own discussions unwittingly reveal the improbability of any conclusions as categorical as those which he espouses. There are three issues in particular where Bennett assumes definite answers to questions which, if I am right, are essentially open.

Objectivity or Sympathy?

The romantic Spinozists unashamedly bond their love of Spinoza with their interpretation of his doctrines, and they will hardly countenance any reading of Spinoza's words which would make them untrue. The effect can be suffocating, and the openness and objectivity of Bennett's approach is a welcome relief. He takes each statement as it comes, trying to determine its meaning before assessing its credibility, and he expresses the deepest scorn for "the courtly deference which pretends that Spinoza is always or usually right, under some rescuing interpretation" (372).

But this clean separation between interpretation and evaluation turns out to be unsustainable. A discussion of what Spinoza meant about personal identity, for instance, obviously presupposes some prior understanding of personal identity in general; and many of Bennett's disagreements with the romantic Spinozists turn on abstract philosophical arguments which might just as well be conducted without any reference to the question of what Spinoza meant. The same applies to Bennett's boldest claim—that the idea of "intuitive knowledge" proposed in the closing pages of the *Ethics* is "a disaster." The puzzle is that Bennett fails to draw the conclusion that the earlier parts of the book—which are obviously meant as an expression of "intuitive knowledge"—must be "a disaster" too. He even adopts an arbitrary textual hypothesis (that the definition of goodness in terms of "an exemplar of human nature" in the Preface to Part Four was written before the earlier parts of the book and represents a view which Spinoza quickly abandoned but forgot to delete) in order to protect his "hypothetico-deductive" interpretation (296). It is hard to avoid the conclusion that Bennett exhibits much the same "courtly deference" in dealing with his favorite passages from the *Ethics* as the romantic Spinozists do when they thrill to the bits which evoke "the intellectual love of God." This suggests that "rescuing interpretations," more or less plausible, may be the normal practice among historians of philosophy (as they clearly are among performing artists), and that the choice between sympathy and objectivity in the interpretation of philosophy is an unreal one.

Logic or Rhetoric?

Bennett's rejection of the romantic interpretation of the *Ethics* issues partly from his preference for philosophical issues which lend themselves to reconstructive paraphrase in brief sentences whose entailment relations can be displayed unambiguously, and each of which can be accepted or rejected at its face value. The romantics, however, see the world of the *Ethics* as controlled by an author who is not, like Bennett, a level-headed, civilized, and clubbable member of a democratic intellectual community, ready to have his claims tested like anyone else. Their Spinoza is a complacent mystic, a self-absorbed saint whom we thank for understanding our difficulties, and never blame for having caused them in the first place. The romantics will not expect their interpretation of the *Ethics* to appeal to someone who has no sympathy with such a figure, and who believes that philosophical thoughts ought always to be represented in a language uncluttered by such complexities as metaphor, narrative, or irony. They may even claim that good philosophy always calls upon forms of representation which involve fictions, and that it can succeed only for readers who are willing to control their disbelief. And they may concede that the necessary fictions (Spinoza's concept of intuitive knowledge, for example) can be incoherent; but they will insist that there are important truths which can be apprehended only by proceeding *as if* they were true. Bennett may complain that they are placing their rhetorical preferences above their serious duty to philosophy. But they will return the charge: to confine philosophy within the bounds of literal statement is itself, they will say, to sacrifice philosophy at the altar of a mere rhetorical preference. And I do not see how this issue, either, could ever be finally resolved.

Internal or External?

Spinoza had an awkward relationship to the traditions, canons, and institutions of European Christian philosophy. He wrote the *Ethics* in Latin, a language he did not learn till he was twenty, and he thought that his ideas about theology and morality would not be tolerated if they were fully understood; and as a Jew he probably had a vivid sense of what such intolerance might mean. He saw his own life as a crucial experiment, a proof that his doctrines were not atheistic, at least in any traditional sense of the term: "For atheists," as he wrote in a letter, "are wont to desire inordinately honors and riches, which I have always despised, as all those who know me are aware."[20]

The earliest biography of Spinoza was written in the two years following Spinoza's death in 1677. Its author, Jean Lucas, was an unrespectable freethinker, but his book was dreary hagiography, depicting an improbable hero "unstained by any blemish."[21] The purpose of the work, presumably, was to shake popular belief in the viciousness of atheists. Bayle's dictionary of 1697 perpetuated the hagiography, though deploring the doctrine; and by 1700 the question whether Spinoza's life, and particularly his death, could possibly be those of an atheist was a standard point of controversy.[22] "His life was a perpetual contradiction of his opinions," says the third edition of the *Encyclopaedia Britannica* (1797), since it "never deviated from the strictest propriety."

It follows that an investigation of the particulars of Spinoza's life, and a self-conscious orientation in the traditions of Spinoza interpretation, is internal to an understanding of Spinoza's philosophical achievement, though it may be external to the history of philosophy, in that it calls upon the knowledge of general historians. Bennett observes quite correctly that "this delving into backgrounds is subject to a law of diminishing returns," but in the case of Spinoza, the returns may be unusually buoyant. His life and reputation stand at the crossroads where modern philosophy found its identity—at the center of the intellectual institutions of Western European Christendom, with all their exclusions along lines of language, religion, race, nation, and gender. Bennett has every right to measure Spinoza's achievement against the standard of "a recognizably worthwhile philosophical project" (374). But it is legitimate to excavate and evaluate this standard itself: what makes a philosophical project worthwhile, and who has the power to recognize it, and how did this come about? In order to investigate these central, internal issues, external "background" is essential.

I began this consideration of Bennett's interpretation of Spinoza by expressing unease about the supposition that historians of philosophy face a choice between fearless anachronism and supine fidelity. Then I discussed the structure of the *Ethics* in the hope of showing that the romantic interpretation is valid in spite of Bennett's skepticism. Finally, I have argued that a work like the *Ethics* may permit or even require a variety of interpretations, so that Bennett's reading of the book, though in conflict with the romantic one, does not necessarily compete with it. This has led me to raise three dilemmas—between objectivity and sympathy, logic and rhetoric, and internal and external history—all of which Bennett would, I think, be inclined to resolve in favor of one of their terms (in each case the first, as I have listed them); whereas they appear to me to be absolutely insoluble: they are the fundamental uncertainties which keep the historiography of philosophy alive.

My own position is that philosophy ought to be interpreted as a part of literature and of general history. This sets me at some distance from Bennett, but at an even greater distance from Spinoza, who affirmed that in the case of Euclid and those who write like him (and Spinoza would have included himself here), "We need make no researches concerning the life, the pursuits, or the habits of the author; nor need we inquire in what language, nor when he wrote, nor the vicissitudes of his book, nor its various readings, nor how, nor by whose advice it has been received." He did acknowledge, however, that the case was different with non-Euclidean works: "If we read a book which contains incredible or impossible narratives, or is written in a very obscure style, and if we know nothing of its author, nor of the time or occasion of its being written, we shall try in vain to gain certain knowledge of its true meaning."[23]

But the truth is that Spinoza's book certainly (and perhaps Euclid's too) is full of "incredible or impossible narratives . . . written in a very obscure style"—notably the story of the three grades of knowledge. Bennett finds it incoherent, while the romantics hold that it is outstandingly elevating; but surely the truth is that it is both.

I started this lecture by referring to people (including myself) who have felt a special bond with Spinoza, like Dr. Fischelson imploring Spinoza to forgive him. I conclude by asking Jonathan Bennett to forgive me for having used the opportunity of commenting on his book to pick quarrels on abstract questions of method, on which he had not written, rather than on concrete questions of philosophy, on which he had; and to forgive me also for having failed to communicate my criticisms to him properly in advance.

NOTES

1. Jonathan Bennett, A Study of Spinoza's Ethics (Cambridge: Cambridge University Press, 1984). The embedded references, which are indicated by parentheses in the text of my essay, correspond either to Bennett's work (cited above) or to Spinoza's Ethics. Page numbers are used to reference the former (e.g., 25), while Bennett's coding is used for the latter. (E.g., "2p7s" should be understood to mean Part 2, Proposition 7, Scholium; and 4d2 names Part 4, definition 2.) Where the part number is made obvious by the text, only its proposition will be indicated [e.g., "p7s"]; such references as "5p23,d" are to be read as Part 5, Proposition 23, and its demonstration).

2. Isaac Bashevis Singer, "The Spinoza of Market Street," in The Spinoza of Market Street (New York: Fawcett Crest, 1980), p. 32.

3. For Jacobi's view of Spinoza, see Leon Roth, Spinoza (London: Ernest Benn, 1929), p. 210. For Schelling, see Alan White, Schelling: An Introduction to the System of Freedom (New Haven, Conn.: Yale University Press, 1983), pp. 32-33. For Hegel, see Lectures on the History of Philosophy, trans. E. S. Haldane and Frances H. Simson, 3 vols. (London: Kegan Paul, Trench, Trubner, 1896). 3: 285, 253, 254. For Coleridge, see John H. Muirhead, Coleridge as Philosopher (London: George Allen, 1930), pp. 46-47.

4. For George Eliot, see her letter to Charles Bray, 4 December 1849, in The George Eliot Letters, ed. Gordon S. Haight (New Haven, Conn.: Yale University Press, 1954), 1: 321. For Matthew Arnold, see "Spinoza and the Bible," Essays in Criticism (1865), in Lectures and Essays in Criticism, ed. R. H. Super (Ann Arbor, Mich.: University of Michigan Press, 1962), p. 181; "Resignation," from The Strayed Reveller (1849).

5. Friedrich Nietzsche, Beyond Good and Evil (1886), §5.

6. Jonathan Bennett, "Substance, Reality and Primary Qualities," American Philosophical Quarterly 2 (1965); reprinted in Locke and Berkeley: A Collection of Critical Essays, ed. C. B. Martin and D. M. Armstrong (London: Macmillan, n.d.), pp. 86-124, 87.

7. Michael Ayers, "Analytical Philosophy and the History of Philosophy," in Philosophy and its Past, by Jonathan Rée, Michael Ayers, and Adam Westoby (Brighton, Eng.: Harvester, 1978), pp. 41-66, 63; see also Michael Ayers, "Substance, Reality and the Great, Dead Philosophers," American Philosophical Quarterly 7, no. 1 (January 1970): 38-49.

8. Maurice Merleau-Ponty, Phénoménologie de la perception (Paris:

Gallimard, 1945), p. ii; translated by Colin Smith, *Phenomenology of Perception* (London: Routledge and Kegan Paul, 1962), p. viii (translation amended).

9. See Paul Edwards, ed., *The Encyclopedia of Philosophy*, s.v. "Spinoza."

10. Cf. *Tractatus Theologico-Politicus*, chap. 7; see R. H. M. Elwes, trans., *The Chief Works of Spinoza*, 2 vols. (London: Bell, 1883), 1: 113.

11. Friedrich Nietzsche, *Der Antichrist*, Gesammelte Werke, Musarionausgabe, vol. 17, p. 187.

12. Wayne Booth, *The Rhetoric of Fiction* (Chicago: University of Chicago Press, 1961), esp. pp. 71ff.

13. For Jacobi, see Roth, *Spinoza*, p. xiv. For Goethe, *Dichtung und Wahrheit* 3; cited in Roth, *Spinoza*, p. 211. For George Eliot, see note 4. For Merleau-Ponty, see *Phénoménologie de la perception*, p. 209, also p. 514; *Phenomenology of Perception*, trans. Smith, p. 179 (translation amended), also p. 451. Bernard Malamud, *The Fixer* (Harmondsworth, Eng.: Penguin, 1967), pp. 70-71.

14. Gilles Deleuze, *Spinoza: Philosophie pratique*, 2d ed. (Paris: Minuit, 1981), pp. 42-43.

15. Ludwig Wittgenstein, *Tractatus Logico-Philosophicus*, trans. D. F. Pears and B. F. McGuinness (London: Routledge & Kegan Paul, 1961), p. 5.

16. Spinoza, *On the Improvement of the Understanding*, in *Works*, trans. Elwes, vol. 2, p. 28.

17. Letter 32, to Oldenburg, 1665; in *The Correspondence of Spinoza*, ed. A. Wolf (London: George Allen and Unwin, 1928), p. 211.

18. Letter 17, to Balling, 1664; in Wolf, *Correspondence*, pp. 140-41.

19. Thomas Paine, *The Rights of Man* (Harmondsworth, Eng.: Penguin, 1969), p. 64.

20. Letter 43, to Jacob Ostens, 1671; in Wolf, *Correspondence*, p. 255.

21. See A. Wolf, ed., *The Oldest Biography of Spinoza* (London: George Allen and Unwin, 1927), p. 74.

22. See Wolf, *Oldest Biography*, p. 168.

23. Spinoza, *Tractatus Theologico-Politicus*, trans. Elwes, pp. 113, 111.

Response to Garber and Rée

Jonathan Bennett

Daniel Garber claims two advantages for studying the history of philosophy. I am struck by the modesty of one of them, namely, that in studying philosophy historically we get a chance to put ourselves and our opinions in perspective, to realize that things we have never questioned haven't always been believed and are therefore accidents (so to speak) rather than the essence of the human mind. Intensive, scholarly historical study is indeed a way of getting those advantages, but it is a rather roundabout one, and there are shorter routes to the same goal.

Secondly, Garber says, the study of the history of philosophy is valuable because of the questions that it suggests to us. That seems to me extremely important. Sometimes I find that historical studies introduce me to questions that I don't think I would have got from anywhere else; so that is one of the things for which I look to the history of philosophy.

The contrast between Garber as looking for questions and myself as looking for answers is one that I don't recognize. If anything in my writings seems to support it, then I apologize; I have never meant to represent myself as interested only in answers and not in questions. Garber quotes me as writing of wanting to "learn philosophy" from what I am studying, and of my studies as "helping us to see things," and I don't take either of those formulations as confining oneself to answers rather than to questions. I'll come back to questions again in a moment. On the matter of answers, yes, I think that one is helped to learn truths from the kind of study of the classical texts that I try to do. This means that one is learning from materials that are themselves often in error, but there is no mystery about that. We all know that error can be instructive. Garber says that a few failures go a long way, and I am not sure that I know what he means by that. I find that I can't have enough illuminating failures: I go on learning things from tackling and sorting them out.

There may be some idiosyncrasy in this. My philosophy studies through M.A. were done in a one-man department in New Zealand. The one man was the late Arthur N. Prior: he was wonderful, and I wouldn't have missed him for anything; but he was so overworked that he didn't have time to learn very much, and I didn't know much of philosophy or its history when I began my graduate studies. Those studies consisted of two years in Oxford in the middle fifties—not the best region of space-time for a sound fundamental philosophical education. I loved Oxford, and learned a lot from Quine (sic!), Waismann, Price, Dummett, Hampshire, Grice, and a few others; but at the end of those years I was still horribly undercooked. Then after one year of teaching in this country I began twelve years in Cambridge, where I was mainly paid to lecture on early modern philosophy. To a large extent I taught myself philosophy through wrestling with those texts, so that for me there was a special reason why they were a source of all kinds of philosophical discoveries and insights. But I am not alone in this. Others too find that they grow as philosophers through engaging with the thoughts of great philosophers of the past, although (and here I agree with Garber) more often than not one is engaging with mistaken thoughts.

In this debate I am not very clear about the difference between "learning questions" and "learning answers." Spinoza holds a doctrine that, if you cut the cackle and put it bluntly, says that there aren't any outright false beliefs, that so-called error is a species of ignorance. One would like to know why a genius should say something as patently false as that, and the usual answers that are given are inadequate. They point to axioms from which, if they are interpreted in a certain way, this follows; but then why accept the axioms on those interpretations if this follows from them? The right answer—the only one that is fit for adult consumption—is that Spinoza had a naturalistic view of the human condition (there is nothing peculiar about human beings as compared with the rest of nature) and accepted a parallelism between the physical and mental realms (there is nothing peculiar about minds as compared with bodies). So he saw that an outright false belief was going to be a part of nature that is false, a false natural object, and he didn't see how there could be one. That generates the question "How could there be a false natural object?" which I think is a wonderful question. I also think that in seeing it as a real question, seeing why it presented itself to Spinoza and not to his contemporaries, seeing what the things are in his philosophy that blocked him from finding the right answer, one can learn a great deal of positive philosophy. This is just one of many examples that make a nonsense of the contrast between learning questions and learning answers.

Descartes's warning against going to books is fascinating and wrong in at least two ways that are relevant to my theme. One is that Descartes writes as though it were a clean-cut choice—either you can get the answer for yourself or you can find it in a book—as though he were unaware of the possibility that one might be able to do a lot of the job oneself but need some help from the works of others. The second point is more important. When Descartes says if you can't do it yourself, then you're not going to be able to "select and order" what you find in the works of others, he makes it sound as though in consulting those works one is looking for pretty pebbles to arrange in a nice pattern (and will fail unless one already has the pattern in one's head). But that's not what it is like to go to the great texts for help with philosophy. One is not selecting and ordering; rather, one is wrestling and struggling and straining and learning and growing, constantly pulling muscles in one's brain. That Cartesian picture is absurd, and I refuse to have anything to do with it.

Garber and I seem to differ in our attitudes to the subject author. He thinks it important to make the author look sensible; I don't. I do want to understand the aspects of the work of Spinoza (say) that make him look like a genius; but what makes him a genius is a set of factors that include courage and intellectual recklessness, sweep and scope of thought, the ability to make connections that wouldn't have occurred to anyone else (without, perhaps, the patience to examine them carefully to see if they really hold). These are not the ingredients of a recipe for seeming sensible.

Jonathan Rée threw several questions at me in his paper at the conference, and I will say what I can in response to them.

How if at all is literary structure relevant to interpretation? I'm sorry, but I have no opinions about that. That is a doctrine of Rée's, and it's for him to instruct us about it. He does oppose his literary picture of the Ethics, in which a lot of attention is paid to rhetoric and poetry and literary devices of various sorts, with my way of looking at it as a hypothetico-deductive structure. Of course, I didn't invent that way of looking at it, though I may have developed it a bit futher than anyone else has. In his paper Rée said that he thought that my hypothetico-deductive picture was a misinterpretation of the Ethics, and that reasons for that could be found in Spinoza's doctrine of the three grades of knowledge. Well, I disagree about that and believe that Rée must have misunderstood the "three grades" doctrine; and on a more suitable occasion he and I might go into that question in detail. As to the thesis that the hypothetico-deductive approach is wrong because of some radically rival way of looking at the entire work, some radically new thesis about how the Ethics is structured, how it is supposed to get its effects, and what those effects are supposed to be—I have nothing to say about that and don't expect to on any future occasion.

Perhaps this is the place to mention something that Jonathan Rée alludes to several times in his paper, namely, the intensity with which

Spinoza has been loved. I want to say two things about that. One is that about thirty years ago when I started working hard on Spinoza I went through my own peculiar version of that. I wasn't overwhelmed by a sense of "this is a wonderful man and I want him for my father," or anything of that kind. Rather, I developed a strong conviction that if only I could understand it, everything in the *Ethics* is true! But I was looking to it for the kinds of things that I still look to it for, not for romantic content; but I had a romantic idea that somehow it ought to be—had to be—right in everything it said. That is what motivated me to work on it so hard: I was going to show a grateful world how right Spinoza was about everything. So clearly the *Ethics* had power to work some kind of magic on me, as well as on George Eliot and many other literary people; I am not in a position to be contemptuous of them.

Indeed, when W. H. Walsh saw a late draft of my book, ending with my disagreeable chapter on the second half of *Ethics* 5, he suggested that I write a further, final chapter that would take away some of the nasty taste. I liked the idea and accordingly wrote a one-section chapter about other ways of looking at Spinoza. I didn't go into detail as Rée does in his paper, and I said nothing specifically about literary form; but I wrote about how Spinoza can be looked to as an examplar, or as a source of wisdom, in the way literary people often have seen and valued him. I offered some of the usual quotations and anecdotes and said that I wasn't quarreling with such attitudes and that for all I knew that approach to Spinoza was more valuable than what I was doing; but (I said placatingly) one uses one's best talents and I was doing what I could do. When I showed this new chapter to my friend and colleague José Benardete, he hit the roof and forbade me to include the chapter in the book. He was right: the chapter was a weak-spirited attempt to wriggle out from under various kinds of disapprobation and dislike that I ought to take on the chin. The things I said in that chapter were true: I do think there are other ways of looking at Spinoza, and I do respect them and don't want to put them down. But it would not have been appropriate in this book to try at the last minute to say that.

The third of Rée's four questions had to do with past and present interpretations. What I have to say about this is fairly prosaic. Obviously, earlier interpretations can simply help. When I can't cope with a passage I will look up such commentators as I think might be helpful, to see what if anything they say about it; and sometimes they'll have noticed something that I had missed. Also, if I have an understanding of some text, and know of a competent earlier worker who interpreted it quite differently, it is a matter of sheer prudence to look at the earlier interpretation and consider the evidence for it. This is just part of the general procedure of testing one's opinions against possible counterevidence.

Rée will find those remarks thin and disappointing: he seems to be

raising a question about one's *responsibility* to account for earlier interpretations. Well, I acknowledge no such responsibility and have nothing
more to say on this topic, except to remark that earlier interpretations
can be dangerous: they can stop one from attending properly to the text
itself. I recently heard Pierre Laberge speak of the tendency to hear the
well-known texts "to the sound of music," and of the kind of commentary
that breaks up the tune and thus makes it easier to understand the words.
The music—I took him to mean—is the lulling, soothing hum of the
received interpretations; and I agree with his implication that these can
be dangerous because they can stop one from listening. Of course, earlier
interpretations are available as an independent subject of historical study:
there could be a good book about what has been made of Spinoza over
the centuries, for instance.

The relevance of societies and institutions to interpretations in
philosophy is not a topic that I have thought about, and I have nothing
to say about it.

The first question in Rée's paper concerns the relevance of evaluation to interpretation: is there a connection, he asked, between my thinking
the second half of *Ethics* 5 is terrible and my not thinking that the rest
of the *Ethics* should be seen as somehow subservient to it and not being
willing to read them in the light of it? I don't think so. Even if I thought
that the closing pages of the *Ethics* were pretty good (and that takes
me to an extremely remote world!), I can't see how that would lead me
to think that that part of the work in any way shapes up the earlier
parts.

Of course the earlier parts of the work have a role in the last part:
in the latter Spinoza uses concepts that are introduced earlier, particularly
that of *scientia intuitiva,* and brings in some of the earlier propositions.
But that's not what Rée was asking about. He was asking whether one
can properly get the hang of what's going on earlier without having a
grasp of what comes later. His answer seems to be no. Mine is yes,
and I would expect to stand by that answer even if I became convinced
that the second half of *Ethics* 5 is much better than I actually think
it to be.

Behind that opinion lies a careful examination of what dependences
there are between the various parts of the *Ethics.* I have an apparatus
that lets me find out in a minute or two the entire deductive progeny,
and the entire deductive ancestry, of any given proposition in the work;
and I have made an enormous amount of use of this. When I wrote my
book I probably knew more than anyone had ever known before about
that aspect of the *Ethics.* I realize, however, that Rée may have in mind
connections and dependences that would not be reflected in the ostensible
structures of Spinoza's arguments.

In a letter that Rée wrote to me recently, but not in his paper, he invokes a contrast between philosophical and exegetical—or reconstructive and exegetical—concerns with a text. I reject that dichotomy, at least as a comment on my work. I am doing exegesis all the way. I do it by reconstruction or paraphrase because there is no other way to do it. (Incidentally, I take issue with Garber about the idea of understanding a past author's text in his own terms. Ayers has criticized me for trying to understand people in my terms and not theirs, and I was pleased to see that Rorty in a recent paper came down on him hard for this, saying rightly that it doesn't make sense. To understand someone's thought you must get it into your own terms, terms that you understand. The only alternative is to parrot his words.)

But a question remains about how central a place should be given in this endeavor to the pursuit of what the author actually meant, and I don't want to be evasive about this.

When dealing with a genius, one is more likely to get illuminating ideas by discovering what he really thought than by forcing onto him thoughts that he didn't have; so from the standpoint of my kind of work, there are strong probabilistic reasons for wanting to get the author right, i.e., to find out what he actually meant. That, of course, treats the author's thoughts as having instrumental value. It would be more conducive to peace if I were to say that understanding the author's intention is always my end, and not just my means; but I cannot in good conscience say that. What I primarily go to these texts for is illumination, insight into philosophical truth; and if an author prompts an illuminating thought in me, seeming to have had it himself though really he didn't, the thought itself is none the worse for that, and perhaps I deserve some credit for having had it.

Let me give an example. In writing *Kant's Analytic* I came across something that I call "the ordering argument." It is a fine, powerful argument, and so far as I know it had never before explicitly appeared anywhere in the literature of philosophy. Its basis in Kant's text was slim, but there were a few small bits that I could understand only as fragmentary expressions of the ordering argument; it was indeed my attempt to understand these that led me to the argument in the first place. It occurred to me that if I was right in attributing the argument to Kant, I had scored an important exegetical coup; and that if I was wrong about that, then I deserved the credit for thinking up a first-rate bit of original philosophy. Well, Peter Strawson in his review of the book described the ordering argument as being better than anything that that part of Kant's text seems on the surface to contain, and praised the quality of my evidence that the argument was Kant's and that I hadn't "put the sixpence in the pudding" myself. I settled for the compliment on my exegetical skills, though I would rather have been told that I had invented the argument myself. My spirits were raised, however, by a paper in which James Van Cleve gives the back of his hand to that part of my book, saying that remarks of Kant's on which I had been relying should be dismissed as casual asides that don't express any considered opinion of Kant's. Perhaps, then, I am entitled after all to the philosophical credit; though Van Cleve might not say so, because he seems not to have noticed what a beautiful thing the ordering argument is.

Who cares? What does it matter? Well, it matters if (for example) Kant did have the ordering argument and this is relevant to how parts of his work should be interpreted. Because if those other parts are misinterpreted then *probably* they will cast less light than they would if they were understood correctly. But this is still to treat knowledge of "what Kant really meant" as instrumentally rather than intrinsically valuable.

Still, because it *is* instrumentally valuable, I want to do as well as I can in finding out what my authors meant. Ayers and Rée and others think that I sometimes go wrong in this by not being historical enough. I'm sure they are right: one can get interpretations wrong by not being historical enough, and it would be amazing if I had never done that.[1]

But I have not been impressed by the specific charges of this kind that have been leveled against my work (I don't mean by Garber or Rée: the former makes no such charge; the latter does, but relies upon Ayers for evidence). For example, Ayers has characterized my understanding of Locke's treatment of "substratum" as "brutal linguistic positivism," a historically insensitive projection onto Locke of twentieth-century preoccupations. Since my reading of Locke's "substratum" texts is exactly the same as Leibniz's reading of them, one can only smile at this warning of the perils of not knowing enough about what went on in the seventeenth century; but my present point is that when Ayers gets down to details regarding Locke on "substratum," his main work is done for him not by special attention to the historical background, but rather by inattention to what Locke actually wrote.[2] Peter Alexander seems, indeed, to have made an almost explicit principle of inattentiveness, of broad-brush impressionism, in reading a text. Locke uses the term "idea" not only to stand for mental items but also to stand for the qualities of extramental things, and he tells us how to unpack statements of the latter kind— he presents them as a kind of short-hand. I have remarked that Locke's rules for unpacking don't work; they have a counterexample in the very passage in which they are given! Alexander offers a weak alternative account of that passage and claims that in the light of that "well-meaning" readers will agree that my point against Locke is a mere "quibble." I call attention to the phrase "well-meaning." Alexander seems to be appealing to readers of Locke who approach his work in the right spirit, namely, with a resolve to make him come out as sensible and respect-worthy, and a reluctance to say loudly that he is wrong, and wrong, and wrong again. I am perfectly willing to be shown how I would do the philosophy better, or get the exegesis more accurate, if I attended more to historical factors; but I am not willing to be fobbed off with a combination of indulgence towards the author and casualness about the details of his text. That combination is indeed the best recipe for becoming comfortable with the text, but I don't want to become comfortable. On the contrary, I want to be supersensitive to every textual detail that seems not to work, that looks contradictory, that seems to be a change of tune, and I want to find out what's going on in there, find out why, draw my own conclusions, and learn and grow in that way.

I am passionately convinced that there are other good ways of coming at the texts. Great philosophers write under an enormous array of different pressures, many of them intellectual, some of them social or moral or emotional. All kinds of different currents come together in one person's mind, and I don't think they have one unitary resultant which is "what he meant." When Locke (say) wrote a particular sentence, there may have been multiple reasons why he was writing a sentence on this particular topic, why he placed it just there, why he used this word rather than that, and so on; and one can only look for some kind of pattern in all this that will meet one's own needs. It is absolutely consistent with my logically structured view of the *Ethics* that the work should also contain the kind of thing that Jonathan Rée finds in it; there is no reason at all why Rée's and my stories should not both be wholly true, in the sense of being true to what Spinoza actually meant.

My choice of what kind of thing to look for is determined by what interests me and, I think, by what I am good at. We all tend to do what we think we can do best, don't we? So I turn my back on these other things; but I'm not early Berkeley, and I don't think that what I turn my back on doesn't exist.

NOTES

1. I am not impressed by Rée's reason for thinking so, namely, that under my interpretations so much of what the author says comes out as false. From the opposite side, Garber questions my use of the great "early modern" texts because, he says, so much of what they contain is false. I will happily hold the towels while Rée and Garber slug it out.

2. For details, see Jonathan Bennett, "Substratum," *History of Philosophy Quarterly* 4 (1987): 197-215.

Part Two

Ancient Philosophy

Rorty on Plato as an Edifier

Daniel A. Dombrowski

INTRODUCTION

One of the most important works written by an American philosopher in recent years has been *Philosophy and the Mirror of Nature* by Richard Rorty.[1] It is a complex work that criticizes most of Western philosophy from the time of Plato to the twentieth century, most notably because of the correspondence theory of truth that dominated, whether explicitly or implicitly, this long period. Dewey, Wittgenstein, and Heidegger emerge as the heroes of the book because of their edifying reactions against the mirror imagery of the philosophic tradition. Curiously enough, however, although "Plato," "Platonism," "Platonic," and the "Platonic urge" are constantly used by Rorty as catchwords for what is to be denigrated in philosophy, it is by no means clear in his book what sort of philosopher Plato himself really was. Paradoxically, Plato may end up being one of the heroes of the book, or at least should be one of the heroes of the book, which is what I will try to show in this article.

I will first examine Rorty's distaste for Plato's philosophy; then I will isolate those passages in Rorty that perhaps indicate Rorty's admiration for Plato as an edifying philosopher; and I will interpret Plato's *Sophist* in a Rorty-like way, for it is in this dialogue that Rorty implies we might see Plato as an edifier. Finally, I will try to put Rorty's view of Plato in a larger perspective.

RORTY'S CRITICISMS OF PLATO

Not everything Rorty has to say about Plato is unique. One of his major criticisms of Plato has been made many times before, i.e., Plato's attempt to talk about adjectives as if they were nouns is muddled (33). He offers this description of how a Platonic Form is constructed:

73

> We simply lift off a single property from something (the property of being
> red, or painful, or good) and then treat it as if it itself were a subject
> of predication, and perhaps also a locus of causal efficacy. A Platonic form
> is merely a property considered in isolation and considered as capable of
> sustaining causal relations. (32)

Also, because of the inadequacy of Plato's assimilation of *ousia* to *idea*
(73), there are few believers in Platonic Forms today (43).[2]

For Rorty, Plato did not discover the distinction between two kinds
of entities, inner and outer. Rather, Rorty claims, relying on George Pitcher,
Plato was the first to articulate the "Platonic Principle" that "differences
in certainty must correspond to differences in the objects known" (156).
This principle is a natural consequence, Rorty thinks, of the attempt
to model knowledge on perception; if it is assumed that we need distinct
faculties to "grasp" bricks *and* numbers, then the discovery of geometry
will seem to be the discovery of a new faculty called *nous*.[3] Although
Plato toyed with "inner space" metaphors (e.g., as Rorty notes, the aviary
image of the *Theaetetus* [242-43]) his thought was "essentially 'realistic'"
rather than introspective:

> The Platonic distinction to which mathematical truth gave rise was meta-
> physical rather than epistemological—a distinction between the worlds of
> Being and Becoming. What corresponds to the metaphysical distinctions on
> the "divided line" of *Republic* VI are distinctions not between kinds of non-
> propositional inner representations, but between grades of certainty attaching
> to propositions. Plato did not focus on the idea of nonpropositional inner
> entities, but rather on that of the various parts of the soul and of the body
> being compelled in their respective ways by their respective objects. (158)

These objects provided Plato with his "foundations of knowledge." Rorty's
antifoundationalism notices that even non-Platonists have traditionally
fallen victim to the Platonic principle by trying to ground knowledge
claims on some incorrigible base like clear and distinct ideas, sense perceptions, a logical use of language, etc. This is the danger that Plato
poses, for if we think of knowledge in this way

> We will want to get behind reasons to causes, beyond argument to com-
> pulsion from the object known, to a situation in which argument would
> be not just silly but impossible, for anyone gripped by the object in the
> required way will be *unable* to doubt or to see an alternative. . . . For Plato,
> that point was reached by escaping from the senses and opening up the
> faculty of reason—the Eye of the Soul—to the World of Being. (159)

> The urge to say that assertions and actions must not only cohere with
> other assertions and actions but "correspond" to something apart from what

people are saying and doing has some claim to be called the philosophical urge. It is the urge which drove Plato to say that Socrates' words and deeds, failing as they did to cohere with current theory and practice, nonetheless corresponded to something which the Athenians could barely glimpse. (179)

There is little epistemology in Plato's thought (222) because, although he was one of the inventors of "idealism" (307), he had a fetish for correspondence. For Rorty (and Kuhn), however, "objective" means "characterizing the view which would be agreed upon as a result of argument undeflected by irrelevant considerations." We have Plato to "thank" for an alternative meaning: "representing things as they really are," and for the concomitant question: "In just what sense is Goodness out there waiting to be represented accurately as a result of rational argument on moral questions?" (333–34). For Rorty, in no sense whatsoever.

The philosophic tradition since Plato, for Rorty, has assumed that the algorithm-no algorithm distinction runs together with the reason-passion distinction (339), such that, at least for Plato, the only way to be "edified" is "to know what is out there." For Rorty, however, the quest for truth is just "one among many ways in which we might be edified" (360). Perhaps because Plato thought otherwise, he defined the philosopher in opposition to the poet (370). Rorty's final judgment seems, therefore, given the aforementioned evidence, to be that "the Platonic notion of Truth itself is absurd" (377) since it condemns philosophers to a Sisyphean task:

> The dilemma created by this Platonic hypostatization is that, on the one hand, the philosopher must attempt to find criteria for picking out these unique referents, whereas, on the other hand, the only hints he has about what these criteria could be are provided by current practice (by, e.g., the best moral and scientific thought of the day). Philosophers thus condemn themselves to a Sisyphean task. (374)

EDIFYING VERSUS SYSTEMATIC PHILOSOPHY

Rorty's attitude toward Plato is by no means clear, however. Consider the following quotation, which opposes the hermeneutical philosopher as conversationalist (Socrates) with the epistemological (or better, in the case of Plato, metaphysical) philosopher as king of culture:

> I think that the view that epistemology, or some suitable successor-discipline, is necessary to culture confuses two roles which the philosopher might play. The first is that of the informal dilettante, the polypragmatic, Socratic intermediary between various discourses. In his salon, so to speak,

hermetic thinkers are charmed out of their self-enclosed practices. Disagreements between disciplines and discourses are compromised or transcended in the course of the conversation. The second role is that of the cultural overseer who knows everyone's common ground—the Platonic philosopher-king who knows what everybody else is really doing whether *they* know it or not, because he knows about the ultimate context (the Forms, the Mind, Language) within which they are doing it. The first role is appropriate to hermeneutics, the second to epistemology. (317–18)

This is the distinction between the edifying and the systematic philosopher, respectively.[4] Since it is the first sort of philosopher that Rorty defends, it would seem that Socrates receives a reprieve that is denied Plato. Rorty thus assumes a solution to the "Socratic problem" both above and in the following passage:

It is so much a part of "thinking philosophically" to be impressed with the special character of mathematical truth that it is hard to shake off the grip of the Platonic Principle. If, however, we think of "rational certainty" as a matter of victory in argument rather than of relation to an object known, we shall look toward our interlocutors rather than to our faculties for the explanation of the phenomenon. (156–57)

The latter sort of rational certainty seems to apply to Socrates and the sophists, who do not see a difference in kind, for Rorty, between "necessary" and "contingent" truths; at most they (along with Rorty) see differences in degree of ease in objecting to our beliefs (157).

Since Plato is our major source of information on Socrates' thought, he might receive a vicarious reprieve as well. But the matter is more complicated than this. In the following remark Rorty reveals an aperture that would grant Plato himself, not just Socrates, the status of an edifying philosopher:

The permanent fascination of the man who dreamed up the whole idea of Western philosophy—Plato—is that we still do not know which sort of philosopher he was. Even if the *Seventh Letter* is set aside as spurious, the fact that after millenniums of commentary nobody knows which passages in the dialogues are jokes keeps the puzzle fresh. (369n)

In addition to having a sense of humor, what enables Plato to possibly be an edifying philosopher is the fact that he started philosophy's (written) conversation, which in a free and leisured way allows the sparks of (Kuhnian) abnormal discourse to fly upward (389):

The fact that we can continue the conversation Plato began without discussing the topics Plato wanted discussed, illustrates the difference between treating philosophy as a voice in a conversation and treating it as a subject, a *Fach*, a field of professional inquiry. The conversation Plato began has been enlarged by more voices than Plato would have dreamed possible. (391)

What is unfortunate is that Rorty gives little indication of what possibly edifying passages in Plato he has in mind. The *Euthyphro*, he tells us, is a work of edifying pedagogy (307), but since this is generally seen as an early dialogue, the edification contained in it might only be attributed to Socrates, not Plato, especially given Rorty's apparent resolution of the Socratic problem. More helpful is Rorty's suggestion of a difference between the *Republic* and *Sophist*: the former is epistemologically (again, metaphysically) oriented while the latter is concerned with "pure" philosophy of language, without relevance to the traditional concerns of philosophy; nor, presumably, with the major concerns of the *Republic* (257). It is Rorty's tantalizing mention of the *Sophist* that inspires the next section of this article, in which I try to find out what sense it makes, if any, to see Plato as an edifier.

EDIFICATION IN THE *SOPHIST*

The beginning of this dialogue finds Socrates and Theodorus agreeing that there is something significant in philosophical discourse; it need not be mere verbal dispute (216B). No doubt Rorty would agree. His suggestion that this dialogue develops a different conception of the philosopher from that found in the *Republic* receives initial support when the philosopher is distinguished not only from the sophist, but from the statesman as well (217A), an un-*Republic*-like distinction. And the *Sophist* is indeed a dialogue (despite the fact that Socrates fades out of the picture early on) in that the major figure, the Eleatic Stranger, prefers dialectical exchanges to long discourses (217C–E).

Most of the dialogue concerns a hunt for the sophist, but *not* because of his inaccurate imitation (or mirroring) of nature, as one might expect. Only the end of the dialogue (266A–268C) is primarily concerned with the art of imitation (*mimetike*—219B), or, if you will, the mirror of nature. The rest of the piece deals with acquisitive arts, where one gains advantage over others, particularly through words (219C). The sophist is a hunter (or fisher) of men who takes money for his supposed ability to educate (223B); he is a trader in virtue (224C). But it is the *way* the sophist trades words that is bothersome to the Stranger and his interlocutor, the young Theaetetus, not the fact *that* he is a conversationalist.

The sophist fosters stupidity (*amathian*), which consists in supposing that one knows when one does not (229C). The instruction needed to get rid of this stupidity is called education (*paideian*—229D), which is roughly synonymous with what Rorty means by "edification," since Rorty's use of this term is related to "education" or Gadamer's *Bildung* (358-60). The Stranger's education is not rough or dogmatic but contains gentle advice (*malthakoteros paramythoumenoi*—229E-230A). If one's interlocutor is conceited, he must be cross-examined through dialectic; from refutation one learns modesty (230B-C). Since this dialogue is placed after Socrates' encounter with the older and wiser Parmenides (217C) in the *Parmenides*, one suspects that it is Plato's own newfound modesty that is alluded to here, as Rorty suggests.

The philosopher's refusal to engage in rough or dogmatic education differentiates him from the philosopher of the *Republic*, yet this raises a problem. The persuasive devices that a philosopher now has to rely on make him resemble a sophist, as a dog resembles a wolf (231A). The questions that must be answered are: how does the sophist foster stupidity, and how does the philosopher educate. To answer the first question, one must at least partially rely on the sophist's inability (or refusal) to create a proper likeness (*eikon*); instead he makes an inadequate semblance (*phantasma*—236B). More importantly, the sophist professes to know nothing of eyesight, image making, or mirrors (!) at all, as he confines himself to what can be gathered from *discourse* (240A). At this point the Stranger's attempt to catch the sophist also seems to be an attempt to catch Rorty. By denying mirror imagery the sophist and Rorty must rely primarily, perhaps exclusively, on discourse. But Plato's own attempt to find out how one can speak falsely, or educate properly, hardly returns unquestioningly to the mirror imagery of the *Republic*.

It is not just the sophist who bothers Plato; the Stranger makes it clear that he is also irked by those who talk about the way things "really are" (*hos estin*—243B). What does the word "reality" mean? Theaetetus asks (243D). Theaetetus quite openly confesses that he is in a wilderness of doubt with respect to theories that claim to give an exact account (*diakribologoumenous*) of what is real or unreal (245E).

The naive foundationalism that the Stranger and Theaetetus oppose is exhibited in a battle between the giants and the gods (246A-249D). The former are the materialists who try to drag everything from heaven down to earth; they affirm that real existence belongs only to that which can be handled: reality is the same thing as body. Rorty's claim that foundationalism aims to get beyond argument to compulsion, to a situation where argument is not just silly but impossible (159), is anticipated in the Stranger's description of these materialists: as soon as one of their opponents asserts that anything that is not a body is real, they are utterly contemptuous and will not listen to another word (246B). It should be noted that for Rorty, too, empiricism can be a type of foundationalism.

The "gods" defend their position somewhere in the heights of the unseen; for them true reality consists in intelligible and bodiless forms; the materialists only defend the moving process of becoming (246B–C). This view is none other than that defended in the *Republic*, which, although a view held by those who are more civilized (*hemeroteroi*) than the giants, needs to be challenged as well (246C). Truth (or perhaps still, for Plato, *the* truth) lies outside these two views (246D).

Plato's solution seems to be in the following statement by the Stranger:

> I suggest that anything has real being that is so constituted as to possess any sort of power either to affect anything else or to be affected, in however small a degree, by the most insignificant agent, though it be only once. I am proposing as a mark to distinguish real things that they are nothing but power. (*dynamis*—247E)

The battle (*mache*) between the giants and gods causes ennui; Plato now seems content to say that *anything* that affects, or is affected by, another is real. Like a child begging for both, the philosopher must declare that reality is both at once: all that is unchangeable and all that is in change (249C–D).

No doubt the giants and gods, and foundationalists in general, will find Plato's "solution" baffling; indeed the Stranger himself still admits that he is "wholly in the dark" about reality. Nonetheless he fancies that he is talking (*legein*) good sense (249D–E; also 250E). It is no more coincidence that the analogy the Stranger uses to determine if, and how, reality combines with other reality is grammar (253A). To say that there is *no* combination at all is self-defeating, for to use the words "being," "apart," or "by itself" implies some sort of connection among things; without such a background of combination these words would not make sense (252B–C)). To say that *all* things combine with all would also be self-defeating, since then one could say *anything*, even that motion is rest, etc. (252D). The only tenable position is that some things blend, some do not (252E).

In the hunt for the sophist, Plato has stumbled on the job of the philosopher, perhaps indicating what Plato's missing (or never written) dialogue the *Philosopher*, which was to constitute a trilogy with the *Sophist* and *Statesman*, was to be about (217A, 253B–D). The philosopher still retains mirror-imaging tasks, like dividing according to natural kinds (253C, 254A), but more importantly, he is supposed to act as a guide on the voyage of discourse, pointing out similarities in different positions, and alerting participants in dialectical dispute of inconsistencies that creep into their arguments (253B). *This* is how he educates.

To illustrate this less-exalted function for the philosopher, the Stranger chooses to analyze some of the most, if not *the* most, important Forms (254C). Since we can affect the contents of our thoughts, and since they can affect us, Forms are real on the criteria of the *Sophist* (248D–249A). The Forms analyzed are *not,* surprisingly, those of the Good, Beautiful, or the like. Rather, attention is paid to Motion, Rest, Existence, Sameness, Difference. The technical details of this dialectical analysis by the Stranger and Theaetetus are not my concern. It should be noted, however, that if anyone mistrusts the Stranger's analysis he is encouraged to produce some better explanation (*lekteon*—259B); little attention is paid to what Rorty would call man's glassy, mirroring essence. In fact, the Stranger suggests that inadequate criticism usually comes from those who have "a too recent contact with reality" (259D).

Since the isolation of everything from everything else would mean the abolition of all discourse, hence the abolition of philosophy, the philosopher must learn how to weave these five central Forms together. The Stranger is quite emphatic that to rob us of discourse is to rob us of philosophy (260A). One of the great achievements of this dialogue is that inadequate discourse is traced not just to imperfect mirroring, to use Rorty's term, but more importantly to the use (or lack thereof) of the Form of Difference or Otherness. The use of this Form not only allows us to talk about non-being (i.e., that relative non-being that things possess with respect to other things), but also about falsity. As long as the sophist can deny any sort of existence for non-being, he can deny that he can ever say falsehoods, since falsity consists in saying what is not is, or vice versa (260C–D). In this manner he fosters stupidity. When the sophist is shown that one *can* talk about non-being without thereby committing parricide on father Parmenides (241D), one is in a position to *begin* an investigation of the nature of discourse (260E–261B), this being claimed by the Stranger late in the dialogue, *after* the criticisms made against the giants and gods.

The fact that Plato sometimes reverts back to the correspondence theory of truth (263B) would perhaps bother Rorty, but he would have to be encouraged by Plato's attempt to explore the elementary conditions of philosophical discourse. The results at first seem rather simple: a statement never consists solely of names—lion stag horse—or solely of verbs—walks runs sleeps (262A–B); there could not be a statement about (absolutely) Nothing (263C); and the meaning of "it appears" would include a blend of perception and judgment (264B). But these small steps add up, and only after one is well versed in what discussion itself is all about can one escape from simplemindedness (268A).

SOME PRELIMINARY CONCLUSIONS

Rorty is on weak ground at some points: for example, (a) when he says (242–43) that Plato only toys around with inner-space metaphors (see

263E); and (b) when he implies that for Plato and other foundationalists, if we are without algorithms we are only left with passion (339)—but Plato's writings, even in the *Republic*, hardly ever exhibit algorithms, rather heuristic devices like dialogues and myths.

From the above evidence in the *Sophist*, however, it can be seen that most of Rorty's suggestions about Plato are useful ones indeed. That is, since edifying philosophy is necessarily reactive (378), depending on systematic philosophy for material to criticize, Plato's status as an edifying philosopher depends on his foundationalism in the *Republic* and elsewhere. Whereas Dewey, Wittgenstein, and Heidegger primarily reacted against the foundational philosophy of others, Plato had the harder task of reacting against his own foundationalism. This is perhaps why the correspondence theory of truth appears every once in a while even in the *Sophist*.

One project remains. Rorty's notion of foundationalism encompasses various positions that claim to have knowledge of "the ultimate context," whether that be the Forms, the mind, sense perception, or language (317–18). What is needed is an explanation of why Plato adopted the particular foundationalism that he did, so as to better understand his edifying reaction.

ORALITY TO VISION TO DISCOURSE

Greek philosophy grew out of an oral-aural culture in which the medium of speech-hearing dominated the other senses. In preliterate society truth was found in the word, i.e., the spoken word of myth. Cultural memory was preserved in the mnemonic devices incorporated into epic poetry. These mnemonic devices made it possible for the Homeric bards to have "memorized" all of the *Iliad* and *Odyssey*. These bards were not just poets or performers, but also encyclopedists preserving expertise in ruling, sailing, religion, war, agriculture, morality, etc., as Plato's *Ion* indicates. The hypnotic effect of the bard's medium led to an approach to knowledge based on formulae that precluded rational analysis. Just as we know the length of the months through the saying "Thirty days hath September . . .," the preliterate Greek preserved all of his knowledge about the world in this fashion.

After hundreds, perhaps thousands, of years of prehistoric, oral-aural culture, a significant shift in the organization of the sensorium, or the sensory apparatus of human beings, occurred. The written word gave prominence to vision in that the word was no longer primarily spoken-heard, but seen on a page. Literacy was not just an aid in the recording of information. It also caused a revolutionary shift in the sensorium. The key figures in this transition from orality to vision were Homer and Plato. Although Homer's myths were written down, it is surprising how few people ever read them.[5] It was the bard who kept these stories alive for so many centuries.

Plato's critique of Homer should be seen in this light, which Rorty, unfortunately, fails to do. Plato's Forms were polar opposites to the oral-aural life-world. Spoken words are events in time, specifically, present time. Their transitoriness contrasts with Plato's Forms, which are outside of time; not heard, but "seen" by the mind's eye. The Greek word *idea* itself means the look of a thing; "phenomenon" also has a visual root. It was only an escape from the constant oral recitation of the mythic stories that allowed science and philosophy to be born in the light of a new day.[6] The separation from the source of oral spontaneity makes possible the life-giving properties of alienation. Reading and writing allow one to keep life at arm's length. Integral to oral culture is the live interaction between speaker and audience, but reading and writing are usually done (and done best) in the absence of others. Without direct audience pressure it is possible for logic to flourish, as in Plato's visually oriented method of collection and division in the *Sophist*.

The shift to a visual domination of the sensorium was connected, perhaps accidentally, with the notion that science, art, and philosophy should offer what Rorty would call mirror imagery. *When Rorty criticizes mirror imagery, he should explore the extent to which the dominance of the visual is necessary for there to be philosophy at all.* Rorty does rightly indicate, but through a glass darkly, that the transition from orality to literacy was not complete in Plato. His teacher, Socrates, left nothing of his philosophy in writing (although he must have *read* Homer). This is difficult to understand from the perspective of more literate culture, but it makes sense against the oral background of ancient Greece.[7] Plato did write, but calculatingly in the dialogue style to preserve the cast of true dialectic, which is basically an oral medium.

CONCLUSION

In short, one cannot react through edifying discourse (as an enlightened type of orality) to *mirror-imaged*, foundational philosophy until philosophy itself escapes from primitive orality.

Plato's dialogues are not merely stylistic devices. The *Sophist* in particular shows that Plato noticed the excesses of the giants (who identify the real with what they see or, perhaps, feel) and the gods (who identify the real with what can be "seen" by the mind's eye). Through the Stranger's concern for discourse, and through his identification of the real with anything that has *dynamis*, Plato has suggested that discourse is a necessary condition for philosophy. The Stranger was quite clear about this: "To rob us of discourse would be to rob us of philosophy" (260A). Rorty's stronger claim (and problematic one) seems to be that discourse is a sufficient condition for philosophy, without any recourse to mirror imagery at all. As he puts it:

> If we see knowing not as having an essence, to be described by scientists or philosophers, but rather as a right, by current standards, to believe, then we are well on the way to seeing *conversation* as the ultimate context within which knowledge is to be understood. Our focus shifts from the relation between human beings and the objects of their inquiry to the relation between alternative standards of justification, and from there to the actual changes in those standards which make up intellectual history. (389–90)

Of course, we do not know what Plato would say about this position, but it might signify for him an unfortunate return to the persuasive, mesmerizing influence of the bards, or at least to the persuasive relativism of the sophists.[8]

NOTES

1. Richard Rorty, *Philosophy and the Mirror of Nature* (Princeton: Princeton University Press, 1979). Numbers in parentheses refer to page numbers in this text. I have used the Burnet edition of Plato, and the translation of the *Sophist* by Cornford, which relies on Jowett, in *The Collected Dialogues of Plato*, ed. Hamilton and Cairns (Princeton: Princeton University Press, 1973).

2. Rorty may be a bit too hasty here. Contemporary philosophy has shown a surprising vitality regarding Plato's Forms, or something like them. Although Whitehead's eternal objects immediately come to mind, we should not forget that Husserl, Frege, and Russell went through periods where they talked about non-material, non-subjective, universal objects of thought (see, e.g., Russell's *The Problems of Philosophy*). The later thought of Popper has emphasized world 3, which has a Platonic character; and recently Jerrold Katz has defended a Platonic theory in the philosophy of language in *Language and Other Abstract Objects* (Totowa, N.J.: Rowman and Littlefield, 1981), et al.

3. See Katz, *Language and Other Abstract Objects*, p. 201, where it is held that "Platonism" does not, of necessity, entail "perceptually inspired accounts of intuition. I think that the traditional claim that knowledge of abstract objects is knowledge by acquaintance cannot be reconciled with the nature of these objects . . . being aspatial and atemporal, they cannot act on a knower through a causal process to produce a representation of themselves in the manner of sense perception."

4. By systematic philosophy Rorty means knowledge of "ultimate context," etc., not a logical fabric of ideas laid out in one cloth, as in Spinoza's *Ethics*. Plato could obviously not be a systematic philosopher in this latter sense.

5. On the relationship between orality and literacy in ancient Greece see, M. I. Finley, *The Ancient Greeks: An Introduction to Their Life and Thought*

(New York: Viking Press, 1963), p. 76; Jack Goody and Ian Watt, "The Conse-
quences of Literacy," in *Literacy in Traditional Societies* (Cambridge: Cambridge
University Press, 1968), p. 42; Alfred Burns, "Athenian Literacy in the Fifth
Century, B.C.," *Journal of the History of Ideas* 42 (1981): 371–87. Especially see
the best work, Eric Havelock, *Preface to Plato* (Cambridge: Harvard University
Press, 1963).

6. In addition to Havelock, see Walter Ong, *The Presence of the Word* (New
Haven: Yale University Press, 1967), especially pp. 34–35.

7. See Ong, *Presence of the Word*, p. 55; also Goody and Watt, "Consequences
of Literacy," pp. 51–53, where it is suggested that for Plato words (spoken or
written) seem inadequate to convey Forms. Although Plato criticizes the written
word (e.g., *Phaedrus* 274 or *Seventh Letter* 344), he must succumb to it in order
to criticize it. That is, there is a connection between writing, on the one hand,
and *logic* and criticism, on the other. The silence ushered in with the triumph
of literacy enhances precision. The oral performer fears having to pause while
composing-reciting; the reader or writer need not have such a fear. His alienation
from the text, as opposed to the social bond created in a mutually engaged-
in dialectic, allows him to attack his text, reread it, rewrite it, treat it as an
object external to himself with formal logical characteristics.

8. The only other treatment (to my knowledge) of the relationship between
Rorty and Plato is in Stanley Rosen's review of Rorty's book in *The Review
of Metaphysics*. Rosen is correct that there "is a thematic of objectivity, Ideas,
and mirroring in Plato" and that "this thematic is embedded within a complex
hermeneutic of human existence," but Rosen is premature in claiming that "Rorty
pays no attention whatsoever" to this hermeneutic.

Commentary on
Dombrowski on Rorty on Plato

Charles L. Griswold

At least three possible answers to the question "Why do philosophy historically?" present themselves. The first is that one cannot philosophize well without conversing with others; since many past philosophers are still worth conversing with, one ought to read their publications. Indeed, we like to assume that our own demise doesn't in itself render our work worthless. A second answer is that we almost always philosophize from within one or another tradition. If we are to proceed self-consciously, then, we must become aware of the "sedimented" presuppositions of the tradition that shape our reflections. One cannot simply turn to "the things themselves" without further ado. A third answer takes this last line of reasoning still further and holds that one cannot philosophize except within a tradition. . The questions and expected sorts of answers that frame philosophizing are, on this account, *always* that of a tradition. There are no "things themselves" that can be apprehended "neutrally," timelessly, outside of history.

Rorty accepts a version of this third answer. For him, philosophy cannot hook onto an "objective world," or some set of "eternal Problems," or "the Mind," or any other discourse-independent entity. Such notions are themselves constructs of the tradition descended, in the West, from Plato. Philosophy properly understood is "hermeneutics," that is, an enterprise whose goal is not Truth but, rather, new and "exciting and fruitful" viewpoints that the interlocutors hadn't thought of before.[1] Philosophy so understood doesn't have any "positions" of its own; its "reactive" character makes it *dialogical* in the strongest possible sense. There are no objective verities to be grasped, just views put forward by others. Hence philosophizing must be bound to interpreting what people are saying and have said, i.e., to the history of philosophy. Rorty's work just amounts, one could say, to a series of brilliant interpretations of the history of philosophy and to the appeal (which by definition cannot be formulated as a further "position" in support of which there exist any "arguments") that we carry on without that history's characteristic rationalizations.[2]

As Dombrowski points out, throughout *Philosophy and the Mirror of Nature* Rorty sets up Plato as the opponent of deconstructed philosophizing. Plato is cast as the chief originator of objectivist metaphysics, and so of the ideas that there are certain basic questions that need to be asked; that there is a difference, marked by the ability to "give a logos," between opinion and knowledge *(episteme)*; that to have *episteme* is to be able, thanks to the "mirroring" nature of the soul, to say something that corresponds to how things really are (the Forms). For Plato philosophy is the "scientia scientiarum" because it possesses knowledge of the principles in terms of which all claims to know must be measured (CP, 222).

Rorty's expressions of praise for Plato are, with one exception, directed to Socrates (presumably the "Socrates" depicted in Plato's dialogues). On those occasions, Rorty distinguishes Socrates from Plato (PMN, 179). Rorty aligns himself with a de-Platonized "informed dilettante, the polypragmatic, Socratic intermediary between various discourses," thanks to whom "disagreements between disciplines and discourses are compromised or transcended in the course of the conversation" (PMN, 317). Rorty goes on to distinguish that role from the role of the "cultural overseer who knows everyone's common ground—the Platonic philosopher-king who knows what everybody else is really doing. . . ." Rorty can align himself with Socrates as against Plato only because he makes two assumptions. The first is that we can distinguish between Plato and Socrates by taking as Plato's views the "epistemological" sounding utterances put by Plato into the mouth of various characters. That is to say, Rorty here pays no attention to the dramatic context of the dialogues. Rorty says nothing to defend this procedure. Second, Rorty holds that one can make sense of "Socratic dialogue" without invoking any of the "metaphysical" theses (such as that of "recollection") that Plato's Socrates regularly invokes in order to explain what he's doing and why he's doing it. That is, Rorty's version of Socratic "conversation" is entirely non-telic (CP, 172; PMN, 317, 391). In my opinion this means that Rortean "conversation" cannot be characterized as "Socratic."[3]

Indeed, on one and only one occasion—in a footnote, in fact—Rorty indicates that the picture with respect to Plato is more complicated. Dombrowski quotes Rorty as remarking that no one knows which passages in Plato are a joke and which are not.[4] That remark is at odds with Rorty's regular identification of Plato with certain philosophical theses, an identification that Rorty presumably thinks elicits the serious, nonjoking side of Plato. Consequently Rorty should feel perfectly able to pick out the joking passages, i.e., those that are at odds with the nonjoking ones. Does not his distinction between Socrates and Plato amount to as much? Had Rorty taken his footnote seriously he would have had to dwell on the complex issue of the literary dimension of Plato's work. For it is surely that dimension (an element of which is the difficulty of determining who, if anyone, in the dialogues "speaks" for Plato) that accounts for the old problem of distinguishing between the playful and serious Plato. Consideration of that dimension would show, in my opinion, that Plato is not a "Platonist" in Rorty's sense.[5]

Inspired by Rorty's footnote, Dombrowski proposes to flesh out Rorty's passing reference to the *Sophist* (*PMN*, 257). On Dombrowski's Rortean reading, the *Sophist* deconstructs the metaphysics of the *Republic*, putting in its place philosophy à la Rorty (the conversation of the edifying hermeneuticist). It seems odd that a dialogue in which Socrates, Rorty's presumed hero, is largely silent, and in which the mathematically inclined Eleatic Stranger (ES) offers a highly technical solution to the problem of non-being—all through the medium of a conversation that, at least on the surface, doesn't look like a real "conversation" at all—should be thought an instance of Rortean "conversation." I am not denying that whatever the ES is doing, it is very different from what Plato has Socrates do in other dialogues. But in order to establish his argument, Dombrowski must overcome a number of objections to his treatment of the matter.

First, he quotes very selectively from the *Sophist*. He acknowledges that the "mirroring" or "imaging" thesis appears at the end of the *Sophist*, but holds that it doesn't appear in the middle (he erroneously implies that it does not figure prominently in the earlier sections of the dialogue; see *Soph.*, 234a-235c). Even if that is true, why take one passage as representing the ES's view and not the other?

Second, there is much talk in the *Sophist* about diairesis and natural kinds, which implies that the ES thinks of epistemic (diairetical) language as hooking onto an objective world. Diairesis certainly sounds like a "commensurating" *techne*.

Third, on the surface the ES does not sound like a "Socratic inter- mediary" at all; he sounds much more dogmatic than Socrates. *Aporia* or "human wisdom" seems alien to him.

Fourth, even if the ES's remarks about *ta onta* as *dynamis* (*Soph.*, 247d8-e4) represent his considered view, it would seem to be a view about "objective reality" every bit as "epistemological" as, for Rorty, Plato's views are.

Fifth, the whole effort of the *Sophist* is to locate the sophist and so to distinguish that type from the philosopher. Can Rorty really admit to a clean distinction of that sort between the two? At one point Rorty remarks that if his program is followed out, "We shall, in short, be where the Sophists were before Plato brought his principle to bear and invented 'philosophical thinking' " (*PMN*, 157).[6]

Sixth, Dombrowski cannot assert without argument that the ES's notion of the philosopher is "less exalted" than that of Socrates without accounting for the very Socratic sounding description of the philosopher at *Sophist* 253c-254b.

Seventh, Dombrowski cannot establish his interpretation without showing that the ES's "megista genē" are non-metaphysical in a way that distinguishes them "ontologically" from Socrates' (Plato's?) "Forms." We would need, that is, to know what an "eidos" is for the ES.

Finally, even if the ES were a Rortean pragmatist, or at least if the *Sophist* proposed a non-metaphysical solution to Socrates' questions, we are not justified in inferring, as Dombrowski repeatedly does, from what the ES says here or there in the dialogue to what Plato thinks.[7] In doing so Dombrowski commits the same error Rorty is guilty of, and thus is no more able than Rorty to account for the truth of Rorty's own footnote about Plato's playfulness. It is perfectly possible, after all, that even if the ES represents all that Dombrowski thinks he does, Plato's point is that the ES's project fails. The *Sophist* has, in fact, been read along these lines, i.e., as a defense of Socrates.[8]

Let me close this telegraphic commentary with several suggestions (the arguments for which I have attempted to formulate elsewhere).[9] By writing in the manner that he did, Plato undercuts dogmatism. The dialogue form keeps metaphysical and antimetaphysical claims situated within a frame of inquiry that is, in one sense, "relative" to the time, place, and interlocutors present. If I could so put it, all of Plato's dialogues are written so as to deconstruct themselves. But the result is not Rortean pragmatism. Our ability to grasp a frame of inquiry as what it is, and so our ability to "react" to or "edify" an inquiry—in short, our ability to engage in philosophical conversations—is for the Socrates of Plato's dialogues evidence of the *presence* of intelligibility and of the soul's mirroring of it. While granting much that Rorty argues, Socrates would want to hold that, even if only at some meta-level, truth claims in the "metaphysical" sense are unavoidable. Socrates and Plato would deny, contra Rorty, that it is possible to have things to say about the having of views without thereby having a view (*PMN*, 371).

Further, Socrates would argue that the rationale for engaging in dialogue at all—the reasons we should give for spending our lives philosophizing rather than, say, tyrannizing—cannot be successfully articulated without an account of (among other things) the "soul." Such an account could not fittingly be stated dogmatically, and it could not be stated except dialogically, indirectly, reactively; but it is still an account that seeks to tell us how things are. That is, a successful explanation of why Socrates acts as he does in Plato's dialogues must lean in part on what Rorty thinks of as "Platonic" metaphysics.[10] This is why for both Plato and Socrates philosophy is not "done historically" in the strong sense of the phrase affirmed by Rorty.

Dombrowski concludes by reminding us that Socrates did not write while Plato did. It is true, as is evident from the *Phaedrus*, that the difference between orality and writing is of deep philosophical importance. But Dombrowski errs in suggesting that "Plato's" Forms are "polar opposites to the oral life-world," and that the mirror of nature thesis is somehow the child of philosophy as written. On the contrary, the Forms are the precondition, for Socrates as for Plato, of reasonable philosophizing whether spoken or written. The *Phaedrus* shows that Plato is as much aware of the dangers of the written word as he is of those of oral discourse. The same dialogue shows, I believe, that Plato's writing is intended to overcome such dangers by recalling us to the measured pursuit of self-knowledge.

NOTES

1. For the "exciting and fruitful" phrase see Rorty's *Philosophy and the Mirror of Nature* (Princeton: Princeton University Press, 1979), p. 318. I shall abbreviate the book as *PMN* and include citations from it directly in my text. I shall also be adverting to Rorty's *Consequences of Pragmatism* (Minneapolis: University of Minnesota Press, 1982), and have abbreviated the title as *CP*. My brief comments about Rorty are based only on these two books. I have discussed Rorty in detail in the works cited in notes 5 and 9 below.
2. Of *PMN* Rorty says, "In this book I have offered a sort of prolegomenon to a history of epistemology-centered philosophy as an episode in the history of European culture" (390). In *CP* Rorty writes,

> Pragmatists follow Hegel in saying that "philosophy is its time grasped in thought." Anti-pragmatists follow Plato in striving for an escape from conversation to something atemporal which lies in the background of all possible conversations. I do not think one can decide between Hegal and Plato save by meditating on the past efforts of the philosophical tradition to escape from time and history. One can see these efforts as worthwhile, getting better, worth continuing. Or one can see them as doomed and perverse. I do not know what would count as a noncircular metaphysical or epistemological or semantical argument for seeing them in either way. So I think that the decision has to be made simply by reading the history of philosophy and drawing a moral. (*CP*, 174)

In the introduction to *CP* Rorty says that in the conflict between pragmatism and intuitive realism "the issue is one about whether philosophy should try to find natural starting-points which are distinct from cultural traditions, or whether all philosophy should do is compare and contrast cultural traditions" (xxxvii; italicized in the original). Rorty chooses the latter; Plato would choose the former.
3. For an interesting argument to the effect that the conversation Rorty envisages is impossible, see D. Roochnik's "The Impossibility of Philosophical Dialogue," *Philosophy and Rhetoric* 19 (1986): 147-65.
4. *PMN*, p. 369 n. 15: "The permanent fascination of the man who dreamed up the whole idea of Western philosophy—Plato—is that we still do not know

which sort of philosopher he was ["systematic" or "edifying"]. Even if the *Seventh Letter* is set aside as spurious, the fact that after millenniums of commentary nobody knows which passages in the dialogues are jokes keeps the puzzle fresh." On p. 77 of this volume Dombrowski also asserts that "'The *Euthyphro,* he [Rorty] tells us, is a work of edifying pedagogy." The reference is to *PMN,* p. 307. As I read the passage, however, Rorty is saying quite the opposite, namely, that the *Euthyphro,* like Moore's *Principia Ethica,* is an effort to establish a specifically "philosophical" or "systematic" sense of "good" that does not "describe current linguistic or intellectual practice," and so is metaphysical.

5. Of course, in Plato's dialogues themselves some passages are characterized as "serious" and others as "playful." For a discussion of the important references of this sort in the *Phaedrus,* as well as of the whole distinction between "play-fulness" and "seriousness," see my *Self-knowledge in Plato's Phaedrus* (New Haven: Yale University Press, 1986), pp. 216-19 *et passim.* The introduction and chapter 6 contain discussions of, respectively, how best to handle the literary dimension when interpreting Plato, and why Plato wrote in dialogue form. Further discussion of these issues may be found in *Platonic Writings, Platonic Readings,* ed. C. Griswold (New York: Routledge and Kegan Paul, 1988).

6. Further, Rorty's assertions that "the application of such honorifics as 'objective' and 'cognitive' is never anything more than an expression of the presence of, or the hope for, agreement among inquirers" (*PMN,* 335), and that "For the edifying philosopher the very idea of being presented with 'all of Truth' is absurd, because the Platonic notion of Truth itself is absurd" (*PMN,* 377), will surely sound, to the Platonist, like a conflation of philosophy and sophistry.

7. For examples of Dombrowski's attribution to Plato of what Plato has characters in his dramas say, see especially p. 79 of this volume ("Plato's solution seems to be in the following statement by the Stranger"; "No doubt the giants and gods, and foundationalists in general, will find Plato's 'solution' baffling"; "In the hunt for the sophist, Plato has stumbled on the job of the philosopher").

8. See S. Rosen, *Plato's Sophist* (New Haven: Yale University Press, 1983).

9. In addition to my *Self-knowledge in Plato's Phaedrus,* see my "Plato's Metaphilosophy," in *Platonic Investigations,* ed. D. O'Meara (Washington: Catholic University of America Press, 1985), pp. 1-33. These publications are the basis for my assertions about Plato in the concluding paragraphs of the present commentary.

10. In an interesting passage in *CP,* Rorty seems to admit to something like this:

> I have not answered the deep criticism of pragmatism which I mentioned a few minutes ago: the criticism that the Socratic virtues cannot, as a practical matter, be defended save by Platonic means, that without some sort of metaphysical comfort nobody will be able *not* to sin against Socrates. William James himself was not sure whether this criticism could be answered. Exercising his own right to believe, James wrote: "If this life be not a real fight in which something is eternally gained for the universe by success, it is not better than a game of private theatricals from which we may withdraw at will." "It *feels,*" he said, "like a fight." For us, footnotes to Plato that we are, it *does* feel that way. (174)

My argument for the interdependence of the "Socratic virtues" and "Platonic" metaphysics, however, wouldn't hinge simply on what Rorty calls "a practical matter," though "practice" is far from being irrelevant to an account of intuitive realism.

Philosophy and Its History

Veatch's *Aristotle*[1]

Jorgé J. E. Gracia

The subject of my inquiry is the nowadays notorious relationship between philosophy and its history.[2] I propose to divide the discussion into six parts that will carry out respectively the following tasks: (1) the formulation of the issue, (2) the characterizations of history, the history of philosophy, and philosophy, (3) a proposal for the solution to the issue, (4) the characterization of Veatch's book on Aristotle in terms of the issue presented, (5) a brief explanation of the rationale that I believe is behind Veatch's own understanding of the nature of his book, and (6) an illustration of how Veatch's understanding of his book affects the theses he defends.

The main theses of the paper will relate both to the issue involved in the relationship between philosophy and its history and to the position with respect to it taken by Veatch. In regard to the first, I shall defend the views (1) that philosophy and its history are not incompatible; (2) that the history of philosophy is not necessary for philosophy, although it is very useful for it; and (3) that philosophy is necessary for the history of philosophy. With respect to Veatch's position, I shall maintain that Veatch's *Aristotle,* contrary to what he seems to think, is primarily a work in the history of philosophy, and (2) that he interprets it as something more than and/or different from that because he tacitly and perhaps unconsciously shares two widespread contemporary prejudices: (a) the view that history is entirely descriptive, and (b) the notion that the history of philosophy has little value for philosophy. Finally, (3) I shall argue that Veatch's understanding concerning the nature of his book and the nature of the history of philosophy undermines the claims he makes about Aristotle's philosophy. Let me begin, then, with the formulation of the issue.

1

The general aim of this conference, if I understand its theme correctly, is to explore the relationship of philosophy and its history. There are two fundamental positions that have been adopted with respect to this issue by philosophers. The first denies that there is or that there should be any relation between them. Those who favor this perspective point out that whatever philosophers do and/or accomplish is irrelevant to what historians do and/or accomplish, and vice versa. For example, they ask: What could what Thales thought about the basic stuff of which the world is made have to do with current questions of philosophy? Indeed, arguing from analogy, they note that no serious astronomer today pays any attention to what Ptolemy thought about the heavens, so why should a contemporary philosopher pay attention to Thales or Aristotle? According to this point of view, there is nothing relevant that the history of philosophy can contribute to philosophy. Something similar could be said concerning the contribution of philosophy to its history. For, so the argument goes, how could contemporarily developed concepts and ideas help in the proper understanding of concepts and ideas developed in a different age and context? Historians of philosophy, then, have no need for philosophy as such.

Still, others go beyond the charge of irrelevance and conclude that what philosophers do and/or accomplish is not just irrelevant but actually downright incompatible with what historians of philosophy do and/or accomplish, and vice versa. Philosophy, like astronomy and the other sciences, is concerned with the investigation of the ultimate nature of the universe and its components, and therefore deals with the truth value of claims about such ultimate natures. But the history of philosophy is concerned rather with what past philosophers have thought about the ultimate nature of the universe and its components *apart from* whether what they thought is true or false. The aims of philosophers and historians of philosophy, therefore, are at odds and cannot be reconciled. The use of history in philosophy leads to confusion, resulting from the simultaneous pursuit of two distinct and conflicting aims that require different and interfering procedures. Likewise, the application of philosophical concepts to its history tampers with historical accuracy, distorting history by presenting it in a light foreign to it.

Of course, just as there are those who reject any relation between philosophy and its history, there are also those who find that such relation is indispensable for the effective pursuit of one or the other. They point out that the study of philosophy is in fact and must always be centered in its past, since from the moment that a view is formulated and/or defended its formulation and/or its defense is already a part of history. So, there is not and cannot be any real cleavage between philosophy and its history; their presumed separation is an artificial one created by those who wish to divide the recent history of philosophy from its more distant history. All philosophy, then, is history of philosophy.[3] Moreover, there are others who argue that on the side of the history of philosophy one can also see its necessary relation to philosophy. For in order to study the history of philosophy, one must study philosophy and understand philosophical notions. Thus, according to this point of view, the history of philosophy requires philosophy, just as philosophy requires its history.

From this brief and necessarily oversimplified presentation of the issue involved in the relation between philosophy and its history, I hope that three points have become clear. The first is that there seem to be two rather incompatible and extreme positions with respect to this relation. One rejects any relation and the other makes the relation necessary.

The second is that the issue can be presented from two different perspectives. On the one hand, it can be presented as the problem of whether and to what extent the history of philosophy can contribute to and/or become integrated with philosophy. And, on the other, it can be presented as the problem of whether and to what extent philosophy can contribute to and/or become integrated with its history. The first perspective is in fact the one reflected in the title of this conference: "Doing Philosophy Historically." The issue posed from this perspective is of concern primarily to philosophers, since it is the nature of philosophy that is at stake. But the same issue can also be presented from a different perspective, although it is often confused with the first and frequently discussed in the same contexts. What is at stake in it is the extent to which, paraphrasing the title of this conference, the history of philosophy can be done philosophically. Posed in this way, the issue concerns primarily the historian of philosophy, for it is the nature of that history that is in question.

Third and last, it should also be clear that in order to bring some clarity into this discussion we must begin by providing a preliminary understanding of the terms of the relation under dispute: 'philosophy' and 'history of philosophy.' Moreover, since the second term of the relation is itself composite, we must also say something about 'history.' Let me begin, then, by providing a brief discussion of history, the history of philosophy, and philosophy, in that order, with the hope that it will help us understand the relation between philosophy and its history.

2

History

The term 'history' is ambiguous in the sense that it is used in the language to mean a number of different things. In one sense the term is used to refer to a series of events or happenings.[4] Thus, for example, we speak of the history of ancient Greece when we want to refer to a series of events that took place during a certain period of time in Greece. We also talk about the history of our lives as comprising such events as birth, marriage, education, accidents, etc. But the term 'history' has also a second meaning derived from the etymology of the original Greek word that meant information, inquiry, and narrative. In this sense the term is used to refer to an account of past events rather than to the events themselves. Insofar as it is an account it goes beyond a simple narrative, chronicle, or annal, for it contains or should contain explanations of the causes and relations among the events in question. History in this second sense is a product of human enterprise. While events themselves may or may not be the result of human action, history as an account of such events is necessarily the result of human action. An earthquake is without a doubt a historical happening that must be recorded in the history books of the particular place where it happened, even though it is also a natural event in whose origin human beings have no role to play. And Caesar's murder by Brutus is also a historical occurrence, although in this case the event is not natural, but rather the result of human will and action. But an account of either event is necessarily the product of human will and action. So, history in the second sense, that is, understood as an account of events, is necessarily the result of human enterprise.

There is still a third meaning of the term 'history' that should not be overlooked, and that results precisely from the human effort to provide an account of events. In this way, 'history' refers to the procedure that is followed in the production of an account of events. By 'history' is meant, then, a certain discipline of learning whose function is both to produce appropriate accounts of events and to devise the rules that, when applied, would yield such appropriate accounts.

From what has been said it would appear that there are important ontological differences among history considered as a series of events, history as an account of those events, and history as a discipline of learning. The first is clearly composed of non-linguistic elements. Caesar's death, for example, is not, regardless of what one might wish to call it, a linguistic fact. On the other hand, the description of such an event yields linguistic facts, namely, propositions such as: 'Caesar died' or 'Caesar was killed by Brutus'.[5] Moreover, history considered as a discipline of learning may involve either an activity, a set of linguistic facts, or

both. The activity occurs when someone is in the process of producing
an account of certain events. Clearly the process is neither the linguistic
account of events nor the events themselves, but rather the activity
whereby the events are described and explained. On the other hand,
history as a discipline may also include a set of linguistic facts or propositions. Those facts and propositions have to be distinguished from the
facts and propositions that propose to give an account of non-linguistic
events. They are, indeed, quite different, for they state, explain, and justify
the rules that need to be followed in order to produce a historical account
of events. For example, one such rule might stipulate that "eyewitness
accounts of events should be given more weight in the establishment
of facts than non-eyewitness accounts of events." Another rule might
establish that "contemporaneous documentary evidence is generally more
reliable than non-contemporaneous verbal evidence." The statement,
justification, and explanation of those rules are what have come to be
called "historiography," in order to distinguish it from history considered
as a series of events, history as an account of those events, and history
as the activity whereby an account of events is produced.

History may be interpreted, therefore, in the following ways:

1. History as a series of events.
2. History as an account of a series of events.
3. History as a discipline of learning:
   A. Activity whereby the account of events is produced.
   B. Rules to which production of the account of events must adhere
      (historiography).

Now, in order to simplify the task at hand, since my time is quite limited,
I shall restrict my understanding of history in this context to meaning
2. Accordingly, history will concern linguistic accounts of events and,
therefore, the object of our study will be the propositions that form part
of such accounts. I consider this a minimalist view of history. History,
as pointed out, may also be something else, but it is at least a series
of propositions that express a certain account of events. More complex
interpretations of history will no doubt complicate the issue under
consideration here, but I do not think they would drastically alter the
conclusions to which we shall arrive.

A general survey of historical propositions, that is, of propositions
that form part of linguistic accounts of events, yields three basic categories. I shall use the terms 'descriptive', 'interpretative', and 'evaluative'
to refer to them. The primary function of descriptive propositions seems
to be to present accurately those events and their relations for which
there is empirical evidence. Thus, they involve descriptions of events
and their relations, descriptions of contemporaneous views concerning

those events and their relations, and descriptions of later historians' views concerning those events and their relations as well as descriptions of the relations of the views of various historians. As examples of these propositions consider the following:[6]

1[h]. X killed Y.

2[h]. X died.

3[h]. X's killing of Y prompted X's own death.

4[h]. M, a contemporary of X, thought that X had not killed Y.

5[h]. M disagreed with N, another of X's contemporaries, concerning M's view that X had not killed Y.

6[h]. R, a later historian, thought that M was right in holding that X had not killed Y.

7[h]. S, another later historian, disagreed with R's view concerning M.

Note that in all cases the function of these propositions is descriptive in the sense specified above, although in some cases the description is of events (1[h], 2[h]) and their relations (3[h]), and in other cases of views about those events and their relations (4[h]-7[h]). On the other hand, the primary function of what I have called "interpretative propositions" is not to describe events for which there is empirical evidence, but rather to go beyond them and reconstruct the fabric of unstated motives, intangible factors, and implicit circumstances within which events take place and for which there is no empirical evidence available. In addition, some of these interpretations contain broad generalizations based on limited evidence but backed up by more or less accepted historiographical interpretative principles, and others include inferences concerning events for which there is no empirical evidence, but which it makes sense to suppose happened. This indicates that there is some descriptive import and intent in interpretative propositions, but the historian is well aware that the description is only based on a reconstruction of elements that fails to adhere to strict evidential empirical criteria. Thus, we find in histories interpretative propositions such as the following:

a[h]. X must have killed Y in order to inherit Y's fortune.

b[h]. That X killed Y meant that X had an intense hatred for Y's mother.

c[h]. The killing of Y gave rise to a series of events that led to the collapse of monarchy.

The use of terms such as 'must have' and 'meant' in the first two propositions and the general character of the third proposition indicate that these propositions go beyond the facts for which there is empirical evidence in various ways. The first proposition (a[h]) presents a conjecture concerning the reasons why X killed Y. The second (b^h) interprets the import and meaning of what X did. The third (c^h) makes a sweeping generalization about the effects of the event with which it is concerned. None of them, then, restricts itself to the description of events for which there is strict empirical evidence. The first two propositions refer to motives that may very well have been the causes of the events in question, but that certainly cannot be regarded as facts for which there is observable evidence, and the third goes well beyond the facts. These propositions, then, describe an edifice of reconstructed circumstances that is used to interpret and make sense of particular historical events within a larger context.

Finally, we come to a third category of historical propositions, the evaluative. These propositions are characterized by the fact that they contain evaluations both of historical events and of the views of historians concerning those events. In this case there is no attempt at description. Moreover, the evaluations in question are based on principles that are part of neither descriptive nor interpretative historical propositions and, therefore, are derived from sources other than history as we have understood it here. They are either part of historiography, which sets the rules for generating history, or they are derived from some other disciplines. As examples of evaluative propositions consider the following:

A^h. X was a bad ruler.

B^h. X's death was advantageous for country C.

C^h. M, a contemporary of X, was wrong in thinking that X had killed Y.

D^h. R, a later historian, who thought that M was right, was wrong.

This third category of propositions is clearly the most controversial, for some historians will want to argue that it is not the business of the historian to issue evaluations of any kind, but simply to describe historical events in an objective and intelligible fashion. The case becomes more controversial in the context of the history of philosophy, as we shall see later. At this point, however, I would like to argue that history involves evaluation both *de facto* and *de jure*. For it is evident, *de facto*, that most historians and certainly all good histories make judgments about the value of historical characters and events. What history of Portugal, for example, would not characterize the eighteenth-century Lisbon earthquake as disastrous? And what historian of the Roman empire would refrain from commenting on the lack of moral restraint of Nero and Caligula? Not only *de facto*, but also *de jure* it makes sense to argue that history without evaluation is not history or at least not good history. And the reason is that values themselves, even though intangible, play important roles in historical development. Therefore, only if historians understand those values *qua* values by judging their appropriateness and validity can we understand the historical process. Evaluation, there-fore, and evaluative propositions must be part of historical accounts.

From all of this we may conclude that history comprises a wide range of propositions and that it is a mistake to think, as some philosophers of history have thought, that history is exclusively descriptive, or inter-pretative, or evaluative. Nor should it be thought, on the other hand, that these categories are meant to be exclusive and exhaustive. They are not exclusive because there are cases in which a particular proposition does not seem to fit any category clearly, and there are others where the proposition would seem to fall into more than one category. In short, I am quite aware that the dividing line between these categories of propo-sitions is tenuous, but I do want to insist that in a large number of cases propositions will clearly fall into one of these categories and into only one. Again, the categories are not meant to be exhaustive, because it may turn out upon further reflection that one or more of these categories need to be subdivided into further categories, or that there may be categories that are not included in the three mentioned. Moreover, there seem to be interpretative and evaluative factors that do not fit the cate-gorical analysis that has been given. For example, it is clear that the historian "selects" materials and that such selection determines in impor-tant ways the nature of the resulting historical account.[7] But where do we put selection? Certainly not in the categories that I have specified, since selection is an act and not a proposition. Indeed, I would classify it as an act based on some historiographical principle itself expressed by a proposition. As such, however, selection influences historical accounts and, since it is not based on empirical evidence, involves inter-pretation and/or evaluation. But selection is not a proposition that is part of the historical account itself. All this should indicate that the analysis of historical propositions into the three categories I have intro-duced here has its advantages but also its limitations.

Let me finish this section, then, by saying that if we look at the examples of historical propositions that have been given, it appears as if they were restricted only in two aspects: temporality and provenance. The aim of history is to give an account of the past, and that aim is carried out through description, interpretation, and evaluation; but in the descriptions, interpretations, and evaluations that result there is always to be found a reference to time as well as to a source or origin. Temporal reference and provenance are of the essence of history.

The History of Philosophy

The history of philosophy, insofar as it is history, should contain de-scriptive, interpretative, and evaluative propositions. Indeed, many of the propositions that form part of histories of philosophy will not be significantly different from the propositions that form part of just histories, and in some cases the same propositions will appear in both. For example, the proposition 'Marcus Aurelius was a Roman emperor' will necessarily appear in a good history of the Roman Empire as well as in a good history of Roman philosophy. Therefore, as far as both history and the history of philosophy describe, interpret, and evaluate events they do not differ.

And yet, from experience we know that there are differences between history and the history of philosophy. It suffices to pick up a history of the Roman Empire and a history of Roman philosophy to realize where those differences are. Indeed, although the information that both histories might contain will overlap on occasion, as we saw in the case of the mentioned proposition, most of the information contained in the history is not duplicated in the history of philosophy. The reason for the difference is that history of philosophy is concerned primarily about philosophy, that is, about a particular set of "facts." I placed the term 'facts' in double quotation marks because the history of philosophy deals with a very peculiar set of facts. Indeed, its primary aim is to describe, interpret, and evaluate the beliefs, doctrines, and arguments of past philosophers together with their internal relations as well as their external relations to and influences on the beliefs, doctrines, and arguments of other philosophers. In short, historians of philosophy are concerned about the history of philosophical ideas and their relations. Naturally, since these ideas do not occur in a vacuum, a history of philosophy will contain references to events and circumstances related to those ideas. As in the example given earlier, it is pertinent to the historian of philosophy that Marcus Aurelius was a Roman emperor, even though the primary aim of the historian of philosophy is to understand Marcus Aurelius's philosophical ideas rather than the political events or positions that affected his life. In general, therefore, the kind of propositions that are contained in a history are different from those contained in a history of philosophy simply because the object of study of the historian of philosophy is only part and parcel of the more encompassing object of the historian. The history of philosophy of a period, then, is part of the history of that period, while only some of the events of the period are relevant for a history of philosophy of the period.

Of course, the history of philosophy does not deal with every sort of idea. For example, although a history of nineteenth-century German philosophy might contain some reference to the development of scientific ideas in physics, astronomy, and psychology in Germany during the nineteenth century, its main concern is not with those ideas, but with philosophical ideas. The distinction between those ideas and philosophy might be a matter of dispute, but that debate is irrelevant to our present task. It is sufficient for us to note in passing that the history of philosophy is not the history of all ideas, but only of those that are philosophical, whatever that may entail.[8]

As was the case with history, the history of philosophy is composed of three types of propositions: descriptive, interpretative, and evaluative. The purpose of descriptive propositions contained in histories of philosophy is simply to present accurately the ideas of particular philosophers as well as to record contemporanous and later views concerning those ideas. In all cases there has to be explicit evidence that the philosophers or those who wrote about them held the views in question, such as written statements to that effect or credible reports of verbal pronouncements.[9] Typical examples of descriptive propositions occurring in a history of philosophy are the following:

1^{hp}. X held that P (where, for example, P = God is omnipotent, omniscient, and benevolent).

2^{hp}. X held that Q (where, for example, Q = God is not the cause of evil).

3^{hp}. X's holding that P is the reason that X gave for holding that Q.

4^{hp}. M, a contemporary of X, held that X did not hold that P.

5^{hp}. M disagreed with N, another of X's contemporaries, concerning M's view that X did not hold that P.

6^{hp}. R, a later historian of philosophy, held that M was right in holding that X did not hold that P.

7^{hp}. S, another later historian of philosophy, disagreed with R's view concerning M.

Historians of philosophy in their descriptive role, then, are primarily concerned with the presentation of ideas for which there is explicit evidence. But those ideas must be understood broadly to include not only beliefs and doctrines, but also arguments. Morever, the descriptive task of the historian of philosophy is not just to describe those ideas and beliefs, but also to present their relations insofar as there is explicit evidence for them. That is, if Y says that he borrowed P from X, then clearly historians in their descriptive role must record that fact. And if X states that he holds that P because he holds that Q, also this must be recorded, even if in fact it turns out that P and Q have no discernible relation. In short, in their descriptive capacity historians of philosophy should not go beyond explicit evidence.

On the other hand, as interpreters, historians of philosophy can and do go beyond explicit evidence furnished by philosophers and other sources concerning their ideas in order to suggest, as already noted in the case of history, hidden relations that in this case hold both among

ideas themselves and between those ideas and the ideas of other philosophers. In addition, the historian of philosophy will draw broad
generalizations that seek to characterize a philosopher's global approach
as well as the overall philosophical perspective of a period. Finally, he
will also try to translate the ideas of earlier philosophers into the language
and conceptual framwork of the present. Thus, we find the following
sorts of interpretative propositions in histories of philosophy:

a^{hp}. X held that Q because X held that P.
b^{hp}. X held that P because Y held that P.
c^{hp}. X's holding that P led to the abandonment of ·Q by subsequent
       philosophers.
d^{hp}. What X meant by C was D.

Interpretative propositions present in the history of philosophy, then,
go beyond established ideas in order to propose hidden relations (a^{hp}),
unstated reasons (b^{hp}), and broad generalizations (c^{hp}). Moreover, they
aim to render the language and conceptual framework of historical figures
intelligible by translating them into a language and conceptual framework
easily understood at present (d^{hp}), although taking care not to distort
the original intent and content of that language and conceptual framework.
How far one can go in this direction is, of course, a matter of controversy
among historiographers. But it is a generally accepted principle of historiography that at least some translation of the sort mentioned is
necessary in any good history of philosophy. Nevertheless, interpretative
propositions should not be confused with those that contain evaluations
of philosophical ideas or of their impact in future history. Such evaluations
are accomplished in a separate category of propositions, which I have
called "evaluative." Consider the following examples:

A^{hp}. X's view, that P, is true.
B^{hp}. X's argument A is valid.
C^{hp}. X's argument A' is unsound.
D^{hp}. X was perspicacious when he asked question q.
E^{hp}. X was right in formulating problem N in the way he did.
F^{hp}. X was unclear on issue I.
G^{hp}. X is an excellent philosopher.
H^{hp}. X contradicted himself.
I^{hp}. X's view, that P, was useful in the development of Y's view,
       that Q.
J^{hp}. M, a contemporary of X, was wrong in thinking X's view, that
       P, was false.
K^{hp}. R, a later historian, who thought that M was right, was wrong.

All these propositions have in common that they in some way evaluate a philosopher, an idea, or an argument. In general, I believe few historians of philosophy would quarrel with propositions such as D^{hp}, G^{hp}, or I^{hp}. Some would go beyond this and also accept propositions such as E^{hp} or F^{hp}. But many would find difficulty in accepting as part of the history of philosophy propositions such as A^{hp}, B^{hp}, C^{hp}, H^{hp}, J^{hp}, or K^{hp}. The reason that they would object to the second and third sets of propositions is that they contain judgments about the truth and value of philosophical ideas, and these historians are under the impression that history is not supposed to make such judgments. The historian, according to them, can at most interpret but never judge. This makes no sense for several reasons. In the first place, even propositions such as D^{hp}, G^{hp}, and I^{hp}, which might seem innocuous to those historians who object to the others, involve value judgments, although such judgments are somewhat veiled. For why would we call a philosopher "perspicacious" or "'excellent" if it were not because he or she somehow reached or at least approached the truth? Isn't the business of philosophy to look for truth? If that is the case, the achievement of truth should be the fundamental criterion to judge philosophical success.

But there is more to it than that, because our understanding of philosophers and their ideas can only go as far as we understand how they succeeded in their task, and philosophers have traditionally interpreted their task as the discovery of truth. Furthermore, it would seem that in order to make past ideas and philosophical positions intelligible we must understand not only their truth value, but also the validity and soundness of the arguments on which they are based, at least insofar as we can.

The history of philosophy, then, contains a wide range of propositions, including descriptive, interpretative, and evaluative propositions. Still, as in the case of history, there is an essential element to all history of philosophy: its concern with the past and its origin. In the case of history it is past events that are the subject of concern, while in the history of philosophy it is only past ideas and the events related to them that are of importance. In either case, however, both time and provenance are of the essence, although they may not always be explicit in all propositions that are part of a history of philosophy. Now let us turn to philosophy.

Philosophy

The first thing that needs to be noted is that the term 'philosophy', like the term 'history', presents us with a certain ambiguity. We found that 'history' had at least the following important meanings: (1) a series of events, (2) an account of a series of events, and (3) a discipline of learning that could in turn be interpreted as (a) the activity whereby the account of events is produced, or as (b) a set of rules to which the production of the account of events must adhere. The last was called "historiography." Moreover, I stated that I would limit my understanding of history in the present discussion to the account of events, and that the account was to be understood linguistically as a set of propositions. Now, the ranges of meanings of the term 'philosophy' coincide with some of these categories but not with all. There is no meaning of 'philosophy' that corresponds to the meaning of 'history' as series of events. True, philosophy deals with the world and human experience, but neither the world nor human experience can be called philosophy. On the other hand, there is some correspondence among the other categories. In the first place, philosophy is a discipline of learning that entails both an activity and a set of rules that governs such an activity. These meanings correspond to the meanings of 'history' as activity and historiography, respectively, although the philosophical counterpart of historiography should be called philosophical methodology instead. Finally, the product of philosophy understood as discipline consists of a comprehensive, consistent, and accurate view of the world, and this product is the counterpart of the view of history as an account of a series of events. Considered as such, then, philosophy should consist of propositions that, like historical propositions, describe, interpret, and evaluate. Regardless of whether one accepts the meaning, objectivity, and truth of philosophical propositions, one would expect that at least most of those authors who have proposed them have intended them to describe, interpret, and/or evaluate. But the threefold distinction with which we have been working in the cases of history and the history of philosophy does not seem to work as well in the case of philosophy. Let me explain.

At first it would seem that philosophy does contain purely descriptive propositions. Indeed, the following examples seem to substantiate that claim:

1^p. P (where, for example, P = God is omnipotent, omniscient, and benevolent).

2^p. Q (where, for example, Q = God is not the cause of evil).

3^p. P, therefore Q.

Still, if we go back to our initial presentation of descriptive and interpretative propositions, we find that the function of descriptive propositions was to present events and ideas *for which there is empirical evidence,* while the function of interpretative propositions was to go beyond empirical facts in order to reconstruct the fabric of unstated motives, intangible factors, and implicit circumstances within which events and ideas occur and for which there is no empirical evidence. Of course, if the distinction is presented in these terms, then clearly none of the examples of philosophical propositions that have been given and which prima facie appeared to be descriptive can be regarded as such, since there is no empirical evidence to support them. What empirical evidence can be brought to bear on the question of God's omnipotence and omniscience, for example? Such propositions must be classified, consequently, as interpretative. And, indeed, a survey of philosophical propositions will show that philosophy as such contains no purely descriptive propositions in the sense we have understood here. Of course, philosophical accounts do contain propositions taken from our everyday discourse that refer to empirical facts; but these propositions are only used as examples or are mentioned and not used. As such, then, they cannot be considered part of philosophical discourse per se. So, the first difference between philosophy on the one hand and history and the history of philosophy on the other is that in philosophy there are no purely descriptive propositions.

On the other hand, philosophy, like history and the history of philosophy, does contain evaluative propositions. The following should serve as examples:

A^p. P is true.
B^p. Argument 3^p is invalid.
C^p. P lacks proof.
D^p. Doctrine 1^p is incoherent.

Finally, there are two other differences between philosophical propositions and those that belong to history or the history of philosophy that need to be noted. The first is that in philosophy there is a third category of propositions that does not appear either in history or in the history of philosophy. The function of these propositions is to describe the relations among ideas or, to put it more exactly, the logical relations among propositions that express ideas. Examples of such propositions would be

1. $P \rightarrow Q$.
2. $(P \cdot Q) \rightarrow P$.

In the first place, these propositions are different from strictly descriptive propositions in that they do not describe events or ideas for which there is empirical and/or explicit evidence. Nor do they describe relations among events or relations among the ideas of this and that author. They describe relations among ideas themselves, without regard to provenance or time. Secondly, they differ from evaluative propositions in that they do not make claims about the value of events or ideas. Thirdly, they stand apart from interpretative propositions in that they do not deal with hidden reasons, broad generalizations, etc., but resemble them in that they make explicit the logical connections among ideas.

Finally, there is a third and most important difference between philosophy on the one hand and history and the history of philosophy on the other. As we saw earlier, two essential characteristics of propositions belonging to history and the history of philosophy were their references to time and provenance. No such references occur in philosophical propositions. Of course, it is possible to find references to provenance and time in philosophy, but when such is the case, the references are immaterial to its main task. For that task, unlike that of the other two disciplines mentioned, is the establishment of philosophical knowledge, and that knowledge, unlike historical knowledge, has nothing to do with occurrences happening at a particular time or place.

In short, what sets philosophy apart from history and history of philosophy is that (1) it does not contain propositions descriptive of events or ideas for which there is empirical evidence, (2) it contains propositions whose function is to describe logical relations among ideas, and (3) its propositions lack reference to time and provenance.

3

Having established these differences we can now go back to the issue presented at the beginning and see whether some solution to it can be found. The issue involved the relation of philosophy and its history and the questions that we asked had to do with whether philosophy and its history are incompatible with and/or irrelevant to each other or whether they are necessarily related. Now, from what has been said concerning philosophy and the history of philosophy, it follows, first, that there is no incompatibility between philosophy and its history. If the propositions of philosophy and those of its history are as different as we have said they are, then it should not be possible to find that they contradict each other and therefore that they are incompatible. A brief perusal and integration into a single set of the non-evaluative propositions of philosophy and the history of philosophy given earlier as examples will illustrate the point.

1^{hp}.   X held that P.
1^{p}.   P.
2^{hp}.   X held that Q.
2^{p}.   Q.
3^{hp}.   X's holding that P is the reason that X gave for holding that Q.
a^{hp}.   X held that Q because X held that P.

3^p.   P, therefore Q.
b^{hp}.   X held that P because Y held that P.
4^{hp}.   M, a contemporary of X, held that X did not not hold that P.
Etc.

Clearly, there is no contradiction in the set, nor do the evaluative propositions of philosophy and the history of philosophy appear to yield any conflict. Putting together our earlier examples of evaluative propositions for both results in the following set:

A^{hp}.   X's view, that P, is true.
A^p.   P is true.
B^{hp}.   X's argument A is valid.
B^p.   Argument 3^p is invalid.
C^{hp}.   X's argument B is unsound.
C^p.   P lacks proof.
D^{hp}.   X was perspicacious when he asked question q.
D^p.   Doctrine 1^p is incoherent.
E^{hp}.   X was right in formulating N in the way he did.
Etc.

Again, there is no contradiction in the set. So much, then, for the charge of incompatibility between philosophy and its history; but we are still left with the question of the usefulness and/or necessity of the relation. In order to answer this question more clearly we must divide the issue in terms of the end pursued, for the end of philosophy is different from that of history. Now, formulated from a philosophical perspective, the question is whether the history of philosopy is relevant and/or necessary for philosophy. And the answer is readily available. First, if on the one hand (1) the function of philosophical propositions, in accordance with what was said earlier, is to present an interpretation of the world in terms of human experience, to describe the logical relations used to present such interpretations, and to evaluate such ideas and their relations and, on the other hand, (2) the aim of the history of philosophy is to present an account of ideas where the reference to time and provenance are of the essence, it is obvious that philosophy is not necessarily dependent on its history. The philosopher *qua* philosopher does not need to refer to the history of philosophy, its actors, and/or its ideas.

Nor will it do to argue against this (1) that all philosophy is historical from the moment that it is formulated, or (2) that philosophy, owing to its dialectical nature, must refer back to its history, or even (3) that the concepts and ideas philosophers use to philosophize have a historical origin and therefore imply a dependence of philosophy on its history. And it does not because, in spite of the spatiotemporal and dialectical character of philosophy and of the historical origin of the concepts and ideas it uses, the philosophical enterprise as such is not concerned with giving an account of the past and does not need to rely on it to go about its business. So, even if philosophy as a human enterprise is itself a historical phenomenon, which moreover engages in dialogue with the past and uses concepts and language that have historical origins, none of that makes of philosophy history or renders it dependent on its history.

That the history of philosophy is not necessary for philosophy does not mean, secondly, that the history of philosophy is irrelevant to philosophy. Indeed, the history of philosophy should be of great use to the philosopher, for it furnishes diverse formulations of positions and arguments that facilitate the philosopher's task. In many instances it may supply the solution or the seeds of the solution that the philosopher was looking for, or it may show that certain views are oversimplistic, or that certain arguments are unsound. The history of philosophy, then, although non-essential for philosophy, is a source of what might be called "raw data" for which the philosopher can find good use. It is where the philosopher does field work, as it were. This can be easily seen if we look back at the integrated sets of propositions in philosophy and the history of philosophy given earlier, for the intimate relationship among them is evident. This does not mean that the history of philosophy is philosophy, or that it becomes philosophy when it is used by philosophers. The history of philosophy remains history, but precisely as such it can be of use to the philosopher.

With respect to history, on the other hand, the situation is somewhat different. For, although the propositions contained in the history of philosophy are different from philosophical propositions in that some of them are purely descriptive and all of them have reference to time and provenance, they also contain philosophical concepts and the understanding of those concepts necessarily falls within the province of philosophy. Thus, the history of philosophy entails philosophy. Otherwise, it reduces to the repetition of terms, phrases, dates, and sources without an understanding of what those terms, phrases, etc., mean. Consequently, while the history of philosophy may only be useful to philosophy, philosophy is essential to its history; for the propositions that compose the history of philosophy entail certain philosophical propositions that are implicit in them. Take, for example, the proposition 'X held that God is omnipotent, omniscient, and benevolent'. Someone could, I imagine, utter that proposition without understanding what the notions of divinity, omnipotence, omniscience, and benevolence are; but that would be equivalent to the utterance of a proposition in a foreign language and, therefore, could not be called understanding and, therefore, history. The history of philosophy entails an understanding of what is being said and, therefore, a conceptual framework and analysis of the terms it uses. And here is where philosophy becomes indispensable for it. The history of philosophy, then, is of necessity philosophical, unless, of course, it is either bad history of philosophy or no history of philosophy at all.

4

Now let us turn to Veatch's *Aristotle* and see how this book fits into the controversy with which we have been dealing and the framework that has been developed.

My argument in the remaining part of the paper will be, first, that Veatch thinks that in his book on Aristotle he is primarily doing philosophy or at least something much more philosophical than just history of philosophy and that he thinks this because his uses of the history of philosophy are philosophical. Second, I shall argue that in fact Veatch is not primarily doing philosophy but rather history of philosophy, even though he uses philosophy in his understanding of that history. Third, I shall point out two misconceptions concerning the history of philosophy which are at the root of Veatch's view concerning the nature of his book and that Veatch shares with many contemporary philosophers. Fourth, I shall indicate how all of this affects at least one of the claims he makes concerning Aristotle's philosophy.

How can it be shown that Veatch thinks that he is not primarily engaged in a historical study? Simply by what he says. The very subtitle of his book, "A Contemporary Appreciation," suggests that he has something more than history in mind. This is supported by explicit statements found throughout the book. He tells us, for example, the "philosopher-historians and historians of ideas continue to write learned books about [Aristotle, but] . . . rather than approach Aristotle in this way, why may we not treat him as if he were a contemporary philosopher . . . ?" (3). A bit later he writes that his "brief account of Aristotle's life and influence . . . is not an account whose purpose is simply to fix Aristotle's place in history; instead it is intended to remind us of just who and what this man is who we claim should once again become a dominant force on the contemporary philosophical scene" (5). And later still, "to preserve Aristotle as a historical figure is really to embalm him as a philosopher" (9).

Thus, it would seem that Veatch regards his aim as not historical or at least not as just historical, but rather either as something different, or at least as something more than that, that is, I take him to mean that his aim is philosophical. And at the basis of Veatch's belief is that he wants to establish the truth of certain views that he claims Aristotle defended.

Now, some historians of philosophy will probably agree with Veatch in that his book contains claims about Aristotle's ideas that they would regard as going beyond what Aristotle said. The primary thesis itself of the book seems to reflect such an interpretative approach, for it claims that "Aristotle is, *par excellence,* the philosopher of common sense" (12) and for most historians of Aristotelian thought, this thesis goes well beyond what Aristotle explicitly held. The reasons are several. In the first place, Aristotle uses no terminology that would express the notion of common sense to which Veatch refers. Indeed, as Veatch himself recognizes, the term 'common sense' is used to translate a Greek term that refers to something that has nothing to do with what Veatch means by common sense. Nor does Aristotle adhere explicitly to the principle that Veatch identifies as fundamental to a commonsense philosophy, the maxim that "what to all men everywhere in their sane moments is known to be the truth is, indeed, really the truth (12). Moreover, if Veatch were right concerning the role of common sense in philosophy, then the function of philosophy would be restricted to the empirical task of finding out what all men everywhere in their saner moments know or think they know to be the truth, but in fact Aristotle engages in no such empirical enterprise.[10]

Moreover, the argument of the historians would continue, the concepts and views that Aristotle proposes in his philosophy are as far from an ordinary commonsensical view of the world as any philosopher can get. It is true that Veatch tries very hard to show that Aristotle's doctrines are commonsensical. But, although he succeeds in many cases, it is just not possible to view all, not even most, of Aristotle's philosophical views as commonsensical. How can one argue the commonsensical character, for example, of Aristotle's doctrine of the ultimate end of human beings as "the whole uninterrupted activity of theoretical knowledge and pure contemplation" (124)? And what of notions such as matter, form, or the unmoved mover? If these are commonsensical notions, then so are Bergmann's bare particular and Scotus's *haecceitas.*

Finally, some historians, and even Veatch himself, might point out that Veatch's book contains judgments about the value of philosophical doctrines. Indeed, the overall conclusion of the book is that Aristotle's philosophy is "perhaps not merely a live option, but even the only option open to a man of healthy common sense with respect to the realities of things generally and of our human situation particularly" (199). In introducing such value judgments, so the argument would go, Veatch has gone beyond history and engaged in philosophizing.

To this I would like to respond that, as we saw earlier, the history of philosophy is not restricted to description but contains also interpretations and evaluations. The presence of interpretations and evaluations in a history of philosophy, therefore, does not render the history less historical. For the interpretations involved are supposed to go beyond what authors have said in order to reconstruct hidden assumptions and views that underlie and explain explicit statements. Thus, Veatch's use of the notion of common sense, even though not explicit in Aristotle, does not render his account unhistorical. It could turn out, of course, that Veatch is wrong about Aristotle and common sense, although I do not think so, but that does not alter the historical character of his enterprise.

Likewise, evaluations involve propositions in which claims concerning the value of the views of historical figures are expressed. Consequently, Veatch's judgments with respect to the value of Aristotle's philosophy can hardly disqualify his account from being primarily historical. Indeed, much of what Veatch is doing is entirely in keeping with what the history of philosophy has done in its best moments and, therefore, should be.

All of this, however, only points out that the considerations that led Veatch to interpret his book on Aristotle as not primarily historical in character are not sound, but that is not enough to establish that the book is not a primarily philosophical book. The proof of that, however, is easily available in that the book concerns Aristotle's ideas, even though those ideas are also thought to be true ones. The thrust of Veatch's account is always concerned with the description, interpretation, and evaluation of Aristotle's views, even though the evaluations involve positive recommendations as to what we should think ourselves. Nor could one argue, I believe, that this is a work of philosophy in which the history of philosophy is used to illustrate the positions discussed. For the book is simply not organized in that way. Indeed, what the book does is to present Aristotle's views in a favorable light and to recommend that we adopt them, but that procedure is still overwhelmingly historical in character, contrary to what Veatch seems to think. Even a superficial perusal of the text will confirm the overriding concern on Veatch's part with the time and provenance of his claims. For, indeed, it is Aristotle's views that are discussed, evaluated, and commended.

5

But we may ask, if what I have said concerning Veatch's book is correct, namely, that what Veatch has carried out in his book on Aristotle is primarily a historical task, why the disclaimers to the contrary? Why should Veatch try so hard to present his account of Aristotle's views as something more than and/or different from simply history of philosophy?

I believe the reasons are two. The first originates in the widespread belief, with which I disagree, that history is entirely descriptive and should contain neither interpretations nor value judgments.[11] The second has to do with a rather poor view of the history of philosophy, in which the discipline is seen as something largely irrelevant and useless, a discipline of interest only to antiquarians. Indeed, the picture of the historian that is indirectly revealed by the first paragraph of Veatch's book confirms my point.

> Poor Aristotle! Having for so many centuries been a dominant force, in Western philosophy and in Western culture generally, he now reminds one rather of an enormous dinosaur. He is not exactly extinct, but he seems hardly to be alive philosophically any more. In consequence, like nearly all dinosaurs, as well as like countless dead philosophers, Aristotle would seem to be reduced to little more than a great, hulking museum piece in the history of Western culture. Classical scholars still translate him and edit his texts; and of course philosopher-historians and historians of ideas continue to write learned books about him; yes, even philosophers themselves—at least during their childhood in the profession—usually find themselves taken around by one of their elders on a tour of the museums of Western philosophy, where they are almost certain to find old Aristotle prominently displayed in a enormous glass case.

But, I hope, Veatch does not hold the views that I have attributed to him. For the history of philosophy is not reducible to mere description, and it has a vital and important function assisting philosophy in its quest.

Veatch's desire to interpret and evaluate Aristotle's philosophy, then, and his wish to make Aristotle's thought come alive for us today need not entail an interpretation of the history of philosophy as philosophy or as something more than what it is, namely, history. We can still have our history of philosophy and also our interpretations and evaluations of the ideas contained in it together with a philosophical understanding of them, as Veatch himself has demonstrated so well in his book.

6

Now we come to the last point I want to make in this paper, namely, that Veatch's understanding of both the history of philosophy and of the nature of his *Aristotle* tends to weaken in some ways the arguments of his book and undermines the main thesis he defends in it.

From the analysis given above, it should be clear that the history of philosophy contains descriptive, interpretative, and evaluative propositions and that it also requires an understanding of philosophy. A good historical account of philosophy requires descriptions that are accurate and historically documented, interpretations that are consistent, lucid, and that enlighten us about the reasons for and the character of certain philosophical ideas, and, finally, sound evaluations of those ideas, their historical impact, and their philosophical worth.

Descriptive accounts that are accurate and historically documented require in turn a careful presentation of historical data backed up with explicit evidence. In the case of philosophy, it is necessary to present and/or refer to not only the primary texts that make explicit the ideas being described by the historian, but also the evidence gathered from the opinions of contemporaries as well as historical authorities who have had something to say about those ideas of their authors.

The development of interpretations that are consistent, lucid, and enlightening requires explanations of how hitherto hidden concepts and ideas explain the nature of the philosophical framework of which an account is being given, as well as the reasons why that particular framework was adopted and defended. If interpretations lack this dimension their use is limited.

Moreover, sound evaluations require clear statements of the criteria used to measure the value of philosophical ideas and an explanation of how those ideas fit the adopted criteria. Otherwise we are unable to judge if such evaluations are appropriate.

Finally, the philosophical nature of the history of philosophy requires the explicit presentation and analysis of the basic concepts used in the description, interpretation, and evaluation sought. Indeed, in order for a historical account to be at all sound it must be presented in the context of a conceptual framework whose tenets and ideas are explicitly discussed. The existence of the framework makes possible the production of an intelligible account, and its explicit presentation functions as a controlling device of the objectivity, fairness, and honesty of the account.

Does Veatch's *Aristotle* adhere to the principles that I have outlined? Does it fulfil the requirements of a sound historical account of Aristotle's philosophy? Clearly most parts of Veatch's account without a doubt are prime examples of what sound history of philosophy should be. But, and this is my main objection, Veatch's account, although generally successful, fails when it comes to the main thesis that he defends. And I suspect the reason is that, as I claimed earlier, Veatch does not quite understand that his task is historical and, therefore, neglects those aspects of a historical account that are necessary for it to be successful. His view that his book is not historical, or at least not primarily historical, leads him to think that he does not need to back up the main thesis he proposes in it with the kind of textual evidence that should accompany sound history, for example. Moreover, most likely for the same reasons, he leaves unstated the criteria of evaluation according to which he measures the value of some of Aristotle's ideas. Finally, and most important, he does not present explicitly the conceptual framework that he uses to interpret Aristotle's philosophy as commonsensical.

A quick look at Veatch's thesis will illustrate these points. The thesis is, as mentioned earlier, that "Aristotle is, *par excellence,* the philosopher of common sense." Clearly, this is a historical thesis that aims to characterize Aristotle's philosophy, it is interpretative insofar as Aristotle did not describe himself or his philosophy as commonsensical, and it involves an evaluative element because Veatch also claims, as we saw above, that Aristotle's philosophy "is not merely a live option, but even the only option open to a man of healthy common sense."

Now, the problem that arises with this thesis is that Veatch's substantiation of it does not fulfil all the requirements of a sound historical account. In the first place, he does not give any textual evidence, either primary or secondary, to support the thesis. Yes, he does show quite successfully that many of Aristotle's basic concepts correspond to concepts present in our ordinary view of the world. Thus, for example, the Aristotelian notion of substance corresponds roughly to the ordinary notion of thing. And so likewise with others. But this is not enough to support the view the Aristotle's philosophy can be best described as a philosophy of common sense. We need the texts from Aristotle that support that view, as well as evidence drawn from existing authoritative interpretations of Aristotle's aims and philosophy.

Secondly, Veatch does not discuss anywhere in the book the criteria by which he is led to conclude that Aristotle's philosophy is the only option available to the man of healthy common sense. He does try and very often succeeds in showing that Aristotle's ideas make sense, but that is not enough to substantiate his much stronger claim at least on two counts: that a view makes sense does not necessarily mean that it is commonsensical, and certainly it does not entail that it is the only view open to individuals with a healthy common sense.

Finally, and this is perhaps the most important weakness that I see in Veatch's substantiation of his thesis, Veatch does not present an explanation of the basic concept of common sense that he uses to interpret Aristotle's thought. Nowhere does he explain in detail what common sense is, and nowhere does he specify for us how to distinguish common sense from personal, social, and cultural viewpoints. How can we judge that Aristotle's philosophy is a philosophy of common sense if we do not know what Veatch means by common sense? Indeed, this is the crux of the matter, because the notion of common sense is one that has been widely discussed in the history of philosophy and no agreement has been reached about it. To use this controversial notion without giving us a clear understanding of it in order to characterize and make intelligible for us Aristotle's philosophy does not make sense. Indeed, I would go so far as saying that it does not seem to be commonsensical at all!

For all we know after reading Veatch's book, then, it may be true that Aristotelian philosophy is a philosophy of common sense *par excellence* and that it is the only one open to a man of healthy common sense, as Veatch claims, but we still have no definite proof that it is so. And this, if I am correct, can be traced to a methodology arising from Veatch's disparaging opinion of the history of philosophy and his view that his *Aristotle* is not a historical work.

Of course, I am sure that Henry will not let my statements go without challenge and that, in his customary understated and self-deprecating manner, he will show both that I am wrong and where I am wrong, treating us in the process to a presentation, both profound and witty, of his own views of the relation between philosophy and its history. That, after all, was the main purpose of my paper, and one that I am looking forward to with pleasure, even if in the process I do not come out looking very well.

NOTES

1. Henry B. Veatch, *Aristotle: A Contemporary Appreciation* (Bloomington and London: Indiana University Press, 1974).

2. The most recent addition to a growing literature on the subject is the volume edited by Richard Rorty, J. B. Schneewind, and Quentin Skinner, *Philosophy in History* (Cambridge: University Press, 1984).

3. There are many other arguments that are given to support the view that the history of philosophy is indispensable to philosophy. For example, Henry Veatch argued in his closing remarks at the conference that the history of philosophy is necessary for philosophy because philosophy is essentially a dialectical enterprise and, therefore, requires that philosophers enter into dialogue with past philosophers. And Carolyn Korsmeyer argued that, although the history of philosophy is not logically necessary for philosophy, it is factually so, since no one can philosophize effectively without taking into account what past philosophers have thought. And the reason for this is that all philosophical reflection involves concepts, ideas, and language that have origins in the history of philosophy.

4. Naturally, reference to events and happenings will also entail references to the persons, things, and circumstances that are involved in those events and happenings.

5. I understand the term 'proposition' to refer to the meaning of sentences that can be true or false, but for present purposes I shall simply use the term to refer to English sentences that express propositions. We need not, therefore, raise the complicated issues involved in the ontology of propositions, since they are only distantly related to the issue that concerns us here.

6. These and the other examples that are provided throughout the paper should not be taken to be paradigmatically exhaustive. They are meant to be precisely what I have called them, namely, "examples" of the sorts of propositions that one finds in histories, histories of philosophy, and philosophy.

7. Kenneth Schmitz raised this question with me.

8. There are some ideas that seem to me to be clearly philosophical. For example, the notion that everything is composed of matter and form seems to me to be a philosophical notion. And there are ideas that do not seem to be

philosophical at all, such as the notion that water boils at 100° Celsius. But concerning many other ideas the case is not so clear.

9. I have substituted 'explicit evidence' in this context for the expression 'empirical evidence' used in the context of history because ideas, unlike events, are subject to perception only insofar as they are stated or reported, that is, insofar as they are made explicit in some way.

10. Of course, other views of common sense and how it functions do not necessarily preclude reaching conclusions that are not part of what "all men everywhere in their saner moments know or think they know to be the truth." For example, G. E. Moore, as Jonathan Bennett pointed out to me, had an important role for common sense in philosophy and yet he reached all sorts of conclusions that were not part of what could be regarded as commonsensical truths. Indeed, as long as those conclusions did not contradict common sense, he felt they were not in conflict with the commonsensical view of the world. However, Veatch seems to hold a much stronger view of common sense than Moore. As I see it, one needs to separate three positions with respect to the use of common sense in philosophy. One holds that all philosophy should begin with the examination of the commonsensical view of the world. In this sense common sense is the origin of philosophy. Another holds that common sense is a strong criterion of philosophical truth in such a way that all philosophical propositions must find counterparts in the ordinary commonsensical view of the world. Consequently, if a philosophical proposition does not have a counterpart in such a view, or if it contradicts a proposition that is part of such a view, the proposition is to be regarded as either nonsensical or false. Finally, there is a view that holds that common sense is a weak criterion of philosophical truth in such a way that philosophical propositions may be true provided that they do not contradict propositions that are part of our commonsensical view of the world. This last view is the one that Moore may have held; the second one could be attributed to Veatch; and the first is the one I believe Aristotle implicitly held.

11. I believe the position that history should not contain value judgments has been forcefully articulated in this conference by Daniel Garber.

Aristotle and Philosophy Now

Some Critical Reflections

Robert G. Turnbull

Henry Veatch in his Aristotle: A Contemporary Appreciation appears greatly to underestimate the importance of Aristotle for contemporary philosophy. There has been in recent years, if anything, an increase in scholarly attention to the texts. And I should be quite surprised if, e.g., John Cooper, Terence Irwin, Montgomery Furth, or Martha Nussbaum would be content to regard their work on Aristotle as unrelated to their philosophy and thus merely antiquarian. And the twentieth century provides many examples of very influential Anglo-American philosophers who can properly be called Aristotelians. John Austin, Gilbert Ryle, Peter Strawson, Elizabeth Anscombe, Peter Geach, and Donald Davidson come readily to mind. At a remove or two Aristotle's influence on the century has been remarkably strong. The Kantian, Hegelian, and phenomenological traditions are heavily Aristotelian. I omit as obvious the large and influential Catholic philosophy group in which I believe Henry Veatch claims membership. Unless he demands submission to the ipsissima verba of the master of those who know, he should recognize that Aristotle's influence on the century has been at least as great as that of any historical figure.

In very large measure Aristotle remains a philosopher who has and should have considerable contemporary appeal. Certainly a large part of the reason for this lies in his obvious respect for and regular attention to what can properly be called 'common sense'. By that expression I mean, as a first approximation, the language or conceptual scheme used by reasonably well educated people for most of the ordinary pursuits of life. In general Aristotle attempts to distinguish, account for, and exhibit the interrelationships of portions of common sense. And he shows no sign of finding philosophical reasons for declaring common sense or parts of it inapplicable or meaningless.

His account of time respects the applicability of tensed expressions.

His account of place respects our ability to locate things. His account of mind introduces no objection to what we ordinarily say about seeing, hearing, learning, remembering, dreaming, deciding, vacillating, exhibiting courage, etc., etc. In *Categories* he is intent on classifying our common-sensical modes of speaking or thinking about things. I could go on. But, without attempting a precise characterization of common sense or adding examples from Aristotle, I think it is clear that he takes it as inviolable and takes pains to account for and exhibit the interrelationships of its parts and thus to exhibit its unity.

So described, Aristotle's philosophy has had perennial appeal. If—as I do—one takes common sense to be philosophically inviolable, it is hard not to fear that, in taking exception to Aristotle, one is challenging the fundamental condition of intelligibility itself. Though Henry Veatch does not express his admiration of Aristotle in quite this manner, my impression is that he may have some such ground for finding what he takes to be the neglect of Aristotle incomprehensible.

Having said this much, I think that there are very good reasons for objecting to Aristotle. I shall first attend to the matter of Aristotelian science, attempting at once to defend and to attack its rationale. My reasons for attacking it will help, I believe, in my second task, viz., criticizing some key features of his metaphysics and philosophy of mind. As we shall see, however, this criticism does not simply grow out of the attack on Aristotelian science. Its major complaint is Aristotle's illegitimate use of what I call 'philosophical entities'.

ARISTOTLE'S SCIENCE

If the proper tests of a science are or include (a) a procedure for investigating nature, (b) a means of arriving at a theory which admits of testing and possible falsification, and (c) a logic suitable for explanation, then surely Aristotle not only developed a theory of science but also engaged in serious science—notably, biological science. Much of the theory of science is developed in *Posterior Analytics*. There, drawing upon Plato's procedure of collection and division and the logic of the *Prior Analytics*, Aristotle laid out a theory of scientific explanation and a procedure for arriving at explanatory middle terms.

The basic syllogism for scientific demonstration is, of course, Barbara in the non-Galenic "C-B-A" form. That is, 'C holds for the whole of B and B for the whole of A'. From that can be read off 'C holds for the whole of A'. In demonstration the premises must, however, be *necessary*, i.e., C must hold *kath auto* for B, meaning that C holds by virtue of the very nature of B. If C holds *kath auto* for B and B *kath auto* for A, then C holds *kath auto* for A. Aristotle's model demonstrative syllogism

has a definitory formula as a middle term, i.e., as 'B' in the "C-B-A"
form. In a simpleminded and obvious case, *three-sided* holds *kath auto*
for *plane figure bounded by three straight lines,* and that formula, in
turn, holds *kath auto* for (the whole of) triangle. (It may be worth noting
in this connection that it does not detract from the necessity to move
from the whole of triangle to *this triangle*. Provided that one has a conceptually associated name as the subject term, the *kath auto* character
of the proposition holds regardless of the quantity of the proposition.
Thus, as should be clear as well from comments shortly to be made
about 'assemblage', Aristotle does not have anything like the standard
"problem of induction.")

Of course, to get an actual demonstrative syllogism, Aristotle needs
terms and definitions. *Posterior Analytics* 2.19, the very last chapter,
contains his account of the etiology of terms. Baldly stated that account
requires that for "the first universal to be in the soul," one must be capable
of sense perception and memory and have "repeated memory of the same."
Such a universal is a concept or conceptual ability, enabling one, on
appropriate perceptual occasions, to recognize, say, a rabbit as a rabbit.
But, of course, such an initial concept is close to sense and is liable to
be inaccurate and somewhat confused. One may in using it, e.g., confuse
rabbits and squirrels. Aristotle supposes that, in addition to our ability
to acquire initial sense concepts, we also have the ability he calls 'epagoge'.
I translate this as 'assemblage' (though it is often and misleadingly
translated as 'induction'). It is the ability to assemble initial concepts
under a genus, those under a higher genus, etc. In the process of assemblage, there is some sharpening and improvement of the initial concepts.
And there is a bringing into play an ability which he calls 'nous' (it
being unclear what connection *nous* here has with *nous poietikos* or *nous
pathetikos* of *De Anima* 3), where *nous* is at least the ability to recognize
kath auto connections. (This is, of course, associated with the idea that
not all knowledge can be demonstrated. To avoid an infinite regress or
argument in a circle, Aristotle thinks there must be such "intuitive" or
"unmiddled" knowledge—as contrasted with the "middled" character of
demonstrative knowledge.)

With the ability to arrive at genera, there comes into play the notion
of definition by genus and differentia. Aristotle describes a procedure
which is akin to Plato's procedure of collection and division (cf. *Philebus*
16Cff.). But he criticizes Plato for failure to test proposed definitions
or definitory formulae by using the latter as middle terms in possible
demonstrations. What emerges is a sophisticated and self-correcting procedure, using our abilities to acquire concepts, arrange them in genera/
species orderings, and try out definitory formulae in the logical form
of demonstrations.

It should go without saying that Aristotle supposes that a very complex battery of concepts can be acquired and improved in the procedure(s), enabling demonstration to be possible for several subject matters. And I think it can be and has been shown that he actually uses the procedure of arriving at definitory formulae and thus demonstrations in, e.g., some of the biological treatises. I should also note that, in all of this, there is an explanation of his distinction between what is evident "to us" and what is evident "in nature," for he thinks that we can move from the former to the latter by using the procedures discussed above—and thus arrive at the definitions necessary for demonstrative science.

Though this account has been all too brief, I think it provides enough backdrop to allow raising the question: But is it science? The answer is, I believe, a highly qualified yes. It does respect observation. It does establish a logical pattern for explanation. It does allow for falsification. And it is reasonably effective for organizing bodies of knowledge.

From the perspective of modern physical and biological science, however, it is severely crippled by its close linkage with what Wilfrid Sellars calls 'the manifest image', i.e., what is available to us by means of our very limited sense organs. Despite Aristotle's realism and recognition that our first universals are not and need not be *of* sensa or ideas (or any other of the entities of modern phenomenalism or idealism), the tie to entities made known through perception virtually prevents access to— much less the discoveries of—modern physics (and, consequently, chemistry and biology).

A related criticism has to do with the Aristotelian appeal to *natures*. A good Aristotelian scientist can substitute for serious microphysics the assumption that the nature of a thing can be determined by noting what happens to it or what it does in a variety of circumstances and then assigning to it a set of abilities which "account for" what has been so noted. Properly done and linked with a classification system or taxonomy, this procedure can yield a great deal of valuable information, and it may have considerable explanatory power. (Improperly done, as persons as diverse as Francis Bacon and Moliére have loudly complained, it can result in the learned nonsense of "explanations" which merely repeat what is to be explained.)

Modern science is, of course, Platonist-inspired, as the writings of such early modern scientists as Galileo, Kepler, and others clearly show. The idea of the classical mechanics that the fundamental processes of the world are mathematically intelligible led by a somewhat tortuous path through Newton, Dalton, and others to what Wilfrid Sellars calls 'the scientific image'. That image forsakes the anthropomorphic empiricism of Aristotle for model-theoretic explanation and appeal to unobservables (except via instrumentation).

ARISTOTLE'S METAPHYSICS

I am exercised generally (i.e., not specifically with Aristotle) about two issues concerning what I shall call 'philosophical entities'. By 'philosophical entities' I mean such purported entities as *qualities, relations, substances, ideas, sense-data,* etc. In the tradition items of this sort are *argued for,* i.e., they are neither the undoubted entities of common sense nor the postulated entities of modern science (whose justification lies primarily in their role in scientific explanation and prediction—and, especially in recent years, detection by a variety of instruments).

I think it is true that, if a person who is not corrupted by philosophy should answer the question, 'What is there?' she or he would not include philosophical entities in the list (though, if conversant with modern science, she or he may include atoms, neutrinos, or quarks in the list). I think it is also true that a person who has been corrupted by philosophy, if asked what, e.g., a tree *really is,* may be hesitant between giving a commonsensical or scientific answer (mentioning commonsensical or scientific entities) and giving a philosophical answer (mentioning philosophical entities). There is considerable oddity, of course, in giving a philosophical answer, e.g., claiming that a tree is a substance together with a number of *qualities* or claiming, with Berkeley, that a tree is a collection of *ideas.* I am reminded of O. K. Bouwsma's story of the apple grower who is informed by an angel that, since apples are substances with such qualities as roundness, mealiness, etc., an alternative to the tedious job of tending the orchard would be learning the trick of joining qualities with substances.

And so my two issues about philosophical entities are these: (1) What sort of connection can there be between philosophical entities and the standard entities of common sense and science? and (2) What sort of status can one give to entities whose existence is established *merely by argument?* My contention is that, given the inviolability of common sense (and, for the present scene, science), philosophical entities should be construed as limning features of our commonsensical (or scientific) representation system, and not as entities among those represented by common sense (or science). The temptation to treat philosophical entities as objects in the world (in addition to or as distinguished from common-sense entities) merits resistance. The reason such entities are *argued for* (and not named or pointed at by standard commonsense means) is that the need for them arises in the effort to show how all of common sense "hangs together" without paradox or contradiction.

One needs to show how one and the same thing can change and yet remain the same (or, alternatively, how two sentences can both be true of the same thing though having contrary or contradictory predicates). So she or he may introduce the idea of distinguishing a thing or substance and its qualities, allowing the thing to have opposed qualities at different times or in different respects. Or she or he may distinguish a thing as a special sort of collection of "ideas" (sensa, what you will) capable of containing "opposites" under specified conditions, Or he or she may speak of each thing as being or made up of "monads" each of which, while maintaining the same nature, generates a sequence of states. Supplying detail for each of these would for the present purpose be otiose. What is important in them is that each is the result of argument, argument designed to exhibit a rationale for common sense (and/or science).

I have elsewhere ("On What There Is: Representation and History," *Synthese* 67, 57-75) argued the case for taking such philosophical entities as classifying our commonsensical (and/or scientific) modes of representing the world and thus belonging rather with represent*ings* than with represent*eds*. With this in mind, it would be a mistake to take philosophical entities as on a par with commonsensical (or scientific) entities and thus to take any of the terms for the former as designating (specifically or generically) any of the latter. It would therefore be an obvious mistake to take Aristotle's categories as philosophical entities and *also* to take the terms for them as designating (generically) common-sensical entities. I think that, since the categories are entities that are *argued for* in the interest of exhibiting the *zusammenhang* of common sense, it is appropriate to take them as philosophical entities and thus not as highest (commonsensical) genera. Taking them as philosophical entities, by the way, enables one to undercut the standard arguments about the status of *categories* (words? concepts? things?).

I regard Aristotle's *form* and *matter,* as well as *potentiality* and *actuality,* as philosophical entities. As argued for in the interest of exhibiting the consistency of common sense, they belong among the modes of representing. Understood in this manner, one might regard *Metaphysics* Zeta as justifying our taking things or sortal terms as our primary means of representing commonsensical things (leaving to one side the issue of mass or bulk terms)—the other terms as (in various ways) derivative means. (This would, incidentally, help to make good sense of Aristotle's doctrine of *pros hen* ambiguity.) The actual text of Aristotle, however, does invite the confusion of commonsensical entities with philosophical entities.

The doctrine of the prime mover (or movers) especially invites the confusion. It is not difficult to give motivation to the potential/actual distinction as allowing us to parse commonsensical talk about changing commonsensical entities without falling into paradox or contradiction. In these cases, however, we speak of entities whose existence is in no way in doubt. In explaining how they can be represented as changing or coming into being, we are not proving their existence. And this is so whether we are talking of human beings, stars, or petunias. But the existence of the prime mover is *argued for,* roughly, on the ground that a given series of changes, construed as actualizations of potentialities, cannot be without a first term and that any candidate for first term *must* be pure actuality or pure form. Given that philosophical entities are ways of organizing our represent*ings*, any such argument, at best, shows only that we cannot use the *actuality/potentiality* distinction for coherently representing commonsensical entities without requiring the representation of an entity for which there is no commonsensical ground, and thus, insofar as the argument for the prime mover falls out of the *actuality/potentiality* distinction, is a *reductio ad absurdum* of that distinction.

Related to the actuality/potentiality distinction is the idea of using *natures* or *forms* or *actualities* for explaining the behavior of various commonsensical things. Though I noted early in this paper that there can be Aristotelian science which appeals to definitory formulae as middle terms, there are stern limits to such science, as modern microphysics shows. And there is a standing temptation to let the use of such formulae as specifying natures cut off further inquiry. Why does x do F? or Why is x F? Because x is G, and it is the nature of G's to do or be F under specified conditions. Though Aristotle's biological works carefully attend to *organa* of various living things as having natures capable of performing the functions of those things and even to the matter of those organs as having appropriate natures, Aristotle stays to the end with explanation by natures. And just *why* the operation of the lower-level natures produces the emergent features of the high-level natures is not only unclear; it is a question which the *nature* pattern of explanation does not allow. Though some limits are set by materials or the materials of parts, things just *have* the natures they have. What I am getting at here is a kind of *hybris* brought on by the relative success of some of Aristotle's philosophical entities in exhibiting the non-paradoxical or non-contradictory character of common sense—a *hybris* which is aided and abetted by the confusion of philosophical entities with commonsense entities.

ARISTOTLE'S PHILOSOPHY OF MIND

I turn to some comments about Aristotle's philosophy of mind. Commonsensically there is no doubt that we can see, hear, feel, taste, and touch various things in our environment. There is no doubt that we can recognize various things as what they are—and that we are capable of making mistakes about what they are. We also can come to know, even to know a great deal. And there is a difference between knowing and believing or opining. We are also capable of memory and recollection, dreaming, and so on.

Of course, Aristotle gives us accounts of all of these. What I wish to attend to here are his use of philosophical entities in some of those accounts and the role they play in his explanations of perception and knowledge.

In the general account of perception, it is assumed that a sense organ has a *passive power* or *potentiality* and the thing perceived has an *active power* or *potentiality*. Both of these are triggered off simultaneously by something *in act,* in the case of vision, the introduction of fire into the medium. In the case of vision, the eye is said to take on the *sensible form* of the thing seen—to take it on without its *matter*. Though I think that Aristotle intends by his use of '*logos*' in this connection the very interesting doctrine that the eye's matter comes to be patterned in the same way as the matter of the thing seen, what I wish to attend to is, once again, the invasion of philosophical entities into the provenance of commonsense entities. And we have an explanation which doesn't really explain anything. What is more, it discourages efforts to produce serious explanation. The contrast in this respect between Aristotle's account and Plato's account in *Timaeus* (which, however crudely, attempts microphysical explanation) is remarkable.

Aristotle is right, of course, to recognize that knowledge is quite different from mere perception (*aisthesis*). And he is right, I believe, in the recognition that conceptualization is not accounted for merely by appeal to perception and memory (whatever accounts are to be given of them)—if only because of the simple evidence that there are animals that are capable of perception and memory and lack conceptual abilities. *De Anima* 3, however, with its appeal to *active* and *passive nous,* once again uses philosophical entities in an egregious manner.

Niceties aside, Aristotle requires that human beings (who are capable of knowledge) have *passive nous,* which is described as the ability to take on the intelligible form (of whatever) without its matter. He even speaks of it as the "place" of forms, though *passive nous* is not linked with any bodily organ. There is, however, no taking on of a form without some appropriate sense experience. Given that we are passive in sense experience, something active is needed to trigger off passive *nous*. That active something is *active nous*. Since *active* and *passive nous* and *forms* are Aristotelian philosophical entities, once again we have Aristotle using philosophical entities as though they were commonsensical or scientific entities and thus, in effect, not only producing an explanation which does not explain but also discouraging serious commonsensical or scientific investigation. (I might note, parenthetically, that the *Posterior Analytics* 2.19 account, which uses '*nous*' in a rather different way, is somewhat less discouraging. In that account, Aristotle does, however, simply announce that it is just some sort of brute fact that we are capable of taking on universals.)

It might well be objected that there is something normative about knowledge and justification of knowledge-claims and that Aristotle, in invoking *active nous,* is taking that into account. So that, in the present case, it is quite justifiable to make use of philosophical entities for explanatory purposes. I readily agree that there is something normative about knowledge but do not agree that explanation by appeal to philosophical entities is more than an *actus fidei.* As for a positive account which makes no such appeal, that is a long story; and there are several such accounts in the present philosophical marketplace, one of which I am prepared to defend.

CONCLUDING COMMENTS

I am painfully aware that the present paper only scratches the surface of a difficult set of issues. Relatively little detail of the matters discussed has been exposed. And nothing has been said about Aristotle's ethics, political thought, aesthetics, etc. I am also acutely aware that I have not fully or even properly explained and defended the philosophical stance taken in the paper. I trust, nevertheless, that the stance taken and the distinctions made within it are relatively familiar to a contemporary audience.

It should be easy to recognize that my way of drawing a distinction between commonsensical or scientific entities and philosophical entities is heavily indebted to Kant and some twentieth-century adaptations of Kant. I think, however, that the distinction stands well enough on its own and that there is no reason to read further Kantian implications into my brief critique of Aristotle.

In the introduction of the paper I gave a description/definition of 'common sense' and characterized it as a first approximation. Let me now, in the light of what has been said, move to a second approximation (at least). The language or conceptual scheme used by reasonably well educated people for most of the ordinary pursuits of life, though I have treated it as philosophically inviolable, need not be and has not been unchangeable or even unchanging. Under the influence of changing social and political institutions, subtler forms of the rude encounter with nature, intercultural contact, change or development of art forms, developing science, and the like, common sense changes. It is fascinating to note, however, that so much of what Aristotle takes into account has the ring of present-day common sense. Historical continuity will explain this in part. But I suspect that, lying rather deeper, there is a similarity between the conditions of life in well-developed cultures which have equally well-developed languages.

Let me end by repeating a major source of agreement with Henry Veatch. I agree that Aristotle exhibits a remarkably good ear for what is and what is not commonsensical. And he exhibits as well a remarkably keen eye for the problems of interrelating the various parts of common sense. Indeed, the problems he isolated remain, in remarkable degree, the continuing problems of philosophy. I also agree with Veatch that Aristotle's reliance on common sense is welcome after so much immersion in the epistemological questing of modern philosophy. Even so, I do not believe that all of this admiration should blind us to Aristotle's anthropomorphic empiricism and to his vacuous use of philosophical entities in a number of crucial explanations.

Response to Commentators

Henry B. Veatch

From the comments and criticisms that we have just been listening to, respecting the inadequacies of my own unhappy efforts, for lo these many years, at trying to be an Aristotelian in philosophy, I wonder if any of you may perchance have noticed the rather marked difference in emphasis and in direction taken by my two critics, Professor Gracia and Professor Turnbull. For I believe it can be said that it was specifically of *my* Aristotelianism that Jorgé Gracia felt he needed to be particularly critical; whereas the terrible and towering Turnbull was critical, I would say, primarily of my *Aristotelianism*. To which my offhand response, first to Jorgé Gracia, would be: "But why did you choose to pick on me, rather than on someone more nearly your own size, say, Aristotle!" And to the terrible and towering Turnbull, my first reaction is: "Is it not significant that you chose to pick on Aristotle at a time when the poor Stagirite had no one better than me, a poor, benighted Hoosier, to defend him!"

But with these opening and, I admit, quite gratuitous aspersions upon, shall I say, the respective characters of my two commentators, let me move at once to their arguments. First, Professor Gracia. For did you not notice that before he opened any fire directly upon me and *my* Aristotelianism, he chose first to mount a rather elaborate and, I must say, a rather cumbersome-seeming apparatus for classifying and judging practically any and all of the specific kinds of enterprises that this conference is concerned with—viz., enterprises that involve "doing philosophy historically"? Moreover, the upshot of Professor Gracia's intricate instructions on this score—arrived at after no little backing and filling—would seem to amount to little more than the truism that to do philosophy historically, of course one cannot very well avoid doing something in the *history* of philosophy; and equally and at the same time, insofar as it is something in the history *of philosophy* that one is doing, one cannot very well avoid doing some philosophy as well.

So much for the truism. Now when it comes to applying these standards to *my* Aristotelianism, it quickly becomes apparent that Professor Gracia would give me quite low marks both on my history and on my philosophy! So be it. Nor would I ever be one to deny that I do indeed deserve low marks on both counts. The only thing is that I wonder if I deserve them for quite the reasons that Jorgé Gracia would appear to want to allege.

Right here, let me remark parenthetically that when Professor Gracia was kind enough to send me a copy of the things he intended to say for this conference, I was at first taken aback a bit. For although there is scarcely anything that I have written throughout the entire course of my professional life, but what it has been directed to the one end of furthering the cause of Aristotelianism in philosophy—at least as I understand this to be—Professor Gracia rather casually announced that, in criticizing my Aristotelianism, he had chosen to look only at one book of mine. This was a little book, published over a dozen years ago, and entitled, *Aristotle: A Contemporary Appreciation.* As it happens, that is a book of which no doubt I should be rather more ashamed than proud. For it is the one book of mine that was written on commission from a publisher! Moreover, the terms of that commission were that the book needed to be "popular," and that at all costs! And popular I indeed tried to make it to be; and apparently, I succeeded, at least to the satisfaction of the publisher. The only trouble was that the populace with whom it was supposed to be popular never responded! So it could well be that Gracia and Turnbull, in trying to ready themselves for this conference, may have been among the first ever even to take a look at that supposed popular book. And isn't that ironic, that the one book of mine, which was designed to be popular and failed, now turns out to be my very undoing professionally? *O tempora, O mores!*

All of this, however, is by way only of an aside. For while I might wish that Jorgé Gracia particularly might have based his research on a somewhat more thorough, not to say discerning, investigation, I dare say that I should be content to go right along with the likes of Pontius Pilate and say, "What I have written I have written," and so take the consequences.

To return, though, to Gracia's criticisms. For I believe that in my little Aristotle book, the sort of thing that would appear there to have turned Jorgé Gracia off was my repeated profession of what I thought was only a befitting modesty. For in seeking to uphold the reputation of Aristotle even in today's philosophical world, I not infrequently tried to cover my own tracks, and doubtless old Aristotle's as well, by protesting that I was no historian of philosophy, and that with respect to Aristotle— i.e., the historical Aristotle—I had really never been particularly concerned with whether I had always, or even most of the time, succeeded in getting

Aristotle right historically. Instead, my concern was rather with whether, whatever it was that Aristotle himself may have said or meant, what I took him to be saying was in any way right philosophically.

Very well, then, what was there about such professions of mine of my relative indifference to mere historical truth, as compared with the all-importance of trying to win through to a genuine philosophical truth, what was there about this sort of thing that would appear so to have set Jorgé Gracia's teeth on edge? Remember that Jorgé is himself a singularly skilled and devoted historian of philosophy. Could it be, then, that he took me to be saying that in the enterprise of doing philosophy historically, all that mattered to me was the philosophical part, the relevant details of the history part being such as to amount to no more than the work of some mere drudge? Well, if such were the reaction of Jorgé to what I wrote in my book, I don't blame him for being irritated! And although such was, I can assure him, in no wise my intended meaning, I do apologize if such was the impression that I gave.

Surely, though, it is more than just injured professional pride that is at the root of Jorgé's dissatisfaction, alike with my history and with my philosophy, in my professed historical-philosophical enterprise of trying myself to be an Aristotelian. For I suspect that what Jorgé Gracia wants to say is that for anyone to be an Aristotelian in philosophy even today, one simply must get one's historical facts straight as to what Aristotle himself actually said, and as to what he thereby really thought and meant. In other words, to do philosophy in this sense just is to do history. And vice versa, I further suspect that Jorgé would also say that for anyone really to become a master of the thought of Aristotle, one cannot at the same time, and even *ipso facto,* avoid being a philosopher, precisely in that one must make judgments as to the truth of what Aristotle was saying. In other words, to do the history of philosophy just is to do philosophy, much as—as we saw just above—to do the history of philosophy in this sense just is to do philosophy.

Nor at this point can I very well refrain from remarking that when I hear Jorgé Gracia saying things such as these, immediately the ancient words of the book of Genesis begin to ring in my ears: "Though the voice be the voice of Jacob, the hands are the hands of Esau" (Gen. 27:22). For surely in Jorgé's implied pronouncement that the history of philosophy is nothing if not itself philosophy; and that philosophy (at least when one does philosophy historically) is nothing if not itself the history of philosophy—is Jorgé here not simply echoing the views of his own great master in both history and philosophy, Father Joseph Owens, as well as of that master's master, the redoubtable Etienne Gilson?

Very well, then, but is this characteristic kind of judgment of the historicist-philosopher and philosopher-historicist—if I might so call him—a true and a sound one? Well, up to a point, I think that I could go along with such a judgment: to do philosophy historically really well, one would certainly need to do both one's history and one's philosophy really well; not only that, but doing the one really well would presumably involve one in doing the other really well too. But right here, I suspect that Jorgé may tend to go rather beyond what the evidence of his own historicist-philosopher's position will legitimately allow him to do, and maybe also beyond what his own mentors in these matters—viz., Owens and Gilson—would allow him to do (though I must admit that on this last point I am not too sure).

For having reached the point just indicated as to how doing history and doing philosophy may well be mutually implicative of one another, I fear that Jorgé then wants to go one step further and affirm that in such instances the ultimate historical judgment is simply identifiable with the philosophical judgment, and the philosophical judgment with the historical one. This, however, I feel sure, is going too far and simply cannot be defended. For suppose, just to take a crude example, that as an expert in Aristotle (which, alas, I am not, and so my supposition is a condition contrary to fact), I am able to determine on the grounds of the historical evidence that Aristotle did indeed hold that change was simply a fact of nature, and that any such change must necessarily be a change of something, from something, to something else. (In other words, invoking the Aristotelian technical terminology, any and all change must involve the three principles of matter, form and privation.) Now let us imagine further that, having established historically that Aristotle did indeed subscribe to such a doctrine, I now go on to affirm that such a doctrine is not just a doctrine of Aristotle's, but that it is also a doctrine that is true—i.e., philosophically true, as well as historically true. Here I suggest that these two judgments—the historical one and the philosophical one—are quite patently different as judgments; and that the evidence that is to be used to support the one is quite different from the evidence that may be used to support the other. For just consider, however well authenticated the judgment may be that Aristotle himself did indeed subscribe to such a doctrine in regard to change and motion, this fact in itself does not in any way establish that the doctrine is true. And vice versa, the fact that this particular doctrine about the character of change in the natural world may have sufficient, and even incontrovertible, rational-empirical evidence in its support, such purely philosophical evidence, if I may so call it, would in no wise, just as such and in itself, suffice to demonstrate that such a truth about the physical world was in fact propounded and taught by Aristotle.

Accordingly, when Jorgé moves over to his specific criticisms of what I argued for in my little book on Aristotle, he singles out for particular and almost sole criticism my having made much of the fact in the book that for people in the present day it might be rather illuminating if one were simply to characterize Aristotle as being somehow a philosopher of common sense. "Not at all!" says Jorgé, for you just cannot get out of the texts of Aristotle that he was ever in any way, and in his own eyes, one who could be regarded as a philosopher of common sense. Nor do the texts lend themselves to such an interpretation even when it is admitted that the interpretation is solely for the purpose of perhaps clarifying things a bit for people in our own day. "No," says Jorgé in effect, "this is simply not allowable!"

To which I would reply, "Granted, but only up to a point." For certainly I must acknowledge that I am but a very indifferent historian of philosophy; and in terms of this qualification, I cannot do other than admit the justice of Jorgé's criticisms. On the other hand, admitting this much, why does that debar me from maintaining on philosophical grounds that something like a commonsense base or grounding for one's philosophy is entirely defensible philosophically? But it is just this that Jorgé will not allow me to do. Nor, if I understand him, would he refuse to allow me to do it, because he thinks he can show that I do it but ineptly and very badly—which maybe I do. No, so far as I can determine, Jorgé's only reason for his prohibition is the seemingly quite doctrinaire one that if one is to do philosophy historically, then one must recognize that the only way one can make philosophical judgments is on the basis solely of the relevant historical evidence. But this, it seems to me, is nothing if not wholly indefensible, since it seems quite to gloss over the simple truth that historical evidence can never and as such suffice to establish a philosophical judgment, any more than evidence of philosophical truth can ever and as such suffice to establish that some figure in the history of philosophy actually did in fact propound such a truth.

With this, though, it would seem that I have consumed time enough, and even too much time, trying to deal with Gracia. So it is not just high time, but past high time, that I turn now to the terrible, towering Turnbull. For he, be it recalled, is the one who would fault me for my *Aristotelianism,* just as it was Jorgé Gracia who would fault me for my Aristotelianism. Nor can I better begin perhaps than by remarking first off that while, like Gracia, Bob Turnbull bases his assessment of my enterprise of doing philosophy historically almost entirely on my little book on Aristotle, still, quite unlike Gracia, Turnbull seems to find that the way I chose in that book to try to rehabilitate Aristotle's philosophical reputation—at least in the popular mind—was a way that was not entirely ill chosen. For Turnbull seems to think it by no means improper that Aristotle be regarded as, indeed, a philosopher of "common sense," taking that term, not in any Reidian sense to be sure, but rather pretty much as I did. That is to say, he takes it not as a technical term of Aristotle himself at all, but rather in the sense of a term that seeks to illuminate, in a rough and ready sort of way for people today, what might loosely be called the general spirit and character of Aristotelian philosophy.

Nor is that all. For again, with reference to that little book of mine, it may be recalled that I have already said that I there took the line that such a "common sensism" might be not just historically illuminating with respect to Aristotle, but could even be regarded as a proper setting for a possibly sound program in philosophy as well. Now consider the sort of thing that Bob Turnbull made very clear in his remarks earlier this morning: "So described, Aristotle's philosophy has had perennial appeal. If—as I do—*one takes common sense to be philosophically inviolable,* it is hard not to fear that, in taking exception to Aristotle, one is challenging the fundamental condition of intelligibility itself" (emphasis added). Do you wonder that to such a comment my first reaction is but to say "Bravo!"?

Very well, given then this not inconsiderable measure of agreement in both our historical and our philosophical assessments of Aristotelianism, where may one say that Bob Turnbull and I differ? For differ we certainly do! And to this challenge, Turnbull would doubtless make prompt response by pointing to the inadequacies of what he would call "Aristotelian science." For Aristotelian science, he says, just cannot get you very far—or indeed cannot get you any place at all—when compared with modern scientific research and investigation. And on this matter I fear I am simply forced to agree.

Not only that, but Turnbull also points out that the key reason for the failure of Aristotelian science in the area of modern scientific investigation is traceable to the fact that, in Aristotelian philosophy and science, its chief resource lay, or lies, in what an Aristotelian would call the natures or essences of things. That is to say, the reason the things and objects of the natural world behave as they do—i.e., act and react as they do—is to be understood in terms of their being the kinds of things they are, i.e., in terms of their natures and essences. However, with respect to this general Aristotelian line of contention, Turnbull is quick to point out that, with the advent of the so-called scientific revolution in the seventeeth century, it soon came to be recognized that not only did explanation of the behavior of things in terms of their natures often not explain anything at all—amounting oftentimes to little more than lazy tautologies; but also it was found that events and occurrences in nature could be much better represented in terms of mathematics and mathematical relationships, rather than explained in terms of the supposed natures or essences that the things in question might be said to have. Here again, I find myself compelled to agree with Turnbull: not only is Aristotelian philosophy and/or science no match for modern science, but also Bob Turnbull, I believe, has put his finger right on what is doubtless the chief cause or reason for the failure of Aristotelian science as compared with modern science. The reason lies in the Aristotelian's reliance upon the natures and essences of things in explanation of those things' actions and behavior.

But now having conceded this much, let me immediately round on Bob Turnbull and say that I just don't see that the conclusion that he would draw from these two main contentions of his, as to the sources of weakness in Aristotelian science, necessarily follows. For his conclusion is that we must simply give over anything like Aristotelian science altogether—at least when it comes to anything like a knowledge of the world of nature—and that instead we must rely exclusively upon modern science, with its radical indifference to explanations in terms of natures and essences, and with its reliance instead upon a mathematized representation of the events and happenings of the natural world.

Right here, though, I would beg to differ: I just don't see that Aristotelian science has no other option than simply to bow out gracefully when it comes to any sort of knowledge of the real world of nature and the natural order, and that here the field must be left exclusively to modern natural science. No, for the sort of knowledge, it seems to me that is mediated in terms of the one view or conception of science is of a very different character and import from that mediated by the other: the one lays claim to being what I might call an ineradicably realistic knowledge of nature and the world as they really are, whereas the other seemingly purports to be no more than a knowledge that is justified merely pragmatically and is thus largely indifferent to whether it reflects the way reality really is in itself or not.

True, until comparatively recently, it was generally assumed that even such a thoroughly mathematized knowledge, as had come to be purveyed by modern physics, was indeed a knowledge of nature as it really is. Yet can such scientific knowledge any longer be so regarded? After all, Sir Karl Popper some years ago got us all accustomed to thinking that a reliance upon induction was not only not susceptible of any logical justification, but in addition, the actual procedures of practicing scientists—at least of the great scientific geniuses—when carefully scrutinized, turned out not to be inductive procedures really at all. Rather, such procedures could only be described as proceeding by the method of hypothesis— where the hypothesis, so far from being based on any evidence, be it either inductive or deductive, is simply dreamed up, or invented, from out of the scientist's imagination, much like the creation of a symphony, or an epic poem, or Michelangelo's ceiling for the Sistine Chapel, say.

And of course, subsequent to Popper, we are all familiar with how the hypotheses upon which our scientific world views or world pictures at any given period are based turn out to be hypotheses that are susceptible neither of verification nor of falsification in experience. Instead, their sole justification would seem to involve no more than an appeal to purely pragmatic considerations. And what does that do if not pretty well scuttle any idea that the scientific picture of the world needs to be taken as being necessarily a realistic picture at all? Far from it. Instead, a scientific account of things, so far from having to be taken as an account of the way the world is, may instead be regarded as justified merely to the extent that it enables us to get around better in the world, or to get better results in terms of technology and our human capacity to control and manipulate nature to our own purposes. Yes, as W. V. Quine once remarked: In terms of "epistemological footing," an account of the natural world in terms of the actions of the gods of Homer, or an account in terms of physical objects, as modern physicists understand these—neither such account of the world is one whit superior to the other, so far as the way things really are is concerned. No, Quine says, the only reason "the myth of physical objects" might be thought to be "epistemologically superior to [other such myths] is that it has proved more efficacious than other myths as a device for working a manageable structure into the flux of experience" (*From a Logical Point of View* [Cambridge, Mass.: Harvard University Press, 1953], 44).

In contrast, Aristotelian science and philosophy, I would suggest, are of a very different nature and character from anything like this. It does not amount to any mere "posit" or "myth" "for working a more manageable structure into experience." Instead, relying as it does upon the natures or essences of things in nature, it affords a real knowledge of why and of what the real causes are for the things in nature behaving and acting as they do. True, such a natural-philosophical knowledge of the real causes of the changes that go on in nature may not be either too extensive or too reliable a knowledge. But such as it is, it certainly is a knowledge of things as they are, and no mere device for "working a more manageable structure into the flux of experience." Yes, if we had time this morning, it would be interesting to see just why it is that a replacement of a knowledge of natural objects, in terms of their natures and essences, with mere mathematical patterns of the occurrence of events and happenings in nature, is bound to result in the displacement of any-thing like a realistic account of nature and the world with but a merely pragmatically justified account. But for this there just isn't still time.

I hope, though, that what there is still time for is a brief rejoinder to that other main feature of Bob Turnbull's way of characterizing Aristotelianism as a philosophy. For not only does he insist that when it comes to natural science, Aristotelian science with its realistic import must simply give way to the modern mathematized type of science with its no more than a purely pragmatic import; but in addition, Turnbull would propose to treat the so-called commonsense core and basic outlook of Aristotelian philosophy proper as itself but just another conceptual scheme, which, like the conceptual schemes and frameworks of science, does no more than impose upon the flux of experience a comparatively manageable pattern and order that enables us to make do in the midst of what otherwise would amount to no more than a wholly unintelligible flux, and even "confusion worse confounded."

True, in this connection I would surmise that Turnbull would avail himself of his master, Wilfrid Sellars's terminology here, according to which the world we inhabit in our everyday lives is the world of the "manifest image." In contrast, when we move from the commonsense world of everyday life to the world of our scientific and technological control over nature, then we must put behind us the "manifest image" and invoke "the scientific image." In the case of either world, however, what we have to do with are no more than myths or cultural posits, mere invented "images," as Sellars might call them.

To all of which I would simply make reply, "But this is all at once gratuitous and unnecessary. For there just is no sufficient warrant either historically or philosophically for supposing that what I would call the commonsense world of Aristotelian physics or metaphysics is no more than a mere image or cultural posit." No, I suggest that Turnbull, like Sellars before him, has been led to such a view simply because, like other contemporary epistemologists, they cannot see how our human experience, or the plain evidence of our senses and our intellectual faculties, can ever lead us to an awareness of anything like the actual physical world of real physical objects and their attributes, of real changes occurring before our very eyes, of real causes producing such changes, etc. In consequence, Turnbull maintains that all such things as substances and their accidents—form and matter, act and potency, the principles and causes of change—are just so many myths or cultural posits, to use Quine's terms. Or to use Turnbull's own term, they are but so many "philosophical entities," which, in their role as cultural posits, have come to be embedded in the uses of ordinary language, and which therefore, as Turnbull says, serve but to "exhibit the *zusammenhang* of common sense." That is to say, they are mere "represent*ings*," and not in any sense "represent*eds*."

And why does Turnbull say this? I suggest that he says it because, as the somewhat uncritical heir of our whole modern epistemological tradition, running from Descartes, through Hume, and then to Kant, and so on right down to the present day, he has tended at once to misconstrue, and then to disregard altogether, the Aristotelian account of what I might call the epistemology of our human experience. For by that account, human experience is in no way limited to acquainting us only with a mere "flux of experience," as Quine calls it. Quite the contrary, involving as it does a coöperation of our sensory and our intellectual faculties, our experience is an experience of no less than the real world of nature—of things and their attributes, of changes and their causes, yes, of the very natures of things, in terms of which it becomes intelligible what things really are, and why things are as they are, and why they act and react as they do.

Now at this point I can already, out of the corner of my eye, catch the terrible, towering Turnbull glowering over at me and saying: "All right, Henry, if you think that your hero, Aristotle, provides an account of what you call the epistemology of our human experience, why don't you tell us what that account is?" To which my reply is, "Sorry, Bob, as you well know, no one here has either time or tolerance for anything like that now. Besides, I have already tried to provide you with just such an account, not once but many times, and in quite a few books and articles. The only trouble is that in preparing your own comments for today, you chose only to look at that one little would-be popular book of mine, and nothing else. And in that book, I must admit that I did fail to provide you with what you now tell me you are looking for, and what I myself think you do stand rather in need of! So sorry, Bob! *Mea culpa!*"

Anachronism in the
History of Philosophy
Daniel W. Graham

The subject I wish to discuss affects all of us as philosophers and historians of philosophy, although it is a subject which few of us ever think about. It is the subject of anachronism. We perhaps like to think of anachronism as a vice that others fall into but which we ourselves scrupulously avoid. Yet the act of coming to grips with our philosophical past requires a complex interaction of present and past concepts that ought to provoke some difficult questions. What is anachronism? Can we avoid it? Ought we avoid it? I shall attempt to illuminate these questions by turning to a classical text in the history of philosophy.

1

Aristotle is the father of history of philosophy; he is also generally recognized as the father of anachronism. Although we do not have all the sources he did, modern scholars feel sufficiently informed to contradict his assessments at key points and to charge him with misconstruing the past in the interests of his own philosophy. Because of the simplicity of his history and the clarity of the criticisms against Aristotle, his *Metaphysics* 1 will provide a good laboratory for examining anachronism at work.

Aristotle's study centers on the development of concepts of cause. Specifically, he wishes to see which of his four causes had been discovered before his time and if any additional causes had been found. He argues that the early philosophers first made use of the material cause, citing water, air, or fire as sources of existent things. This did not suffice; led on by the truth itself, philosophers glimpsed a second cause, the efficient cause. Anaxagoras came close to discovering the final cause

137

but failed to exploit his insight. The Pythagoreans and especially Plato discovered the formal cause, which indeed Empedocles had already used without recognizing.

Modern students of the Presocratics have been quick to criticize Aristotle's history:

> Book A of Aristotle's *Metaphysics* . . . which both directly and through Theophrastus had greater influence upon the subsequent ancient histories of philosophy than any other single work, interprets all previous philosophy as a groping for his own doctrine of fourfold causality and is in fact intended to be a dialectical argument in support of that doctrine, which itself implies a question that could not have been formulated before Plato. . . . [T]o suppose that such an inquiry is historical, that is, to suppose that any of these systems was elaborated with a view to that problem as formulated by Aristotle, is likely to lead to misinterpretation of those systems themselves and certainly involves the misrepresentation of the motives and intentions of their authors.[1]

In this influential statement, Harold Cherniss argues that Aristotle seriously misrepresents his predecessors insofar as he is attempting to give a historical account of their theories. There seem to be two possible problems: (1) the concepts Aristotle uses are his own sophisticated notions of cause, which form part of a complex theory of his own; (2) his account suggests that his predecessors were interested in the same project as he was, namely, to distinguish the different kinds of explanation. In other words, Aristotle's account misrepresents the aims and intentions of the philosophers he studies.

The criticism thus suggests two possible ways in which a history of philosophy might go wrong: it might read into earlier thinkers concepts that are not appropriate to them; and it might read into them intentions and objectives that they did not have. I would like to identify these two alleged kinds of mistake as two forms of anachronism, which I shall call conceptual anachronism and intentional anachronism, respectively. The two kinds of anachronism seem to be independent of one another inasmuch as one might commit either one independently of the other as well as both together.

Is Aristotle actually guilty of anachronism? The one kind of defense that supporters of Aristotle have given consists largely in showing that he is careful to distinguish his own views from those of his subjects.[2] This suggests a limited defense of Aristotle against the charge of conceptual anachronism. However, it remains true that he elucidates the philosophers in terms of his own conceptual distinctions. Can this practice itself be justified? Furthermore, what about the more serious charge of intentional anachronism?

I would like to propose a more ambitious defense of Aristotle than that of showing piecemeal how he is careful to observe nuances in his subjects' thought. Although the standard defense is promising as far as it goes, it does not go far enough. What I would like to argue is not that Aristotle is reliable on the details, but that his approach as a whole is quite unobjectionable. I wish to claim that he is not only good on the empirical data, as it were, but correct in his methodology. The defense that I shall make of Aristotle's methodology is to show that he does precisely what we do when we do history of philosophy. Thus if we are justified in our practices, so is Aristotle; and by understanding how he is justified, we shall understand how we are justified.

2

In order to understand the problem better we must make another distinction. The distinction I have in mind is an obvious one—almost too obvious. We must distinguish between *applying* a concept to a philosopher and *attributing* that same concept to him. It is one thing to employ a contemporary concept to elucidate a historical figure, and another thing to claim that that figure uses the concept himself. Of course there are problems even with applying a concept to a philosopher. But the important thing is that it involves a much weaker commitment on the interpreter's part than does attributing the concept. For in one limiting case, I may apply the concept to an earlier philosopher only to show that the concept does not fit within his position at all.

This limiting case suggests a further point. When a question arises as to whether we should attribute concept C to philosopher P, the only way to answer the question is to *apply* C to P's philosophy and see what happens. If C can be identified with some term T, and if T is used in a way that approximates C, we have positive evidence for the attribution. If there is no corresponding term T but the functions associated with C can be found in some theory, we still might have some evidence for attribution. But if we found no corresponding functions at all in the system, we would have evidence against the attribution. For instance, it can plausibly be argued that the Greek atomists are pluralists because they recognize the plurality of atoms; it can be argued that they are materialists even though they lack a word for matter, because they deny mental properties to the atoms; but one cannot plausibly attribute materialism to Empedocles because he ascribes mental properties to material objects, most notably to the "Sphere" in which the four elements are perfectly mixed.

But is it not anachronistic to apply modern concepts to ancient texts? In one sense of "anachronistic" it certainly is; but in this sense anachronism is not at all vicious. To think that it is wrong to use modern concepts on ancient texts is to confuse historical explanation with a kind of naive doxography. The very practice of explaining presupposes a situation that is puzzling or problematic and requires a language that is regarded as perspicuous and unproblematic into which the problematic statement of the problem situation must be rendered. And for historical explanation in particular the temporal and cultural setting of the text are part of the problem. To explain the historical text is at least in part to make it intelligible to our age and our society. If we do not allow ourselves the luxury of our own conceptual scheme, we make the past inaccessible to us. An extremist who would not admit modern concepts into his explanations will end up, for instance, having to explicate Aristotle in Aristotelian terms. (More likely than not his allegedly Aristotelian terms will be scholastic or neoscholastic.) Even this is not enough; for the English terms will be but imperfect renderings of the Greek. Thus to be faithful to the program one must explicate Aristotle in Greek. But not just any Greek will do; it will have to be fourth-century Attic Greek—written by a native speaker of an Ionic dialect, and so on.

It seems then that we are sometimes justified in applying later concepts to earlier texts. That provides us some working room to deal with conceptual anachronism. What about intentional anachronism? Is there a corresponding distinction to be made between applying and attributing intentions? I can obviously attribute intentions to earlier thinkers, but it appears to be anomalous to apply my intentions to them. Yet there is at least one sense in which I as an interpreter can manipulate the intentions of my subject: I can simply ignore them. But how can I be justified in ignoring them? Clearly I cannot if it is my aim to reproduce the thought of my subject along with its rationale. But suppose this is not my aim. Suppose that what I want to do is not to clarify the theory of my subject by itself, but to show how it fits into a larger historical pattern. I may find that there is no continuity in the intentions of philosophers P_1, P_2, P_3—as is often the case—yet that there is considerable continuity in conceptual and theoretical development in the thought of those philosophers. For instance, Locke wants foundations for knowledge without innate ideas; Berkeley wants to defend against atheism; Hume wants to save the world from the sophistry and illusion of school metaphysics; and Kant wants to save the world from skeptics like Hume. Yet there are multiple lines of continuous theoretical development: the commitment to foundationalism, the refinement of empiricism, the decline and fall of substance metaphysics, the articulation of the mind-body problem. We all can and do tell our students interesting stories about how Locke begat Berkeley, Berkeley begat Hume, and Hume begat Kant. We do so by systematically ignoring the considered aims of the philosophers in favor of our pet developmental scheme.

There is then a place for ignoring philosophers' intentions, at least in our curriculum. The place is within a set context, a genre of history of philosophy. In this genre what is at stake is not the coherence of the philosopher P_1's thought as a whole, but its coherence with the thought of P_2 and P_3 in a genetic sequence—in a tradition. We get the required coherence only by suppressing the intentions of the philosophers themselves. Is the recognition of a tradition bad history? Only, I would say, if we claim that P_1 was setting out to arrive at where P_3 is. That mistake would be somewhat analogous to attributing to P_1 a concept not found until P_3 developed it. But we can reconstruct the tradition without making any such mistake. The genre in which it is appropriate (and indeed essential) to ignore a philosopher's intentions I shall call schematic history of philosophy. In this genre the historical pattern is the thing, and to discern the pattern we must treat the sequence of philosophers schematically, as though the form of their thought were basic, their intentions at most ancillary.

We have distinguished some senses in which historical concepts and intentions can be treated legitimately and some senses in which they cannot. We might limit the term anachronism to the illegitimate uses. But there is a sense in which even the legitimate ones are anachronistic: they require a perspective on the past that unavoidably introduces present concepts and schemas. They structure the past in terms of the present. Consequently, I do not dispute, but rather welcome, the suggestion that even the legitimate cases we have examined are cases of anachronism. But if we accept this suggestion, we must realize that not all cases of anachronism are vicious. Some are highly productive.

3

Does Aristotle distinguish between his own concepts and intentions and those of his subjects? In other words, does he apply his own concepts and schemes without naively attributing them to his subjects? Clearly he does make the requisite distinctions. For instance, in dealing with the emerging efficient cause, Aristotle notes, "to seek this is to seek the second cause, as we should say."[3] Here he recognizes that a certain train of thought leads to positing a new form of explanation that fits into a certain order in his own scheme. But he carefully distances the original inquiry from his own schematization.

Aristotle's critical distance from his subjects can be seen clearly in a passage at the end of Metaphysics 1. Noting that Empedocles gives something like a formal cause in describing the ratio of the elements in bone, Aristotle observes, "But while he would necessarily have agreed if another had said this, he has not said it clearly."[4] There is an important point behind this remark. Empedocles did not articulate the notion of a formal cause, perhaps because he did not have the philosophical sophistication to do so. But we can imagine a counterfactual situation in which some later philosopher clarified to him the options and asked him if he would accept the cause in question. Such a thought experiment allows one to neutralize the conceptual differences between the present and the past and to ask whether a present concept is appropriate to a past philosopher despite the theoretical discrepancy. This exercise is an attempt to bridge the generation gap while acknowledging that the gap is there.

Aristotle is aware of the conceptual inadequacies of earlier philosophy—which "pronounced everything with a lisp as it were, because it was in its infancy."[5] Early philosophers pose their questions "darkly," "obscurely and unclearly," "only faintly glimpsing" their objects, like untrained soldiers in battle.[6] His remarks can be taken as exhibiting a chauvinistic self-satisfaction. But they can equally, and more charitably, be taken as evincing Aristotle's awareness of his predecessors' lack of theoretical development. The point is not that Aristotle's theory is so wonderful but that those of his predecessors are so underdeveloped. Aristotle presents the early philosophers as groping for answers that are not given until Aristotle expounds his four-cause theory. But it does not follow that he portrays them as *aiming* at his four-cause theory. Indeed, the groping metaphor suggests just the opposite: those who grope are in the dark about where they are and even what path they are on. Their path may be taking them to places that they do not intend to go. Aristotle nowhere suggests that the Presocratics are pursuing a theory of cause. More likely he thinks of them as groping along precisely because they have no metatheoretical awareness of what they are trying to explain. This suggests that he realizes their intentions are different from his own. He is not attributing his intentions to them but merely remarking their lack of any objective more subtle than merely explaining the physical phenomena.

Yet there are Aristotle's troublesome statements about philosophy being *forced* by the *truth itself* into envisaging new causes.[7] What sense can we make of them? There is an element of overzealousness here, to be sure, but the problem is not a problem of anachronism per se. It is rather a problem of imposing a teleological schema on history. Yet even this teleological leap is not so indefensible as it might at first seem. I have already pointed out that it is a well-established practice to ignore philosophers' intentions in schematic histories of philosophy. But I have oversimplified. The fact is that to compose a schematic history is in part to create a sequential structure in which the sequence is conditioned by the final stage. The history aims at making it evident how we got from there to here—how the events between the first and the last chapter constitute a progression that has a rationale. The story as told must make philosophical sense. Thus the schematic history comprises a teleological structure in which the episodes can be viewed as stages in the plot. Consequently it is not simply an accident that each episode can appear as a step along the way. The story itself imposes such an order on events. What the schematic historian does then is not simply to ignore the original intentions, but to construct them systematically in terms of the final act of the drama. The story has a logic of its own, a dialectic of development, and relative to that logic the relevant intentions can be postulated.

At this point it sounds as if the kind of relativism I am promoting is excessively subjective, as if by retelling the story I can invent any motives I want. This is not what I have in mind. Although the story we historians of philosophy tell depends on the point of view we choose to tell it from, given the concepts and schemes we employ, the questions about what our subjects said are empirical questions. We could have asked different questions using different presuppositions; but once we commit ourselves to a set of presuppositions, the questions about where our subjects stand are empirically decidable. Furthermore, I would claim that an empirical inquiry into the philosophical position of our subject will reveal certain harmonies and conflicts, certain entailments and contradictions, advantages and disadvantages. By assessing the strengths and weaknesses of the position the historian can characterize the dynamics of the position: this advantage is to be exploited, that conflict to be eliminated. For each such problem there are different options. But the ideal philosopher would modify his position so as to minimize difficulties and optimize advantages. And from our privileged vantage point we, as ideal observers, can describe what would be the proper moves in the game and the reasons—the philosophical motivations—for making them. Accordingly, the motivations we as historians identify are, though relative to our point of view, objectively determinable. Although they are part of our picture of the problem situation, they have reference to real challenges and conflicts. Thus, our historical recreation of a philosophical position generates potential motivations for philosophical change that constitute a set of intentions appropriate for certain dialectical moves.

The construction of ex post facto and hence anachronistic intentions for philosophical positions corresponds to the application of modern concepts to historical philosophies. By this means we impose our point of view on the past. But again the effort need not be viciously anachronistic. Given the motivations derived from our scheme we can check the philosopher's subjective intentions, stated goals, and apparent historical aims against what relative to our picture would be a rational, forward-looking motivation. Even if the philosopher fails to measure up, we can point out the effect that his work had on the tradition, though that effect was unanticipated by the philosopher. In the case that several different motivations are possible, we may also use the data to discover which motivation was operative on the philosopher. In any case, our construction of motivations appropriate to the scheme of development as we see it offers us reference points for the further investigation of a historical position. They need not lead us astray if we use them carefully; rather, they may provide a deepened appreciation of the philosopher's options and projects.

The view I have sketched of a nonvicious kind of conceptual and intentional anachronism, in which the anachronisms are actually beneficial as heuristic and evaluative tools, is perfectly compatible with Aristotle's practice in *Metaphysics* 1. He distinguishes his concepts from those of his predecessors; he recognizes that they were not necessarily in a position to articulate the concepts by which he explains and measures them; and he recognizes that they had no clear foresight of the end toward which reason was leading them. Yet one can still ask whether Aristotle's historical account is really adequate. For it is not only Aristotle's general procedures but also his actual account itself that critics have objected to. If Aristotle's methods are as unobjectionable as I have made out, his history should not be badly in error. Thus we cannot rehabilitate Aristotle as a historian of philosophy without to some degree vindicating his history.

4

The best way to vindicate or to denigrate Aristotle is to see how his history of early philosophy compares with our own. In a sense, critics of Aristotle score their points precisely by reappraising the early history of philosophy vis-à-vis Aristotle's account. Can Aristotle stand up to this kind of scrutiny? Before we answer the question, however, we must note again the genre to which Aristotle's history belongs. It is a schematic history of philosophy. This means that it is designed to provide a rational ordering of previous thought. Furthermore, Aristotle's history is not meant to deal with all developments or all aspects of the overall development of Greek philosophy. It is a history of the development of causal concepts. Accordingly it is not incumbent upon him to examine other lines of development in early philosophy except as they illuminate the history of the notion of cause.

There is one further preliminary task to formulating a history of philosophy to rival Aristotle's. That is to identify the point of reference from which the history is to be written. For as I have noted, schematic histories are written from some backward-looking perspective. We have decided that we must sketch a history of concepts of causation. But what is the touchstone of adequacy to be, the point of comparison? Whose set of concepts shall we use as the final set? Hume's? Kant's? Some contemporary set? Any set of these concepts is a legitimate possibility, but in order to evaluate Aristotle's success or failure, we can only compare the early concepts with Aristotle's own. Any other choice of a reference point would alter the emphases so radically that it would not provide an evaluation of Aristotle's history. What we must do in order to appraise Aristotle's efforts is to set the variables as close to his own as possible and then see if his account provides a fair and accurate assessment of his predecessor's contributions.

Accordingly, we must determine what Aristotle's theory of cause is. Although there are alternative interpretations, the most attractive and popular account of Aristotle's theory is one that identifies his causes as "becauses"—logically different types of explanation. This does not mean that the causes are merely linguistic items, which they are not, but that real causal factors are to be classified by the logical form of the explanation in which they are described. Thus the material cause is a causal factor that answers the question "Why?" by stating that from which a thing came. Why does the knife cut? Because it is made of steel. The formal cause, by contrast, answers a why question by telling what a thing is or what form it has. Why does the knife cut? Because it is sharp. Thus different causes presuppose different types of explanation, and one who holds the four-cause theory will have a pluralistic view of explanation.

Given the Aristotelian background theory, we as modern interpreters can construct an independent account of the history of Greek concepts of cause. We can ask to what extent Aristotle's predecessors anticipated or prepared the way for his theory. The procedure is perfectly defensible, and indeed scholars often ask what contributions Plato or some other predecessors made to Aristotle's understanding of cause. Note that this procedure still gives rise to a schematic history of philosophy since it requires us to overlook or play down other elements in the history of philosophy *including the intentions of the philosophers themselves.* We should purposely put aside questions whether the philosophers in question had any metatheoretical views about cause or whether they could have answered a question about what their theory of cause was. Those issues would not matter. All that would matter is whether their own explanations of events could intelligently and accurately be described as exhibiting some explanatory pattern. In other words, all we need to know is whether their explanations embody some principle of explanation, not whether the philosophers were in a position to articulate that principle.

In what follows I shall give the barest outlines of a reading of the ancient notions of cause, a mere recipe. As an exercise the reader should construct his or her own version. The point here is to see how a modern account might conform to the requirements of a schematic history and how it might compare to Aristotle's.

In order to explicate the development of causal notions, I would first divide Presocratic philosophy into three successive periods: the era of the Milesians, an era of criticism, and an era of pluralistic thought. The Milesians predominantly explain natural phenomena by reference to their components. In the clearest and most developed version of the approach, that of Anaximenes, the cosmos is described as composed of air, which through processes of dilation and compression can assume the forms of all other physical substances. Thus the phenomena are explained by referring to the material from which they are composed, and this is material-cause explanation.

The Milesian scheme was severely criticized from two different perspectives. Heraclitus argued that the ultimate reality was process, rather than any set substance,[8] where this process suggests a kind of structural feature of the universe that prefigures the formal cause. Nevertheless, he fails to exploit his process as a new mode of explanation, tending to fall back into a discourse involving material-cause explanation. Parmenides, on the other hand, rejects the Milesian approach as incoherent because it requires the positing of not-being. If reality consists only of what-is, its distinguishing marks must be formal or structural properties and explanation must be by formal causes. But like Heraclitus, Parmenides lapses back into a mode of discourse that suggests that what-is is characterized by its material composition. One destabilizing effect of the Parmenidean critique is to make matter more substantial and to separate it from notions of agency, process, and self-change.

Under pressure from the Eleatic critique, the pluralists accepted the claim that what is cannot come to be or perish. Yet they preserve the possibility of change by allowing for a plurality of eternal and internally changeless substances that vary in their relationships to each other. Since the notion of matter has been dissociated from the notion of power, they posit external agents such as Love, Strife, and Mind to provide an impulse for change. Thus they introduce the first distinct efficient causes. And since matter does not change internally the external structural relationships of matter must change. Hence further hints of structural explanation appear, introducing the formal cause.

Finally Plato, driven by a desire to explain the order and constancy in this Cratylean world of perception, elevates structural features to the highest ontological estate in his cosmos and similarly advances formal-cause explanation to the highest rank. Plato decries the lack of final-cause explanation in Presocratic philosophy, but his own constructive alternative limits explanation to formal-cause accounts, so that he fails to discover final-cause explanations.[9] Thus none of Aristotle's predecessors discovers the four causes as a group, and none has more than a subset of them, which in all cases provides only a tacit theory of cause.

My schematic account of early Greek theories of cause differs from

Aristotle's in providing more of a motivation for the conceptual developments. It also cautiously avoids positing a recondite teleology in the evolutionary process. Nonetheless, it does identify a kind of progress, one determined by the dialectic of the debate itself: criticisms of material-cause explanations forced natural philosophers to articulate first the efficient cause and then the formal cause. Thus my account envisages a progressive conceptual development, even if the progression is not teleologically grounded. Moreover, the general results of my survey substantiate Aristotle's findings: the sequence of discovery is precisely the same in both accounts.

Now if you accept my account, or if you accept the possibility of such a schematic account in principle but prefer a different interpretation—say, in terms of the one and the many or the contrast of reason and experience—in any case, you are committed to accepting conceptual and intentional anachronism. For the categories in terms of which the account is developed are anachronistically applied to the early philosophers. They did not recognize the four causes, or indeed in most cases an abstract notion of cause at all; nor did they recognize the salient categories in terms of which we might retell their story to satisfy ourselves. Furthermore, in order to tell the story—whether in Aristotle's way or in my way or in yours—we must systematically ignore the temporary objectives of the philosophers in question. These may be whimsical, arbitrary, totally unknown to us; they may be harmonious or conflicting with each other or with our objectives; but the point is that we don't care about the immediate motives per se. We reconstruct the dialectical situation—e.g., trying to defend natural philosophy against the Eleatic challenge—and then we *infer* the strategic reasons for positing a new cause. The reasons that emerge are thus certifiably philosophical reasons, part of a philosophical story of progress.

The mistakes Aristotle made were in overlooking some of the internal dialectic of the Presocratic movement and in inventing a self-serving teleology to govern the development he found. His mistakes do not include viciously anachronistic readings of his predecessors. The kinds of anachronism Aristotle employed are the same kinds of anachronism we all allow ourselves. Thus if we are justified in our strategic use of anachronism, so is Aristotle; if he is not justified, neither are we. But I would maintain that we are justified: it is precisely the constructive use of anachronism that makes it possible for us to have a link to our predecessors, to see ourselves as their heirs. If we are not their heirs, they have philosophized in vain; if no one can become our heirs, we shall have philosophized in vain.

I have examined one early and undeservedly infamous example of a schematic history of philosophy. The moral of the example and the general line of argument I have been pushing is somewhat surprising:

that history of philosophy is anachronistic and, indeed, I should say, essentially anachronistic. But on the other hand, this is only to say that we must understand the past in light of our own categories if it is to be meaningful for us. This does not mean that we must foist the present on the past; for a good historian of philosophy will notice where our categories fail to fit as well as where they succeed. Accordingly, I see nothing vicious in the anachronism that is essential to history of philosophy. History of philosophy, as presumably is the case with any species of history, grows out of a confrontation between the past and the present. The past cannot be historical without a contrasting present; the present cannot be historically conscious without appreciating the differences of the past. To do any kind of history, and in particular to do history of philosophy, is thus to engage in a certain kind of anachronism. And so, in order for Aristotle to become the father of the history of philosophy it was necessary for him to be the father of anachronism.[10]

NOTES

1. Harold Cherniss, "The Characteristics and Effects of Presocratic Philosophy," in Studies in Presocratic Philosophy, ed. D. J. Furley and R. E. Allen. (London: Routledge & Kegan Paul, 1970), 1: 2f. Cf. J. B. McDiarmid, "Theophrastus on the Presocratic Causes," ibid., pp. 180f.

2. W. K. C. Guthrie, "Aristotle as a Historian," in Furley and Allen, Presocratic Philosophy, pp. 239-54, provides a valuable discussion of Aristotle along these lines. See also Julia Annas, "Aristotle on Inefficient Causes," Philosophical Quarterly 32: 311-26, defending an Aristotelian criticism of Plato.

3. 984a25-27, Oxford tr.

4. 993a22-24, Oxford tr.

5. 993a15-17, my tr.

6. 987a10, 985a13, 988a23, 985a15f.

7. 984a18f, b8-11.

8. Of course he said that fire was the ultimate reality; that identification can be taken either as asserting against the Milesians a new generating substance or as providing a symbol of a reality that is antisubstantial. There is a tension in Heraclitus's thought at this point, but I choose to read him in the latter, more radical, and forward-looking manner. Cf. A. P. D. Mourelatos, "Heraclitus, Parmenides, and the Naive Metaphysics of Things," in Exegesis and Argument, eds. E. N. Lee et al. (Assen, Netherlands: Van Gorcum, 1973).

9. Plato criticizes the Presocratics at Phaedo 97C-99C and develops his own alternative account at 100Bff.

10. I have received valuable suggestions for this paper from my colleagues at Brigham Young University, particularly from Brian Poll. I am grateful to Josiah Gould for acute criticisms in his comments presented at the SUNY conference, and to conference participants for stimulating suggestions.

A Response to Graham's
"Anachronism in the
History of Philosophy"

Josiah B. Gould

To ascribe a metaphysics of substance to Thales, to refer to Vitruvius's distaste for Gothic architecture, to applaud Cicero for his crisp discussion of the distinction between sense and reference, and to commend Abelard for his succinct formulation of the axiom of separation all count, I think, as clear and egregious cases of anachronism, which one should take pains to avoid. Professor Graham, I assume, would concur. Yet he argues that anachronism in some of its forms is highly productive and, as regards a certain kind of history of philosophy, inescapable. He embeds this argument in a larger project—that of giving a stronger defense than has been given heretofore of Aristotle as a historian of philosophy.

I want, first of all, to say what I think is wrong about Graham's position and, secondly, to suggest that Graham has nonetheless opened up, for me at least, an intriguing line of thought about ways in which philosophers might fruitfully reflect on the writings of their predecessors.

Graham distinguishes, on the one hand, concepts from intentions, and, on the other, application from ascription of them, which obviously yields four possibilities. As regards the application of modern concepts in the study and exposition of an earlier philosopher's thought, Graham rightly supposes that there is no alternative unless one chooses to work on editions of the text. But unlike Professor Graham, I think that to apply, say, the use/mention distinction in the exposition of an Aristotelian text is not only sometimes appropriate and useful, but it is also not a case of anachronism. As regards the attribution of modern concepts, Graham holds that one can safely ascribe a concept to an earlier philosopher if "the functions associated" (p. 139, this volume) with the concept can be found in his theory. If Aristotle in an appropriate context uses a string of Greek marks to express the negation of both necessity

149

and impossibility, then he is wielding the concept of contingency. Such an ascription is not only true and useful, but again it is not a case of anachronism. There is a question here about how much or how explicitly one has to wield in order to merit an ascription but that, I think, is independent of questions about anachronism.

Turning to intentions, Graham points to the anomaly in applying one's own intentions to earlier philosophers, and this seems right. Graham has no objection to ascribing to their authors what we take to be their intentions, and I gather that he means we can make such attributions nonanachronistically. But I find puzzling Graham's sentence, "Yet there is at least one sense in which I as an interpreter can manipulate the intentions of my subject" (p. 140). For I am not sure what the adversative "yet" is opposing. If I may presume to ascribe an intention to Professor Graham, I suppose that he is intending to say that although one cannot apply one's own intentions to earlier thinkers, one can nonetheless manipulate those intentions. Graham claims that one can manipulate the intentions of one's philosophical predecessors simply by ignoring them. Manipulation, in this sense, it seems to me, might affect or infect our understanding of an earlier philosopher's thought, but to leave out of account a thinker's intentions is not, in any obvious way, to produce an anachronism. Graham has, then, pointed to several activities, each of which he claims is harmless and sometimes useful in doing the history of philosophy, but none of these, contrary to his claims, constitutes producing anachronism—i.e., "representing something as existing or happening at other than its proper or historical time," a use of the expression Webster records.

Graham justifies neglecting the intentions of earlier philosophers, or at least assigning them an ancillary position, by appealing to the genre of history one is doing. This he calls "schematic history of philosophy" (p. 141). Working in this genre one is not aiming to represent the thought of one's subject and its attendant rationale. One is not trying to discover and to represent the coherence and integrity of a philosopher's thought, but rather to depict the coherence of that thought with the thoughts of a second and third philosopher in what Graham calls "a genetic sequence" (p. 141). Finally, in doing schematic history one is not aiming to explain the philosophical theory of a given thinker but instead is trying to make evident how that theory is accommodated in a larger historical pattern.

What becomes apparent in Graham's characterization of schematic history of philosophy is that it is not a substitute for a nonschematic, more garden-variety type of history in which one is simply trying to represent accurately the claims, arguments, motivations, and objectives of the philosopher one is writing about. So far from supplanting this "get-it-right" variety of doing the history of philosophy, schematic history presupposes that the groundwork has been done. And, indeed, it may have been done by the same historian, who then makes a return sweep through his materials to show how they exhibit the march of the Absolute through history, the rise and fall of foundationalism, or the stepwise emergence of a quadruple explanatory grid.

Graham's defense of Aristotle as a historian of philosophy is, I think, flawed by his assumption that in doing schematic history of philosophy one is at the same time somehow doing the "get-it-right" variety. Certainly if in doing the first Aristotle was also doing the second, then his success at doing the first would have to count as his success at doing the second.

In his 1935 study of Aristotle's criticism of presocratic philosophy (New York: Octagon Books, 1983) Harold Cherniss concludes by outlining seven sources of error in Aristotle's discussions of the presocratics. Cherniss is eager to emphasize these errors because of the influence they have had upon subsequent interpretations of presocratic thought. Graham tries to justify Aristotle's account of presocratic philosophy in *Metaphysics* 1 by referring to the account that we—presumably we moderns—give of that history. If, however, as Cherniss fears, Aristotle's history has biased and rendered erroneous the accounts we have given, then it is not surprising that these accounts agree with Aristotle's. Suppose Thucydides erroneously reports that the Greeks conquered Syracuse in the Peloponnesian War. We would not take his account to be confirmed by a modern historian who, influenced by Thucydides, reports Syracuse's capitulation to the Greeks. So, likewise, we should not take accounts of modern historians of philosophy influenced (even indirectly) by Aristotle to confirm Aristotle's reports.

Cherniss and Graham agree about Aristotle's immunity from criticism for lack of a historical sense in *Metaphysics* 1. As though anticipating Graham, Cherniss wrote in 1935,

> The historical account in Metaphysics A is no different from the other passages in which earlier doctrines have been reinterpreted for a special purpose; it has been well described as "a hymn of triumph in honor of the four types of causality." Here, too, when the purpose is understood, it is impossible to criticize Aristotle for misrepresentations or lack of "the historical sense." (357)

But Cherniss goes on to point out what he has monumentally demonstrated in the first three hundred pages of his study: that "it is likewise impossible to use his [Aristotle's] groupings and representations of the affinity and relationship of various doctrines as historical evidence" (357). And here of course Cherniss's view diverges from Graham's.

Cherniss was not then, to use Graham's terms, criticizing Aristotle's schematic history of philosophy. He was rather attacking Aristotle as a historian of philosophy. As a historian doing the "get-it-right" species of history of philosophy Aristotle, Cherniss argues at length, got it wrong. And nothing in Graham's paper undermines that charge.

Graham's remarks have, however, provoked in my mind a speculation about different ways in which one might approach the writings of one's philosophical predecessors. One way is that riveted upon by Cherniss that I have, rather tendentiously, called "get-it-right" history of philosophy. Another involves either charting or laying out possible lines of philosophical thought. Here one is not attempting to represent, at any rate entirely, what a philosopher's doctrines, arguments, aims, and motivations were in fact. One is aiming rather to depict or to construct how his thoughts might have gone. Here the project can go in one of two separable, though probably not separate, ways. In the first one tries to lay out a system of propositions and concepts, some of these apparent to the philosopher under study. This map, accessible from all vantage points, would be published presumably with the claim that the philosopher in question was acquainted with it or with some stretch of it. The opening sentence in this kind of work is usually something like, "I don't know anything about the details of Kant's philosophy, but . . . " In the second way one tries to set forth a possible set of motivations and aims, which while it may not fit the actual motivations and aims of the philosopher under study, nonetheless helps to highlight a possible sequence of thought. This strand, unlike the other, would not be timelessly present in all states of affairs but would appear with the claim to represent one facet of some one possible state of affairs. I am not sure how Graham's schematic history of philosophy fits into my classification. I suspect that both it and much of *Metaphysics* 1 fall into that way of doing philosophy in which one is more interested in representing some possible alignment of ideas or some possible sequence of motivations or some possible set of aims rather than in charting some segment of the past of the actual world. Schematic history, as represented by Professor Graham and as exhibited in *Metaphysics* 1, is mainly concerned with nonactual motivations and aims, but it is nonetheless illuminating, certainly nonparochial, and eminently worthwhile doing.

Part Three
Descartes

The Limits of Cartesian Dualism

Georges Dicker

INTRODUCTION

In his book *Descartes Against the Skeptics*, E. M. Curley speaks of "a persistent feeling that there may be something in Descartes's argument for dualism."[1] My purpose in this paper is to exhibit what is plausible in Descartes's argument, and to show that even if it is sound, it lacks the weighty implications that might reasonably lead one to reject it. Further, I shall argue that Descartes himself understood the limitations of his argument; he was not fooled by its impressive look.

A RECONSTRUCTION OF DESCARTES'S ARGUMENT

Descartes presents his proof of the Real Distinction between mind and body in the following paragraph of Meditation 6, which I have divided into three segments:

[A] And first of all, because I know that all things which I apprehend clearly and distinctly can be created by God as I apprehend them, it suffices that I am able to apprehend one thing apart from another clearly and distinctly in order to be certain that the one is different from the other, since they may be made to exist in separation at least by the omnipotence of God; and it does not signify by what power this separation is made in order to compel me to judge them to be different:

[B] and, therefore, just because I know certainly that I exist, and that meanwhile I do not remark that any other thing necessarily pertains to my nature or essence, excepting that I am a thinking thing, I rightly conclude that my essence consists solely in the fact that I am a thinking thing [or a substance whose whole essence or nature is to think].

[C] And although possibly (or rather certainly, as I shall say in a moment) I possess a body with which I am very intimately conjoined, yet because, on the one side, I have a clear and distinct idea of myself inasmuch as I am only a thinking and unextended thing, and as, on the other, I possess a distinct idea of body, inasmuch as it is only an extended and unthinking thing, it is certain that this I [that is to say, my soul by which I am what I am], is entirely and absolutely distinct from my body, and can exist without it. (HR 1, 190)[2]

In segment [B], Descartes returns to a line of argument that he introduced in Meditation 2: that since he did not know with certainty that any property other than thought belonged to him, therefore he was essentially a thinking thing.[3] This argument does not significantly differ from the notorious "argument from doubt" that Descartes seems to use in his *Discourse on the Method* and *Search After Truth:* I cannot doubt that I exist; I can doubt that any body exists; *ergo* I am not a body (Cf. HR 1, 101, 319). But in the more careful second meditation, Descartes recognized that this is an *invalid* argument. For directly after stating it, he went on to admit that, for all he knew, he might be a body (HR 1, 152). As the phrase "and, therefore" ("*ac proinde,*" L. V.; "*et partant,*" F. V.) at the beginning of [B] indicates, however, Descartes now thinks that the material in segment [A] somehow *legitimizes* the reasoning in [B]. The material in [C], as I shall argue in a moment, also contributes to the legitimization of [B]. In any case, the paragraph as a whole is at least partly intended to show that an argument that was deemed unsatisfactory at an earlier stage, when supplemented by further principles, can be safely accepted. This reading is confirmed by what Descartes says in the "Preface to the Reader." He notes that an objection to the *Discourse* had been that

it does not follow from the fact that the human mind reflecting on itself does not perceive itself to be other than a thing that thinks, that its nature or its essence consists only in its being a thing that thinks, in the sense that this word *only* excludes all other things which might also be supposed to appertain to the nature of the soul. (HR 1, 137)

After complaining that this objection is based on a misinterpretation of his intentions in the *Discourse* (a complaint that need not detain us here), he adds, significantly: "But I shall show hereafter how from the fact that I know no other thing which pertains to my essence, it follows that there is no other thing which really does belong to it" (HR 1, 138).

This certainly raises a question of interpretation, for if an argument is invalid, then nothing can transform *that very argument* into a valid one. At best, the addition of new premises can only yield a new argument that includes the premises of the old one and that is valid. But segments [A] and [C] do not seem to stand even in that relation to the argument in [B]. So what does Descartes mean by suggesting that the reasoning in [B] has now been vindicated? To answer this question, we must first examine what Descartes says in segments [A] and [C].

The first part of the first sentence in [A] can be formulated as follows:

(1) If I can clearly and distinctly conceive X existing in a certain way, then X can really exist in that way, at least by God's power.

This opening premise follows directly from Descartes's criterion of truth. In the next part of the sentence, Descartes derives an important principle from (1): that if he can clearly and distinctly conceive X existing apart from Y, then X is really different from Y. The inference from (1) to this principle, however, requires two intermediate steps. The first one is elliptically stated in the clause "since they can may be made to exist in separation at least by the omnipotence of God." Untelescoped, this says that

(2) If I can clearly and distinctly conceive X existing apart from Y, then X really can exist without Y, at least by God's power.

This follows directly from (1) and leads to Descartes's principle. To obtain that principle, however, the second intermediate step is required. This is a premise that Descartes leaves wholly unstated:

(3) If X really can exist without Y, at least by God's power, then X and Y are really two different things.

The idea behind (3) is that if X can really exist without or apart from Y, then *even if it takes so much as God's power for this to happen,* X and Y must be different things. For not even God could make a thing exist without or apart *from itself,* since that is not even logically possible. (Of course, here I deliberately ignore the view—often ascribed to Descartes—that an omnipotent God could do the logically impossible. Descartes never mentions this doctrine in the *Meditations,* and it would certainly ruin the present argument.) From (2) and (3), we can now derive Descartes's principle that

(4) If I can clearly and distinctly conceive X existing apart from Y, then X and Y are really two different things.

Now, the references to clearness and distinctness in (1)–(4) are absent from segment [B] of our passage. But they are picked up again in segment

[C], where Descartes advances another premise and then draws two conclusions. The premise, worded so as to make it connect clearly with (4), is that

(5) I can clearly and distinctly conceive myself, as a thinking and unextended thing, existing apart from (my) body, as an extended and unthinking thing.

This premise rests on Descartes's long and careful discussion of the self in Meditation 2. For surely, if anything was established by that discussion, it was that Descartes could form a clear and distinct conception of himself as simply a "thing which thinks." But with the help of (5), the two conclusions that Descartes draws at the end of segment [C] can be derived. For it follows from (4) and (5) that

(6) I am really a different thing from my body.

And, it follows from (2) and (5) that

(7) I can really exist without my body, at least by God's power.

Before discussing the argument, let me address the question of interpretation raised above: How is this argument, which is extracted only from segments [A] and [C], supposed to legitimize the reasoning in segment [B]? Compare steps (5)-(7) with [B]. In (5)-(7), Descartes goes from the premise that he can clearly and distinctly conceive himself existing as only a thinking thing, to the conclusion that he is distinct from his body and could exist without it. This certainly *resembles* the argument in [B], where he goes from the premise that he knows with certainty only that he is a thinking thing, to the conclusion that he is essentially only a thinking thing. But we can go further: we can say that the argument in [B] is merely a preliminary, abbreviated version of the argument extracted from [A] and [C]. In the first place, the two arguments' *premises* are intimately related. For surely, Descartes's claim in Meditation 2, that he knew for certain only that thought belonged to him, already had much more content than the words "I know only that I am a thinking thing" reflect. What more? Well, he had a clear conception of his thinking; he was forming a clear conception of body; he could appreciate the difference between those two conceptions, and he could conceive, through the doubt, the possibility that the object of the former conception might exist though the object of the latter did not. Now this is virtually what Descartes asserts in (5). In the second place, the two arguments' *conclusions* are intimately related. For, as Descartes uses these notions, to say that X can exist without Y entails that Y is not part of X's essence: "in my opinion nothing without which a thing can still exist is comprised in its essence" (HR 2, 97). Thus, when Descartes affirms in (7) that he can exist without his body, this entails that extension is not part of his essence, which leaves only thinking as his essence. This is just the conclusion of [B]!

Of course, the argument in [A] and [C] differs from the one in [B] by presenting the general principle, namely, (4), that is supposed to legitimize the inference from a clearly and distinctly conceived distinction between mind and body, to a Real Distinction between them. And it also justifies that principle, by appealing ultimately to Descartes's criterion of truth. But none of this should stop us from seeing that the argument in [B] is a rough, enthymematic statement of what Descartes fully and adequately presents in (1)-(7). This reading is confirmed by the "and, therefore" at the start of [B], especially when this phrase is read in light of Descartes's previously cited remarks in the "Preface to the Reader." For the phrase can very naturally be interpreted as indicating that segments [A] and [C] constitute a kind of second-order commentary on [B], telling us that the enthymematic, intuitive sketch in [B] is now legitimate because it serves as a stand-in for the more complex argument in [A] and [C]. Finally, when Descartes responded to a request that he present his main arguments "in geometrical fashion," he gave, as his demonstration of the Real Distinction, essentially the argument in [A] and [C], omitting the one in [B] altogether (HR 2, 59). For these reasons, I conclude that the former is Descartes's finished, "official" argument for dualism.

WHAT FOLLOWS FROM THE ARGUMENT

In order to assess the argument, I shall first present a pruned or stream-lined version of the argument, which I believe captures the most important intuitions on which Descartes's own argument turns. Second, I shall argue that even if this streamlined argument is sound, it does not have the weighty implications associated with Cartesian dualism—implications that some dualists prize and that materialists shun. Third, I shall argue that these implications do not follow from Descartes's own argument either. Finally, I shall show that Descartes was aware of this.

Descartes's argument turns on three basic intuitions: the conceivability of the separate existence of the mental and the physical, the principle that what is conceivable is logically possible, and the principle that the logical possibility of separate existence implies distinctness or nonidentity. Thus, the streamlined version of his argument starts from the premise that

(8) For any x and any y, if x is a conscious state (i.e., a thought, desire, mental image, sensory experience, etc.) and y is a physical state or process (e.g., a brain event), then it is conceivable that x exists and y does not exist.[4]

This premise resembles, and rests on the same considerations as, Descartes's richer premise that he can clearly and distinctly conceive himself, as a thinking and unextended thing, existing apart from his body, as an extended and unthinking thing. The second premise is

(9) For any proposition p, if it is conceivable that p, then it is logically possible that p.

This premise, except for omitting any reference to God's power, is close to Descartes's principle that whatever he can clearly and distinctly conceive as existing in a certain way can really exist in that way, at least by God's power. The third premise is

(10) For any x and any y, if it is logically possible that x exists and y does not, then x is not identical with y.

This is close to Descartes's premise that if X can really exist without Y, then even if it takes so much as God's power for this to happen, X and Y are really two different things. The basic point, as before, is that nothing could possibly exist without or apart from itself. The conclusion that follows from (8)–(10) is

(11) For any x and any y, if x is a conscious state and y is a physical state or process, then x is not identical with y.

Although this conclusion may seem weaker than Descartes's own conclusion that he, as a thinking thing, is not identical with his body, in a few moments we shall see that the difference does not matter very much. For the moment, however, I need only emphasize that (11) does, of course, assert a *dualism* of the mental and the physical. For it implies—assuming that any conscious states and physical states exist—what all materialists deny; namely, that in addition to material things and processes, there are purely mental existents.

This streamlined argument can doubtless be attacked. For example, some philosophers think there are counterexamples to (9), and perhaps some would, even in the wake of Kripke's work, attack (10) by appealing to the notion of "contingent identity."

Although I find these objections unpersuasive, I shall not insist that the argument can withstand them. For although I think the argument is quite powerful, my thesis is not that it is sound. My thesis is, rather, that even if it is sound, the implications are not very significant. For even if the logical possibility that conscious states might exist apart from physical states shows that conscious states are not identical with physical states, it does not show that it is causally possible for conscious states to exist apart from physical states. Thus, for all that the argument can show, consciousness may exist only as an effect of certain sorts of brain processes, i.e., may never exist apart from the physical processes that cause it. This may be so even if (as interactionists maintain and epiphenomenalists deny) mental events causally affect brain processes or events. For it may be that those mental events are in turn caused by prior brain events and never occur unless caused by these brain events. Thus James Cornman, drawing on C. D. Broad's suggestions about mind-body interaction, points out that the causal relationships between mental and brain events might be as shown in figure 1:

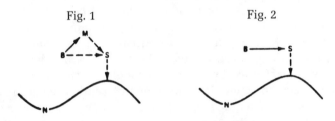

Fig. 1   Fig. 2

B = brain event
M = mental event
N = nerve impulse
S = change of electrical resistance in synapses
x ———►y = x causes y
x -----►y = x causally affects y
⌒⌒ = path of nerve impulse[5]

If this is the way mental and brain events are interrelated, then there are two notable consequences. First, as Cornman emphasizes, a scientist could give an adequate neurological explanation of human thought and behavior without ever mentioning the mental events. For although M causally affects S, M is in turn caused by B. So if a neurophysiologist knew that B was occurring, he could predict and explain S and N without ever mentioning M, and indeed even if he were a materialist who denied M's existence and believed that matters stand as in figure 2.[6] Second, since on this view M would not occur unless B (or some other brain event) produced it, consciousness is totally dependent on a functioning brain for its existence.

Once these points are recognized, some of the objections that recent materialists have raised against dualism seem strangely empty and rhetorical. For example, J. J. C. Smart's chief objection to dualism is that it postulates "an irreducibly psychical something," a "ghost stuff . . . or . . . ripples in an underlying ghost stuff," thereby multiplying entities unnecessarily.[7] But if dualism concedes that mental existents may be completely causally dependent on physical ones, then it is hard to see much force in this complaint. To be sure, if the argument for dualism is sound, then conscious states cannot be reduced to brain states: in that sense they are irreducibly mental. But phrases like "irreducibly psychical something" and the like also suggest a kind of independence of the mental that is wholly belied by such a dualism. And while the notion of theoretical simplicity is doubtless a complex one, its applicability here is questionable. For it seems reasonable to hold that its sphere of application is limited to entities that are held to play some essential *explanatory* role, though there is no independent evidence of their existence. The other side of the coin, of course, is that if the dualist concedes that mental existents may be completely causally dependent on physical ones, then it is hard to see the metaphysical significance of dualism. For such a dualist agrees with materialists who think that a complete neurophysiology could causally explain human thought and behavior, and that there is good reason to believe that consciousness ends when brain activity ceases. He insists only on the logical possibility of consciousness existing apart from brain activity and its consequent nonidentity with brain activity. This is to abandon some of the ideas commonly associated with dualism, e.g., that the mental component of human beings stands in the way of any adequate scientific explanation of human thought and behavior and offers some positive evidence for immortality. Thus, the objections of materialists are blunted only at the cost of foregoing some of the cherished ideas commonly associated with dualism. The disagreement between dualists and materialist seems to become at least partly a verbal one, over labels like "spiritual" and "material" and associated ideological beliefs that do not logically follow even if the case for dualism is sound.

Appearances to the contrary notwithstanding, much the same assessment holds for Descartes's own proof of the Real Distinction. To see this, it is crucial to understand, first of all, that Descartes is not claiming to have proved, in (7), that his mind *does*, at any time, exist without his body. Rather, he is claiming to have proved that his mind *could* exist without his body. As previously mentioned, Descartes holds that the mere logical possibility that mind can exist apart from body is enough to establish that they are different things.[8]

Even in light of a proper grasp of the Real Distinction, it may still seem that Descartes's argument has weightier implications than my pruned version of it. This is because Descartes's proof concerns the distinctness of a thinking *thing* from matter, and he understands this thing to be a *substance.* The term "substance," especially, is associated with a permanence, durability, even indestructibility, that can make it look as if Descartes's argument, if sound, would establish a dualism that would support traditional beliefs about the causal independence of the soul from the body and the soul's prospects for immortality. Of course, empiricist criticisms of the concept of substance have cast a shadow over Descartes's reliance on this concept. But the important point is that even if we do import the notion of mental substance, my basic assessment of Descartes's case for dualism still holds. For the two chief arguments for substance, namely, the argument turning on the need for a subject that persists through qualitative change, and the argument turning on the need for a subject of predication, do not justify assuming that a mental substance would be causally independent of the body, or indestructible, or anything of the sort. It follows that nothing in the concept of substance, at least insofar as its employment is supposed to be justified by these arguments, entails that a mental substance and its states must be causally independent of a material substance and its states. Now Descartes does not base his espousal of substance on any arguments other than these two; indeed, insofar as he *argues* for substance, he seems to rely only on the argument from qualitative change (notably in the wax passage of Meditation 2 and in the "Synopsis"). Moreover, the proof of the real distinction itself contributes nothing that might strengthen the concept of substance; it only uses the concept of substance that was already operative in Meditation 2. So far as Descartes's case for dualism goes, then, mind might be totally dependent on matter. For mental properties, without which there can be no mental substance, might be completely causally dependent on material ones.

In concluding, it should be noted that whatever might be said about the medieval inspiration or the naiveté of Descartes's metaphysics, he recognized the limitations of his case for dualism. It is true that in the *Principles of Philosophy* he defines substance as "a thing which so exists that it needs no other thing to exist" (HR 1, 239). This may seem flatly to contradict my claims about the possible causal dependence of one substance on another. However, in the next sentence Descartes admits that this definition applies only to God; created substances, by contrast, need God's constant concurrence in order to exist. Now in so qualifying his definition of substance, Descartes does not explicitly differentiate between saying that (a) created substances exist only if God sustains them, and (b) created substances exist if only God sustains them. The former is consistent with one created substance's causally depending on another; the latter is not. However, even if (as seems almost certain) Descartes holds (b) as well as (a), it does not follow that he has shown, or believes that he has shown, that the mind *is* a substance in the sense stipulated by (b). That he has not shown this is, I think, obvious from what has already been said about his rationale for using the concept of substance. More interestingly, there is excellent evidence that Descartes realized he had not shown it. In the "Synopsis" of the *Meditations,* he issues a *caveat* to those who might "expect from me in this place a statement of the reasons establishing the immortality of the soul." Then he makes this crucial comment:

> I have not . . . dealt further with this matter [i.e., immortality] in this treatise, both because what I have said is sufficient to show clearly enough that the extinction of the mind *does not follow from* the corruption of the body, and also to give men the *hope* of another life after death, and also because the premises from which the immortality of the soul may be deduced *depend on an elucidation of a complete system of Physics.* This would mean to establish in the first place that all substances generally—that is to say all things which cannot exist without being created by God—are in their nature incorruptible, and that they can never cease to exist unless God, in denying to them his concurrence, reduces them to nought. (HR 1, 140-141; my emphasis)

Descartes here represents the thesis that substances are naturally incorruptible, i.e., need only God's concurrence in order to exist, *as something to be established.* Thus, he is prepared to admit that for all his metaphysical arguments in the *Meditations* have shown, neither the soul nor body is incorruptible. Even more significantly, Descartes here says that proving the immortality of the soul depends upon the completion of his *physics.* Now although it may be hard to see how a physics could show that a purely mental substance is incorruptible, the vital point is that Descartes's statements imply that any knowledge we could have of the soul's immortality must rest on a completed natural science, which might reveal as yet unknown causal connections and dependencies between mind and body. Descartes realized that the logical possibility of the mind's existing without the body, and its consequent nonidentity with the body, which is all he had argued for in the *Meditations,* is consistent with the mind's causal dependence on the body. He knew, and he openly acknowledged, how far his case for dualism comes from establishing beliefs that he himself undoubtedly held and cherished.[9]

NOTES

1. E. M. Curley, *Descartes Against the Skeptics* (Cambridge, Mass.: Harvard University Press, 1978), p. 193. For differing recent assessments of Descartes's argument, see: Curley, *Descartes Against the Skeptics,* pp. 193-206; Anthony Kenny, *Descartes: A Study of His Philosophy* (New York: Random House, 1968), pp. 79-95; Bernard Williams, *Descartes: The Project of Pure Inquiry* (Middlesex,

England: Penguin Books, 1978), pp. 102–29; Margaret D. Wilson, *Descartes* (London: Henley; Boston: Routledge & Kegan Paul, 1978), pp. 185–200. Curley and Wilson give rather similar reconstructions of the argument, but Wilson qualifiedly endorses Descartes's argument while Curley rejects it. Kenny also rejects it, but for quite different reasons than Curley. Williams gives a very different reconstruction, whose faithfulness to Descartes's intentions is well questioned by Wilson in her review of Williams's book, *The Journal of Philosophy* 76, no. 8 (1979):431–35.

2. All quotations from Descartes are from *The Philosophical Works of Descartes*, trans. Haldane and Ross, 2 vols. (New York: Dover Publications, 1955 [1931]). I follow the usual conventions of using "HR1" to designate volume 1 and "HR2" to designate volume 2, and of including these references in parentheses in the text.

3. My interpretation here follows Ferdinand Alquié, *Oeuvres Philosophiques de Descartes*, (Paris: Garnier, 1967), 2:448 n. 1, and Curley, *Descartes Against the Skeptics*, p. 196.

4. For economy's sake, I suppress the reference to clarity and distinctness throughout the argument, but "conceivable" should, of course, always be understood to mean "clearly and distinctly conceivable."

5. James W. Cornman, Keith Lehrer, and George S. Pappas, *Philosophical Problems and Arguments: An Introduction*, 3d ed. (New York and London: Macmillan, 1982), p. 172. I have made one slight modification in the key of abbreviations.

6. Ibid., pp. 171–72.

7. J. J. C. Smart, "Sensations and Brain Processes," in *The Mind-Brain Identity Theory*, ed. C. V. Borst (New York: St. Martin's Press, 1970), pp. 52–66, esp. 53 and 64.

8. This point is well made by Margaret D. Wilson, *Descartes*, p. 190.

9. An earlier version of this paper was read at the fall, 1986, meeting of the Creighton Club. I am grateful to Fred Feldman, C. L. Hardin, and Robert Van Gulick for their helpful criticisms and comments.

Some Thoughts on
"The Limits of Cartesian Dualism"

José Benardete

Has anyone ever doubted that the issue of materialism is one of the most important questions of philosophy? Or that a decisive argument refuting materialism could hardly fail to constitute a major achievement? Well, Professor Dicker appears to be doing just that. On the one hand, he argues that, properly understood, Descartes's famous argument "lacks the weighty implications that might reasonably lead one to reject it." But he also argues that "it implies" something that "all materialists deny, namely, that in addition to material things and processes there are purely mental existents." How, then, to reconcile these two theses?

My bafflement was soon to abate on my receipt of the January 1987 edition of the *Proceedings and Addresses of the American Philosophical Association* 60, no. 3, where Professor Dicker is found to be in the most distinguished company. Reminiscing about G. E. Moore, Brand Blanshard writes:

> At the junior seminar on a rainy and chilly fall day only one student appeared, and he a major in physics. Moore asked him what he would like to discuss, and he answered: the mind-body problem. Very well, said Moore, let us take your sensation of blue. How do you think it is related to what is going on in your brain? There is no relation involved, said the student; what I call the sensation is the change in my brain. At this the veins in Moore's head began to stand out. As I remember, he briefly tried to show the student that he was talking nonsense, but without success. Then he fell silent and would not go on. I led him away, boiling with impatience at the "stupe," to use his own term. May I add that I quite agree with Moore about this?

Blanshard concludes by remarking on the "inability" of the poor stupe "to see one of the most obvious of all distinctions, the difference between consciousness and matter." *Autres temps, autres moeurs.* At the present time the prevailing view is that, far from being "obvious," this distinction, so far as it might be taken to militate against the physics student and his identity thesis, is in fact largely an artifact of the Cartesian revolution from which we are fortunate enough to be liberated. Our own sympathies lie with the student, and we are especially bemused by the failure of even so acute a philosopher as Moore to entertain the following hypothesis. Granted that the student was badly mistaken in his views, might not his error be charitably explained by a lack of proper acquaintance with what Professor Dicker calls "the long and careful discussion of the self in Meditation 2"? Why suppose that a mere physics student should have instant access to the kind of insight that the professional philosopher acquires only after years of study? Irony aside, my point of course is that Moore failed to recognize how his own conviction presupposed fairly complex considerations that had accumulated in the interim over centuries of Cartesianism. For if we look simply to Descartes's contemporaries— Mersenne, Hobbes, Arnauld, and Gassendi—we find that all of them remained unconvinced by Meditation 2, let alone the rest of the work on the point at issue.

Then as now the point at issue remains the same, though precisely *what* it is Professor Dicker's reconstructions of Descartes's argument go a long way toward concealing, thanks indeed to their being so superbly faithful to Descartes's thought. What has not been noticed, I believe, is that in Aristotle can be found an argument that exactly reproduces Descartes's strategy. The argument Aristotle in effect attributes to Hesiod, and its value for us lies in the fact that the weaknesses (and strengths) of the strategy are much more evident in Hesiod's version than in Descartes's. Turning then to the first chapter of *Physics* 4:

> The existence of place is held to be obvious from the fact of mutual replacement. Where water now is, there in turn, when the water has gone out as from a vessel, air is present . . . so that clearly the place or space into which they passed was something different from both. . . . Hesiod too might be held to have given a correct account of it when he made chaos first . . . implying that things need have space first. . . . If this is its nature, the potency of place must be a marvelous thing, and take precedence of all other things. For that without which nothing else can exist, while it can exist without the others must needs be first; for place does not pass out of existence when the things in it are annihilated.

A good argument, certainly, as far as philosophical arguments go! But it is one that most philosophers, including Aristotle and Descartes, have finally rejected, doubtless for a variety of reasons. I remain to be persuaded that Descartes's argument is any better then Hesiod's, as the one argues that mind and the other that space can be clearly and distinctly conceived to exist in the absence of all body. The example is particularly apposite to the present occasion, seeing that it positively celebrates the rewards of doing philosophy historically.

Descartes's Answer to the Problems of Empiricism

Is This a Philosophic or a Historical Issue?

Frederick P. Van De Pitte

When we turn our attention to the history of philosophy, we intend to learn something about philosophy, as well as about history. But what is it that we expect to learn about philosophy, as distinct from its mere "history"? An exhaustive examination of texts and related sources may very well turn up unexpected results, but such research, and its results, must surely be classed as getting *history* straight. Is there not something else at issue when we speak of learning something about philosophy itself?

A step in the right direction was provided by Kristeller when he stated that the "ultimate purpose of the history of ideas" is to "acknowledge the inherent 'absolute' significance of many ideas and achievements which for some reason or other failed to have any visible influence."[1] This suggests that there were moments in the past when someone achieved an insight that has never again been attained. That is, there may have been genuine contributions to philosophy—real progress in the field— of which we have no awareness at all. This insight could have been the result of personal genius, or it might have been merely the recognition from a particular perspective, that what had previously seemed complex and intricate is actually very simple. Of course, if there have been such moments of insight, the task of the historian of philosophy is to capture once again the required perspective. For if we could recognize these contributions, we might very well learn something new about philosophy itself, in addition to something about its history. However, this is a result for which the requirements of sound scholarship may be offered as necessary, but can hardly claim to be sufficient, conditions. Perhaps the best way to make this whole matter clear is to offer an example.

For this purpose, it will be useful to focus on the philosophy of Descartes. We are constantly surprised by additional dimensions of his thought that had not previously been recognized. There is now clear evidence, for example, that Descartes was not only a necessary condition for the perspective later developed by Immanuel Kant, but in fact we also find that Descartes himself had already brought into play the essential ingredients of transcendental philosophy.[2] Again, rather than understanding Descartes to be merely a source of inspiration for Husserl's phenomenology, we can now demonstrate exactly how Descartes himself employed the essential methodological procedures of phenomenology.[3] These particular insights have not been disclosed by any esoteric techniques of investigation. They are simply a recognition of what is explicitly stated by Descartes when we look for clear answers to simple questions. This should be kept in mind as we now look at an even more interesting aspect of Descartes's work.

It is well known that Descartes was a fine mathematician. The discovery of analytic geometry, and the devising of a coordinate system to display the properties of algebraic equations are only two of his accomplishments in this area. It is not surprising, therefore, that two of the most widely repeated clichés of modern philosophy are that Descartes employed a mathematical method, and that he defined physical substance as extension in order to ensure the application of abstract mathematical principles to material reality. Yet Descartes himself tells us that what he is interested in is not at all ordinary mathematics.[4] It is interesting to see what conclusions we are led to when we simply accept his statement.

The precise character of the distortion that has taken place here is not hard to define. Roger Verneaux tells us that: "The origins of Cartesianism are to be sought in the project of a universal mathematics. This idea, or rather this ideal, serves as a focal point around which the other aspects of his system—his entire philosophy—are organized."[5] Mathematics is therefore extremely important for Descartes's philosophy, but how is this vision of a "universal mathematics" to be understood? Pierre Boutroux maintains that Descartes was attempting to develop a method that would imitate the purity of mathematics, i.e., a method that would be purely intellectual and (ideally) entirely free of the imagination.[6] The significance of this point becomes apparent when we find Charpentier assuming in Descartes's thought the traditional conception of mathematics: "Everyone knows that geometry studies order and measure; everyone knows also that it considers them not in really existing objects, but in purely ideal objects."[7] The final step is provided by Jean-Louis Allard (after referring to the passage from Charpentier): "As in mathematics, the intelligibility of science will be independent of sensible experience."[8] We find here the essential elements that prompt even the most competent scholars to see Descartes either as himself caught in idealism, or at least as initiating the movement by which philosophy would slide inexorably into idealism in the eighteenth and nineteenth centuries.[9]

That conclusion is based on the assumption that Descartes had adopted the traditional view of mathematics as an abstract discipline dealing exclusively with ideal objects. Since there is good reason to challenge that assumption, let us try reading Descartes in a somewhat different manner. Mathematics was indeed important in Descartes's intellectual development, but there are grounds for rejecting assertions that he sought a universal mathematics or employed a mathematical method. These rather common assertions are the result of a long tradition of incorrect translations of Descartes's term *Mathesis universalis* as "Universal mathematics." The translation ignores the Greek root of the term *Mathesis* (of which Descartes was clearly aware), which would permit us to read instead "Universal process of learning," or simply "universal method."[10] Scholars have recently concluded that the term *Mathesis* should not be translated at all,[11] but if it is, then the result must make it clear that his method ranges far beyond the limits of even a universal mathematics. Descartes sought out the cognitive principles that give mathematics its certainty and applied these not merely to matters of quantification, but even to metaphysical issues.

Secondly, a close reading of the *Regulae* makes it clear that the imagination plays a very important role in Descartes's method. Jacob Klein has helped us to see that, in fact, mathematics itself requires an imaginative process according to Descartes.[12] Therefore, if his method is seen as patterned on mathematics, it would certainly employ (rather than reject) the imagination. In this respect, Boutroux has clearly led us astray. Consequently, one might very well agree that, for Descartes, mathematics and science have the same degree of objective validity, without agreeing that this knowledge is of an abstract or ideal realm.

In fact, when we look more closely, Descartes's statements about mathematics and mathematical objects would not at all prompt us to accuse him of idealism. Let us consider a few textual examples. In one context Descartes says: "Figures of geometry are considered not as substances, but as the boundaries within which substance is contained."[13] This means not only that he does not recognize such figures as separately existing substances, but more importantly that figures are also considered *precisely* as the limits of substances. We see this more clearly elsewhere, as for example when he says: "Quantity and number differ only in thought from that which has quantity and is numbered."[14] Again, he says, "order and number are not really different from the things ordered and numbered; they are only the modes under which we consider these things."[15] And finally, "Geometrical figures are entirely corporeal [*omnino corporeae*]."[16]

These are not casual statements by Descartes, nor is he expressing himself badly. Because he maintains that figures and numbers—indeed all universals—are simply modes of thought, his position is entirely clear.[17] We need only realize how he wants us to understand the relationship between physical substances and the mere modes under which we think these entities (e.g., figure, number, motion, etc.). In general, his position is that we cannot have a conception of such modes without a conception of the substance.[18] "This is a peculiarity," he says, "of those things which exist only in something else, and can never be conceived without the subject."[19] We can of course think of such modes in some fashion or other. But his point is that we "cannot think of the motion *in a complete manner* apart from the thing in which the motion is, nor of the figure without the object in which the figure is."[20] Therefore, within the context of his method (where complete conception is so important) Descartes makes the general statement: "Be warned that by extension we do not here mean anything distinct and separate from the extended object itself"; and he adds: "nor in general do we recognize those philosophical entities which are not subject to the imagination."[21] In what follows, he rejects the use of terms such as extension, figure, number, superficies, line, point, unity, etc., when they "have such a restricted significance as to exclude something from which they are not really distinct."[22]

Thus Descartes rejects any conception of mathematics that is not actually concerned with concrete objects; and the results of this restriction are very important. He recognizes that if we consider mathematical concepts—or abstract figures and numbers—in isolation, we are only able to grasp those relations that are explicitly in the abstractions considered. Therefore, he sees the complete object (or the physical context) as a means by which we can ensure that no important aspect of the matter is ignored. Wherever possible, he tells us, we must bring the imagination into play to provide this assistance for the understanding.[23] What Descartes is attempting to express here may be seen as his version of what Kant will later call the problem of synthetic judgments a priori. Descartes is adopting the physical entity itself as the underlying medium that will ensure that merely analytic relationships among concepts can be complemented by additional relationships not entailed by the concepts, but equally necessary in the context.

The result would be a system of mathematical relations, embedded in sensible objects, that nonetheless retains the essential necessity of mathematics as it is traditionally conceived: an abstract, formal system. After discussing the necessity of the relationship expressed by the equation "$3 + 4 = 7$," Descartes goes on to say: "Nor does this necessity reside only in sensible matters."[24] So there is no doubt that he understands this concrete system of mathematical relations to retain the necessity we associate with mathematics. Therefore, he concludes that "whatever is demonstrated of figures or numbers is necessarily bound together with that of which it is affirmed."[25]

Descartes would think it very strange, therefore, that we have chosen to understand his position as one that requires him to define material substance as extension *in order* to assure a proper "fit" when abstract mathematics is applied to physical things. Rather, these abstractions are possible only because there are particular things to which they apply— and on which they necessarily depend[26] —and it is inappropriate (i.e., methodologically wrong) ever to divorce these mathematical entities from their physical context. In this respect, the received view of Descartes is precisely upside down.

But is this a reasonable reading of the text? It is indeed; in fact, we find that it is the only appropriate interpretation of Descartes's position if we focus on a single key issue. Throughout his work, Descartes systematically rejects abstraction because it results in inadequate ideas.[27] In the present case, abstract mathematics deprives us of the full implications of the concrete context. Descartes rejects abstract mathematics, therefore, because it does not provide clear and distinct ideas and thus is too weak a tool for his purposes.[28] It deals merely with logical possibilities (and thus its necessity is merely the necessity of consistency); the more rigorous necessity that Descartes requires for his method is still lacking. Concrete mathematics gives us the relationships among actually existing entities (and among their properties), and therefore questions regarding possibility, fit, and correspondence simply do not arise. Whatever conclusions are drawn will be necessary not merely by logical criteria, but also because they are *necessarily true,* i.e., they will express actual states of existing things.

This is why Descartes speaks so disparagingly of formal mathematics in Rule 4, and again in Rule 14. In the first instance, he speaks of "the solution of vacuous problems with which logicians and geometers have been accustomed to toy idly,"[29] and the futility of "busying oneself with bare numbers and imaginary figures so as to appear content with such trifles."[30] In the second, he suspects that in spite of his long comments, one doing arithmetic will continue to believe that numbers are "really distinct objects of the imagination"; and the geometer will continue "to obscure the clarity of his subject with incompatible principles."[31]

At this point, however, Descartes's position seems to leave us with a major difficulty. How is *any* knowledge possible without abstraction? With respect to mathematical knowledge, at least, the answer is fairly clear. First of all, Descartes maintains that it is of the very nature of the mind to move from the particular to the universal (or from the particular case to the general principle).[32] In several places he mentions the power of the mind to form ideas on the basis of a particular experience. For example, he explicitly discusses how we form the universal idea "two," and how we form the universal conception of a triangle.[33] But how does this process work? Abstraction is rejected, and because it seems to be on the basis of only a single example, it cannot be an empirical generalization in the usual sense. Moreover, Descartes maintains that these ideas are not derived from sensory experience in the simple sense that they are reducible to data perceived.[34]

Descartes's answer to this problem is to insist that there is a special class of ideas—"innate" ideas—that are in principle not reducible to sensory data. We must acknowledge that there is a certain justice to his claim; for a triangle presented to us on paper does not bear the kind of necessity that we recognize in mathematics. Moreover, we must not succumb to the illusion that innate ideas are merely a convenient solution for an epistemological dilemma (i.e., ideas born with the mind). When he is forced to defend his position,[35] he consistently maintains that these ideas are formed by the mind, not simply found in it. With respect to the triangle presented on paper, he says that the true triangle "is contained in this figure only in the way that the figure of Mercury is contained in a rough piece of wood."[36] His point is that whatever is in the sensory example could not pass through our nervous system to the brain (and thus to the mind) in any direct way. More importantly, the properties of a triangle (straight lines, points, true angles) could not be abstracted from such an example, because they are not there to be abstracted. With respect to each of these elements, the mind literally must "invent" a true conception before it can even begin to structure the more complex concept of a triangle.

It is not necessary to discuss this process in detail, since it has already been presented elsewhere.[37] It is enough to mention that it is a complex process of imaginative variation, which permits the subject to isolate invariant (essential) aspects of a phenomenon, and then to recognize how these essential components mutually limit each other in context to form a rigorous configuration, or concept. The result is a kind of complete induction by which we can have necessary knowledge of objects. In this way, Descartes is able to claim that these "innate ideas" or concepts of mathematical entities are not only based on experiential objects, but even that they reveal the essential aspects of such objects, and thus are true. Even more important, as we have already suggested, this process is (in principle) extendable to all experiential objects and is therefore not just a mathematical procedure, but valid for epistemology in general. Indeed, if it were not applicable to objects generally, then it would not serve for mathematical objects either; and this is clearly an area where it does work. Thus, at a single stroke, Descartes brings mathematics back into the physical realm from which it had been abstracted and demonstrates that all our other knowledge (when rigorously deduced) can have the same degree of certainty—even the necessity—that had been attributed to mathematics alone.

Now we can begin to appreciate more clearly the significance of the original insight that Descartes shifts from abstract to concrete mathematics. For example, this insight helps us to sort out a good deal of clutter in our general interpretation of Descartes's thought. It helps us to recognize that Descartes was not concerned with a mathematical *method*; rather he focused on mathematics only in order to disclose the epistemological foundations (such as concept formation) that are essential to all areas of knowledge.[38] In addition, this perspective helps us finally to grasp what he means by innate ideas, and to appreciate the full historical significance of this innovation. That is, we are able to recognize that this is not a mysterious procedure to avoid, e.g., the epistemological consequences of his mind-body dualism. Consequently, when we recall that Descartes defines ideas as *forms*,[39] we are able to appreciate that— while he rejected *substantial* forms, and similiar occult or "philosophical entities"[40]—he carried the epistemological significance of the doctrine of forms into the modern period by demonstrating how the mind can provide its own forms.[41] We find, therefore, that what seemed at first to be merely a mathematical insight turns out to shed a good deal of light on other aspects of Descartes's work as well.

It should be apparent, however, that this insight would have even broader consequences. For example, if this interpretation of Descartes is valid, it will significantly alter our evaluation of the work of the classical empiricists. That is, the kind of empiricism offered by Descartes might be seen to obviate much of the effort expended by the British empiricists, and it would certainly provide new dimensions to our conception of how empiricism should be done. Thus, this historical insight would also make a genuine contribution to our understanding of philosophy itself.

Now, therefore, we can return to our original question of historiography. The consideration of our example tends to confirm our normal intuition that we must investigate a historical matter as one that offers (potentially) a genuine contribution to philosophy, while simultaneously viewing the matter as enmeshed in a variety of historical relations. But the question remains as to how we are to recognize this genuine contribution, and how we are to sift the wheat from the chaff of superfluous historical data. We can bring a great deal of technical apparatus, and much philosophical insight, to bear on a figure like Descartes with no guarantee that the true significance of his work will be disclosed.

The difficulty lies in the fact that the past may very well have provided the paradigm for solving a particular problem. That is, there may have been a unique historical vantage point from which the issue could be viewed in the proper perspective. Due to the advantage of this special perspective, the problem might seem utterly simple—or at least remarkably simpler than one would expect. But once that vantage point was lost, it would be extremely difficult to regain it *as history*. Subsequent events would make it virtually impossible to reconstruct the precise

176 Part Three: Descartes

perspective. However, while the historical aspects of the context might become increasingly problematic with time—perhaps ultimately intractable—there is no reason to think that the essential *problem* will have changed. Recognizing that it is often not possible to determine what historical data is essentially relevant and what is not, we may consequently find ourselves forced to accept the view that minimal reconstruction of the context is sometimes heuristically preferable to the very complex.

In the case of Descartes, it might be suggested that a certain common-sense attitude prevailed during this period, in virtue of the practical results that characterized the "new science." Because of this, the occult aspects of Scholastic philosophy simply could not be taken seriously any longer—and this would include the occult status attributed to abstract mathematical entities. Equally important, the epistemological complexities that we associate with the rationalist and empiricist movements had not yet appeared on the scene. In this lull between the storms of philosophical obscurity, therefore, it is possible that Descartes had sufficient good sense to take advantage of his privileged perspective. That is, the interpretation offered here would suggest that he was able to recognize the obscurities and occult entities of Scholastic philosophy, and to replace them with a much more simple conception of mathematics—and consequently of epistemology in general. Concrete mathematics would replace previous abstractions; concept formation would replace substantial forms. If this is in fact what took place, it would not be surprising that his contemporaries were unable to appreciate his new philosophy.

The result that this hypothesis suggests is very close to what we now recognize to be the case. The most significant contributions that Descartes made to modern philosophy seem only now to be emerging, after having been lost for three hundred years. The response of his contemporaries to his thought could only mislead us, since it was based on a misunderstanding; and the systematic responses of the rationalists and empiricists would tend to confirm our misunderstanding. Therefore, since we would be unable to reconstruct the historical perspective, the only apparent remedy open to us would be to adopt the good sense that permitted Descartes to grasp the basic philosophical problem clearly in the first place—irrespective of his, or any other, historical context. For if we could, by adopting this perspective, understand the problem clearly, there is every reason to believe that we would be able to appreciate the way it would be viewed, or how individuals would attempt to solve it, in a variety of historical contexts. Without this clarity of *philosophical* vision, it is unlikely that we would be able to comprehend properly at all either the problem, or Descartes's solution.

This is not, of course, a very helpful suggestion. For even if, as Descartes says, good sense is the most equitably distributed of all the world's goods, we must nonetheless acknowledge that it is not the most frequently employed, or even easily identified. We may very well be left with an uncomfortable feeling, therefore, if we conclude that it is essential to our cause. It would be disquieting, that is, for us to find that while technical ability and a good nose for solving historical puzzles may be important to our enterprise, it is still necessary to recognize an essential role for old-fashioned virtues like simplicity and good sense in the investigation of the history of philosophy.

NOTES

1. Paul Oskar Kristeller, "The Place of Classical Humanism in Renaissance Thought," *Journal of the History of Ideas* 4 (1943): 62-63.

2. See, for example, Franz Bader, *Die Ursprünge der Transzendental-philosophie bei Descartes*, 2 vols. (Bonn: Bouvier Verlag H. Grundman, 1979-83); and F. P. Van De Pitte, "Descartes et Kant: Empirisme et Innéité," *Les Etudes Philosophiques*, 1985, pp. 175-90.

3. See K. Wüstenberg, *Kritische Analysen zu den Grundproblemen der transzendentalen Phänomenologie Husserls unter besonderer Berücksichtigung der Philosophie Descartes'* (Leiden: Brill, 1985); and F. P. Van De Pitte, "Descartes's Innate Ideas," *Kant-Studien* 76 (1985).

4. *Regulae*, Rule 4 *(Oeuvres de Descartes*, ed. C. Adam and P. Tannery, rev. ed. [Paris: Vrin, 1964-76], 10, p. 374, lines 1-7; *The Philosophical Works of Descartes*, ed. E. S. Haldane and G. R. T. Ross [Cambridge: Cambridge University Press, 1911], 1, p. 11).

5. R. Verneaux, *Les Sources cartésiennes et kantiennes de l'Idéalisme francais* (Paris: Beauchesne, 1936), p. 15.

6. P. Boutroux, *L'Imagination et les mathématiques selon Descartes* (Paris: Alcan, 1900), esp. p. 35.

7. T.-V. Charpentier, *Essai sur la méthode de Descartes* (Paris: Delagrave, 1869), pp. 95-96.

8. J.-L. Allard, *Le Matématisme de Descartes* (Ottawa: Université d'Ottawa Press, 1963), p. 49.

9. "By turning the concrete into a mosaic of clear ideas, the mathematical method of Descartes raised difficulties whose solution was sought throughout the whole of the seventeenth and eighteenth centuries; in the nineteenth century it led in the end to despair—despair of philosophy itself." Etienne Gilson, "The Distinctiveness of the Philosophic Order," *A Gilson Reader*, ed. Anton C. Pegis (Garden City, N.Y.: Doubleday Image Books, 1957), p. 52.

10. See my "Descartes' *Mathesis Universalis*," *Archiv für Geschichte der Philosophie* 61 (1979): 154-74.

11. Jean-Luc Marion, for example, argues strongly against translation in his edition of the *Regulae: Règles utiles et claires pour la direction de l'esprit et la recherche de la vérité* (La Haye: Martinus Nijhoff, 1977), pp. 156-58 n. 31; and pp. 160-63 n. 34.

12. Jacob Klein, *Greek Mathematical Thought and the Origin of Algebra* (Cambridge, Mass.: The M.I.T. Press, 1968), pp. 197ff.

13. *Reply to Objections 5* (AT 7, p. 381, lines 17-19; HR 2, p. 227).

14. *Principles* 2, 8 (AT 8-1 p. 44; HR 1, p. 258).

15. Ibid., 1, 55 (p. 26, lines 15-18; HR 1, p. 241).

16. *Reply to Objections* 5 (AT 7, p. 385, lines 9-10; HR 2, p. 229).

17. *Principles* 1, 58 (AT 8-1, p. 27; HR 1, p. 242).

18. Ibid., 1, 61 (AT 8-1, p. 29, lines 27-31; HR 1, p. 244).

19. Rule 14 (AT 10, p. 444, lines 7-9; HR 1, p. 58).

20. *Reply to Objections* 1 (AT 7, p. 120, lines 28ff.; HR 2, p. 22), emphasis added.

21. Rule 14 (AT 10, p. 442, lines 25-28; HR 1, p. 57).

22. Ibid. (AT 10, p. 445, lines 4-5; HR 1, p. 59).

23. Ibid. (lines 17ff.; HR 1, pp. 59-60).

24. Rule 12 (AT 10, p. 421, lines 17-18; HR 1, p. 43).

25. Ibid. (lines 15-17).

26. In Rule 6, Descartes tells us that the universal "depends upon individuals in order to exist" (AT 10, p. 382, line 24; HR 1, p. 16).

27. A sample of texts: *Reply to Objections* 1 (AT 7, p. 120, lines 20-21; HR 2, p. 22); *Reply to Objections* 4 (AT 7, pp. 220-21; HR 2, p. 98); Rule 12 (AT 10, pp. 418-19; HR 1, p. 41); *Letter to Clerselier* (AT 9-1, p. 216). Note also Descartes's distinction between abstraction and a clear and distinct operation of the intellect: *Reply to Objections* 1 (AT 7, p. 117, lines 12-14; HR 2, p. 20).

28. This is the only appropriate conclusion to be drawn from his statements taken together (notes 17-19 and 27).

29. AT 10, p. 373, lines 27-28; HR 1, p. 10.

30. Ibid., p. 375, lines 13-16; HR 1, p. 11.

31. Rule 14 (AT 10, p. 446, lines 17ff.; HR 1, p. 60). See also p. 445, lines 28ff.

32. *Reply to Objections* 2 (AT 7, p. 140, lines 28ff.; HR 2, p. 38).

33. *Principles* 1, 59 (AT 8-1, p. 27, lines 23ff.; HR 1, p. 243).

34. *Reply to Objections* 5 (AT 7, p. 380, lines 16-20 and p 381, lines 20-22; HR 2, pp. 226-27).

35. See, for example, the *Notae in Programma*: "I have never written or accepted that the mind requires innate ideas which are somehow distinct from its faculty of thinking" (AT, 8-2, p. 357, lines 26-28; HR 1, p. 442). In what follows he mentions our ability "to form these ideas by means of an innate faculty . . ." (ibid., p. 359, lines 3-5; HR 1, p. 443).

36. *Reply to Objections* 5 (AT 7, p. 382, lines 6-8; HR 2, p. 228).

37. See my "Descartes' Innate Ideas," note 3, above.

38. This point is discussed in "Descartes' *Mathesis Universalis*," note 10, above.

39. See *Reply to Objections* 2 (AT 7, p. 160, lines 14-16; HR 2, p. 52); and *Reply to Objections* 3 (AT 7, p. 188, lines 14-16; HR 2, p. 73).

40. See, e.g., *Letter to Morin*, 12 September 1638 (AT 2, p. 367; *Descartes: Philosophical Letters*, ed. Anthony Kenny [Oxford: Clarendon Press, 1970], p. 61); and *Letter to Regius* (AT 3, p. 502, lines 1-5; *Letters*, p. 128).

41. See my "Descartes' Epistemological Revolution: A Modern Realist Transformation of the Doctrine of Forms," *Proceedings of the American Catholic Philosophical Association* 59 (1985): 132-48.

Commentary—Whig's Progress

Richard A. Watson

Professor Van De Pitte provides an example of doing philosophy historically that is both exemplary and provocative. It is exemplary of a specific approach to historical figures and texts, and it is provocative because he challenges a standard interpretation. I believe that the standard interpretation is more correct than Professor Van De Pitte's interpretation, but I shall not argue the case here. Instead, I shall concentrate on the general method and on its results.

Professor Van De Pitte advocates searching in historical texts for genuine contributions to philosophy that have been neglected. Such neglect could stem from the obscurity or difficulty of the text, or through misinterpretation, as Professor Van De Pitte proposes in the case of Descartes. The goal is to "learn something new about philosophy itself," that is, to find solutions to philosophical problems. In Professor Van De Pitte's terms, such new solutions constitute genuine contributions to philosophy, and to search for them is to do philosophy historically.

He asks, then, "How we are to sift the wheat from the chaff of superfluous data"—a phrase that broadcasts his whiggish adherence to progressive history—and recommends that we should use "a great deal of technical apparatus, and much philosophical insight." We must also try to see texts and philosophical problems in historical context. But, he says, our ability to comprehend historical context becomes "increasingly problematic with time—perhaps ultimately intractable." Nevertheless—and this is his key point—"there is no reason to think that the essential *problem* will have changed." This leads him to what I take to be his central methodological principle. He puts it this way: "recognizing that it is often not possible to determine what historical data is essentially relevant and what is not, we may consequently find ourselves forced to accept the view that a minimal reconstruction of the context is sometimes heuristically preferable to the very complex."

Let me now take these elements to propose a reconstructed key principle of Professor Van De Pitte's method. It is this: Look for historical texts that can be reconstructed (with whatever technical apparatus is helpful) to provide new solutions to perennial problems of philosophy. A lemma to this principle is that because historical contexts are very difficult to recover, and thus it is very difficult to make out the sense of a historical text as it was intended and understood in historical context, one should attempt to provide only a minimal historical context in working on a historical text. I think an implication of this principle is the following: Both the historical nature of the texts being searched and the historical context of the texts are of negligible importance to doing philosophy; because they are so problematic, they may even be obstructive to the examination and reconstruction of a text for the purpose of discovering new solutions to ahistorical philosophical problems.

Professor Van De Pitte will surely say that I am interpreting him too rigidly, but about the example he himself provides he remarks that the response of Descartes's contemporaries "could only mislead us, since it was based on a misunderstanding," a misunderstanding that he believes was continued by the rationalists and empiricists.

It is clear that my reconstruction of Professor Van De Pitte, in the historical context of the present—while being a highly defensible reconstruction of his methodological *obiter dicta*—is not accurate to his practice in the example he provides. Professor Van De Pitte does not primarily reconstruct Descartes's position on the mathematical or philosophical method, keeping his presentation of the historical context to a minimum, but in the bulk of his paper he presents the case in historical context with the intention of demonstrating just how and why Descartes's contemporaries misunderstood him. Professor Van De Pitte's argument about the historical circumstances is essential because only if it is persuasive will we be convinced that his reconstruction of Descartes is acceptable.

Acceptable to whom and on what grounds and for what purpose? Acceptable to those who, in Professor Van De Pitte's words, are interested in "getting history straight." Unless this were not also a major concern of Professor Van De Pitte himself—one that emerges from his practice if not from his statement of method—he would not have gone to such length to try to show that in historical context Descartes can and should be understood in a way different from the way he was understood by his contemporaries and four centuries of commentators. Instead, he would have kept the historical commentary to a minimum and would have presented a reconstruction of Descartes's text in contemporary technical terms that exhibits a new solution to an ahistorical problem in philosophy. Instead he uses historical data to exhibit a solution in contemporary technical terms, and he seems to be at least equally as concerned to convince us that the position he presents really is *Descartes's* position, as he is to show us that interpreted in his way it offers a new solution to an old problem.

One could say that my reconstruction of Professor Van De Pitte's method as purely a search in historical texts for new solutions to old problems is an extreme that does not represent doing philosophy historically at all, but is merely a description of a technique for mining historical texts for concepts, arguments, and structures that, when adapted to contemporary terminology with contemporary techniques, are useful in solving problems, much in the way physicists and biologists sometimes skim mathematical journals for ideas —completely out of mathematical context—of how to represent, analyze, or solve problems in physics and biology.

To do philosophy historically, one might contend, at a minimum would be to take the historical context and historical nature of both the texts and the problems as essential elements in the reconstruction of texts. If you ignore the historical elements, you can certainly do philosophy using historical texts, but you would not be doing philosophy historically. In the case Professor Van De Pitte examines, whether or not his reconstruction of Descartes solves a philosophical problem, our evaluation of that reconstruction is going to rest as much or more on whether or not it is a defensible interpretation of the historical texts in historical context, as it is on whether or not the reconstruction itself solves a philosophical problem. That is inevitable given the concern Professor Van De Pitte himself exhibits for historical matters in the presentation of his reconstruction. He wants to convince us that he is exposing what Descartes really meant.

I think there are extremely few pure philosophers who are never influenced by the history of philosophy, and that there are extremely few pure historians of philosophy whose goal is to do nothing more than get history straight. Philosophers and historians of philosophy alike are constantly reconstructing historical texts with the goal of showing how philosophical problems can be or have been solved or not. You cannot not do philosophy historically.

Now I am prepared to challenge Professor Van De Pitte's interpretation of Descartes, but, alas, my time is up.

Descartes, Omnipotence, and Kinds of Modality

Lilli Alanen

This paper discusses Descartes's theory of the creation of eternal truths and the views of modality attributed to Descartes in recent readings of this theory. Two main lines of interpretation can be discerned. According to the first, Descartes would hold that there is no absolute necessity—there is only necessity for us or epistemic necessity.[1] This kind of reading, it has been claimed, commits Descartes to a radical universal possibilism, inconsistent with other fundamental tenets of his philosophy. Many scholars, to avoid this conclusion, have tried to attenuate the consequences of Descartes's doctrine by a distinction between different kinds of necessary or eternal truths, exempting some eternal truths, the necessity of which is taken to be absolute, from the doctrine of the creation of truths.[2] Both lines of interpretation involve difficulties. To the extent that they share assumptions of rationality Descartes rejects, they fail to do justice to Descartes's theory. In my view, Descartes's theory is radical indeed, but it is not incoherent, and it does not commit Descartes to any irrationalist voluntarism. It raises interesting and important questions concerning the nature and foundation of rationality and conceivability. It is only against the background of these questions that Descartes's original doctrine can be fully understood and assessed.[3]

I will first recall, briefly, Descartes's statements of his controversial doctrine and then look at different ways of reading them and the difficulties they involve.[4] I end by sketching out some differences between Descartes's view on the nature and origin of modality and the Scholastic view he opposes. The reasons for which Descartes opposes this view, as I will try to show, arise both from theological and logical considerations.

1

Descartes's statements of the doctrine that God has freely created the eternal truths are found in his correspondence. It is announced for the first time in a famous letter to Mersenne, where Descartes asserts that the mathematical truths, called eternal truths by Mersenne, are posited by God and entirely dependent on him. He also asks Mersenne to "assert and proclaim everywhere" that these truths are laid down by God in nature, just as a king lays down the laws in his kingdom, and that they are also inborn in our minds (and hence fully intelligible to us), just as a king would imprint his laws on the hearts of his subjects if he had enough power to do so.[5]

The mathematical truths established by God are the ones on which Descartes's new physics is based, and therefore he can speak about them as laws of nature too. None of the mathematical truths inborn in our minds and exemplified in the order of the universe is necessary or unchangeable in itself. Descartes writes: "It will be said that if God has established these truths he could change them as a king changes his laws. To this the answer is: Yes he can, if his will can change" (loc. cit.).

In explaining these ideas to Mersenne again some weeks later, Descartes uses expressions directly or indirectly derived from Suarez's *Disputationes*.[6] He writes:

> As for the eternal truths, I say once more that *they are true or possible only because God knows them as true or possible. They are not known as true by God in any way which would imply that they are true independently of him*. . . . In God willing and knowing are a single thing in such a way that *by the very fact of willing something he knows it and it is only for this reason that such a thing is true*. So we must not say that if *God did not exist nonetheless these truths would be true*; for the existence of God is the first and most eternal of all possible truths and the one from which alone all others derive. (To Mersenne, 6 May 1630, AT 1, 147, K, 13. Passages in italics are in Latin in the French text.)

It is not very clear how the remark that the eternal truths are "true or possible only because God knows them as true or possible" (*verae aut possibiles*) should be read.[7] As it is here understood, Descartes's formulation is meant to emphasize his opposition to the view defended by Suarez that the eternal truths are necessarily true independently of God's infinite intellect. According to Descartes there is no distinction between God's willing and knowing the eternal truths, and it is not only their necessity but also their possibility as objects of knowledge (i.e., their conceivability) that depends on God's willing and knowing them.

God's sovereignty is not limited by any necessary truths about possible objects, because the very possibility of things depends to the same extent as their existence on God's knowledge, will, and power.[8] The necessary truths are produced by God as freely as he has created the world.[9] Descartes, in claiming this, is aware that the notions of causality and creation are inappropriate in accounting for the way in which the eternal truths depend on God.[10] The important thing for Descartes is not to know how they depend on God, for this is something we cannot in fact understand, but to know that they depend entirely on him.[11] The position outlined in the letters to Mersenne is not opposed only to Suarez's conceptualist view on the origin of modality, it also conflicts with common Scholastic assumptions about rationality and the conditions of intelligibility in general.

The Scholastics distinguished God's absolute power from his ordinary power, considering God's absolute power coextensive with the logically possible. God's omnipotence, interpreted in terms of absolute power, has no limit other than that imposed by the law of contradiction: anything that can be described without implying a contradiction in terminis can be created or actualized by God's power. God could have created another world or changed the laws he has ordained in the actual world. But God could not violate the laws of logic. This restriction on purely logical grounds of God's absolute power does not, as generally understood, involve any impotence in God, for, as Aquinas and his followers stressed, what implies contradiction is neither feasible nor possible: it is nothing. Also, one should not say of what is impossible in this sense that God cannot do it; rather one should say, since it involves contradiction, that it cannot be done.[12]

But God's power, as Descartes understands it, seems to have no restrictions whatsoever—not even logical ones. To say that God has created or established the necessary truths as a free and efficient cause is to make the necessary as well as the possible contingent upon his will: it is, in a way, to abolish the very distinction between the necessary, as that which cannot possibly not be, and the possible, as that which may or may not be. Truth and logical consistency are separated, for Descartes not only says that God can make necessary propositions untrue, but he also says, repeatedly, that God can make contradictories true together.[13]

The interpretation of the crucial passages is, however, controversial. Is Descartes talking about real or epistemic possibility and necessity? Although the notion of "eternal truth" is never explicitly defined, it corresponds, in Descartes's use, to the one of necessary truth in the traditional sense of a truth the denial of which involves logical contradiction. It covers both mathematical and logical principles and also general metaphysical principles.[14]

2

One interpretation, which Edwin Curley somewhat misleadingly labels the "standard" interpretation, ascribes to Descartes the view that there are no eternal truths in the above sense of necessary truths. This interpretation, as Curley construes it, involves the thesis that anything whatsoever is possible, from a strictly logical point of view, for the Cartesian God.[15] There are, Curley rightly observes, serious systematic reasons for rejecting this reading: Descartes could not defend a universal possibilism without giving up central tenets of his philosophy and science, indeed, without giving up his whole philosophical enterprise.[16] Descartes, as we have seen, insists that the eternal truths are "imprinted" in our minds in the way "a king would imprint his laws on the hearts of all his subjects if he had enough power to do so" (to Mersenne, 15 April 1630, AT 1, 145, K, 11), and hence considers them somehow facts about the constitution of the human mind or understanding. But they are not contingent in the sense of historical and changeable facts. Rather, Descartes seems to regard them as some kind of immutable, a priori conditions for rational thinking and science, which also have a counterpart in reality since the laws of nature can be derived from them. Not only are all the things in this world disposed by God according to these truths, but if God created several worlds they would be true in all of them. (AT 11, 47, AT 6, 43, HR 1, 108). This is what justifies the application of a deductive, mathematical method to the sciences of nature.[17] But how, then, should the necessity or immutability Descartes ascribes to the eternal truths be accounted for? For although God, according to Descartes, can change the eternal truths if his will can change, God's will is immutable, and therefore, Descartes writes, the (created) truths are eternal and unchangeable (to Mersenne, 15 April 1630, AT 1, 145, K, 11).

The reason Descartes calls necessary the eternal truths that he holds to be freely established or produced by God seems to be that God has willed them to be true in any world God would create—i.e., in all possible worlds.[18] It is not necessary that there are any necessary, universal truths or more restricted, contingent truths. Nevertheless, because of God's free act of the will, the modal structure he has produced is eternally in power. The modal theory or model chosen by the Cartesian God is, interestingly, more similar to the Scotistic than to the Aristotelian one.[19] Statements are not called necessary simply because they are eternally true. There are eternally true statements that are necessary and others that are not necessary. This fact as such is regarded as totally dependent on God's free will: "though God has willed that certain truths be necessary, that is not to say that he has willed them necessarily. For to will that they be necessary and to will necessarily, or to be necessitated to will them, are completely different" (to Mesland, 2 May 1644, AT 4, 118-19, K, 151).

Curley, following Peter Geach, reads this passage as involving "not a denial that there are necessary truths, but a denial that those which are necessary are necessarily necessary." According to Curley the best and most charitable way of stating Descartes's doctrine would be in terms of iterated modalities.[20] This line of interpretation, however, is not satisfactory. It seems to water down Descartes's doctrine to the view Plantinga (1980) characterizes as a "limited possibilism," according to which *modal* propositions (propositions ascribing modality to other propositions) would be within God's control, but not the necessary truths themselves. God could not have made "2 + 2 = 4" false, "he could only have made it the case that he could have made it false. He could have made it *possibly* false."[21] This, however, is in conflict with Descartes's explicit claim that God could make it untrue, for instance, that all the lines from the center of a circle to its circumference are equal, or that the three angles of a triangle are equal to two right angles (to Mersenne, 27 May 1630, AT 1, 152, K, 15, cf. AT 7, 435–36, HR 2, 251, to Mesland, 2 May 1644, AT 4, 118, K, 151). Why would Descartes have opposed Suarez's antivoluntarist, conceptualist theory of necessary truths, if his own view of God's power had been restricted to this kind of "limited possibilism"? Plantinga observes that Descartes did not distinguish between a "limited" and a "universal possibilism" in stating his view, but thinks that the latter is more in accordance with "Descartes's deep conviction that all things are dependent upon God and hence within his control."[22] But readings that ascribe a radical, universal possibilism to Descartes seem equally unacceptable, both for textual and systematic reasons, and make his position not only incoherent, but also utterly unintelligible.

We seem to be faced with the following awkward choices: (1) Read Descartes's enigmatic statements as committing him to universal possibilism and declare his position inconsistent, unintelligible, and extravagant. (2) Read them as involving merely a limited possibilism, thereby saving Descartes's respectability, but at the same time cutting off the very edge of his doctrine. (3) Conclude that Descartes had no clear and distinct idea of the nature of necessary truths and was simply confused about their status.

Let us turn to a recent interpretation by Hide Ishiguro that purports to escape this kind of dilemma. Ishiguro takes her starting point in Martial Guéroult's (1968) suggestion that Descartes's theory of modality foreshadows the distinction made by Leibniz between absolute necessity and necessity *ex hypothesi*. However, the distinction between absolute and hypothetic necessity in Descartes does not, she argues, coincide with the Leibnizian distinction between the laws of logic and mathematics on one hand and those of physics on the other, but occurs in a very particular form. It is a logical distinction arising "from the way Descartes understands negation and from the fact that we are bound by our thought and the expressive powers of our language."[23]

Descartes's eternal truths, Ishiguro argues, can be described as "rules or forms of the working of the mind freely created by God." They depend on the constitution of our mind and are, in Kantian language, given "as a priori forms of thinking."[24] God could have constituted our minds in some other way and hence created other eternal truths, but given the way our minds are constituted, the eternal truths are immutable and necessary. Their necessity is, absolutely speaking, contingent, but once they have been "created" or "instituted," they cannot be denied without contradiction. Descartes would not reject the notion of "absolute non-epistemic modality," for he holds that the actualization of what is contradictory is absolutely impossible.[25] This reading allows Descartes to have it both ways: he can hold that the eternal truths could be other than they actually are, without committing himself to the problematic claim that actual contradictions could be rendered true by God's omnipotence.

Ishiguro's reading is perplexing, for the denial of a necessary truth is usually understood as equivalent to a contradiction. To say that a proposition is necessary is to say that its denial implies contradiction. Now if the impossibility of actualizing a contradiction (making a contradictory proposition true) is absolute, the impossibility of negating a necessary truth would seem absolute too. This, however, is not the case according to Ishiguro, who wants to show that there is, on the contrary, an interesting asymmetry between the status of necessity and that of impossibility in Descartes's theory. The asymmetry arises partly from Descartes's view that the eternal truths are contingent upon our concepts and the constitution of our minds, partly from Descartes's use of negation. Ishiguro takes Descartes to treat negation not as a content of a proposition, but as an operation carried out on the proposition. But Ishiguro is not very explicit on the use of negation she ascribes to Descartes, and I must admit that I find this point unconvincing.[26]

Consider the standard example of a necessary truth discussed in this context, "2 + 2 = 4." Its necessity is here supposed to be contingent upon the way our minds are created. Descartes's God could render it false, he could make its negation true. To say that the negation of a necessary proposition is a logical possibility is to say that God could have created our mind in some different way. He could have created minds without any arithmetical or mathematical concepts and rules; and he could also, presumably, have created minds working according to quite different rules or concepts in terms of which those truths that are necessary given the concepts we actually use could not be intelligibly stated at all. The history of mathematics provides an illustration of how Descartes's assertion that God is free to make contradictories true together should be understood according to Ishiguro. Consider the claim that God can make it untrue that the three angles of a triangle are equal to two right angles (note 13). After the discovery of non-Euclidean geometries we know that the number of angles in a triangle can add up to more or less than two right ones. Ishiguro writes:

> Indeed we can see how the above proposition would be true in a Euclidean geometry and false in general in Riemannian geometry. Thus, as Descartes writes, God could instantiate two apparent contradictories (e.g., when each belongs to a different geometry). We learn that each of the apparent contradictories were conditional truths, dependent on distinct, different antecedent conditions, and not contradictories.[27]

But are we really using, as Ishiguro seems to think, the same concept of triangle in different geometries? And is not Descartes's point, in the statement referred to, precisely to deny that the possibility of making a self-contradictory proposition true can be understood at all by our limited intellects?[28] As to the denial of the truth of a necessary proposition, it is not a real possibility unless the antecedent conditions, i.e, the language or mental constitution on which its content and truth depends, are by the same means annihilated. The negation of any particular necessary truth is in itself as unintelligible and impossible as the instantiation of any of the absolute contradictions discussed by Ishiguro.[29]

If this is granted, it is difficult to claim that there is any real asymmetry or difference in principle between the negation of a necessary truth and the assertion of a contradiction, e.g., between "it is not the case that '1 + 2 = 3' " on one hand, and "I + 2 = 4" or "p & -p" on the other. Necessity as well as impossibility are both hypothetical or conditional, for they are both relative to the language and concepts in which they are formulated, or, if you prefer, to the constitution of our mind. However, once the antecedent conditions on which the content and truth of a proposition depend are assumed or given, its modal status (necessity and possibility as well as impossibility) is absolute. The asymmetry, if there is one, is, rather, in the scope of what God can do. Talking of languages (conceptual systems) we could perhaps say that God can create infinitely many languages that are mutually incompatible and, as it were, incommensurable, actualizing within one language what appears as absolutely incoherent or impossible in terms of another. In this sense God can render apparent contradictories true together, but God could not make a real contradiction true.

The advantage of the reading proposed by Ishiguro is that it seems to render Descartes's enigmatic claims about modality somehow intelligible without committing him to assumptions about any a priori limits constraining God's omnipotence. God is free to create minds that use other concepts and rules incompatible with those conditioning our thinking, however, given the rules and the contents of the concepts within the language he has chosen to create, even God cannot bring about what contradicts these notions. This reading too has its drawbacks. For what, it might be asked, have we gained, if we look back at the three alternatives facing Descartes's interpreters mentioned earlier? If, as I have argued, there is no real asymmetry of the kind Ishiguro assumes between the Cartesian notions of necessity and impossibility, then the assumption that there is a distinction between absolute and contingent modality in Descartes must be reconsidered. All modality is hypothetical, in the sense of depending on the conceptual systems or mental constitutions that God chooses to create. But given these antecedent conditions, modalities are absolute. We seem to have ended up with another version of the second interpretation, open to the same criticism as can be raised against Curley's interpretation: it leaves Descartes's most radical statements of the doctrine difficult to account for. Of the interpretations here considerd, only the one defended by Harry Frankfurt (1977) takes full account of those statements.

Frankfurt, like Ishiguro, understands the necessity of Descartes's eternal truths as a necessity relative to the contingent nature of the human mind.[30] Differently from Ishiguro, Frankfurt takes Descartes's statements about the unintelligibility of God's unlimited power seriously and does not attempt to explain away Descartes's enigmatic claims about God's ability to make what involves logical contradiction true and is, therefore, inconceivable to us. On the contrary, he takes those claims quite literally and admits, as I think one should do, that the power Descartes attributes to God to make, e.g., the radii of a circle unequal, or any other self-contradictory proposition true, surpasses our understanding. To seek a logically coherent explication of such assertions is, as Frankfurt recognizes, a mistake.[31] But I think the implications of this view are rather different from those that have been associated with it.

Contrary to what Curley thinks, the reading defended by Frankfurt does not commit Descartes to any radical *logical* possibilism as expressed in the formula Curley uses to describe what he calls the "standard interpretation."[32] This, I want to stress, is not to say it commits Descartes to some other kind of possibilism. Descartes's doctrine, properly understood, involves neither a limited nor a universal possibilism. What is implied by Descartes's thesis is that there are no possible or necessary truths before God decides to make them. The idea of iterated modalities presupposes that modalities are given, which is precisely what Descartes wants to question. Nothing precedes and nothing predetermines the modal structure created by God. The necessary truths are, once and for all, created by God and constitute the absolute limits of conceivability to which finite, created minds are confined: they cannot constitute limits for what God, who creates them, could conceive or do.[33] It does not follow that anything whatsoever is possible to the Cartesian God, or that there are no limits at all to God's omnipotence. What follows is that since God creates the modal structure to which our thinking is bound, there is no absolute frame in which questions about what is possible independently of this frame can be posed. There are no independent absolute standards of rationality or possibility shared by created rational beings and God against which the acts of God's infinite intellect and will can be measured.

3

From a very broad historical perspective one could roughly distinguish three general views or accounts of the foundations of modality and conceivability: the ancient realist model found in Aristotelian and Platonist doctrines, the conceptualist model developed by the late Medievals, and voluntarist or constructivist accounts. By the realist model I mean the view according to which modalities are ontologically founded in the invariant intelligible structure of the universe as contained in the divine intellect (or essence) and exemplified in the natural kinds, potencies, and tendencies of real things in the world. The conceptualist view, as here understood, is a secularized, "detheologized" theory of the foundation of modality. Necessity and possibility are here dissociated both from real powers and potentialities of things as well as from any other kind of ontological foundation in the divine intellect. They are identified instead with semantic and logical relations between the terms of modal propositions.[34]

Suarez defends a version of the modern conceptualist view. The eternal truths, in this view, are construed as conditionals that are necessarily (analytically) true not because they are eternally known by God, but in virtue of the content and the relations of their terms. The contents and relations between the terms of conditional truths about possible essences depend, according to Suarez, on the natures or essences they denote. Although these essences are conceived by the eternal intellect from all eternity and can therefore be described as being produced by or having some kind of intellectual being in God's intellect, they are possible or conceivable in and of themselves, independently of whether any intellect, eternal or created, actually conceives them. The truth of conditional propositions describing these essences depends neither on the existence (in real or intellectual being) of these essences, nor, Suarez insists, on the divine intellect who conceives them eternally; for the relations between the terms of such propositions would remain the same even if, to assume the impossible, there were no eternal intellect to conceive them.[35]

The meaning of modal notions is here spelled out without reference either to God's will or power or to his intellect. It is assumed instead that the eternal truths are founded on formal (logical) relations of compossibility or mutual exclusion between possible beings that, as mere possibilities, are given prior to and independently of God. Descartes saw this as an arbitrary restriction of God's infinite and incomprehensible power, leading to the "heretical" assumption that God's intellect is somehow on a par with our finite intellect. Why should the acts of an infinite and incomprehensible being satisfy the criteria of intelligibility to which our rational thinking and understanding of the world have to conform? To take this for granted is not only to presume that God has created the human intellect to resemble his own (the only difference between a finite and an infinite mind would be a difference in scope), it is also to say that God *could not* have created the human mind in a different way. Any intellect or mind would be bound to the same set or sets of possibilities. Such consequences are unacceptable to Descartes because they are incompatible with what he considers a true conception of God's nature.[36] Part of that conception is Descartes's view of the radical freedom of the divine will and his denial of any distinction between the acts of God's intellect, will, and power.[37]

In some texts Descartes seems to give the priority to the will and hence to reverse the traditional ordering of God's faculties.[38] His position, on this ground, has been characterized as an extreme voluntarism. This label as I see it is inadequate or at least not very illuminating: it makes sense only given traditional distinctions between reason and will that Descartes rejects. Voluntarism as ordinarily used presupposes not only a distinction, but also an opposition between reason and will, and because of this contrast, it is usually associated with irrationalism.[39] We cannot, however, talk of the rationality versus irrationality of what God understands and wills without presupposing a standard of rationality, the one God has actually willed and imposed on our minds. But for this reason it cannot be used as a standard shared by the human and the divine (or any) intellect, a standard *against* which God's will could be opposed or measured. Descartes's claim that the area of possibility and hence conceivability is freely set by God and could therefore be different from what it is does not imply any contradiction, because in his account the notions or propositions chosen to be necessary or possible do not, in themselves, have any modal status. They are, one could say, modally indifferent.[40]

NOTES

Earlier and more extensive versions of this paper were read at philosophy colloquia at Columbia University, Ohio State University (April 1986), and University of

Helsinki. My thanks are due to Nuel Belnap, Harry Frankfurt, Simo Knuuttila, Fred Stoutland, and to the members of these colloquia for helpful discussions on the subject.

1. Recent versions of this reading are found in Harry G. Frankfurt, "Descartes on the Creation of the Eternal Truths," The Philosophical Review 86 (1977):36–57; A. Plantinga, Does God Have a Nature (Milwaukee: Marquette University Press, 1980); Jean-Luc Marion, Sur la théologie blanche de Descartes (Paris: Presses Universitaires de France, 1980); and J. Bouveresse,"La théorie du possible chez Descartes," Revue International de Philosophie 146 (1983):293–310.

2. See, e.g., Martial Guéroult, Descartes selon l'ordre des raisons (Paris: Aubier Montaigne, 1968); Amos Funkenstein, "Descartes, Eternal Truths, and the Divine Omnipotence," Studies in the History and Philosophy of Science 6 (1975): 185–99; and more recently, Edwin M. Curley, "Descartes on the Creation of the Eternal Truths," The Philosophical Review 93 (1984):569–97; and H. Ishiguro, "The Status of Necessity and Impossibility in Descartes," in Essays on Descartes' Meditations, ed. A. Rorty. (Berkeley and Los Angeles, Calif.: University of California Press, 1986), pp. 459–72.

3. The only interpretation in recent Anglo-American literature that does justice to this doctrine is the one defended by Frankfurt (1977). His subtle and penetrating analysis of Descartes's view and its difficulties has not received due attention, and it has also been partly misunderstood. Frankfurt's interpretation is discussed in section 2. For conclusions similar to those reached by Frankfurt, see the extensive and richly documented work of Marion, Sur la théologie blanche de Descartes, especially pp. 296–304.

4. The interpretations on which I will be focusing are those of Edwin Curley (1984), Hide Ishiguro (1986), and Harry Frankfurt (1977).

5. To Mersenne, 15 April 1630, AT 1, 145, K, 11. Whenever possible, a multiple reference is given to the texts of Descartes: to Charles Adam and Paul Tannery, eds., Oeuvres de Descartes, 12 vols. (Paris: Leopold Cerf, 1897-1913) (here quoted as AT); to the standard English translation by E. S. Haldane and G. T. Ross, The Philosophical Works of Descartes, 2 vols. (London: Cambridge University Press, 1911, 1978) (cited as HR); and to Anthony Kenny, trans. and ed., Descartes, Philosophical Letters (Oxford: Clarendon Press, 1970) (cited as K).

6. See Francisco Suarez, Disputationes Metaphysicae, reprinted from his Opera Omnia, Vives, Paris 1856-1878 (Hildesheim: G. Olms, 1965), Disp. 31, 2:224–312. The theory endorsed by Suarez corresponds to the view of modality developed by John Duns Scotus and shared by many late medieval thinkers. See, e.g., Timothy J. Cronin, "Eternal Truths in the Thought of Descartes and His Adversary," Journal of the History of Ideas (1960):553–59; Geneviève Rodis-Lewis, L'Oeuvre de Descartes (Paris: J. Vrin, 1971), 1:125–40, and Lewis-Rodis, "Quelques compléments sur la creation des vérites éternelles" in M. Couratier, ed., Etienne Gilson et nous: la philosophie et son histoire (Paris: J. Vrin, 1980), pp. 72–77. Suarez's theory, as Marion has shown, was largely accepted also by Descartes's contemporaries (Jean-Luc Marion, Sur la théologie blanche de Descartes (Paris: P.U.F., 1981), p. 27ff. and passim.

7. Marion takes aut as disjunctive and assimilates this distinction to the one made elsewhere by Descartes between the essence and the existence of

creatures. Anthony Kenny thinks that "the most consistent way to take the expression is as meaning 'necessarily true of actual or possible objects.'" See Marion, *Sur la théologie blanche*, p. 30.; Anthony Kenny, *The God of the Philosophers* (Oxford: Clarendon Press, 1979), pp. 17-18.

8. Cf. L. Alanen, "Descartes, Duns Scotus and Ockham on Omnipotence and Possibility," *Franciscan Studies* 45 (1985), sect. 2; cf. also L. Alanen and S. Knuuttila, "The Foundations of Modality and Conceivability in Descartes and His Predecessors," in *Modern Modalities: Studies of the History of Modal Theories From Medieval Nominalism to Logical Positivism*, ed. Simo Knuuttila (Dordrecht-Holland: Kluwer Academic Publishers, 1988), pp. 1-69.

9. ". . . just as He was free not to create the world, so He was no less free to make it untrue that all the lines drawn from the center of a circle to its circumference are equal" (to Mersenne, 27 May 1630, AT 1, 152, K, 15, cf. AT 7, 435-36, HR 2, 251).

10. "There is no need to ask what category of causality is applicable to the dependence of this goodness upon God, or to the dependence upon him of other truths, both mathematical and metaphysical. For since the various kinds of cause were enumerated by thinkers who did not, perhaps, attend to this type of causality, it is hardly surprising that they gave no name to it. But in fact they did give it a name, for it can be called efficient causality, in the sense that a king may be called the efficient cause of a law, although the law itself is not a thing which has physical existence, but is merely what they call a 'moral entity' "(AT 7, 436, HR 2, 251; cf. To Mersenne, 27 May, K, 15).

11. "Again, there is no need to ask how God could have brought it about from eternity that it was not true that twice four make eight, and so on, for I admit this is unintelligible to us. Yet on the other hand I do understand, quite correctly, that there cannot be any class of entity that does not depend on God; I also understand that it would have been easy for God to ordain certain things such that we men cannot understand the possibility of their being otherwise than they are" (AT 7, 436, HR 2, 251).

12. ST 1a 25, 3. Cf. the papers referred to in note 8 and Marion, *Sur la théologie blanche*, especially note 34, pp. 303ff.

13. Compare the following statements: (1) ". . . I now turn to the difficulty of conceiving how it was free and indifferent for God to make it not be true that the three angles of a triangle were equal to two right angles, or in general that contradictories could not be true together" (To Mesland, 2 May 1644, AT 4, 118, K, 151); (2) "But I do not think that we should ever say of anything that it cannot be brought about by God. For since everything involved in truth and goodness depends on His omnipotence, I would not even dare to say that God cannot make a mountain without a valley, or that one and two should not be three. I merely say that He has given me such a mind that I cannot conceive a mountain without a valley, or an aggregate of one and two which is not three, and that such things involve a contradiction in my conception" (To Arnauld, 29 July 1648, AT 5, 224, K, 236); (3) "I boldly assert that God can do everything which I conceive to be possible, but I am not so bold as to deny that He can do whatever conflicts with my understanding—I merely say that it involves a contradiction" (To More, 5 February 1649, AT 5, 268, K, 241. Cf. AT 7, 436,

HR 2, 251). Cf. also the passage quoted in note 11.

14. Cf. the discussion in Funkenstein (1975).

15. Using the symbolism of modern modal logic, Curley thinks it can be expressed as the thesis that for "any proposition p, p is logically possible" (p) $M(p)$, Curley, "Descartes on the Creation of Eternal Truths," 570.

16. Curley, ibid., 570ff. It is not clear to me who the proponents of this "standard" reading, as it is stated by Curley, are. Curley himself incorrectly attributes it to Harry G. Frankfurt. See note 32.

17. AT 6, 43, HR 1, 108, cf. Curley, "Descartes on the Creation of Eternal Truths," 571–573.

18. AT 11, 47, AT 6, 43, HR 1, 108. Curley notes that Descartes seems in fact to be anticipating the idea of necessary truths as true in all possible worlds usually credited to Leibniz, and insofar as the textual evidence goes, Curley is certainly right that the grounds for crediting Descartes with this idea are as good as those for crediting Leibniz with it. The idea in fact is to be found already in Duns Scotus, although he does not use the term *possible worlds*. One difference between Descartes's notion of several possible worlds and that of Leibniz according to Curley is that Descartes does not seem to conceive his alternative worlds as mutually exclusive (Curley, "Descartes on the Creation of Eternal Truths," 575). Another is that Descartes's God is the creator not only of the actual (world or worlds), but also of any possible world, contrary to the Leibnizian God who chooses to create one (the best) of an infinite number of possible worlds that are given eternally in God's intellect, which Leibniz describes as the "land of possible realities" (G. W. F. Leibniz, *Discours de métaphysique et correspondance avec Arnauld* [Paris: J. Vrin, 1957], pp. 120ff.). Cf. the discussion in Bouveresse, "Théorie du possible chez Descartes," 293–310.

19. Cf. Alanen and Knuuttila, "The Foundations of Modality and Conceivability."

20. Curley, "Descartes on the Creation of Eternal Truths," 581–83, 589ff. Instead of the formula $(p)M(p)$, representing what Curley takes to be the "standard" interpretation of Descartes's doctrine we would have (p) $MM(p)$. Curley thinks an exception must be made for the truths concerning God's nature, which Descartes holds to be not contingently but "necessarily necessary," that creates the additional difficulty of accounting for the relation between two sets of necessary truths, those which are necessarily necessary and those which are contingently necessary. Curley, ibid., 581–83 and 589ff. I have discussed this interpretation in my "Descartes, Duns Scotus and Ockham on Omnipotence."

21. See Plantinga, *Does God Have a Nature?* pp. 112–13.

22. Plantinga, *Does God Have a Nature?* pp. 112–13, 103–104.

23. Ishiguro, "Status of Necessity and Impossibility," pp. 463–64; cf. Guéroult, *Descartes selon l'ordre des raisons*, 2:39, and Bouveresse, "La théorie du possible."

24. Ishiguro, "Status of Necessity," 460–61.

25. Ishiguro, ibid., 467. Descartes, Ishiguro argues, never asserts that a logically inconsistent affirmative proposition, e.g., "2 + 3 = 6," could be a necessary truth, or that God could have made it the case that 2 + 3 = 6. What he says is that God could have made necessary truths not to be true (Ishiguro, ibid., p. 460.) Support for this is provided, e.g., by the quote given in note 9. Passage

(1) quoted in note 13 is obviously problematic for this interpretation. It continues: ". . . It is easy to dispel this difficulty by considering that the power of God cannot have any limits, and that our mind is finite and so created as to be able to conceive as possible only things which God has wished to be truly possible, but not to be able to conceive as possible things which God could have made possible, but which he has nonetheless wished to make impossible. The first consideration shows us that God cannot have been determined to make it true that contradictories cannot be (true) together, and therefore he could have done the opposite. The second consideration shows us that even if this be true, we should not try to comprehend it since our nature is incapable of doing so." (To Mesland, 2 May 1644, AT 4, 118, K, 151).

26. The evidence Ishiguro invokes—the discussion of error in Meditation 4— is, at best, inconclusive. See Ishiguro, "Status of Necessity," 468-69.

27. Ishiguro, ibid., 468.

28. Cf. the difficult passage in the letter to Mesland, AT 4, 118-19, K, 151, and the discussion in Frankfurt, "Descartes on the Creation of Eternal Truths."

29. E.g., "2 + 2 = 5," or "1 + 2 = 4." Ishiguro, "Status of Necessity," 467.

30. Frankfurt, "Descartes on the Creation of Eternal Truths," 45. This, as I understand it, is not to say that the necessity of these truths is epistemic in the sense of relative to our subjective state of knowledge or to other historical conditions. If they can be characterized as subjective at all it is, presumably, in a Kantian sense of relative to any rational mind: they constitute a kind of a priori conditions of rational thinking and science.

31. Frankfurt, "Descartes on the Creation of Eternal Truths," 44. Cf. Marion, *Sur la théologie blanche*, pp. 296-303.

32. Curley, "Descartes on the Creation of Eternal Truths," 570. It does not, as Harry Frankfurt has pointed out to me, attribute to Descartes the claim that there are no necessary truths the denial of which involves contradiction, but takes him to claim merely that the necessary truths do not constitute a priori limits of what God can conceive or do. See Harry Frankfurt, "Descartes on the Creation of Eternal Truths," 42ff.

33. What contradicts our concepts is inconceivable to us, but nothing justifies the assumption that what is inconceivable to us is impossible to God. See, e.g., AT 4, 118-19, K, 151; AT 7, 152, HR 2, 46-47.

34. This "modern" view of modality is expressed in its most radical form in the idea that the only necessity is verbal or linguistic necessity. The first explicit identification of necessity with analyticity has been traced to the writings of Duns Scotus. Cf. Calvin Normore,"Ockham, Possibility and the Past," forthcoming, *Franciscan Studies* 45, and Simo Knuuttila, "Time and Morality in Scholasticism," in *Reforging the Great Chain of Being*, ed. S. Knuuttila (Dordrecht: D. Reidel Publishing Co., 1981), p. 225 nn. 151, 170.

35. Suarez, *Disputationes metaphysicae* 31, xii, 40, *Opera omnia*, vol. 35 (Paris 1866; reprinted Hildesheim: Georg Olms, 1965). See Alanen, "Descartes, Duns Scotus and Ockham," and Alanen and Knuuttila, *Modern Modalities*.

36. Cf. the passage quoted on p. 183 above which continues: "It is easy to be mistaken about this because most men do not regard God as an infinite and incomprehensible being, the sole author on whom all things depend; . . . Those

who have no higher thoughts than these can easily become atheists; and because they perfectly comprehend mathematical truths and do not perfectly comprehend the truth of God's existence, it is no wonder that they do not think that the former depend on the latter. But they should rather judge on the contrary, that since God is a cause whose power surpasses the bounds of human understanding, and since the necessity of these truths does not exceed our knowledge, they must be something less than, and subject to, the incomprehensible power of God" (To Mersenne, 6 May 1630, AT 1, 148, K, 13-14).

37. In God, Descartes insists, "willing, understanding and creating are all the same thing without one being prior to the other even conceptually" (ne quidem ratione) (To Mersenne, 27 May 1630, K, 15).

38. "In God willing and knowing are one single thing so that *by the very fact of willing something he knows it and it is only for this reason that such a thing is true.*" The passage in italics is written in Latin. To Mersenne, 6 May 1630, AT 1, 149, K, 13-14.

39. See, e.g., Frankfurt, "Descartes on the Creation of Eternal Truths," pp. 53ff.

40. Leaving God out of this account of the foundation of necessary truths, Descartes's view, on the interpretation here defended, is not very different from the position taken by Georg Henrik von Wright in his recent writings on logical truth and modality. See G. H. von Wright, *Truth, Knowledge and Modality*, vol. 3 of *Philosophical Papers* (Oxford: Basil Blackwell, 1984), pp. 104-16. I am grateful to Georg Henrik von Wright for having drawn my attention to this. Descartes's position could, with certain reservations, be seen as a first step towards modern "conventionalist" or "linguistic" views of modality.

Commentary on Lilli Alanen's "Descartes, Omnipotence, and Kinds of Modality"

George I. Mavrodes

One's initial reaction to Descartes's scattered comments about the eternal truths is likely to be that the position he seems to espouse is incoherent, and that it would be fatal to his own rationalistic projects in science and metaphysics. In the previous paper, Lilli Alanen claims that Descartes's position is *not* incoherent, and that it is not irrationalist. For all I know, Alanen might be right about that. I think that I do not really understand the proposed interpretation well enough to tell—nor do I sufficiently understand the Frankfurt interpretation to which it is closely related. This paper of mine is an attempt to generate a somewhat clearer idea of these interpretations.

My strategy here will be to propose what I take to be an anti-Cartesian thesis about the structure of the human intellect. I will call it the "Madman's Thesis." Then I will suggest, and explore briefly, some possible Cartesian rejoinders to this thesis. Perhaps then Alanen, or other Cartesian scholars, can identify one of these as the genuine Cartesian position. Or if not, then perhaps they will suggest some other rejoinder that I have not thought of.

Well, what is the Madman's Thesis? Put briefly it is

(MT) The structure of the human intellect (though perhaps not its scope) is identical with that of the divine intellect.

I intend this thesis to entail that the acts of God should satisfy the criteria of intelligibility to which our own rational thinking conforms. Human minds and the divine mind alike are bound to the same set, or sets, of possibilities. The standard of rationality, that is, the one God has willed and imposed on our minds, is the very same standard that is shared by the divine intellect.

You will recognize that the language with which I have chosen to express and expand the Madman's Thesis is taken from page 191 of Alanen's paper in this volume. I have done that in order to formulate a thesis that is incompatible with the position that Alanen there attributes to Descartes. I intend MT to assert some of the things that Alanen explicitly denies, or vice versa.

The Madman's Thesis, however, does not deny everything that Alanen asserts. As I understand it, Alanen's version of Descartes's position includes three elements or claims. They are

(1) The truth and/or the necessity of the "eternal truths" is/are a function of the structure of the intellect that considers those propositions and may be different relative to different intellects.

(2) The structure of created intellects is determined by God, and it was (is?) within the power of God to give those intellects a structure different from the one they actually have.

(3) Finite minds—or human minds, at any rate—have a structure radically different from that of the divine mind.

The Madman's Thesis is intended to be incompatible with the third element of this set.

I attribute this thesis to a madman because I want to think of it as being put forward without supporting argument, without a reason. It is just a madman's raving, but even a madman, I suppose, may sometimes rave the truth. Might MT be the truth after all?

I can imagine some possible Cartesian rejoinders to MT. One of them would be

(CR 1) We know that MT is false, because God *could not* create a finite mind with the same structure as His own infinite mind.

You will recall that on page 191 Alanen ascribes to some anti-Cartesian the view that God *could not* have created a human mind whose structure did not resemble that of His own infinite mind. My madman, of course, has not asserted any thesis nearly that strong. He has claimed only that God *did not* create human minds with a different structure from that of the divine mind. Here it is the Cartesian whom I imagine putting forward the strongly modalized proposition: he claims (perhaps, indeed, with some reason?) that the structure of the divine intellect *cannot* be mirrored in a finite human intellect. To create a human mind of that sort is completely beyond the power of God.

I said that I could imagine CR 1 as a Cartesian rejoinder to MT, but perhaps that was too hasty. For on second thought, does not CR 1 seem to be completely lacking in the Cartesian spirit? Would not the assertion of CR 1 by a Cartesian seem to imply that this Cartesian— a human being, after all—has identified an impossibility that binds even the omnipotence of God? So, at least, it would seem to me. So CR 1 does not appear to be promising for the Cartesian.

Let us try something else.

> (CR 2) We know that MT is false because we know that in fact God has created human intellects with a structure not shared by His own intellect.

This rejoinder is similar to CR 1, but without the introduction of impossibility. It claims only that God did not do something, not that He could not have done it.

CR 2 may have several variants. Some Cartesian, for example, may claim to know that the structure of the divine mind differs from that of the human. Relative to our intellect, "1 + 2 = 3" is a necessary truth; but relative to God's intellect, it might be claimed "1 + 2 = 3" is false. Or perhaps, though it is true, it is not *necessarily* true. If we knew either of these things then we would have reason to think that divine and human minds differ radically in their structure.

It might be held, on the other hand, that the difference between the divine and the human mind consists of the fact that the divine mind has *no structure* at all. Standards of rationality, and things of that sort, are imposed by God on His creation, but He Himself has no analog to them at all. He does not embody a different standard; he embodies *no* standard. Therefore, relative to the divine intellect, "1 + 2 = 3" is neither necessary or contingent nor impossible, and it is there neither true nor false.

Perhaps CR 2 is not so lacking in the Cartesian spirit as its predecessor. Maybe, in fact, it embodies that spirit rather fully. Its main difficulty—for me anyway—is that of finding any plausibility in the suggestion that we might know any such thing as that "1 + 2 = 3" is false (or contingent, etc.) relative to the divine mind. How is a Cartesian supposed to discover the divine mathematics? How could we come to any such knowledge? But if we do not have such knowledge, then we would seem to have no reason for thinking that CR 2 is true.

In a letter that Alanen quotes, Descartes says that God could make (or could have made?) it untrue that all the radii of a circle are equal (page 186). On the Alanen interpretation, as I understand it, this means that it is (or was?) within the power of God to create human intellects with different propensities from the ones they actually now have. We might have had, that is, a propensity to accept different geometrical axioms, or different patterns of arithmetic. If we had those different propensities, then we would accept different propositions as necessary truths. Well, maybe it is within the power of God to create intellects of that sort; but that seems to have nothing to do with the question of what sort of intellect God Himself has. Consequently it cannot settle the question of whether the human intellect, the way in which it actually is right now, does or does not mirror the divine intellect. But CR 2 commits us to a claim about the factual relationship between divine and human intellects.

This might suggest a third possible rejoinder, one that retreats somewhat from the categorical force of its predecessors:

(CR 3) We don't know whether MT is true or false.

With this rejoinder the Cartesian may turn the tables, challenging any defender of MT to produce a reason in support of it. How, that is, has the madman managed to probe into the divine epistemology and rationality? A good question, no doubt, but I have already said that the madman, my madman anyway, will have no answer to this. He has no reason for MT—it is just a raving. That is why he is a madman. But CR 3 suggests that the Cartesian, having turned the tables, must now find himself in the same boat. After all, if he had a good reason for a thesis contrary to MT, then he would be in position to know that MT was false. If he just doesn't know whether MT is true or false, then he must not have any satisfactory reason for a thesis contrary to MT. If he holds such a thesis anyway, then he must be no better off, in this regard, than the madman.

Now, maybe Descartes is in that position (on Alanen's interpretation). He has a hunch that the divine intellect is radically different from that of humans, but he has no reason to back up that hunch. Or maybe there is some entirely different way to go, some way that I haven't thought of. Maybe, indeed, such a way will develop out of our discussion here.

Part Four
Kant

What—If Anything—
Is Transcendental Synthesis?

John I. Biro

1

It is an interesting irony that the great influence Kantian ideas continue to exert on contemporary philosophy is accompanied by a frequent dismissal of much of what he actually wrote as scientifically outdated and philosophically confused. One example is the oft-heard accusation that he is held captive by an outmoded and sterile picture of logic, one that places strains on one of the central parts of the critical philosophy, the doctrine of the categories. Another, the one I shall discuss in this paper, involves the theory of transcendental synthesis, a part of his philosophy Kant himself regarded as one of the most important.[1] Many think that Kant's position in the latter case is as unsalvageable as in the former. The theory of synthesis has been dismissed, and not only by historically insensitive readers, as expressing his commitment to an obsolete scientific framework in general, and to the hopelessly wrongheaded project— Strawson calls it "the imaginary subject"—of transcendental psychology in particular. Subtle and sympathetic a commentator as he is, Strawson has dismissed the doctrine of the threefold synthesis as an "aberration" and has recommended that we purge Kant's philosophy of it, much as we would chemistry of alchemy. Only thus, he urges, can we come to appreciate the revolutionary character of the critical philosophy, which is to have anticipated twentieth-century conceptual analysis:

> Whenever [Kant] found limiting or necessary general features of experience he declared their source to lie in our own cognitive constitution; and this doctrine he considered indispensable as an explanation of the possibility of knowledge of the necessary structure of experience. Yet there is no doubt that this doctrine is incoherent in itself and masks, rather than explains, the real character of his inquiry; so that the central problem in understanding

the *Critique* is precisely that of disentangling all that hangs on this doctrine from the analytical argument which is in fact independent of it.[2]

It is true that Kant thought of himself as investigating the general structure of ideas and principles which is presupposed in all our empirical knowledge but he thought of this investigation as possible only because he conceived of it also, and primarily, as an investigation into the structure and workings of the cognitive capacities of beings such as ourselves.[3]

Strawson is not alone in taking a dim view of Kant's project understood in this way. Jonathan Bennett distinguishes a "genetic" and an "analytic" interpretation of the doctrine of transcendental synthesis. The picture of synthesis drawn by the former is much like the version Strawson criticizes, a picture Bennett describes in similarly unfriendly terms, progressing from "a mistake" through "desperately unpromising" to "a quagmire."[4] In a more recent discussion of the B deduction as refutation of Cartesian skepticism, Edwin McCann endorses the strategy of dispensing with "the hoary transcendental psychology in terms of which Kant tended to put his points," especially the claim "that there are atemporal acts of transcendental synthesis," which he, too, regards as merely obscuring the lines of Kant's real and deeper analytical argument.[5]

Out of date as Kant's psychology undoubtedly is, I think it is not uninteresting to speculate on its similarities with, if not anticipations of, psychological theories we take very seriously today. Be that as it may, whether his philosophical doctrines can be sterilized in the way Strawson suggests is another, and more serious, question. I have, in an earlier paper, argued that they cannot, and that in excising the theory of synthesis from his account of experience we are throwing out the philosophical baby along with the transcendental bath-water.[6] I urged that Kant's speculations about synthetic activity are not only central to his philosophy of experience but are also philosophically well motivated: no experience of the sort we actually have could occur without some active contribution from us of the sort he postulates. Thus the doctrine of transcendental synthesis, as developed in the A deduction especially, must be taken seriously and accorded a central rôle in our understanding of Kant's philosophy.

Doing so, of course, leads to a difficulty, which is one of the chief reasons why commentators such as Strawson and Bennett wish to have no truck with the genetic interpretation of the theory of synthetic activity. Again, I quote Strawson:

The theory of synthesis, like any essay in transcendental psychology, is exposed to the *ad hominem* objection that we can claim no empirical knowledge of its truth; for this would be to claim empirical knowledge of the occurrence of that which is held to be the antecedent condition of empirical knowledge.[7]

The difficulty is actually deeper. Not only can we not have empirical knowledge about synthesis—this would not be too worrying in itself, since Kant surely allows for other kinds of philosophical knowledge. The real trouble is that it is hard to see how transcendental synthesis can be thought of as taking place in the phenomenal world at all, as it clearly must be if it is to be assigned the kind of causal-constitutive rôle vis-à-vis experience the "genetic" interpretation envisages for it.

This is the problem I wish to address in this paper. I shall argue that on the most plausible construal in modern terms of transcendental synthesis, namely, as the workings of the nervous system, this seemingly fatal difficulty may not in fact be insuperable.

2

Contemporary cognitive psychology tells us much about the mechanisms of experience, about how various mental processes—mostly non-conscious—are related to the phenomena of consciousness, perception, memory, concept formation, belief fixation, and so on. So did Kant—about some of these, at least. His transcendental story involved the whole machinery of the categories, synthesis and schematization. As we have seen, some balk at taking some of that story literally, despite Kant's talk of this machinery as *productive* of experience; they urge us to regard it only as an archaic way of groping one's way toward an *analysis* of its conceptually necessary features.

Contemporary neurophysiology tells us something about the various physical processes that may underlie the mental process the cognitive psychologist talks about. These physical processes, too, are conceived of as *productive* of those parts of our mental life that Kant is referring to when he uses the term "experience" (or its variant, "empirical knowledge"). And in spite of some well-known and powerful arguments to the contrary, some still cherish the hope that a mature cognitive science may be able to tell us how the laws governing psychological processes are related to the physical laws governing physiological ones, on the assumption that, at some level, they describe the same things. The thing they describe is, on this picture, a member in good standing of the phenomenal world. Hence our problem: this thing cannot be what Kant's transcendental story is about. That story must be about something "outside" the world of phenomena, and the application of causal language to it is, if taken literally, a category mistake from which we must save Kant by reinterpreting him.

The proposal to straightforwardly identify transcendental synthesis with neural processes is an alternative to this defeatist conclusion. To make the proposal plausible, I must show that, contrary to first appearance, such an identification may not be incompatible with the critical turn. If that is correct, we may continue to take seriously Kant's talk of the *productive* rôle of transcendental synthesis.

Such a proposal of course raises complex questions about the interpretation of many aspects of Kant's philosophy, and it is not possible in a paper of this length to do justice to all of them. So I shall restrict my discussion in several, I hope not too misleading, ways. I shall consider only the kind of synthetic activity involved in the perception of the external world, and in the most basic levels of such perception at that. Thus the focus will be, as it is in at least some of Kant's own discussions (most notably in the A deduction section on the threefold synthesis), on what is minimally involved in perceiving the sort of enduring physical objects we naturally take to populate the external world. No doubt that level of perception is accompanied—"suffused" might be a better word— by layers of the more complicated and reflective mental activity normally yielding the much richer actual perceptual and conceptual content of our experience, with all its sortal and aspectual discriminations and inferential potential. But we can still distinguish those aspects of synthesis that are responsible for the most basic and necessary elements of that experience, necessary in that without them the objectivity that is its hallmark would be missing. It is, I think, to these elements that Kant is addressing himself in the threefold synthesis described in the A deduction, especially in its first two levels, and it is with these that I am concerned here.[8]

This, perhaps artificially narrow, focus on basic perception will still allow us to evaluate the central objection to my proposed identification of Kant's transcendental synthesis with the activity of the nervous system. What I shall seek to show is that we can indeed make this identification without doing violence to an important aspect of Kant's thought, namely, a sharp conceptual separation of the phenomenal from the transcendental.[9]

3

Kant himself was not unaware of the issue. There is evidence that he was quite willing to take seriously proposals of the sort I am advancing, though he could not see a way of solving the difficulty they carried with them.

In 1796, a famous German anatomist, Samuel Thomas von Sömmerring, published a book with the title *Über das Organ der Seele,* concerning his researches into the structure of the brain and the rôle of "brain-water" in both the operations of the various sense organs and in the unification of these operations in one consciousness.[10] As Kant, to whom Sömmerring had sent the manuscript prior to publication and whose comments on it were included by the author as an appendix, put it:

> we have to do . . . with the material which makes possible the unification of all sense presentations in the mind. The only material which is so qualified (as *sensorium commune*) is, according to the discovery made through your profound anatomical skill, contained in the brain cavities and is mere water. This is the immediate organ of the soul which, on the one hand, separates the nerve-bundles terminating there, so that the sensations conveyed through these are not confounded with one another and, on the other hand, effects a thoroughgoing community between these . . . .[11]

In the remainder of his letter, Kant, not unnaturally, goes on to point out to Sömmerring the essential incommensurability between an attempt to give a physiological account of these separating and unifying functions of the nervous system and a philosophical argument concerning the need for a unified consciousness in experience. He expresses qualms about locating "the unity of self-consciousness (which belongs to the understanding) in the spatial relations of the soul to the organs of the brain (which belongs to outer sense)." This project, one common in precritical metaphysics, is essentially that of giving a "local presence" (= spatial location) to an entity experienceable only in inner sense (= time)—a task not only insoluble by metaphysics, but in itself contradictory:

> the desired solution to the problem of the seat of the soul, which was expected from metaphysics, leads to an impossible magnitude $(\sqrt{-2})$, and one can exclaim to whomever undertakes to solve it, in the words of Terence, "You will get no further with that than if you tried to be sanely insane."[12]

4

The stumbling block Kant is here calling to Sömmerring's attention is, of course, the very same one Strawson is emphasizing, one that seems to present an insuperable difficulty for the project of using neurophysiological knowledge in a properly Kantian theory of experience, no matter how much more sophisticated such knowledge may be nowadays. Any attempt to think of the transcendental "machinery"—responsible, in the Kantian account, for experience—as the physical machine investigated by the neurophysiologist must, it seems, run into this seemingly fatal objection. Given the general principles of the critical philosophy, the attempt involves a gigantic category mistake. The behind-the-scenes synthetic activities of the understanding and of the imagination are not and cannot be themselves *objects* of experience—only their *products* ("appearances" = objects) are. On the other hand, the brain and the whole nervous system and its workings are themselves appearances, proper phenomenal objects, located in space and time. We can observe them as we observe any other empirical object. To do so is indeed the business of the neurophysiologist; but nothing in his observations can yield knowledge about the transcendentally presupposed—and transcendent-to-experience—activities on which *all* observation depends. Thus, the nervous system and the transcendental machinery *cannot* be identical, since they are radically different sorts of entities (if, indeed, the latter can be said to be an *entity* at all).

Yet with our increasing knowledge about the nervous system and the part it plays in producing experience, the temptation to use that knowledge in understanding synthesis and *its* productive rôle is not hard to explain. First, there is the reluctance I have already expressed to jettison the entire transcendental story as hopelessly metaphorical, obscure, obsolete, and incoherent. Surely, attempting to reinterpret it in contemporary terms, even if the attempt is necessarily somewhat speculative, has more interest than turning one's back on it entirely. Second, there is a desire in some way to extend physical explanation to the realm of the mental, as part of a generally physicalist outlook to which we might like to read Kant as being as committed to as are we (a commitment his response to Sömmerring indeed suggests). Third, a narrower, but perhaps more compelling, reason: there appear to be striking similarities between the effects we would expect to follow from certain kinds of malfunctioning in the nervous system, on the one hand, and what Kant tells us about the consequences of a failure of transcendental synthesis, on the other.

Consider what Kant calls "recognition in a concept." This is required for normal experience in the sense of subsuming our possible sensations both under the "concept of an object in general" (the "transcendental object") and under the empirical concept of this or that particular (kind of) object. Without such recognition (or at least the former of these), Kant suggests, our "experience" would not be experience, but "a rhapsody of sensations." Compare this with the sort of description of "experience" one sometimes hears in cases involving some malfunctioning of, or interference with, certain parts of the brain. These suggest that if the pattern of firings among one's synapses is abnormal, the world may no longer be experienced as a world of distinct and independent objects, but rather as a "world" that is a succession of changing states of one's self. Conversely, the sense of the self, that unity of consciousness which looms so large in the B deduction, is sometimes said to go missing as a result of alterations in the normal functioning of the brain, leading to what is sometimes called a "merging" of self and world. In such cases, it does not seem implausible to suggest that the same phenomena are being addressed by the transcendental philosopher and the empirical scientist, albeit from different points of view, the first perhaps focusing more on effects, the second more on causes.

Thus it may not be too fanciful to suggest that the sort of features that are, on Kant's view, necessarily involved in our experience—roughly, certain kinds of objectivity and unity—are very much the features that go missing if the nervous system fails to function properly. In fact, this is a very weak claim: some such connection would be recognized by any reasonable account of the mental. The special feature of Kant's version of the claim is the insistence on locating the sources of objectivity and unity in synthetic *activity*. This is why he suggests that the failure of such activity, that is, the failure of some or all of the levels of the synthesis he describes in the A deduction, would reduce the subject to a "rhapsody of sensations."

5

Kant's own rejection of the possibility of a physiological account of the sort Sömmerring offers is, of course, to be seen in the context of the science of his day and cannot be taken as indicating what his response would be to more recent developments. But the fact that he is clearly willing to take Sömmerring's efforts seriously is prima facie evidence that he would be at least willing to entertain more sophisticated versions of a physiological construal of synthesis, if only he could see a way around what we might call the critical objection. If it can be shown that that objection is not compelling, *we* can cheerfully accept a neurophysiological account without feeling that we are thereby losing the insights of the critical philosophy.

I want to suggest that the key to doing so lies in relativizing the empirical/transcendental distinction to individual subjects. When worrying about what can or cannot be part of our knowledge, as the objection bids us do, we should note the plural pronoun in expressions such as "our knowledge" and "our experience" that figure prominently in the usual formulations of the objection. That pronoun hides a complexity that, once recognized, can be seen to yield the key to the apparent paradox. In order to see this, we have to bear in mind the limitation I have imposed on how "knowledge" is to be understood in the context of this discussion. Whatever kinds—inferential, theoretical, etc.—of knowledge other than basic perception may count as empirical in Kant's (or anyone else's) sense, and whatever the extent to which such kinds of knowledge about my nervous system may be available to both you and me, it seems that *perception* of the relevant aspects of the workings of that nervous system is not possible in the same way for the two of us. The knowledge *in that sense* that you can have with respect to the workings of my nervous system may not be knowledge that I can have of it (and so, of course, in reverse).

First, it seems that there are contingent reasons why I can never have empirical knowledge of those activities of my nervous system that have an allegedly transcendental function vis à vis my current experience. For even if I could observe the firings of my own synapses, etc., the firings I would be observing would not be identical with those firings involved in and responsible for these very observings. What I would be observing would be some *past* (if only fractionally past) firings. It seems physically impossible for me to "catch up" perceptually with my own nervous activity (just as in the more standard perceptual situation I do not see the movement of my hand until fractionally after it has begun)—and this because of perfectly general physical laws concerning the speed of light and of electrical impulses.

While this physical impossibility is of course a merely empirical fact, it is nevertheless enough, I suggest, to recommend relativizing the empirical/transcendental distinction. However, this way of drawing the distinction is unsatisfactory for at least three reasons. First, the time lag responsible for the physical impossibility of observing the nervous activity producing present experience extends to third parties, too. I cannot observe the events in *your* nervous system that are involved in your experience *now*, until fractionally after they occur. What I observe now are events relating to earlier—if only slightly earlier—experience. (This would also be true of you, were you to observe those events in the way I do, as in principle you might.) Second, for reasons closely related to the last point, on this way of drawing the empirical/transcendental distinction, we could apply it only to an experience-at-a-moment. Third, and most important, it would be nice if one could also argue that the physical impossibility is paralleled by some stronger conceptual barrier, especially in view of Kant's typical concern with necessities rather than mere contingencies. Add to this the fact that Kant believed the speed of light to be infinite, and the need for a construal of the impossibility of experiencing the relevant events in one's nervous system as something stronger than mere physical impossibility becomes even more pressing.

Is there, then, some deeper reason to think that that which is transcendentally necessary for experience cannot itself be part of the content of that experience? I think so, though I have to admit that I don't know how to make a case that Kant had anything like it in mind. When we talk, as we earlier saw Strawson doing, about transcendental activity being "antecedent" or "prior" to experience, what sort of priority do we have in mind? It would be unfair to deny to the real Kant the very nontemporal sense of priority that Strawson allows his proto-analyst Kant. We could, instead, say the following. The reason why I cannot observe my *observings* resides not in some physical fact—perhaps we *could* do it with mirrors—but in the fact that even when I observe the events in my nervous system that cause those very observings, I can do so only through their effects, namely, by having the experience they cause. This is not so when I observe your observings, even though, of course, I must be doing that, too, through *my* observings. But the direct effects of what I observe in the latter case are beyond me, as it were: *they* can never be part of my experience.[13]

There is thus a fundamental asymmetry between the access I have to my own synthetic activity and that which you have to it, and it is this asymmetry that the relativized empirical/transcendental distinction captures. It is not that I cannot observe my own brain as an empirical object: it is that I cannot observe it in its relevant function, *qua* synthesizer. It is in that function that synthesis is transcendental with respect to the experience it produces. This does *not* mean that it is transcendent in the bad noncritical sense, something inexperienceable, outside the phenomenal realm. The brain events that produce *my* experience do, however, transcend *that* experience: this is what is meant by saying that they are transcendental *for me.*

You, of course, can observe my brain also only as an empirical object. In this we are alike, and since the brain *is* an empirical object, so we should be. The difference is that for you, there is nothing to which it is transcendental, since its workings are not causally connected with your experience.[14]

So perhaps we have found a way of grounding the kind of relativization of the empirical/transcendental distinction I am recommending on more than contingent facts such as the speed of light. If so, we may, I suggest, have taken the sting out of the objection to physicalizing synthesis that both Kant and Strawson saw as insuperable. The objection rested on the assumption that if the nervous system is part of the phenomenal world, from which it follows that our knowledge of it must be empirical, we can no longer hold that *one's own* knowledge of the necessarily transcendent-to-experience activity of one's nervous system is—and must be—merely transcendental. But once this assumption, hidden by the ambiguity of the phrase "our experience," is spelled out, it may be seen to be unwarranted; for it takes no account of the special circumstance of the knower's relation to his own nervous system, a circumstance that necessarily permits only transcendental knowledge on his part of the relevant activities of that system. This is true for each of us, so that there is a sense in which the knowledge each of us has of these of activities is and must be *through* the experience to which they relate, even if we can have no such knowledge of them as *part* of the content of that experience. In this sense are they "outside" experience, a sense captured by Kant's term "transcendental." So understood, the transcendentality of synthesis, far from standing in the way of identifying it with the workings of the nervous system, is just what makes such identification plausible. Indeed, the point of this identification is to draw attention to just this feature of experience: that its dependence on synthetic activities that lie "outside" it has a remarkable parallel in the dependence scientific discovery has shown it to have on the activities of the nervous system. There is no reason whatever for thinking these two kinds of dependence to be incompatible rather than complementary.

6

Among the many objections that may be leveled against this admittedly rather speculative account, the following is, to my mind, the most serious. Isn't this talk of neural events taking place in a world of real space and time dogmatic metaphysics of precisely the sort the critical turn was designed to take us away from? How, then, can we give a Kantian answer to the skeptic who exploits the ever-present possibility of a gap between the cognizer's picture of the world and the way the world really is? According to the skeptic, one may experience spatially and temporally, with space and time only subjectively real; one may think that every event has a cause, when it doesn't. If so, one's beliefs about the world could not reflect synthetic a priori truths about that world, in the way that Kant thinks some of them do. Whatever gains my interpretation may garner us in understanding Kant's doctrine of synthesis, it does so at an unacceptable price, if it makes the closing of this gap between the subjective and the objective impossible.

However, I don't think the objection is decisive. Perhaps we *can* have our cake and eat it, too. The fact that from a subjective point of view it is impossible *to tell* that one's experiences are really of an objective world doesn't mean that they aren't so and, more importantly, that they aren't so *necessarily*. We can argue, as Kant does, that in order for one's experience to be the way it is, it *must* relate to such a world in such and such a way (else it couldn't *be* that way). But one's experience does not *create* the world to which it must so relate. Kant is no solipsist trying to get out to a shared, public world. (Nor does he worry about other minds much, interestingly enough.) He is an empirical realist describing the relation between subjective experience and the real world. That world, of course, cannot be conceived of by any of us in terms other than those that derive from our subjective experience and constitution. But this doesn't mean that every part of the world must be open to every single experience, much less that only those that are comprise it. My brain is part of *the* empirical world whether or not *I* experience it as an empirical object, as long as cognizers constituted much like I am do. Its workings are responsible for my experience of other parts of that same world, whether I know this or not. And they are transcendental, in a perfectly good sense, *to* my experience, even to my experience of it *qua* phenomenal object, should I have such. There is, then, no need to read Kant as confusedly talking about admittedly unintelligible things such as "the atemporal workings of noumenal mechanisms" (Bennett) or "atemporal acts of synthesis" (McCann). It is a virture of the interpretation offered here that we can take his talk of combining, unifying, producing, etc., literally, referring to perfectly ordinary, though nonconscious, non-reflective (in modern parlance, subpersonal, subdoxastic) acts of the experiencing subject that have a very special relation—intimate yet external, in a word, transcendental —to the subject's experience.

7

In this short paper I have been able to do no more than suggest a direction one might take in dealing with the chief difficulty that seems to stand in the way of our taking seriously both Kant's claims about transcendental synthesis and the attractions of seeing some aspects of his philosophy of mind and epistemology in the context of modern neuroscience. In doing so, I have virtually ignored those aspects of Kant's account of mental functioning that can be seen as constituting an argument against a Cartesian or Humean skeptic. Some will say that this is to ignore what is philosophically most interesting about that account. They may be right. But there is also a *theory of experience*, one that is surprisingly in line with modern theories about it, and it is one that is not un-Kantian philosophically, as many commentators allege. Taking it seriously means making the antiskeptical assumption all scientific theorizing requires. It means naturalizing Kant's epistemology and philosophy of mind much as we want to do our own these days. Not all of Kant is captured this way, but interesting things are that otherwise would not be.[15] In particular, I have suggested that one and the same process—synthesis—can be both phenomenal and transcendental-for-a-subject, and thus both empirically and transcendentally knowable—though from different points of view. Put the other way around, we can see how something that is transcendental for a particular knower can be part of the phenomenal world that is shared by many. So we do not have to worry about the question, which would otherwise be very reasonable and, as far as I can see, unanswerable, "Well, if it's not part of the phenomenal world, what world *is* it part of?"[16] To talk about activities transcendental to my experience is a legitimate way of talking about some things that are—and must be—

part of *the world I experience,* even if they are not—and cannot be—part of *my experience of that world.*

Thus perhaps we *can* avoid the uncomfortable dilemma Strawson and other critics pose for us. The options they give are both unattractive. On the one hand, we can opt for the "more acceptable face of the *Critique*," the face of conceptual analysis, providing "the framework of a truly empiricist philosophy, freed . . . from the delusions of transcendent metaphysics." On the other, we can take the work seriously "as an investigation into the structure and workings of the cognitive capacities of beings such as ourselves" and pay the price of having to swallow its "more questionable doctrines": a metaphysics at odds with empiricism.[17] What I have suggested is that these are not our only options; in fact, that we, and Kant, *can* have it both ways.[18]

NOTES

1. Not the most important: of the "two sides" of the transcendental deduction (emphasized in the A and the B versions, respectively), the objective side is clearly held to be more central by Kant. Nevertheless, he regards the entire two-sided deduction as a unity and as together forming the core of the critical philosophy. (Preface to the first edition of the *Critique of Pure Reason,* A xvi-xvii. In citing from the *Critique,* I shall use the Kemp Smith translation.)

2. P. F. Strawson, *The Bounds of Sense* (London: Methuen, 1966), p. 32 et passim. Strawson's general approach is shared by many others, including Jonathan Bennett (see his *Kant's Analytic* [Cambridge: Cambridge University Press, 1966]) and M. Gram (in *Kant, Ontology and the A Priori* [Evanston, Ill.: Northwestern University Press, 1968]). For a contrary view, see Lewis White Beck's "Lewis' Kantianism" in Beck's *Studies in the Philosophy of Kant* (New York: Methuen, 1965).

3. Strawson, *Bounds of Sense*, p. 19.

4. Bennett, *Kant's Analytic*, pp. 111-13.

5. Edwin McCann, "Scepticism and Kant's B Deduction," *History of Philosophy Quarterly* 2, no. 2 (January 1985): 71.

6. J. I. Biro, "Kant and Strawson on Transcendental Synthesis," *The New Scholasticism* 53, no. 4 (Autumn 1979).

7. Strawson, *Bounds of Sense* p. 32.

8. *Critique of Pure Reason*, A98-106. In an earlier passage, Kant had defined synthesis as "the act of putting different representations together, and of grasping what is manifold in them in one [act of] knowledge" (A77=B103). He goes on to insist that this activity occurs mostly at the subconscious level, much as the processes of interest to the cognitive psychologist and the neurophysiologist do.

9. This separation lines up with the distinction between the contingent a posteriori and the necessary a priori components of our knowledge. Any interpretation of Kant, however adventurous in other respects, must respect this fundamental division: I shall claim that, contrary to first expectation, an interpretation of synthesis along neurophysiological lines *can* do so.

10. Sömmerring sent a copy of his manuscript to Kant, who acknowledged it in a highly complimentary letter on November 1790 (*Kant's Gesammelte Schriften,* Band XIII [Briefwechsel, Band III], Brief 671, pp. 30-35 [Königliche Preussischen Akademie der Wissenschaften]). Kant attached to this letter of acknowledgment some remarks on the manuscript, giving Sömmerring permission to make them public. When Sömmerring came to publish his work, he appended Kant's remarks to it, dedicating the book to "Our Kant."

11. The text of Kant's remarks is to be found on pages 31-35 in volume 12 of the Academie-Edition. This exchange was brought to my attention by David Lachterman, whose translation of 1971 is the source of my citations. I am grateful to Lachterman and to Rod Stewart for making me aware of this material.

12. See *Eunuchus,* 61-2: "Invecta haec si tu postules ratione certa facere, *nihilo plus agas quam si des operam ut cum ratione insanias*" (Kant quotes the italicized segment). The rhetorical force of Kant's citation is not altogether clear. Is he saying that the project is altogether hopeless, or that while it seems to be so, there is nevertheless a rational point in pursuing it? (Should we stress "cum ratione" or "insanias"?) His *final* remark following the quotation from Terence is that "one cannot hold it against the physiologist, who is satisfied to have traced the simple dynamic presence, as far as possible, to an immediate sensible presence, for having urged the metaphysician to make good what is still missing."

13. A not too—albeit slightly—misleading way to put the difference is that I cannot have the kind of acquaintance with your neural events that you do, acquaintance via the experience they produce. The point is related to that made by those, for example, Nagel and Jackson, who insist on the essential subjectivity of experience, though I would not draw the conclusion they often do, namely, that experience is ultimately description and theory resistant. See T. Nagel, "What is it Like to be a Bat," *The Philosophical Review* 83, no. 3 (October 1974); F. Jackson, "Epiphenomenal Qualia," *The Philosophical Quarterly* 32, no. 127 (April 1982); also C. McGinn, *The Subjective View* (Oxford: Oxford University Press, 1983).

14. There is a sense, of course, in which they *are* causally connected, in that they cause your perceptions of it, but that is not the sense of causal connectedness in question here.

15. An attempt to capture some similarly interesting things in Hume is made in J. I. Biro, "Hume and Cognitive Science," *History of Philosophy Quarterly* 2, no. 3 (July 1985).

16. It must be remembered that for Kant things transcend*ental* are not to be thought of straightforwardly as transcend*ent.* That is, synthesis isn't obviously a "process" in the noumenal world, either; indeed, such a way of thinking is incoherent.

17. Strawson, *Bounds of Sense,* p. 19.

18. I am grateful to Chris Swoyer for many helpful discussions of earlier versions of this paper.

"What Is the Ground of the Relation of That in Us Which We Call 'Representation' to the Object?"

Reflections on the Kantian Legacy in the Philosophy of Mind

David G. Stern

> What is the ground of the relation of that in us which we call "representation" to the object? . . . Our understanding, through its representations, is not the cause of the object (save in the case of moral ends), nor is the object the cause of the intellectual representations in the mind (*in sensu reali*). Therefore the pure concepts of the understanding must not be abstracted from sense perceptions, nor must they express the reception of representations through the senses; but though they must have their origin in the nature of the soul, they are neither caused by the object nor bring the object itself into being.[1]

In the letter to Marcus Herz from which this passage is taken, Kant says that the question of the ground of the relation of representation to its object "constitutes the key to the whole secret of hitherto still obscure metaphysics." The obscure metaphysical question which occupied Kant was the problem of understanding how knowledge is possible. Knowledge is a matter of our representing the world correctly. But if mind and world are separate, how can we know that the mind represents the world correctly? In response to the conflict between rationalism, which dogmatically asserts that the mind has knowledge of the world, and empiricism, which leads to skepticism about our knowledge of the world, Kant insisted we must first understand how the soul grounds the relationship between our representations and their objects.

While philosophy has since become uneasy about the soul, the thesis that the nature of the mind is crucial to metaphysics has been an enduring

Kantian legacy. For Kant's conception of the soul includes two major contributions to our understanding of the mind. First, he decisively rejected any conception of the mind as consisting of objects: representation is a rule-governed activity, and an account of representation must consist in an analysis of those rules. Second, the rules which constitute the mind also constitute the world. Mind and world are so interrelated that they must either be understood together or not at all.

But what is the relationship between such programmatic commitments and a specific theory of mental functioning? Kant's exposition of his Copernican revolution is embedded in an aprioristic psychological theory, a theory that has since been discredited. This forces us to make a choice: either we ensure that Kant's insights are put on a philosophical basis that is independent of psychological theory, or we integrate them into empirical psychology. While Kant scholars have explored the first alternative, most philosophers of mind have embraced the second. In this paper, I approach the vexed question of the relationship between empirical psychology and the view of the mind which we have inherited from Kant by way of a discussion of Kant's argumentative strategy in the Transcendental Deduction.

In the *Critique of Pure Reason*, Kant set himself the task of providing a philosophical justification of our claim to have knowledge of the world. His justification relies on a distinction between three types of argument about the relationship between mind and world: empirical, dogmatic, and transcendental arguments.

"Empirical" reasoning makes use of empirical statements about the origin of our knowledge. Kant called such an argument an "empirical deduction." It "shows the manner in which a concept is acquired through experience and through reflection upon experience, and . . . therefore concerns, not its legitimacy, but only its *de facto* mode of origination."[2] So while it may tell us how we arrived at our present beliefs, it cannot show that they are true.

"Dogmatic" reasoning analyzes the logical relations that hold between our beliefs. It can lead to conclusions which are logically necessary, but its conclusions are analytic. It can only tell us of the relations that hold between our thoughts, while what we need is to show that certain thoughts about the world are true. "For such a purpose, the analysis of concepts is useless, since it merely shows what is contained in these concepts, not how we arrive at them *a priori*."[3]

Kant concluded that neither "empirical" nor "dogmatic" reasoning could bridge the gap between mind and world. Dogmatism is particularly instructive here, for it assumes we can make use of the principles we apply in experience without first investigating in what way and by what right reason has come into possession of these concepts. Dogmatism is thus the dogmatic procedure of reason, *without previous criticism of its own powers.*[4]

The dogmatist will reply that it is entirely reasonable to start from the standards we ordinarily employ. But to agree with common sense is not to vindicate it: we need a *justification* of the standards we ordinarily employ. An "appeal to the common sense of mankind [is] an expedient which always is a sign that the cause of reason is in desperate straits,"[5] and so Kant holds that the problem of knowledge calls for a critique of pure reason. We must understand the power and limits of pure reason before we can say what it can and cannot achieve. One can also speak of answering the skeptic: Kant calls the skeptic "the taskmaster who constrains the dogmatic reasoner to develop a sound critique of the understanding and reason."[6] The skeptic is a methodological device, a pointed way of putting the epistemological challenge. This character personifies Descartes's position at the end of the first Meditation, doubting everything that can be doubted, challenging us to justify any claim to knowledge that goes beyond immediate experience.

Kant's third mode of argument, the transcendental or critical argument, is designed to reach substantive conclusions about matters which skepticism doubts while accepting its starting point. In such an argument "the game played by idealism has been turned against itself."[7] For a critical argument aims to show that skeptical doubt depends on accepting conditions that skepticism claims to repudiate. Jonathan Bennett calls this skeptical point of departure the "Cartesian Basis," the "intellectual situation in which one attends to nothing but one's mind and its states."[8] Kant, like Bennett, thinks this is the correct starting point in philosophy:

> While . . . the skeptical procedure cannot of itself yield any *satisfying* answer to the questions of reason, none the less it *prepares the way* by arousing reason to circumspection, and by indicating the radical measures which are adequate to secure it in its legitimate possessions.[9]

So, a transcendental argument starts from a characterization of immediate experience and shows that this characterization commits one to more than the skeptic thinks. This calls for

(a) A characterization of some aspect *a* of experience.
(b) An argument that *a* is not possible unless some condition *b* obtains.

The skeptic may, of course, challenge our choice of *a*, arguing that there could be experiencing subjects whose experience does not include *a*.[10] For example, Strawson gives an argument which starts from the premise that a subject must be able to distinguish those states that are one's own and those that are not.[11] The skeptic can reply that we can imagine subjects that do not satisfy such high standards of self-awareness. Indeed, there are many possible values for *a*: it has even been argued that we can imagine experience in a spaceless and timeless world.[12]

This suggests that we need to add to our argument schema

(c) An argument that *b* is also a condition for every characterization of experience.

But this move does not so much fix up the preceding argument as open it up to further objections. How, for instance, could we be sure that we had exhausted all the possible alternatives? To meet this difficulty, we must look for aspects of experience that are essential. If we had an analysis of the necessary conditions for something's being an experiencing subject, then the problems (c) was designed to remedy could not arise. We would then have the following argument schema:

(A) An argument that possession of characteristic *a* is a necessary condition for something's being an experiencing subject.
(B) An argument that *b* is a necessary condition for *a*.

If we can find a pair of arguments that fit this schema, we will have a transcendental argument. To meet the skeptic's demands, *a* must be an aspect of experience which even the skeptic cannot dispense with; to fully answer the skeptic, *b* must affirm what the skeptic denies. For instance, it might be a claim such as "I am part of a spatiotemporally extended world" or "I am part of a community with a shared language."

Let us look at Kant's reasons for thinking that a certain conception of experience must be accepted by the skeptic, part (A) of the argument schema. Kant holds that philosophy deals with the limits of possible experience, where "experience" is taken to be the *conceptualized experience of a judging subject.* But can't we be conscious without judging, without being self-conscious?[13] Imagine being in an accident in which one suffered such severe injuries that one was kept alive by machinery, unable to speak or think. With the disappearance of the ability to think and judge, there would be no "I," no judging subject. All that would be left would be a body on a life-support system. Something which is conscious and has sensations but has no conceptualized experience would be "merely a blind play of representations, less even than a dream"— there would be no judgment, and hence no subject.[14] How is Kant to establish this distinction between mere sensation and experience proper?

First, it must be *conceptualized* experience, experience in which concepts are applied in making judgments. The skeptic will grant that judgments of the form "It seems to me that p" are made within the Cartesian Basis but does not see this as a concession to Kant. Kant's reply is that judgment has a larger role than the skeptic admits. While most experience does not involve explicit judgment, judgment enters into all experience, for all experience is potentially judgeable. As Kant cryptically puts it, "it must be possible for the 'I think' to accompany all my representations."[15]

Second, it must be the experience of a judging *subject*. Although I do not "perceive something simple and continu'd"[16] which is my "self," my experiences are *my* experiences only because they stand in certain relations to each other. These connections are what constitute the synthetic unity which obtains between a person's experiences. For

> As *my* representations (even if I am not conscious of them as such) they conform to the condition under which alone they *can* stand together in one universal self-consciousness, because otherwise they would not all without exception belong to me.[17]

The relations between our representations lead us to think of them as coordinated toward that *focus imaginarius* which is the transcendental ego.

In the Transcendental Deduction, Kant sets himself the task of showing that the formal aspect of experience which makes it a subject's experience can be identified with the formal aspect which makes it judgeable, that the two conditions I have outlined—judgeability and subjectivity—are ultimately one and the same. But how is this claim to be established? It seems to say that for a representation to be my representation, I must be able to judge that it is mine. Indeed, some commentators have alleged that this thesis rests on an equivocation. The charge can be set out as follows. Kant starts from the trivially analytic

(1) All my representations are my representations.

This leads to the equally uncontentious claim that

(2) All my representations must be such that they satisfy the conditions in virtue of which they are my representations.

Kant then slips without justification to the much stronger claim:

(3) All my representations must be such that I can judge them to be my representations.

But, his critics respond, if I can have a long-lost cousin without being able to recognize her as my cousin, why can't I have a representation that I can't recognize as mine?[18]

One cannot defend Kant by saying that (3) is part of what he means by a representation, or that he defines a representation as judgeable. For this would be a retreat to dogmatism and the skeptic will reply that no reason has been given for it. If (3) is to be justified, Kant must concede that an unjudgeable representation is a logical possibility; and so he must consider the possibility that

> there might exist a multitude of perceptions, and indeed an entire sensibility, in which much empirical consciousness would arise in my mind, but in a state of separation, and without belonging to a consciousness of myself.[19]

In that case the manifold of sense would lack "affinity," and the mind would be unable to unify it. What, then, would happen if the mind were to be presented with such an unsynthesizable manifold? Kant's answer is that as the mind cannot unify it, it would be "nothing to me."[20] For a representation to be a thought of mine, it must stand in whatever relation to my other thoughts which is constitutive of my identity. If I cannot judge it, then it cannot enter that circle. The skeptic's conception of a subject that only judges part of the time rests on an inadequate conception of the self: for experience to be assignable to a self at all, it must be at least potentially judgeable. In the B Deduction Kant says that

> The thought that the representations given in intuition one and all belong to me, is therefore equivalent to the thought that I unite them in one self-consciousness, or can at least so unite them; and although this thought is not itself the consciousness of the *synthesis* of the representations, it presupposes the possibility of that synthesis. In other words, only in so far as I can grasp the manifold of the representations in one consciousness, do I call them one and all *mine*.[21]

From this vantage point, the outline of Kant's path to the thesis that the categories must be applied in all experience is clear. All experience must be judgeable, it must be possible to attach an "I think" to it, and so the manifold must be such that it can be combined and so brought to the unity of apperception.

> For without such combination nothing can be thought or known, since the given representations would not have in common the act of the apperception "I think," and so could not be apprehended together in one self-consciousness.[22]

To judge is to apply the categories: if all intuition is judgeable, then the categories are applicable to all intuition.

Judgmental experience must have a certain formal structure, and this structure, it turns out, is what makes it subjective. Whatever differences there may be between any two subjects, they must have this structure in common. This, then, is Kant's justification for the selection of *a*, that aspect of experience on which his argument is to turn. Regardless of the gradations between the most sophisticated consciousness and the most rudimentary, we can draw a sharp line between possible conceptions of experience by means of the criterion of self-conscious experience: is the experience the conceptualized experience of a judging subject? This criterion does not force us to say that creatures that do not make judgments cannot have experience. It only requires that we sharply distinguish two kinds of experience.

Although we can raise the bare possibility of an alternative synthesis of the manifold, philosophical reflection has led us to see that it is not a real possibility, for it is ruled out by the train of thought we have just examined. This thinning out of the skeptic's speculative psychologies has its limits, however. For instance, it still leaves open the possibility that there might be subjects which satisfied Kant's criterion but whose experience was phenomenologically quite different. For the criterion is metaphysical: it tells us what conditions something must satisfy for it to be a subject. It does not, in itself, give any answer to related epistemological questions about identifying subjects, or what things are like for a subject. In this connection we might consider familiar examples, such as people who lack a sense or have heightened sensitivities, or more exotic alternatives, such as having eyes on two separate bodies, or the sensations of bats, which orient themselves by listening to the way in which the high-pitched sounds they emit are reflected back by the objects around them.[23] The last cases are so different from our own that we may well be unable to imagine what such experience is like.

Kant does not trouble himself with such questions, perhaps because he thinks that the rejection of skepticism yields much more than the bare criterion of self-conscious experience. In his hands, the argument also leads to a detailed account of the operation of our mental faculties in synthesizing experiences. Once that account is in place, such vertiginous alternatives are no longer possible.

The train of thought I have just sketched suffices, I believe, to set out much of what is most powerful in Kant's account of the relationship between judgment and self-consciousness in the Transcendental Deduction. What role does the synthetic activity of the mind play in his argument? Do we really need an account of how it operates? For if we ignore his detailed theory, we can allow our reconstructed argument to rely on the bare thought that there are processes that underlie our experience and leave the task of specifying those processes to neuro-physiology. Kant's insights into the nature of the mind might in this way be separated from his mistaken theory. But once we attempt to reconstruct his argument without his transcendental psychology, we have to ask ourselves whether the reconstructed argument can stand alone.

Kant not only tells a detailed psychological story about how the mind constitutes the world, he also makes continual use of it in the course of his argument. Indeed, in the first edition of the *Critique of Pure Reason,* he gave an elaborate description of the way in which the mind synthesizes the manifold of sense into sensory experience. Much of this transcendental psychology was eliminated in the second edition. In particular, the new exposition of the Transcendental Deduction leaves out most of the detailed description of the operation of the faculties to be found in the original version. The first-edition exposition gives the central role to the constitutive activity of the imagination; in the second, the concept of judgment occupies center stage.

Six years of further work on his system had given Kant a clearer idea of his argument. At first sight, it looks as though he had taken the opportunity to remove unnecessary commitments to faculty psychology. In support of this reading, one can point to §§15–20 of the B Deduction, which contains a very clear exposition of the line of argument I have just set out. The sections that follow make it equally clear that Kant thought of this as only a part of his overall argument. In §21 he tells the reader that in §20 "a beginning is made of a deduction of the pure concepts of understanding."[24] So far, he says, he has abstracted from the spatiotemporal nature of human sensibility, an omission that must be made good before the proof can be completed. Only in §26 will the "*a priori* validity of the categories in respect of *all* objects of our senses" be made good.[25]

The first part of the argument of the B Deduction concludes with §20, which is a brief and well-organized summary of the overall course of the argument. The title of the section is a statement of what Kant has to prove: "*All sensible intuitions are subject to the categories, as conditions under which alone their manifold can come together in one consciousness.*"[26] To see why he thinks the argument can only be completed in §26, let us look one by one at each sentence in §20.

Kant starts by reminding us that

> The manifold given in a sensible intuition is necessarily subject to the original synthetic unity of apperception, because in no other way is the *unity* of intuition possible.

This amounts to a summary reminder of an argument we have just met: unless the manifold were synthesizable, it would be "as nothing" to me and hence could not be my experience. Next, he makes the point that synthesis is a matter of judgment:

> that act of understanding by which the manifold of given representations (be they intuitions or concepts) is brought under one apperception, is the logical function of judgment.

Having brought these two main strands of his argument together, one might expect that Kant would bring in the relationship between judgment and the categories—

> Now the *categories* are just these functions of judgment, in so far as they are employed in determination of the manifold of a given intuition.

—and so reach the desired conclusion:

> Consequently, the manifold in a given intuition is necessarily subject to the categories.

Indeed, in §§15–19 of the B Deduction, this is what he has already done. However, between the first two sentences of §20 and the last two, Kant inserts his caveat:

> All the manifold, therefore, so far as it is given in a unified empirical intuition, is *determined* in respect of one of the logical functions of judgment, and is thereby brought into one consciousness.[27]

This raises anew the possibility of an unsynthesizable manifold being given to sensibility. For if there were a manifold of sense that could *not* be "given in a unified empirical intuition," it need not be "determined in respect of any of the logical functions of judgment." The preceding argument has shown that whatever is given in a unified empirical intuition—immediate experience—must be judgeable. This is insufficient, for it leaves open the possibility that the sensory material which is initially presented to the mind may be so chaotic that it cannot be synthesized into a unified empirical intuition.

Kant's caveat makes it quite clear that he would not have been content with the logical reconstruction of his deduction that I gave earlier. For in abstracting from any consideration of the precise nature of synthesis, it can have nothing new to say in reply to the suggestion that our initial sensory input, rather than the content of sensory experience itself, might be unjudgeable. It can only reply that both suggestions are equally inconceivable, for in either case we are talking about experience which would be unjudgeable and so "as nothing" to me.

In §26, Kant says that the first half of the argument only shows that the categories are applicable in all knowledge of "objects of an intuition in general."[28] This leaves the task of showing that "whatever objects may *present themselves to our senses*" can be brought under the categories.[29] In other words, he still has to show that every manifold of sense must be unified by a synthesis which employs the categories and cannot merely be collocated by empirical laws of association.

Now we can see the force of the remark in §21 that the preceding argument involves abstracting from the spatiotemporal nature of our sensibility. The argument leading up to §20 draws out the connections between the subject and object of experience in a wholly general way, while the subsequent argument will turn on considering the fact that experience is spatiotemporal. Kant's account of the spatiotemporal constitution of experience provides the basis for the second half of his argument.

Kant's solution turns on an appeal to the synthetic activity of the mind. Space and time are the forms of all our sensibility, so everything that is given to us in sensibility is presented under at least one of these forms. The Transcendental Aesthetic has shown that we also have a priori intuitions of space and time. Any intuition presupposes the existence of a synthesis which has brought about the unity of that intuition.[30] As the categories are applied in constituting the intuitions of space and time, which in turn contain the entire manifold of sense, all intuition presupposes a synthesis by means of the operation of the understanding. But if the categories are applied to the entire manifold of sense in constituting space and time, then the categories must be applicable to everything given in that manifold.

Even if Kant never deviated from considering transcendental psychology an indispensable part of his argument, this hardly settles the question whether he was right to do so. The problem he tries to solve in the second half of the B Deduction only arises once one accepts that there is a need for an account of the constitution of sensory experience. The solution to his problem is ad hoc, too. It requires a substantial and unjustified revision of the introductory account of space and time given in the Transcendental Aesthetic—Kant summarily asserts, contrary to the Aesthetic, that formal intuition presupposes a synthesis.

If the problem and the solution are equally spurious, why should we let this confusion worry us? At the very least, it is a sign that Kant felt an acute need for an account of the processes in the mind which make judgment possible. Further, it points to an underlying difficulty: while Kant spurned opinions and hypotheses, he nevertheless made claims about the mind which we now judge to be false, insofar as we can understand them at all. Lacking his unquestioning acceptance of faculty psychology, we will say that it is not a description of the nature of the mind and that its true locus is the Kantian texts themselves. If we put aside the exegetical exercise of trying to understand the role of transcendental psychology in those texts, we are left with the question of what we can salvage from the Kantian program.

Kant says that transcendental arguments can only tell us about the constitution of the phenomenal world, not things in themselves. Strawson and most subsequent Kant commentators advise us to disregard transcendental idealism as a part of the metaphysical strand of the *Critique* which has not stood the test of time. Talk of the mind constituting the phenomena is to be rejected as part of Kant's psychologistic tendencies. On this "austere" reconstruction, transcendental arguments simply establish how things must be if experience is possible.

In this spirit, we might try to reconstruct a transcendental argument along the lines I sketched out earlier. Such an argument moves from a, a characterization of the experiencing subject, to b, the conditions that must obtain if there is to be such experience. If the argument is valid, then the only way to avoid its conclusion is to reject the premise. To do that is to hold that a is not essential to experience. Kant and Strawson charge that the skeptic has been caught out. To reply, the skeptic would have to show that we can dispense with the subject. But the skeptic's starting point, the Cartesian Basis, is the situation in which one attends to *nothing but* one's mind and its states.[31]

Richard Rorty had described such an argument as an "anti-parasite" argument.[32] It moves from the chosen a to some condition of its employment. Should the skeptic set out a conception of experience that lacks b but still contains a, then one can show that the conception is not self-sufficient, being "parasitic," for skepticism must also accept a. Such an argument is only a standing challenge to the skeptic to find an autonomous conception of experience, one that lacks a and so lacks b. In any case, the skeptic is unlikely to accept the claim that transcendental arguments establish how things must be. Instead, he or she will argue that even a successful transcendental argument would only show how we must think of the world, not how it is in itself, and so leaves open the possibility that we must think of it wrongly.

One might think that the verification principle could be used to bridge the gap: if a statement's meaning consisted in a method for ascertaining its truth, to understand b is to be able to tell if it is true.[33] However, the verification principle is of little use against the skeptic, who can argue that b is meaningless rather than false. In any case, a verification principle strong enough to underwrite such an argument could only make the argument valid at the price of making it obviously unsound.

If a transcendental argument is not the final answer to the skeptic, but only one move in a continuing struggle, then it no longer has the decisive power Kant promised. In that case, we may well return to the form of argument I mentioned briefly toward the beginning of this paper: empirical reasoning. The empirically minded philosopher thinks that some principles must underlie the functioning of the mind, and that psychology, neurology, or artificial intelligence will eventually enable us to understand them. Many contemporary philosophers of psychology have turned to such theories. They believe that science will set out the rules on which the mind operates and so enable us to understand the mind and its place in nature. However, most formulations of this approach depend on assumptions about the nature of the mind that are as unjustified as any to be found in dogmatism or transcendentalism. For they assume that there are processes in the brain which can be correlated with mental processes. Yet we have no neurophysiological theory that actually does this. Why should we expect that theory will in due course arrive at some such correlation between terms referring to mental tokens and terms referring to physical tokens? Current work on connectionist theories of neural functioning strongly suggests that no such principles will be found.[34]

Perhaps the questionable move in the Kantian argument about the ground of representation on page 220 (this volume) is the first inference, the one we took for granted. Starting from the premise that "All my representations are my representations," we inferred that all my representations must satisfy whatever the conditions are for them to be my representations. In making that move, both Kant and the empiricist tacitly assume that the psychological phenomena are grounded in an underlying order. But "why should there not be a psychological regularity to which no physiological regularity corresponds? If this upsets our concept of causality then it is high time it was upset."[35] We have simply taken for granted the assumption that the relationship between our representations and their objects must be grounded in a certain kind of psychological theory. Like the Ptolemaic belief that the sun goes around the earth, Kant's faculty psychology, or the phrenologists' account of the nature of the mind in terms of the size and shape of the skull, this is a natural interpretation, an inexplicit assumption, not a scientific result. Once we see that it *is* an assumption, we may wonder why we were so convinced it was true.[36]

NOTES

1. Letter to Marcus Herz, February 21, 1772. *Kant—Philosophical Correspndence 1759-99,* ed. and trans. Arnulf Zweig (Chicago: University of Chicago Press, 1967), pp. 71-72. See L. W. Beck, "Kant's Letter to Marcus Herz," *The Philosophical Forum* 13 (1955): 96-110.

2. Immanuel Kant, *Kritik der Reinen Vernunft* (Hamburg: Felix Mayer Verlag, 1956). *Immanuel Kant's Critique of Pure Reason,* trans. N. Kemp Smith

(London: Macmillan, 1933), A85/B117. References to the first *Critique* are to the pagination in the 1781 "A" edition and the 1787 "B" edition.

3. B23.

4. Bxxxv.

5. A783–84 = B811–12.

6. A769 = B797.

7. Jonathan Bennett, *Kant's Dialectic* (Cambridge, 1974), p. 66.

8. B276.

9. A769 = B797.

10. This anti-Kantian strategy is the theme of chap. 4 of John Mackie's *The Cement of the Universe* (Oxford: Oxford University Press, 1974).

11. Peter Strawson, *Individuals* (Methuen, 1959), chap. 2.

12. Ralph Walker, *Kant* (Routledge and Kegan Paul, 1979), chap. 3, §2–§3.

13. Cf. Mackie, *Cement of the Universe.*

14. A112.

15. B131.

16. David Hume, *Treatise of Human Nature,* ed. L. Selby-Bigge (Oxford, 1888), p. 187.

17. B132–33.

18. On pp. 83–84 of *On What There Must Be* (Oxford: Oxford University Press, 1974), Ross Harrison puts this objection very clearly, but he seems to consider it obvious enough that he does not bother to argue for it.

Dieter Henrich holds that this error vitiates the argument of the A Deduction. See Henrich, "The Proof Structure of Kant's Transcendental Deduction," *Review of Metaphysics* 22 (1968–69): 640–59, and especially pp. 654–55.

19. A122; cf. A89/B122ff. The passage continues with the words: "This, however, is impossible." We have yet to see how this can be shown.

20. B132.

21. B134. Cf. A117a.

22. B137.

23. See Thomas Nagel, "What Is It Like to Be a Bat?" *Mortal Questions* (Cambridge: Cambridge University Press, 1979).

Wittgenstein thought that visual experience with two bodies was inconceivable and that this pointed to an important epistemological asymmetry, an asymmetry between self-knowledge and knowledge of others:

> What would it be like if I had two bodies, i.e. my body were composed of two separate organisms?
> Here again, I think, we see the way in which the self is not on a par with others, for if everyone else had two bodies, I wouldn't be able to tell that this was so.
> Can I imagine experience with two bodies? Certainly not visual experience.

Ludwig Wittgenstein, *Philosophical Remarks* (Oxford: Blackwell, 1975), §66.

24. B144.

25. B145. My italics.

26. B143. I have omitted Kemp Smith's capitalization of the nouns. All of §20 is on p. 143 of the B edition.

27. The German reads:

Also, ist alles Mannigfaltige, sofern es in Einer empirischen Anschauung gegeben ist, in Ansehung einer der logischen Funktionen zu Urteilen bestimmt, durch die es nämlich zu einem Bewusstsein überhaupt gebracht wird.

Henrich argues that Kemp Smith's translation of *"Einer"* by "single" is too weak. For "in German the indefinite article *(ein)* and the word unity *(Einheit)* have the same root. This made it possible for Kant to express through the capital letter not the distinctness of any arbitrary intuition as opposed to others (singularity), but rather its inner unity." Henrich, "Proof-Structure of Kant's Transcendental Deduction," p. 645.

The same point applies to the second sentence on page B144.

28. B159.

29. Ibid.

30. See B159-60. In a footnote, Kant recognizes that this is a revision of the account of pure intuition he has given in the Aesthetic.

31. At this point, the skeptic may attempt a revisioning of the Cartesian Basis in terms of a subjectless conception of experience.

32. Richard Rorty, "Verificationism and Transcendental Arguments," *Nôus* 5 (1971): 3-14.

33. See Barry Stroud, "Transcendental Arguments," *The Journal of Philosophy* 65 (1968): 241-56.

34. Connectionists study mathematical models of neurological functioning in which brain structure is represented by a network of multiply connected nodes. Nodes and connections are initially given small random values on an arbitrarily chosen scale, and a single invariant function determines the value of each node at time t+1 in terms of its value at time t and the value of its neighbors at time t. By varying the input to the network at certain assigned input nodes and observing the effect of those variations on the output nodes, one adjusts the values of the connections in order to teach the network to respond to each of a variety of inputs with the corresponding output.

On this model, a system can learn to respond correctly to a wide range of inputs without the information being represented by one specifiable pattern in the network. Some neurologists have argued that this model enables us to understand many of the differences between human perception and memory and a digital computer's information processing and storage: for instance, we generally recall information in a relevant context. The following references are by no means exhaustive; they do provide an introduction to some of the main areas of current research: Hubert and Stuart Dreyfus, "Making a Mind vs. Modeling the Brain: AI at a Branch Point," *Daedalus* (Winter 1988); Israel Rosenfeld, "Neural Darwinism: A New Approach to Memory and Perception," *New York Review of Books,* 9 October 1986; David Rumelhart et al., *Parallel Distributed Processing,* vol. 1 (Cambridge: Bradford/MIT Press, 1986).

35. Ludwig Wittgenstein, *Remarks on the Philosophy of Psychology,* ed. G. E. M. Anscombe and G. H. von Wright, trans. G. E. M. Anscombe (Chicago: University of Chicago Press, 1980), vol. 1, §906. In §908, Wittgenstein presents his point by means of the following parable:

> Imagine the following phenomenon. If I want someone to take note of a text that I recite to him, so that he can repeat it to me later, I have to give him paper and pencil, and while I speak, he makes lines, marks, on the paper; if he has to reproduce the text later he follows those marks with his eyes and recites the text. But I assume that what he has jotted down is not *writing*, it is not connected by rules with the words of the text; yet without these jottings he is unable to reproduce the text; and if anything in it is altered, if part of it is destroyed, he gets stuck in his "reading" or recites the text uncertainly or carelessly, or cannot find the words at all.—This *can* be imagined!—What I called jottings would not be a *rendering* of the text, not a translation, so to speak, in another symbolism. The text would not be *stored up* in the jottings. And why should it be stored up in our nervous system?

The conclusion is more striking in the German: "stored up" translates "niederlegen," which can also mean to lay down, or to write down. I discuss this passage at much greater length in a paper on "Models of Memory: Wittgenstein and Cognitive Science."

36. I would like to thank Simon Blackburn, Patrick Maher, Bob Brandom, Janet Broughton, Hans Sluga, Elizabeth Calihan, Bert Dreyfus, and Nancy Mullenax for their comments on previous drafts of this paper.

Inner States and Outer Relations

Kant and the Case for Monadism

James Van Cleve

My text in this paper is the fascinating, but seldom studied, little corner of the *Critique of Pure Reason* entitled "The Amphiboly of the Concepts of Reflection." In this section, which occurs as an appendix to the chapter on "Phenomena and Noumena," Kant presents his criticisms of the philosophy of Leibniz, arranged under the four headings of "Identity and Difference," "Agreement and Opposition," "The Inner and the Outer," and "Matter and Form." I wish to concentrate here on Kant's discussion of "The Inner and the Outer," which contains an argument for monadism more satisfying and explicit than anything I have ever found in Leibniz. Kant does not endorse this argument, but he evidently deserves the credit for constructing it, so I shall refer to it in what follows as Kant's.

The paper is divided into four sections: (1) reconstruction of the argument, (2) Kant's assessment of it, (3) my own assessment of it, and (4) a conclusion.

1. RECONSTRUCTION OF THE ARGUMENT

Kant presents the Leibnizian argument in three separate passages, the first version beginning at A265/B321, the second at A274/B330, and the third at A283/B339.[1] The reader may wish to number the sentences in each of these paragraphs, since I will refer to them by number presently.

The fullest version of the argument occurs the third time around. I here reproduce the first five sentences of it.

(1) According to mere concepts the inner is the substratum of all relational or other determinations. (2) If, therefore, I abstract from all conditions of intuition and confine myself to the concept of a thing in general, I can abstract from all outer relation, and there must still be left a concept

231

of something which signifies no relation, but inner determinations only. (3) From this it seems to follow that in whatever is a thing (substance) there is something which is absolutely inward and precedes all outer determinations, inasmuch as it is what first makes them possible; and consequently, that this substratum, as no longer containing in itself any outer relations, is *simple*. (4) (Corporeal things are never anything save relations only, at least of their parts external to each other.) (5) And since we know of no determinations which are absolutely inner except those given through our inner sense, this substratum is not only simple; it is likewise (in analogy with our inner sense) determined through *representations*; in other words, all things are really *monads*, simple beings endowed with representations.

I will omit for the time being such qualifications as "according to mere concepts" and "abstracting from intuition." As we shall see later, these are phrases that Kant thinks vital if the argument is to be sound, but we can more readily understand the argument if we ignore them the first time around.

The premise on which the entire argument turns is that the "outer" in some sense presupposes the "inner": if you take away all "outer relation," there must still be left something "inner," something that "signifies no relation." What exactly does this mean? The key to my interpretation of Kant's argument is that it means *two* things. His leading premise is systematically ambiguous in a way that has not been pointed out (so far as I know) by previous commentators.

To bring out the two meanings, we must ask two questions: what are the "outer relations" that we are to imagine taking away, and what is the something "inner" that must still be left? I believe that there are two possibilities in each case, generating four combinations in all. They may be represented as follows:

Take away all

1) relations of a thing to other things *outside* it

2) relations of part to part *within* a thing

and there must still be left

a) some nonrelational properties, i.e., some *qualities*.

b) some things capable of standing in relations, i.e., some *terms*.

Of the four resulting possibilities, the two that figure in Kant's argument are 1a and 2b. The idea expressed by 1a is that nothing can have its whole nature exhausted by the relations in which it stands to other things; on the contrary, everything must have some qualities.[2] The idea expressed by 2b is that there cannot be a thing whose existence derives from the relatedness of its parts, whose existence in turn derives from the relatedness of their parts, and so on, without end. In other words, nothing can have the property that Bradley found so disconcerting about space: that of being "essentially a relation of what vanishes into relations, which seek in vain for their terms."[3] Kant uses the second of these principles to argue for the existence of simples (i.e., entities without parts), and the first to argue that the simples must be endowed with representations.

In accusing Kant of systematic ambiguity, I do not mean to accuse him of equivocation. He does not, for example, argue *for* the outer-inner premise in one of its meanings and *from* it in another. He simply uses two independent assumptions for which he has only one mode of expression. This makes the real structure of his argument hard to discern, but it does not issue in a fallacy of equivocation.

If you find it hard to believe that Kant would conflate principles as different as 1a (the "qualities" principle) and 2b (the "ultimate terms" principle), I invite you to read carefully through Kant's three presentations of the argument. Here is what I think you will find: In the version at A265/B321, the qualities idea figures in sentence 5, the ultimate terms idea in sentence 8. In the version at A274/B330, the ultimate terms idea figures in sentences 2 and 3, the qualities idea in sentence 4. Finally, in the version at A283/B339, the qualities idea figures in sentences 5 and 12, the ultimate terms idea in sentences 4, 8, 9, and 16. Certain other sentences—e.g., the first sentence of paragraph 3, with which our discussion began—could be read either way.

I might add that the conflation of which I am accusing Kant occurs also in the famous chapter on "Quality and Relation" in Bradley's *Appearance and Reality*. Bradley argues that qualities cannot be reduced to relations on the ground that a relation cannot "precipitate its own terms," thus confounding the idea that relations demand independent terms with the idea that relations demand independent qualities *in* the terms. In Bradley's case, there is perhaps some excuse for the conflation in his having adhered to a "bundle theory" according to which terms are just complexes of qualities. If relations demand independent terms and terms are just bundles of qualities, then relations demand qualities. But Kant did not accept the bundle theory, so there is no similar explanation in his case.

Let me now proceed with my reconstruction of the argument. Some terminology will be useful. Let us say that a thing is *constituted by relations* if its existence derives from the fact that certain other things stand in certain relations, and that it is constituted *entirely* by relations if each of its parts is also constituted by relations. More precisely:

D1. w is *constituted by relations* = Df for some individuals x_1 through x_n and some relation R that is accidental to them, w is necessarily such that it exists iff x_1 through x_n are related by R.

D2. x is constituted *entirely* by relations = Df x and all of its parts are constituted by relations.

The starting point of the argument can now be put very simply: nothing can be constituted entirely by relations. This implies that there must be some things that are not constituted by relations at all, and these (on the assumption that everything composite is constituted by relations) will have to be simple.

We next go on to argue that the simples must have some qualities, and that the only qualities available to them are psychical. Some more terminology will be useful. Logicians often use the terms "nonrelational" and "monadic" interchangeably, but I am going to use them to mark a distinction.

D3. P is *nonrelational* = Df it is possible for something x to have P even if no individual *discrete* from x (i.e., having no part in common with x) exists.

D4. P is *monadic* = Df it is possible for something x to have P even if no individual *distinct* from x (i.e., not identical with x) exists.

Shapes are nonrelational properties, since an object could be round or square even if nothing existed outside it. They are not monadic, since an object can have a shape only if it has parts that stand in certain relations to each other, and thus only if there are entities distinct from it.[4] It is going to turn out, of course, that a monadic property is one suited to a monad.

Kant distinguishes between two species of nonrelational property, the "absolutely inward" and the "comparatively inward." The former involves "no relation whatsoever (so far as its existence is concerned) to anything different from itself" (A265/B321), whereas the latter "is itself again composed of outer relations" (A277/B333). I should like to understand this distinction in terms of the distinction just drawn, as follows:

D5. P is *absolutely inward* = Df P is nonrelational *and* monadic.
D6. P is *comparatively inward* = Df P is nonrelational, but *not* monadic.[5]

Shapes, as already noted, are examples of comparatively inward properties; so are colors.[6] What would be an example of an absolutely inward property? The only examples we know of, Kant says, are "those which [our] inner sense presents to [us]"—namely, psychic properties, or properties that involve the having of representations (A266/B321).

We are now in a position to set forth the rest of the argument. According to the qualities version of the outer-inner premise, everything whatsoever must have some nonrelational properties. (A thing must have *some* properties, and since they cannot all be relational, some must be nonrelational.) In the case of composite entities, this demand can be filled by comparatively inward properties, such as color and shape; but in the case of simple entities, it can only be filled by absolutely inward properties—properties that do not require the existence of anything distinct from their bearers. So a simple thing must have some absolutely inward properties. But the only such properties we know of, Kant says, are either *thinkings* or properties analogous to thinkings (A266/B321). So the ultimate constituents of the universe must be "simple subjects with powers of representation—in a word, MONADS" (A266/B322). Q.E.D.

Here is the entire argument set down explicitly, with the steps numbered for later reference:

1. Nothing can be constituted entirely by relations. (Ultimate terms version of the outer-inner premise)
2. There are things that are not constituted by relations at all; everything else is composed of these. (From 1, D1, and D2)
3. Everything composite is constituted by relations. (Premise)
4. There are things that are not composite; everything else is composed of these. In other words, the basic constituents of the world are *simple*. (From 2 and 3)
5. Everything must have at least one nonrelational property. (Qualities version of the outer-inner premise)
6. The only nonrelational properties a simple thing could have are absolutely inward properties. (Premise)
7. The only absolutely inward properties a simple thing could have are properties that involve the having of representations. (Premise)
8. A simple thing must have *representations*. (From 5, 6, and 7)
9. The basic constituents of the world are "simple beings endowed with representations," i.e., *monads*. (From 4 and 8)

As I remarked above, I know of no arguments in Leibniz as explicit as this one, but it is possible to discern something like it in the opening paragraphs of the *Monadology*. The first half (steps 1-4) may be regarded as an unfolding of paragraph 2, "There must be simple substances, because there are compounds"; and the second half (steps 5-8) may perhaps be regarded as an unfolding of paragraph 8, "Simple substances must have some qualities." These qualities, as we learn in the ensuing paragraphs, can only be perceptions and their changes.

2. KANT'S ASSESSMENT OF THE ARGUMENT

Kant's attitude toward the argument may be summed up very briefly: he thought it would be entirely sound as regards *noumena,* but that it fails in the case of *phenomena.* What is not so clear is whether he thought the argument sound as applied to *things in themselves.*

Implicit in the preceding paragraph is a distinction between noumena and things in themselves. Noumena (in the *positive* sense of the term— see B307) are entities completely knowable by a pure intelligence or, as Kant also puts it, entities "determinable through mere concepts" (A285/ B341, sentence 15). Things in themselves are things that exist independently of human consciousness. According to Kant's mature philosophy, we have no right to assume that things in themselves are noumena in this positive sense, or even that noumena exist at all. So in conceding that Leibniz would be right about noumena, Kant is not automatically conceding that he would be right about things in themselves.

Surprisingly, however, there are places in which Kant seems to imply that Leibniz *would* be right about things in themselves:

> Leibniz took the appearance for things in themselves, and so for intelligibilia . . . and on that assumption . . . could not be disputed. (A264/B320)

> The simple is therefore the basis of that which is inner in things in themselves. (A274/B330)

> Appearances are not included as things in themselves among the objects of pure understanding. (A279/B335)

> The argument of the monadists would indeed be valid if bodies were things in themselves. (A442/B470)

In the first and third of these passages, Kant seems to be implying that Leibniz is right about things in themselves *because they are noumena.* If so, he is lapsing into his "pre-Critical" views, and the remarks may be dismissed. But in the second and the fourth passages, he seems to be implying that Leibniz is right about things in themselves directly, without any need to assume that they are noumena. Did Kant really believe that? If so, he was as thoroughgoing a monadist as Leibniz himself. His only ostensible point of dissent would be that the *phenomenal* world contains no monads, but Leibniz did not believe otherwise. The phenomenal world is not *composed* of monads, according to Leibniz; it is a construction out of their perceptive states.

I shall not try to settle here the question *why* Kant thought Leibniz would be right about noumena, nor the question *whether* he thought Leibniz would be right about things in themselves. I shall only take up the question why he thought the argument fails for phenomena.

I note first that on my interpretation of Kant (which is too phenomenalistic for some, but I cannot go into that here) there is no question *that* the argument fails. Phenomena (appearances) are either "internal accusatives" of intuitings (e.g., patches of color) or more complex objects constructed out of these (e.g., houses and ships). In either case, phenomena exist only in relation to human consciousness. This puts it entirely out of the question that the phenomenal world should contain any monads, since one conscious being cannot exist only in relation to the consciousness of another.

If the conclusion of the monadist's argument is false, at what point does the argument break down? The only premise Kant seems to challenge is the outer-inner premise. But that premise, as we have seen, is really two principles rolled into one. Which of them does Kant wish to deny?

At A265/B321, he seems to be denying *both* of them. In regard to *substantia phaenomenon* in space, he says, "Its inner determinations are nothing but relations, and it itself is entirely made up of mere relations." That is, a phenomenal substance need not have any qualities, and it may be constituted entirely by relations. (This, by the way, is the only sentence I have found in the entire Amphiboly section that clearly distinguishes, by devoting a clause to each, the two strands in the outer-inner premise.) On a closer reading, however, it appears that Kant is not denying the need for a phenomenal substance to have nonrelational properties. He is only denying the need for it to have *absolutely inward* properties. Since phenomenal substances are always extended in space, they may have the *other* species of nonrelational property, the comparatively inward ones:

> All that we know in matter is merely relations (what we call the inner determinations of it are inward only in a comparative sense). (A285/B341, sentence 13)

Evidently, then, Kant thinks the argument fails only at its first step.

He thinks it is possible after all for a phenomenal substance to be constituted entirely by relations. This raises the following question: if there were any reason to think that the first premise of the argument *did* hold in the case of things in themselves, what feature of phenomena would make them exempt from the premise? I would like to suggest the following answer: a phenomenon can be composed of parts inside parts *ad indefinitum* (with no ultimate ground for its existence *within*) simply because, as a phenomenon, it has the true ground of its existence *without*, i.e., in the occurrence of perceptive acts by a perceiver. A thing in itself, on the other hand, must be entirely self-subsistent, so if it has no ultimate ground for its existence within, it has none at all. This, I conjecture, is one reason why Kant may have thought the endless dependence of part upon part tolerable for phenomena, but not for things in themselves.

The same suggestion would explain away an apparent inconsistency between the Amphiboly and the Second Antinomy. In the Amphiboly, as we have just seen, Kant is apparently willing to allow that phenomenal substances can be composed of parts within parts forever, with no need for ultimate simples; but in the "Proof of the Thesis" of the Second Antinomy, he purportedly refutes that very possibility. My reconciling suggestion is that what Kant refutes in the Antinomies is not the absence of simples *überhaupt,* but the absence of simples in anything that exists *an sich.* It would thus be left open that phenomena could contain nothing simple.

I acknowledge the following difficulty with my suggestion: if it is correct, the Transcendental Idealist can escape the antinomy by evading the refutation of one of the antinomial alternatives. Kant's official position seems rather to be that *both* alternatives are refutable, and that the Transcendental Idealist escapes because he need not embrace either one of them.

3. INDEPENDENT ASSESSMENT OF THE ARGUMENT

I wish now to consider the argument on its own merits, independently of any special doctrines of Kant's. As I have set it up, the conclusions (steps 2, 4, 8, and 9) all follow validly from what has gone before, so it is necessary only to consider the premises—steps 1, 3, 5, 6, and 7.

Premise 1 (Nothing can be constituted entirely by relations). This premise owes its plausibility to considerations of the following sort. A thing constituted by relations would apparently be an *ontological parasite*—something that would not exist unless certain other things did and whose existence consists in those other things being related in a certain way. For example, a fist does not exist unless there is a hand whose fingers are clenched, and a valley does not exist unless there are two mountains adjacent to each other. Now if a thing constituted by relations is a parasite in this sense, it follows that a thing constituted *entirely* by relations would be a parasite on parasites that were themselves parasites on parasites, and so on, without end. That is unsettling. If there are parasites, must there not be *ultimate hosts,* that is, hosts that are not themselves parasites?

There is one conception of parasites according to which the answer is easily seen to be yes—the conception of them as *mere logical constructions.* In saying that As are merely logical constructions out of Bs, I mean that (i) all truths about As are re-expressible as truths about Bs, and (ii) the As do not exist except by courtesy of such paraphrase. That is to say, the As enter our world of discourse only via paraphrase and not by way of identification with any already recognized entities. They exist only nominally or in a manner of speaking. The stock example of such a merely nominal existent is the average plumber, who is said to have a fractional number of children. We all know how to paraphrase away such talk and would not dream of finding an entity already in our ontology with which to *identify* the average plumber. Other candidates for merely nominal existents are *holes* and *shadows.* We can paraphrase away our talk of such things, but would be hard pressed to find anything in our ontology with which to identify them.[7]

If one thinks of parasites as mere logical constructions, the idea of parasites on parasites forever is indeed out of the question. In order for some things to have nominal existence, there must be others that have real existence![8]

The question that must now be asked, however, is whether all things constituted by relations are parasites in the above sense, i.e., mere constructions. I do not think it is obligatory to regard them so. Take the fist again: it might be regarded as an entity in its own right, though a dependent one. It is, so one might say, an *ontological supervenient* or an *ontological emergent*—a genuinely new entity that comes into being when old entities are suitably related.[9] Since it is not simply a *façon de parler,* we no longer face the specter of nominal existents anchored in no real existents.

Of course, if one accords such "emergent" status to fists, one will naturally also have to accord it to semi-fists, quarter-fists, and so on, with the consequence that myriads of beings come and go with each twitch of a finger. This is an extravagant view. Suppose, then, that we stay with the more austere position that regards things constituted by relations as mere constructions. Would we then be forced to admit the existence of simples? No, for as we shall now see, premise 3 may be challenged, too.

Premise 3 (Everything composite is constituted by relations). In other words, wholes are parasites on their parts. This may seem obvious, for every whole is dependent on its parts for its existence. If w is a whole and p one of its parts, w cannot exist unless p exists.[10]

But this is not enough to make wholes or composite entities things constituted by relations, as this notion was defined above. According to the definition, things constituted by relations have a *double* dependence on their parts: they depend for their existence both on the existence of their parts and on how the parts are related. Not all composite entities exhibit this twofold dependence on their constituents; some composite entities depend for their existence only on the fact *that* their parts exist, not on *how* they exist. The continued existence of a teacup may depend on its halves being related in a particular fashion, but the same is not true of the collection of clay particles of which the cup is composed. The mere existence of all the particles, however widely scattered, suffices for the existence of the original collection. We can say, then, that there is one kind of composite entity—sheer material aggregations, as opposed to compounds of matter and essential form—that is not constituted by relations. So premise 3 is false.[11]

Now it might be objected to what I have just said that there is one relation among its parts that is essential even to the existence of a sheer aggregate—namely, the relation of *coexistence,* or existence within the same universe. Note, however, that the relation of coexistence is *essential to its terms:* it cannot cease to hold unless at least one of the terms ceases to exist. But it is stipulated in D1 that the "constituting" relation must be *accidental* to its terms. That is, it must be possible for the terms all to exist outside of the relation. So the objection is blocked.[12]

Note that nothing forces us to say that aggregates are mere constructions. It may well be that any truth about an aggregate can be restated as a conjunction of truths about its parts, but that is not enough to make it a *mere* construction. Recall our test above: is there any entity with which the purported entity may be identified? If the answer is yes, we have not got a mere construction. For an aggregate, the answer is indeed yes, since an aggregate may be identified with the sum of its parts. (Such identification is made possible by the indifference of the sum to all rearrangements.)

We have now identified two strategies for avoiding the admission of simples. One is to deny that things constituted by relations are mere constructions, giving them instead the status of ontological emergents.[13] The other is to maintain that some composites are *not* constituted by relations in the relevant sense. In effect, the second strategy holds that the disconcerting downward regress ceases to be disconcerting when we reach entities that no longer possess essential form—in other words, when nothing matters but matter.[14]

Premise 5 (Everything must have at least one nonrelational proper-

ty). A famous thesis often attributed to Leibniz is the "reducibility of all relations." What he seems actually to have held in this regard is this: whenever any relation holds between two or more concrete individuals, there are qualities whose presence in the relata entails the holding of the relation.[15] To illustrate with an obvious example, if a is darker in color than b, this will be because a is red and b is orange, or a orange and b yellow, etc. If *all* relations were like this, as Leibniz maintained, we would have an easy argument for premise 5: to exist at all, a thing must either have qualities or stand in relations, and if it stands in relations, it must have qualities.

Now in my opinion, *not* all relations are grounded in qualities. Some relations are purely "external," spatial and temporal relations being the most obvious examples. But I do not think that a thing could stand in external relations *exclusively*. If you knew all about a thing's external relations, you would still know nothing about *what it is*. Imagine the following exchange: "What have you got in your pocket?" "Something that is thirty inches from my big toe, placed there by my own hand, inquired about by you . . ." Nothing could be fully described by predicates like this; on the contrary, everything must have some intrinsic nature. So despite not agreeing with the Leibnizian underpinning Kant probably had in mind for premise 5, I find the premise itself quite compelling.[16]

Premise 6 (The only nonrelational properties a simple thing could have are absolutely inward properties). This premise is virtually analytic. Here is an informal demonstration of it. Suppose that a simple thing, x, has a nonrelational property, P, that is *not* absolutely inward. Since P is not absolutely inward, x can have P only if something distinct from x exists. Since x is simple, the only things distinct from it are also discrete from it (i.e., lie wholly outside it). Therefore, x can have P only if something discrete from x also exists. But this contradicts the initial supposition that P is nonrelational.[17]

Premise 7 (The only absolutely inward properties a simple thing could have are properties that involve the having of representations). We come now to the most vulnerable premise in the second half of the argument. To the premise as it now stands, there are dozens of counterexamples. Being nongreen, being either red or nonred, being an individual—these are properties whose exemplification does not require the existence of anything distinct from their bearers, but they are not properties that involve the having of representations. (For short, they are not psychic properties.)

Yet the properties just cited are so boring and bloodless that one suspects there might be something to Kant's claim after all. To help the argument along, I propose to circumscribe the meaning of "property" so that the boring properties just cited will no longer count as properties in the relevant sense. For this purpose, I will employ the following definition, used by R. M. Chisholm in a related connection:[18]

D7. P is a *character-conferring property* = Df P is a property
such that: (a) only individual things can have it; (b) anything
that can have it can have it, or fail to have it, at any time
it exists; and (c) it can be such that some individuals have
it and some do not.

None of the properties listed above qualifies as a character-conferring
property. Negative properties, such as *being nongreen,* are excluded by
clause (a); universal properties, such as being red or nonred, are excluded
by clause (a) and again by clause (c); the property of being an individual
is excluded by clause (c). I believe that most other exceptions to D7
that the reader can think of will also be excluded. For example, *being
identical with this very individual* is ruled out by clause (b); so is the
property of having come into being at a certain time.

A word is in order about my strategy at this point, since it may
appear that I am trying to remove counterexamples by stipulation. I am
not. The definition itself, of course, is purely stipulative, but the premises
containing the defined term are not. They must be assessed on their own
merits. So what we must do now is go back and satisfy ourselves that
the three premises containing the term "property" remain acceptable when
"property" is given the meaning of "character-conferring property."

Premise 7, of course, is *more* defensible; to make it so was the very
purpose of introducing the definition. Premise 6 is unaffected, since it
was demonstrated independently of the meaning of "property." It is
Premise 5 that acquires a stronger import through the new definition,
so we must make sure it remains plausible. I think it does. The reasons
for saying that a thing could not have its nature exhausted by relations
are equally reasons for saying it could not have its nature exhausted
by relations together with such nondescript attributes as being nongreen,
being such that 2 + 2 = 4, and so on.

Having disposed of the boring counterexamples to premise 7, I now
wish to consider two classes of putative counterexamples that are more
interesting. The first is *colors.* Colors would not normally be thought
of as absolutely inward, but there is a view that makes them so. I have
in mind the conception to be found in Berkeley and Hume of the *minimum
visibile.* A minimum visibile is supposed to be without parts (hence its
minimality), yet possessed of color (hence its visibility). If such a thing
were possible, color would not imply the existence of parts within its
possessor and would thus count as absolutely inward. But it is not
psychical, so premise 7 would be false.[19]

In response to this suggestion, I must simply be dogmatic. The following principles both seem to me to be self-evident: (a) whatever is colored
is extended, and (b) whatever is extended has parts. Hence minima
visibilia as conceived by Berkeley and Hume are impossible; what has

color must also have parts.[20]

The other class of putative counterexamples to premise 7 is *dispositions*, or powers to affect and be affected by other objects in various ways. Such powers may qualify as properties in our narrow sense, and they are arguably possessable by simples, yet they need not be psychic. Since Kant in his writings on the foundations of natural science ascribes repulsive force to pointlike particles, he may perhaps be taken to have raised this counterexample himself.

The dispositions of a thing are typically specified by reference to other things or kinds of things. For example, fire has the power to melt wax, and a key has the power to open a certain kind of lock. Are these not then relational properties, hence not absolutely inward, hence not counterexamples after all? The answer is that in a sense these properties are relational, but not in the sense that is relevant here. Fire would have the power to melt wax even if there were no wax, and a key might be such that it *would* open any lock of a certain description even if there were no locks of that description in existence. So in the sense I have defined (which requires the *existence* of a discrete relatum), dispositions need not be relational. They remain as potential exceptions to premise 7.[21]

Nonetheless, if dispositions are the *only* exceptions to premise 7, Kant's argument needs only two minor modifications to succeed. First, let us modify the premise to admit the exception:

7'. The only absolutely inward properties a simple thing could have are either psychic properties *or dispositions.*

Next, let us add to the argument the plausible premise that every disposition must have a "categorical basis." In other words, the dispositions of a thing depend on and are determined by its *nondispositional* properties: there are no "brute dispositions." If we accept this idea, we can still reach the original conclusion by the following route. The dispositions referred to in premise 7' must be nonrelational, and the categorical basis of a nonrelational disposition must itself be nonrelational. (Otherwise, the original disposition, in depending on a property that requires the existence of something outside its bearer, would itself require the existence of that thing and hence be relational.) Any simple thing possessing a nonrelational disposition must therefore also possess some property P that is both nonrelational and nondispositional. Since P is nonrelational, it must (in virtue of premises 6 and 7') be either psychic or dispositional; and since it is nondispositional, it must be psychic. So a simple thing must have psychic properties after all. Q.E.D.

It may seem a strange consequence of the argument just given that a psychic property, such as thinking a thought or feeling a sensation, should be the ground of a disposition. It would be more plausible to insist that the ground of a disposition must be some *structural* property— some configuration of atoms or brain circuits. But if we thus insist on structural bases for dispositions, we bar simples from having dispositions to begin with, in which case we could have dismissed the counterexample at the outset.

One last point needs to be discussed in connection with the second half of the argument. What the argument clearly needs is the premise that the only absolutely inward (and nondispositional) properties *there are* are psychic; but all that Kant actually asserts, and all that I have defended, is the thesis that the only such properties *we know of* are psychic. This, of course, opens up a gap, for there may well be absolutely inward properties of which we can form no notion.[22] It seems that what we should really conclude at the end of the argument is this: the basic constituents of the world are either (i) *monads* or (ii) *something, we know not what.*

CONCLUSION

I should like to close by contrasting my view of Kant's argument with the view one gathers Wittgenstein would have taken toward it at the time of the *Tractatus.* Evidently, he would have gone along with the first half of the argument, but balked at the second. At 2.024, he says, "Substance is what subsists independently of what is the case."[23] Since anything composite exists only insofar as its components stand in certain relations—i.e., dependently on what is the case—it follows that Tractarian objects must be simple. (This is affirmed at 2.021.) But Wittgenstein would evidently deny the need for the simples to have a qualitative nature. He holds (at least according to the interpretation of Guido Küng) that any qualities in a thing must reduce to interrelations of its parts, and from this it evidently follows that a thing without parts must also be without qualities.[24] "In a manner of speaking," Wittgenstein says, "Objects are colorless" (2.0232).

My own view is just the opposite. I am not convinced of the need for simples to begin with, but if there are any, they must surely have a qualitative (even if not a psychic) nature.[25]

NOTES

1. All such references are to Immanuel Kant, *Critique of Pure Reason,* trans. Norman Kemp Smith (New York: St. Martin's Press, 1965).
2. Of course, one should not really make this point by saying, "If you took away all relations, there would still be left some qualities." The presence of *any*

qualities in a pair of things would automatically induce some relations of qualitative similarity or dissimilarity, so if you took away *all* relations, you would have to take away all qualities, too.

3. F. H. Bradley, *Appearance and Reality* (Oxford: Oxford University Press, 1969), p. 32.

4. I am presupposing here, with Pierre Bayle, that "Every extension, no matter how small it may be, has a right and a left side." (See Pierre Bayle, *Historical and Critical Dictionary,* ed. Richard Popkin [Indianapolis: Bobbs-Merrill, 1965], q.v. "Zeno of Elea.") Kant agrees: "Everything real that occupies a space contains in itself a manifold of constituents external to one another, and is therefore composite" (A436/B464).

5. I find confirmation of my interpretation in Kant's discussion of the word "absolute" a few pages beyond the Amphiboly section. He says that the word "absolute" may be used to indicate either (i) "that something is true of a thing considered *in itself*" or (ii) "that something is valid in all respects" or "in every relation." For example, the absolutely possible in the first sense would be that whose nature is internally possible (i.e., free from contradiction); the absolutely possible in the second sense would be that whose existence is not precluded by anything else. He goes on to say that he will use the word "absolute" in the second sense, "opposing it to what is valid only comparatively, that is, in some particular respect" (A326/B382). Applying this to the phrases at hand, an absolutely inward property would be one involving no relations at all, and a comparatively inward property would be one involving no relations of a specified sort. Taking the specified sort to be relations of a thing to other things outside it, we get the concept defined in D6.

6. I presuppose here that only extended things can have colors—something that Berkeley and Hume may have denied. See note 20.

7. It has been suggested (by one of the characters in David and Stephanie Lewis's "Holes," *Australasian Journal of Philosophy* 48 (1970): 206–12), that holes be identified with hole-linings, but this will not do. When you plug a hole, the hole is no more, but the lining remains. In a similar vein, it might be suggested that shadows be identified with shadowed surfaces. This will not do either, since when a shadow moves, no surface moves with it.

8. Strictly speaking, it is not the idea of parasites on parasites forever that is absurd, but the idea of parasites with no ultimate hosts. An endless chain of parasites would be all right, provided the entire chain were anchored to something outside the chain.

9. Such a view is defended by Ernest Sosa in "Subjects Among Other Things," *Philosophical Perspectives: Metaphysics,* ed. by James Tomberlin.

10. What I have just asserted is not the innocuous "You can't have wholes without parts," but the more controversial "You can't have *this* whole without *these* parts," which is the thesis of mereological essentialism. For the (in)significance of this fact, see the next note.

11. Given the way D1 is presently framed, premise 3 implies mereological essentialism, or something close to it: every composite thing has a partitioning into parts each of which is essential to it. This may provide for some an additional ground on which to deny the premise. It would be an extraneous ground, however,

inasmuch as I could have framed D1 in such a way that mereological essentialism is *not* implied by premise 3. For example, I could have said that a thing is constituted by relations = Df it exists iff certain things *or their successors* are related in a certain way. The rest of the argument would be unaffected.

12. This objection was suggested to me by Ernest Sosa—before I had added the clause to D1 that now blocks it. Note that the addition is not simply *ad hoc.* It is in keeping with the traditional notion that the statue is an *accident* of its matter: the existence of the statue consists in the obtaining of a relation among the chunks of matter that is accidental to them, though essential to the statue. And as Kant notes at A434/B462, "Composition, as applied to substances, is only an accidental relation."

13. But could there really be emergents from emergents *ad infinitum?* Some may balk even at this. All I can say here is that the envisioned regress does not have for me the same evident impossibility that attaches to some other regresses—for example, the regress involved in there being a conjunctive proposition each of whose conjuncts is again a conjunction, and so on forever. That would be "form without matter" in a wholly unacceptable way.

14. Here, perhaps, is another way to make the regress of part depending on part less disconcerting. Suppose we are Spinozist enough to believe that the entire material cosmos is a necessary being, but not so Spinozist as to deny the existence of parts within this being. Then we could allow that although in one sense every whole is a parasite on its parts (it would not exist unless they did), in another sense it is not (for, not being contingent at all, it is not contingent *on them*).

15. In contemporary jargon, he held that relations *supervene* on qualities of the related terms: this is weaker than a reducibility thesis in not requiring there to be reciprocal entailment between a relational fact aRb and its basis, Fa & Gb.

16. Perhaps the premise should be restricted to *concrete* objects. According to Moritz Schlick, the nature of a concept is exhausted by its relations to other concepts, and according to Paul Benacerraf, the nature of a number is exhausted by its relations to other numbers. See Moritz Schlick, *General Theory of Knowledge,* trans. by A. E. Blumberg (La Salle, Illinois: Open Court Publishing Company, 1985), p. 34, and Paul Benacerraf, "What Numbers Could Not Be," *The Philosophical Review* 74 (1965), 47–73.

17. In working out a formal proof of premise 6, I have found it necessary to use one extralogical assumption: that nothing can be simple in one possible world and composite in another. So premise 6 is not strictly analytic, but it is certainly a necessary truth.

I see now that for the proof to be valid, I must use a stronger definition of 'P is nonrelational' than D3. The definiens must not merely say that it is possible for there to be *something* that has P even though nothing discrete from it exists; it must also say that *anything* that had P could have it even though nothing discrete from it existed.

18. Roderick M. Chisholm, "On the Nature of the Psychological," *Philosophical Studies* 43 (1983): 155–64. I have coined a new name for the definiendum. Chisholm's more developed views are contained in "A Logical Characterization

of the Psychological," in *Proceedings of the Ninth Annual Wittgenstein Symposium* (Vienna: Holder-Pichler-Tempsky, 1985), pp. 156–61.

19. For Berkeley, a dot of red exists only if someone perceives it, so in the sense defined by D3, redness turns out to be relational. For this reason, it may be that only Humean minima visibilia will generate counterexamples to premise 7.

20. Hume denied (a) of my syllogism, and Berkeley is generally taken to have denied (b). For a discussion of these matters, see David Raynor, " 'Minima Sensibilia' in Berkeley and Hume," *Dialogue* 19 (1980): 196–200. Raynor argues, contrary to the usual interpretation, that Berkeley denied (a) rather than (b).

21. In the first paper referred to in note 18 above, Chisholm defends the thesis that every "purely qualitative" property is psychological—a thesis very similar to my premise 7. He defines purely qualitative properties in part by the condition that they "include every property they imply or involve," and this turns out to exclude dispositional properties. I could therefore have made my defense of premise 7 easier by adopting Chisholm's definition of the "purely qualitative" as my definition of the "absolutely inward." Had I done so, however, I would have made it *harder* to defend premise 6, since it is by no means obvious that the only nonrelational properties a simple could have are purely qualitative in Chisholm's sense.

22. In *The Principles of Mathematics* (New York: W. W. Norton & Company, Inc., 1903), sec. 428, Bertrand Russell makes the following remark: "There is no difficulty, so far as I can see, in supposing an immediate difference between points, as between colors, but a difference which our senses are not constructed to be aware of."

23. Ludwig Wittgenstein, *Tractatus Logico-Philosophicus*, trans. Pears and McGuinness (London: Routledge and Kegan Paul, 1961).

24. G. Kung, *Ontology and the Logistic Analysis of Language*, rev. ed. (Dordrecht, Holland: D. Reidel Publishing Company, 1967), ch. 6; cited in D. M. Armstrong, *A Theory of Universals* (Cambridge: Cambridge University Press, 1978), vol. 2, p. 82.

25. I have benefitted from the suggestions of Kenneth Barber, Jonathan Bennett, John Biro, Roderick Chisholm, Philip Cummins, Georges Dicker, George Mavrodes, David Raynor, Ernest Sosa, David Stern, and Michael Zimmerman.

Part Five
Hegel

Why Philosophy Must Have a History
Hegel's Proposal

Kenneth L. Schmitz

Hegel sets forth his most formal consideration of the relation of the history of philosophy to philosophy itself in the Introductions to his *Lectures on the History of Philosophy*.[1] For he outlines therein the indispensable contribution of the history of philosophy to the practice of philosophy itself. He tells us that he is not interested in merely "external reflections on the history of philosophy" (93/64:1825). In his review of the existing *Histories*,[2] he finds much that is extraneous. In any event, the only proper sources for the history of philosophy are the writings of the philosophers themselves, the primary texts, the more so, since the history of philosophy is just that—the history of *philosophy*, and not the history of philosophers. This marks off the history of philosophy from ordinary history. For ordinary history must take historians as its direct sources, and not the events and personalities that they record; whereas the history of philosophy deals directly with what we may call the "philosophical events," that is to say, with the published *thoughts* of the philosophers themselves. These are the "deeds" that have occurred in the history of philosophy, and the great philosophers are the "heroes" of thought (252ff./184ff.:1825). As to the utility of such a history, Hegel is content to let it show itself indirectly, once we consider it in an appropriate way (93/64:1825).

But, how are we to consider it appropriately? If we are to approach the study of the history of philosophy *philosophically,* so that it may produce something of philosophical and not merely of general scholarly worth, we must already have in mind some idea of what philosophy is or can or should be. However, the very question of what philosophy is is problematic, in a way in which the idea of mathematics or biology is not. Nor can we turn to the extant histories of philosophy, since in them the trace of what philosophy is is too faint and obscured by scholarly details to be easily made out. Hegel laments, too, the current state of philosophy, and sets as the task of the history of philosophy: to "rescue" philosophy itself from the shallows into which it has drifted (5/2:1816). It will not be easy, however, especially since Hegel insists that what philosophy is cannot be decided upon beforehand.[3] On the other hand, if we do not have a firm purchase on what we mean by philosophy, we will drift through the history of philosophy as a ship without rudder or compass. This is the paradox of Scholasticus who wished to learn how to swim before he entered the water.[4]

Moreover, the trouble is complicated by the fact that people think they know what philosophy is, just because they can speak the name before they know the thing. What must be rejected first is the common assumption that the history of philosophy is a compendium of mere opinions (7-10/5-8:1816).[5] Hegel plays upon the German word for opinion, Meinung: to the extent that a thought is an opinion, it may be mine or yours; it is optional, and one thinker may frame one opinion, another a different one. To the extent that Plato or Kant had opinions, these opinions belong to them and may be safely buried with them. But they are great philosophers only because they gave expression to thoughts that are necessary and objectively true. Such thoughts belong to everyone, or rather to humanity as a whole (27/17:1816; 86ff./58ff.:1823).

So we come to a second paradox: philosophy has a history, but it has no past. We must address this in three steps. First, Hegel operates out of the intuition: once true, always true. That is, given the needed qualifications of tense and circumstance, something that is once true remains so: Caesar is not now crossing the Rubicon, the deed is over and done with; but if he actually did, then *that* he did remains true and is not over and done with. Hegel likes to say both that a truth is always true, and that truth transcends time, is eternal. If the truth in history transcends time, so much the more does truth in philosophical knowledge. He puts it in these words:

> [In the history of philosophy] we have not to do with the *past*, but with thinking. . . . Thus it is not history proper that we are concerned with, or rather, it is a history which at the same time is not history, since the thoughts, principles, ideas confronting us are something present [i.e., something still valid for us]. (133/98-99:1825)

For all that—and this is the second step—Hegel warns us that each philosophy "belongs to its own time and is caught in that time's restrictions," since it speaks only to, and out of, its own era and situation (72/49:1820). That is why he considers it wrongheaded to try to revive the philosophy of Plato or of Aristotle or any other (72-75/49-52:1820), and equally wrongheaded to load up an earlier philosophy with questions of which it never dreamed (68-69/47:1820).[6] This is indeed a puzzle:

philosophy has a history, has no history, has only a history.

And so, we pass on to the third step in the form of a question: how is it that philosophy, which seeks what is presently and always true—how is it that it has a history at all (7/5:1816)? How does that which is always true appear in the form of that which passes away? In Hegel's succinct, if to us puzzling, language: why and how does the eternal come to be in time? Hegel speaks of an "inner contradiction" in the very enterprise of the history of philosophy:

> Philosophy aims at knowing what is imperishable, eternal, and absolute. Its aim is truth. But history relates the sort of thing which has existed at one time but at another has perished. (14/11:1816)

If time and history give us problems, so too does the variety and diversity of philosophies. Hegel does not suppose that philosophy is one in any simple fashion, but if it is a genuinely integrated body of knowledge at all or, better still, a consistent way (*habitus*) of knowing—then we have a right to expect that *in some sense* philosophy is one. But if philosophy is one, does that mean that one philosophy is true and the others false? And if so, which one? and on what basis do we select that one? He remarks:

> It is . . . a fact that there are and have been different philosophies. Yet the truth is *one*: this invincible feeling or faith is possessed by the instinct of reason. Thus too there can be but *one* philosophy. And because philosophies are so different, it is concluded that the others must be *errors*. (28/17:1820)

Not surprisingly, the one that is held to be true is likely to turn out to be one's own philosophy, let the devil take the others. Hegel's answer, on the other hand, is rather different: it is that not this or that philosophy is true philosophy. On the contrary, what is required if we are to speak of philosophy is the totality of philosophies; not this or that one, but *all* comprise the truth of philosophy. The question is, how are we to understand this?

Hegel unfolds his own understanding of the oneness of philosophy with the help of three central concepts: the famous Hegelian negation, the notorious Hegelian Idea, and the notion of development.

Negation. The variety of philosophies expresses the difference of each from the others. But by the very fact of being different from others, a particular philosophy must contain "not only its *one* immediate specific character, but its *other* also" (31/20:1820). We discover this when we try to explain a particular philosophy in terms of its concrete situation; we inevitably set it off from others, especially from those that almost

254 Part Five: Hegel

agree with it. In a controversial move Hegel takes this negation to be more than merely an external setting apart and exclusion of the one from the other. Instead, he argues that this very exclusion is as much constitutive of the meaning of a particular philosophy as are its own positive positions. By way of analogy, Hegel remarks that to say of something that it is a cause (*Ursache*) is to include within its meaning the relation to what is precisely *not* a cause, i.e., a potential or actual effect; without that intrinsic reference, it remains merely a thing (*Sache*) (31/20:1820). We may infer, then, that Aristotle's philosophy is intrinsically related to Plato's as well as to the Stoics'. Now, these particular philosophies are more or less contemporaneous and have actual causal links; but we would miss Hegel's point, it seems to me, if we insisted upon relations of actual influence among all the philosophies Hegel discusses. The negative relation of one philosophy to another is intrinsic and constitutive in the first instance as a relation of the *difference in meaning* of one philosophy to another within the unity of philosophy as such. In this inclusive sense of negation lie the seeds of the Hegelian dialectic, which transforms the simple, analytic understanding of sheer identity into "speculative" identity, i.e., identity that confirms itself only in and through what stands in opposition to it. There also hides the more positive prospect of that inclusive totality of meaning that we call the Hegelian system (33/21:1820). How can these conceptions of negation, speculative identity, and system be put to work in determining the role of the history of philosophy?

Idea. Hegel is conscious that he is writing a preface to a philosophical history of philosophy. Without a pre-understanding of what philosophy is we have no basis for accepting or rejecting what in that history puts itself forward as philosophy; yet we have seen that to simply impose one more conception of philosophy upon the materials would violate Hegel's own stated aims. Hegel finds the key to the solution in what he calls the *Idea*. He proposes it provisionally to account for why there are many philosophies and why philosophy has to have a history. The Idea receives "the strict and speculative proof . . . in the science of philosophy itself," i.e., in the *Science of Logic* and the *Encyclopedia of the Philosophical Sciences.*[7] Nevertheless, I think we would miss both Hegel's meaning and his intent if we thought of the Idea as merely an hypothesis, without further qualification.[8] He does speak of the Idea as a presupposition (*Voraussetzung*) operative in his inquiry; and he speaks of "an advance statement" (*ein vorher Auszumachendes, eine vorausgeschickte Angabe*) that will be proven in the examination of the history of philosophy itself. As we read on, however, we sense a peculiar kind of definiteness or content and, at the same time, a peculiar kind of emptiness in his guiding Idea.[9]

As the guiding idea that Hegel brings to the study of the history of thought, Hegel acknowledges the indispensable role of the individuals who alone exist; but he defines the significance of the community in terms of the thinking that animates it and that constitutes it as a community of rational discourse.[14]

Hegel tells us that the community of thought upon which the history of philosophy rests could only emerge after a long period of development. To what in our experience can we turn in order to find analogs and anticipations of these great self-sustaining realities about which Hegel is so fond of speaking? What he considers most fundamental to *organic life* is that it is not merely a collection of individual organisms, each of which happens to be alive. Rather, what is fundamental is the interlocking web of life on this planet: the cycle of reproduction, the dynamism of the food chain, in which individuals sustain not only themselves and their successors, but in which, actively and passively, they also carry on the great forces of organic life itself. It is not that the individuals are unimportant; indeed, they are indispensable, for there is no life force without individual organisms. A disembodied life force would simply not exist at all. What is most distinctive and essential— in a phrase, what holds fast in and through time—is the common flow of vital energy in which the present organisms share.[15] Now, when Hegel insists that philosophy is somehow *one*, because "thinking is essentially one," he has something similar in mind. Of course, because philosophy is the science of pure thought, its dynamic unity must realize itself in conceptual, rational form.

Where do we turn to find the essence of thinking? We could turn first to *culture*, which includes a certain kind of consciousness within it, primarily at the level of feeling, imagining, and representing. This modality of consciousness shows itself in art, myth, and religion.[16] A still clearer exhibition of the essence of thinking is to be found in what we might call the community of *language*, which requires individual speakers to situate themselves within a flexible matrix of linguistic possibilities, a matrix that bends the speakers in accordance with its primary tendencies and possibilities. Indeed, Hegel is not above complaining about the strictures of just such a matrix. But more clearly still, Hegel has in mind something like the *community of scientific research*. A particular discovery by an individual scientist is meaningful only in the context of scientific laws, discoveries, theories, hypotheses, experiments, and observations, along with the techniques, methodologies, logic, and fundamental philosophy that underlie the context. Not only does the meaning of the discovery depend upon such a web of thought, but the very possibility of such a discovery coming to be and coming to be recognized also supposes such a context. Now, it is in this sense that Hegel speaks of what is essential to thinking. The work of scientific discovery is always the work of individual minds, or groups of them, but they function precisely as members of a community of scientific research. Philosophy is not different in this respect, except that in philosophy—according to Hegel—thought reaches its purest rational, conceptual form. If we ask what "purest" means here, Hegel will say that in philosophy thought is least distracted by alien factors, is most attentive to its own standards, and translates everything into the universal, conceptual categories of rational discourse. This is precisely what he means by the "essence of thinking," and he calls this living community of thought *spirit*. Of course, he does not mean by "spirit" the Latin *spiritus*, at least not in a disembodied, immaterial sense; he means the Germanic *Geist*, and it is for him in its actual existence always embodied.

A living community of thought is not, of course. a *thing*, nor can we really speak of the "products" of thought as though they could be sustained apart from their being recognized by thinking. Thoughts may be said to reside in books or in other artifacts, but strictly speaking they are present only in minds, and they are actually present only in minds that think them. It is *activity* that sustains thoughts; they are not independent objects that have any reality in themselves. Nevertheless, the demand for the translatability of perceptions, images, and feelings into the categories of thought is the demand that *they* be translated in their objective truth, as they really *are*. Although thoughts are not things that exist independently of the minds that actually think them, nonetheless those minds must think in accordance with objective reality if they are to think truly. So, on the one hand, Hegel catches the autonomy and the energy of thought when he insists that the Idea "determines itself entirely out of its own resources [*sich nur aus sich*]" (99/69:1825). On the other hand, he catches the objective content of thought by insisting upon the need for consciousness to take cognizance of the objective world out of which it has arisen and within which it both lives and thinks (121/90:1825).

Philosophy begins when thought is able to raise the question of the meaning of reality as a whole, and when it expects to answer that question in the conceptual categories of rational discourse. Now, this occurs in time when a people is able to rise beyond its particular interests. It does not simply set them aside, of course, since it must survive. Nevertheless, it must regard them as not absolutely primary, and it must build institutions upon the expectation inherent in rational discourse. Only in this way will it be conscious that it is a *free* people. Then—and only then—can the historical conditions be favorable to the development of philosophy. Freedom is inseparable from the realization of rational discourse. Hegel thinks that this beginning occurs in Greece and constitutes the first epoch of the history of philosophy.[17]

The second epoch belongs to what he calls "Germanic" philosophy, which we would more clearly call "European" or "modern" philosophy.

Prompted by the Christian insistence upon the infinite value of the individual person, modern philosophy joined to the Greek development of objective rational discourse the inseparability of self-consciousness from such discourse. With this (the spirit of the autonomy of thought sponsored by the Enlightenment), the need for freedom is recognized; for it consists in "not being in the hands of a stranger . . . but being at home with oneself": "nicht bei einem Anderen, Fremden zu sein . . . sondern bei sich zu sein" (233/172:1823).[18] The stranger is not only another human being (slavery), or an oppressive social order (tyranny), or the capricious forces of nature (barbarism), but is all the residue of unmediated otherness, all that is not translated into the categories of thought. Throughout the history of rational discourse the principle of the autonomy of thought has been at work: the Greek discovery of rational discourse first promulgated the hegemony of thought, and self-consciousness in the modern form of a critical, progressive community of thought is indispensable to its completion.

We are now in a position to say why philosophy must have a history. Thinking must begin objectively in an individual by occurring at some definite time and by attaching itself to a definite place. This is merely the general requirement that all existing beings must take their rise in time and space. Moreover, the beginnings—even of thought in its proper, conceptual form—must be poor and empty, just because they arise immediately out of the sensuous life of man's physical, animate, sentient nature. Immediately: that is, the first thoughts are not yet analyzed and articulated in the realm of thought, which can only be accomplished by the thinking of further thoughts. It is this immediacy that makes both possible and necessary the development of thought in time and place.

As we have seen, however, the condition that is intrinsic and proper to rational thought itself is that the finite interests of the individual and the merely particular interests of a people must give way to more general and essential concerns. Only this transcendence of private and social particularity introduces a people into the sphere of the universal. This sphere is also the sphere of freedom. In order to fulfil freedom, however, thinking must proceed from its poor, abstract beginnings through an accumulative development in which partial truths are translated into the discourse that constitutes the history of philosophy. This discourse is multifaceted and yet, properly understood, is recognized as an integrated achievement. It is nothing less than the realization of the project announced by Hegel in his Einleitung, and which he called the Idea. He adds that "the Idea is just what we call truth—a big word [ein grosses Wort]" (99/70:1825). Knox renders it more sedately: "a great word." Others might want to say an [all too] grand word. But however embarrassing some philosophers might find the claim today, it would be a betrayal to hand it over without a struggle to dogmatists, fanatics, or ideologues. It is difficult to know what business philosophy will have left to itself if it severs ties with such a "grand" enterprise. Even skepticism is haunted by the word.

As to the *diversity* of philosophies, only the examination of the history of philosophy under the lead of the Idea can hope to demonstrate that each philosophy, developed in its own time, continues to contribute as a stage or moment of philosophy as a whole; and that each is part of the developed *system* of thought that coincides with philosophy itself. Not only, then, does philosophy *have* a history, but the history of philosophy *is* philosophy (119/88:1825).

Hegel brusquely puts aside the complaint that thought has taken too long to produce such a result. Time and toil belong to the restricted sphere of limited ends, and not to the realm of discourse itself, which takes all the time it needs. As Knox puts it, in the realm of spirit there are no "upstarts" popping up overnight like so many mushrooms. Instead, spirit often meanders in a roundabout way toward the true and tested knowledge that results (61–63/42–43:1820).[19]

In the light of the foregoing, what can it mean to make use of the history of philosophy "in the Hegelian manner"? It can mean, of course, that one considers the history of philosophy to be important, but such a general interest is not peculiar to Hegel and is not sufficiently specific to be dubbed "Hegelian." There is, it seems to me, at least in English-speaking philosophical circles, a rough division of approach to "doing philosophy historically." On the one hand, it consists in the *use* of past texts in the history of philosophy, especially of great or influential philosophers. Through the study of them we benefit from the acquisition of new ideas, the refinement of ones already held, the detection of flaws in the arguments put forth, the discovery of unrecognized premises or presuppositions, and the pursuit of implications and consequences. This is, if I may so call it, the *instrumental* approach to the study of the history of philosophy. The history of philosophy is a useful instrument in the development of a philosophical habit of mind, but it remains incidental and external to the real business of philosophy proper. On the other hand, the second approach to the history of philosophy makes a stronger claim, since it insists that the history of philosophy is itself in some way *constitutive* of philosophy. Now, this second approach is taken by Hegel, for he insists that the history of philosophy constitutes an integral part of what philosophy *is*. The approach is by no means exclusive to him, and the precise nature of the relation between philosophy and its history will differ from one philosopher to another. If the danger of the first approach is the introduction of anachronisms into the text under analysis, the threat of the second is the concession to relativism and historicism. It is clear that Hegel thinks he has forestalled the charge of relativism and historicism by proposing the Idea as the indispensable expectation of true knowledge.

In addition to the importance Hegel accords the history of philosophy and in addition to its constitutive character, there are more specific aspects to Hegel's approach. Thus, for example, despite what at first glance may seem to be a purely theoretical interpretation of philosophical knowing, he does take account of the practical modalities of knowing insofar as he insists upon the relation between freedom and rational discourse. What is more, he gives emphasis to the primarily social character of theoretical as well as practical knowing and anticipates the concern about the sociology of knowledge. Indeed, he recognizes the close relation between the history of thought in a given era and the actual events and course of history. At the same time, he takes pains to distinguish the philosophical study of history and civilization (*Weltgeschichte* or philosophy of history) from the study of pure thought (*Geschichte der Philosophie* or history of philosophy). Finally, he insists upon the power of the negative in developing the course of thought. It may well be that in following the later *Einleitung* I have not given enough emphasis to the negative in Hegel's philosophy.[20] It is certainly prominent in his own thought, and it is much stressed today; but it is less prominent in the sphere of pure thought which is the province of the history of philosophy. There it is manifest more through the one-sidedness of time-bound philosophies than through their polemical confrontation. It must be added, however, that Hegel's emphasis upon the Idea may well have led him to place a too irenic emphasis on unity in the *Einleitung*, a unity whose reconciliation of opposites can only be displayed in its concreteness by following through the actual course of the history of philosophy that is to be found in the subsequent lectures.

Still, the importance of the history of philosophy, its constitutive role, the inclusion of the practical, social, and negative are not of themselves peculiar to Hegel. Other dialectical philosophies—many of them descendants of Hegel's—contain these features too.

Special applications of Hegelian categories arose in part after the appearance of Nicolai Hartmann's volume of *Das deutsche Idealismus* (1929), which was given over to Hegel. The book had a considerable impact on young French philosophers at the beginning of the fourth decade of this century. They learned that they might draw upon Hegel and his interpretation of the history of philosophical thought without—to put it bluntly—accepting the "baggage of the System." This "baggage" had weighed heavily upon some earlier Hegelians, notably among the British. This neglect of the systematic "pretensions" of the Hegelian system opened up the use of some aspects of Hegel's analysis and method to what might be called "situational" analyses, often yielding brilliant vignettes, especially among the Existentialists. Others—and these were eventually to become the neo-Marxists, whether of the French, East European, or

Frankfurter variety—were struck with the transposability of the power of the negative, so that the force of the dialectic permitted fresh approaches to previous philosophical positions and to present-day human situations. None of these, it seems to me, would satisfy Hegel, for the systemic drive was overpowering in his thought. The recognition of such a drive should not in itself brand one a "right-wing" Hegelian, any more than the recognition of the power of the negative should brand one a "left-wing" Hegelian. These categories are too simplistic for a mind as subtle as Hegel's, and it is the work of that mind that has been the object of this paper. Considering the use we have just seen him make of the Idea as the leading hermeneutic principle for the interpretation of the history of philosophy, we might well expect him to consider its suspension in the cited "situational" analyses as one more instance of a lack of seriousness in the pursuit of philosophy.

On the other hand—there is always another hand in dialectic—we might well reply that Hegel's own philosophy has been overcome from within on the basis of its own principles; for he has told us that reality must change before philosophy can change (72/49:1820; 26/39-40:1820; 225ff./165ff.:1825). Now, it is not too much to say that reality has changed in significant ways since the days when Hegel lectured on philosophy and its history in Berlin. The question he leaves us with is whether the philosophical Idea he proposed—which I have called "rational discourse"—can be transformed to serve today, or whether the situation has changed so much that his Ideal of rational discourse has ceased to "hold fast"—if it ever did—against the ravages of time and history?

NOTES

1. For the time being, the best available German text of the several versions of the Introduction is that edited originally by Joh. Hoffmeister (1940) but revised and somewhat abbreviated by Fr. Nicolin: Einleitung in die Geschichte der Philosophie, 3d ed. (Hamburg: F. Meiner, 1959). A new semicritical edition is underway. We have two translations into English based upon the Hoffmeister text and drawing especially upon the lecture course of 1825-26: Hegel's Introduction to the Lectures on the History of Philosophy, trans. T. M. Knox and completed for publication by A. V. Miller (Oxford: Clarendon, 1985), based upon the 1940 text; and with a more extensive introduction and a slightly different selection, Hegel's Idea of Philosophy, trans. Q. Lauer (New York: Fordham, 1971). The older translation: Hegel's Lectures on the History of Philosophy, trans. E. S. Haldane and Frances H. Simson, 3 vols. (London: Routledge and Kegan Paul, 1892-96), is based upon Michelet's text in the Werke, 2d ed., 1840. Unless otherwise indicated, references henceforth will be included in the body of the paper, the first figure giving the reference to the Nicolin (1959) revised German edition, followed by a slash, and the page number of the Knox translation, followed by a colon to indicate the year of the course from which the passage has been taken.

For literature on the topic, see K. Duesing, *Hegel und die Geschichte der Philosophie* (Darmstadt: Wiss. Buchgesellschaft, 1983), and *Hegel and the History of Philosophy*, ed. Jos. O'Malley et al. (The Hague: M. Nijhoff, 1974.

The choice of the *Einleitung* as the basis of my presentation is not without its problems, both textual and hermeneutic. The first concern the authority of the text, since Hegel published neither the *Einleitung* nor the subsequent lectures, and many of the sources of the early posthumous editions are no longer extant. We do have about a quarter of the text of the *Einleitung* in Hegel's own hand (1816, 1820), and the remainder (1823, 1825, 1827; and 1829) is drawn from notebooks written for the most part by known and reliable students. (See the *Vorbemerkungen* in the German edition, pp. xi–xv.) The present text, however, is a continuous composite text constructed by the modern editor, though the German edition does provide marginal indications of the course year in which each passage was recorded. The second set of questions are hermeneutical in nature and arise largely in the milieu of poststructuralist French writing. They touch especially upon the problematic character of the Preface as a literary genre; for in the Preface the author must say what he is not entitled to say. Hegel was himself aware of this difficulty and expressed it in each of the Prefaces to his works. Mark C. Taylor, ed., *Deconstruction in Context: Literature and Philosophy* (Chicago: University of Chicago Press, 1985), provides an informative essay and a useful collection of background selections on this discussion. For a principal development of the problem see, Jacques Derrida, *Of Grammatology*, trans. and with an introduction by G. C. Spivak (Baltimore: Johns Hopkins, 1976), and also by Derrida, *Margins of Philosophy*, trans. A. Bass (Chicago: University of Chicago Press), especially "The Pit and the Pyramid: Introduction to Hegel's Semiology," pp. 69–109.

Despite these difficulties, if we are to get at Hegel's general view of the relation between philosophy and its history, the *Einleitung* to his lectures on the history of philosophy remains the most formal consideration we have from his pen.

2. Especially those of Thomas Stanley (1655), J. J. Brucker (1766–67), Dietrich Tiedemann (1791–97), J. G. Buhle (1796–1804), and Tennemann's twelve volumes (1798–1819) (252/184:1823, 1825, 1827).

3. This is a constant position with him. See, for example, the Preface and Introduction to the *Phenomenology of Spirit*.

4. *Enzyklopaedie der philosophischen Wissenschaften, 1830*, ed. F. Nicolin and O. Poeggeler (Hamburg: F. Meiner, 1959), p. 43, n. 10.

5. The German reads: "*Die Geschichte* [der Philosophie ist] *nicht eine Sammlung zufaelliger Meinungen, sondern* [ein] *notwendiger Zusammenhang, in ihren ersten Anfaengen bis zu ihrer reichen Ausbildung.*" On "deeds" [die Taten], see 71/49:1820.

6. "One must adhere strictly, *historically*, precisely, to the *very own* words of [the author], not draw conclusions [and so] make something different out of them" (Ibid).

7. Speaking of the identity of philosophy and the history of philosophy, Hegel admits that, in the Introduction to the *Lectures on the History of Philosophy*, such an identification is as yet only an assertion: "*noch eine Behauptung*" (119/88:1825).

8. Although he does speak of the history of philosophy as that which affords an empirical proof (den empirischen Beweis) of its identity with philosophy as system (119/88), everything nevertheless turns on what he means by "empirical."

9. The point is important enough to provide the essential text: "Therefore this introduction is to premise [vorauszusetzen] the conception both of philosophy and also of the subject-matter [des Gegenstandes ihrer Geschichte]. . . . What can be said in this introduction is not so much something to be made out in advance [ein vorher Auszumachendes] but rather something which can be justified and proved [gerechtfertigt und erwiesen] solely by the treatment [Abhandlung] of the history itself. Simply for this reason these preliminary explanations [vorlaeufigen Erklaerungen] cannot be classed in the category of arbitrary pre-suppositions [willkuerlichen Voraussetzungen]. But to premise [voranzustellen] them, though when justified they are essentially results, can only have the interest which an advance statement of the most general subject-matter of any science may have [eine vorausgeschicte Angabe des allgemeinsten Inhalts einer Wissenschaft ueberhaupt haben kann]" (10/7–8:1816).

10. As far as I know, J. E. Erdmann, Grundriss der Logik und Metaphysik. Eine Einfuehrung in Hegels Wissenschaft der Logik (1841; Leiden, 1901), first proposed this term to identify that "harmless presupposition" that Hegel brought to the supposedly "presuppositionless" beginning of the Science of Logic.

11. Hegel makes a similar suggestion in the Introduction to the Lectures on the Philosophy of History: "The sole thought which philosophy brings to the treatment of history is the simple concept of Reason" (Reason in History, trans. R. S. Hartman [Indianapolis: Bobbs-Merrill/Library of Liberal Arts, 1953], p. 11). For the German text: Die Vernunft in der Geschichte, ed. Joh. Hoffmeister (Hamburg: F. Meiner, 1955). This proposal is more daring in the matter of history proper, perhaps, than it is in regard to the matter of the history of philosophy, which is the history of thought attending to itself.

The challenge of skepticism is later faced by Hegel, who assigns to it a specific and necessary role in the development of philosophy. Of course, the radical skeptic can protest that such a domesticated doubt is merely a house pet; but if the wild variety can be baited out of its lair to engage in the enterprise of rational discourse, it must be caught eventually in the trap of self-contradiction.

12. The language undoubtedly strikes us as high flown. It is not unusual today to disclaim any pretensions to an all-embracing system, let alone one that unites all philosophies; and there are proven difficulties in systematic grandeur. In the absence of such a claim, however, we are left with strategies, including (a) to select or produce one view and ignore others (dogmatism); (b) to treat other views as simply wrongheaded, confused, mistaken, neurotic, or even to attribute stupidity, softheadedness, or bad will to their proponents (at its best, sectarianism; at its worst, fanaticism); (c) to integrate other views into our own (imperialism); (d) to modestly lower our claim to one view among others, no better or no worse (mild skepticism). These strategies are not mutually exclusive. Many think Hegel guilty of philosophical imperialism. He would undoubtedly reply that he is attempting none of the above, but rather to bring all philosophical insights together in the unity of rational discourse. We might wish to answer that pluralism is both a theoretically realistic and practically civil strategy, but

he would undoubtedly add that no project other than integration can be considered philosophically serious.

13. Hegel tells us that the most general thoughts can be expressed in myths, symbols, and similes, but that developed, concrete thoughts cannot. Speaking of myth, he says: "This form is not the correct, appropriate one for philosophy. The thought which has itself as its object must itself also be objective in its form; it must have raised itself above its natural form [i.e., above imagery drawn from nature]; it must also appear in the form of thought [i.e., in rational, conceptual form]. . . . Once thought has been so strengthened as to gain its existence in its own proper element, myth is a superfluous decoration, whereby philosophy is not advanced" (211-12/156-57:1823; cf. 238-39/176-77:1823, 1825).

14. For a recent presentation and discussion of a wide variety of approaches see, *Rationality To-Day: La Rationalité Aujourdhui*, ed. Th. F. Geraets (Ottawa, 1979). Cf. K. L. Schmitz, "Are there things more important for the human race than survival? The Greek Heritage: Rationality," in *Das Europaenische Erbe und Seine Christliche Zukunft*, ed. N. Lobkowicz (Koeln: Hans Martin Schleyer-Stiftung/Pontificium Consilium pro Cultura, 1985), pp. 348-56 (German, pp. 95-104).

15. Of course, this dynamic unity remains implicit in the actual web of organic life. There it is only imperfectly realized and is made explicit only by and in thought (102-103/72-73:1827; 106-108/76-78:1825, 1827; 127/94-95:1825). This is because it is of the nature of thought alone to hold together factors that may be separated in themselves: for example, the beginning of a process in nature is separate from its end, or the different members of an organism are in themselves separate from one another. When we come to properly human (Hegel calls it spiritual) life, however, we have a more or less explicit holding together of such factors in the living things themselves; as, for example, in the cultural memory of a people, or in more conceptual terms, at the various stages of scientific research in which the prior findings are gathered up as a provisional result and adverted to in setting out the problem.

16. This is why Hegel says that we can no longer wholly ignore the implicit presence of thought in these forms of human life and judge them to be simply erroneous (53/36:1820). "In the history of philosophy, however, we have to do solely with reason as it is set forth in the form of thought. Philosophical affirmations contained merely implicitly in religion [and mythology] are therefore not our concern" (205/152:1823). "Philosophy can have nothing to do with them [i.e., the implicit philosophical affirmations] because even in such myths thought is not the first thing; what is predominant in them is the form of imagery" (208/154:1823; cf. 210-16/156-59:1825, 1833, 1823). Even in the Christian religion—just because it accepts what is true as a *given* revelation received from without—*the self-determining activity of rational discourse* is not what counts as the absolute basis and norm; and so Christianity does not qualify as philosophical thinking, nor is it the concern of the history of philosophy (216-19/159-60:1825, 1823). Myth and religion are prephilosophical because of the element of unresolved *immediacy* that is in them: they are simply given, received from another source than rational thought. Speaking of Greek religion, he remarks that "for another thing, these thoughts have not won their proper form. The form required [for

the fully rational discourse of philosophy] is the form of thought, and what is expressed in that form must be ultimate and the absolute foundation" (217/159:1823). Speaking of the writings of the Fathers of the Church and the Schoolmen, he says: "The content is true in itself, but it is not self-dependent, not dependent on thought as such . . . not self-dependent, justified through thinking as such" (218–19/159–60:1825, 1823). This element of positivity is found in popular philosophy as well, which retails received opinions (sometimes profound, sometimes banal) (221–23/162–63:1823). Indeed, even the natural sciences, which rightly pride themselves on the autonomy of judgment (159/117:1825), attend to natural processes that—however mediated by theory they may be—present themselves in the form of external observations (158–66/116–23:1825, 1823; 219–20/160–61:1825, 1823).

17. "Philosophy's history begins where thought comes into existence [Existenz] in its freedom, where it tears itself free from its immersion [Versenktsein] in nature, from its unity with nature, when it constitutes itself in its own eyes [sich fuer sich], when thinking turns in upon itself and is at home with itself [in sich geht und bei sich ist]" (224/164:1825). "Philosophy strictly begins when the Absolute is no longer regarded pictorially [als Vorstellung], but when untrammelled thinking [der freie Gedanke] does not merely think [denkt] the Absolute, but apprehends [erfasst] the Idea of the Absolute, i.e. the being . . . which thought recognizes as the essence of things, as absolute totality, and the immanent essence of everything" (224/164:1833). "Philosophy begins where thinking emerges in its purity, where it is universal, and where this purity, this universal is what is essential, genuine and absolute, the essence of all that is (224/165:1827; Knox tr. slightly altered). Hegel recognizes, of course, that Greek society is flawed by its dependence upon the institution of slavery (235/173:1823).

18. That the Enlightenment and its sequel have actually realized such a concept of reason is denied by at least some who adopt a thoroughly instrumental understanding of reason: see, Max Horkheimer and Theodor Adorno, Dialektik der Aufklaerung, Theodor W. Adorno: Gesammelte Schriften 3 (Frankfurt am Main: Suhrkamp, 1981). An English translation exists of the essay and the two appendices: The Concept of Enlightenment. Cf. also, Kant's essay What is Enlightenment?

19. "Yes, it is a long time; the length may surprise [auffallen] us, but the spirit needs it to work out [erarbeiten] philosophy. I said at the beginning that our philosophy today is the result of the labor of every century. . . . If the length of time surprises us we must realize that this time has been spent on acquiring these concepts—this could not have happened so well previously. . . . As for the slowness of the world-spirit, we must reflect that it did not have to hurry; it had time enough. . . . There is a trivial saying that nature goes to its end by the shortest route—correct. But the route of the spirit is roundabout, mediation [Umweg, Vermittlung]" (61–62/42–43:1820). Yet, it is "labor, activity directed on something present and transforming it" (65/44:1820).

20. See the excellent commentary by James Lawler and Vladimir Shtinov.

Hegel's Method of Doing Philosophy Historically: A Reply

James Lawler and Vladimir Shtinov

It is possible to separate two matters joined initially in Dr. Schmitz's paper. One is the very general issue of "why philosophy must have a history," and if it must, what it means "to do philosophy historically."[1] The other matter concerns the problem of how "to approach the study of the history of philosophy *philosophically*."[2] Whereas the first is a general question regarding the nature of philosophical practice as a whole, the second appears, on the surface at least, to be a partial issue, an issue for those philosophers who happen to have a special interest in the history of philosophy.

One can show, as Dr. Schmitz has done in connection with Hegel, that it is possible, and at least plausible, to understand the history of philosophy in a philosophical manner. We can do this by viewing that history as a quest for truth made by reasonable men, building on one another's accomplishments, correcting their predecessors' mistakes, defining more precisely the limits within which previous ideas have validity, improving in this way on the truth of the ancestors on whose shoulders we stand and with whom we form a kind of community of truth seekers.

But once having risen to a certain level of accomplishment, we may think we can push away the ladder—to change our metaphor slightly— that brought us up to the sunny heights of philosophical mastery. When Wittgenstein applied this metaphor not just to past philosophy but to his own preceding arguments,[3] he might have said more accurately that we—certain nonhistorically minded philosophers at least—pull out our stakes as we climb. According to such a perspective, philosophy may indeed have a history, and one that can be studied philosophically, but this is far from implying that it is necessary or philosophically obligatory to pay any attention to that history, or "to do philosophy historically."

It is often argued that awareness of the origin or genesis of the philosophical ideas and methods we use today does not guarantee or establish their truth, and philosophical truth, as Hegel himself tirelessly repeated, is independent of time and space. To trace the history of this truth may be an interesting and gratifying occupation. We may even be able to accomplish this exercise by explicitly invoking very little of contemporary theory and by using only the arguments of our ancestors, repeating the course of the history of thought until we arrive at our own standpoint. But all this can be done differently, it seems, less circuitously, by nonhistorical reasoning.

The charge of "historicism" has been so vehemently laid against Hegel[4] that it is sometimes easy to overlook the fact, brought out early in Dr. Schmitz's paper, that Hegel considered the historical existence of philosophy to be something of a scandal. Reason is eternal—Hegel repeated this axiom of his own philosophical heritage. But Hegel did not draw from this belief that "truth is truth," the conclusion that, given the diversity of philosophical positions, one philosophy must be true and the rest false. Certainly he did not support the skeptical conclusion of popular educated opinion in his time that *none* of them can be true, that philosophy consists in historically relative "opinions." Hegel's own solution to the contradiction between the unity of truth and the diversity of philosophical positions was to reject the notion that truth is an all-or-nothing affair, and to advance the idea of a developing historical progression of "relative truths."

Nevertheless, despite this acknowledgment of its historical character, Hegel regarded philosophy in the highest sense to be a matter of philosophical Logic—i.e., the study of what might today be called the logic of our basic or most general concepts. Such Logic not only does not depend on historical evidence, but it also even consists, Hegel writes, in the "exposition of God as he is in his eternal essence before the creation of nature and a finite mind."[5] As Dr. Schmitz has mentioned, such idealistic exaggeration has not prevented thinkers of various philosophical trends from seeking, in the spirit of Hegel himself, the rational kernel in Hegel's own theory without "the baggage of the System."[6]

Our question therefore takes the form of asking whether for Hegel himself a historical approach is something basically intrinsic to philosophical activity in this proper "logical" understanding. Granted that Thales can indeed be said to be a philosopher in more than a nominal sense. This is so not primarily because Thales' philosophy contains significant truths by today's standards—the approach to the history of philosophy taken by so-called "rational reconstruction"—or because Thales' philosophy is "intelligible" in the light of contemporary beliefs, the approach of "historical reconstruction."[7] Thales is significant because his ideas can be situated at the start of some minimal grade of rationality that leads eventually, and not necessarily by the straightest path, to the emergence of contemporary standards of rationality. Even so, why need we, in doing philosophy today, turn back to the primitive ideas of Thales?

Hegel's Introduction to the lectures on *The History of Philosophy* gives some credence to the view that philosophy can do without history. Philosophy, in some sense, must already be presupposed to the study of its own history—otherwise, how could we recognize whether what we are studying is a philosophical doctrine? Even if the "Idea" with which we begin to study the history of philosophy is a "reduction" of the Idea of the Logic, as Dr. Schmitz suggests, does this not support the belief that if we want the full truth, we should turn to the Logic itself and not bother with its watered-down approximations?

Yet in his Introduction Hegel speaks of a twofold premise to the history of philosophy—not just the premise of preexisting philosophy, but the premise of "the subject-matter of its history."[8] Likewise, Hegel speaks of two methods of finding philosophical truth, an historical method and a logical method. Rather than separate the two, Hegel sees them to be necessarily connected: "This [double method] is the only worthy way of studying philosophy." But then he adds, characteristically, "Logic is the true way because it works through the *concept* of the thing."[9]

Because of the particular subject matter and objectives of his *History of Philosophy,* Hegel is naturally more concerned with the question why the history of philosophy should be understood philosophically than he is with the question why philosophy itself should be understood and practiced historically.

If we look at Hegel's actual philosophical arguments as developed in other works, Hegel's understanding of the connection of the logical and the historical methods stands out more sharply, perhaps, than in his explicit discussion of the history of philosophy.

In his Preface to the *Phenomenology of Spirit* Hegel explains his conception of the nature of philosophy primarily through a criticism of his predecessor, presumably Schelling, whom he doesn't mention by name.

Schelling—or a philosophical trend of which Schelling was the foremost representative—sharply criticizes the Enlightenment conception of scientific knowledge as a collection of special investigations, as a body of particular information or truths. Authentic science must be one, unified, a whole, Schelling asserts in reply. Hegel does not disagree with this general statement, but with the way in which it is set against the opposing view as though it were the pure light of truth dispelling ignorance and stupidity. In Schelling's abstract understanding of truth, the opposing view is false, his is true—and that is all there is to it.

This conception of the nature of science was linked with a larger romantic, mystical or intuitivist movement of those days that involved, Hegel writes, "The strenuous, almost over-zealous and frenzied effort to tear men away from their preoccupation with the sensuous, from their ordinary private affairs, and to direct their gaze to the stars; as if they had forgotten all about the divine, and were ready like worms to content themselves with dirt and water."[10]

In reply to this unhistorical approach to the criticism of a historical opponent, Hegel charges that such a negative attitude toward the particularism, sensualism, and materialism of Enlightenment thought has failed to appreciate fully the standpoint that it is opposing.[11] We can remedy this failure by recalling the fact that medieval other-worldliness forms the background to modern empiricism and Enlightenment this-worldliness. The cult of feeling, the rejection of "formalistic" knowledge, as well as the Schellingian one-sided insistence on the unity of science all imply contempt for what in fact constituted an enormous advance for the human spirit—the development of the capacity to find intelligibility and interest in the world we see before us. If we remind ourselves of what went before the early modern scientific outlook and try to understand how this outlook advanced beyond what preceded it, we will not dismiss it so thoughtlessly.[12]

Now, however, Hegel says, it appears that the pendulum has swung in the opposite direction.[13] But in its quest for something more than the piecemeal accumulation of particular bodies of information, this trend (exemplified by Schelling's pronouncement that in the Absolute all is one) presents the need to make an advance as though it were already an accomplished fact. Its intrinsic abstractness reflects its failure to understand the fundamental contributions of the empirical sciences and the empiricist-materialistic point of view in philosophy.[14]

Indeed Schelling presents as an accomplished result what is only the starting point of the task of philosophical thought: not to engage in empty talk about the unity of science, as though such talk was that unity itself, but to realize in fact a great work of unification of the natural and social sciences.

The particularism of empiricist science that was so unceremoniously set aside by Schelling gets revenge for this mistreatment by reemerging within his work. It is not possible to write an interesting book in which one simply repeats one's insight into the Absolute. So Schelling fills up pages by going over previous scientific knowledge, demonstrating at each turn that some particular fact or concept is not the absolute truth. Such dipping of particular truths in the Absolute may make diverting reading for a general audience that picks up information in this way— especially if the examples are carefully chosen—but this does not constitute any real advance over what has been achieved.

If science must be unified, there must first be something to unify. The "speculative" task of unifying the diverse fields of knowledge is only possible thanks to the work that has preceded it. Moreover, as Hegel writes elsewhere, given the nature of the preceding medieval outlook, Newton had reason indeed to say, "Physics, beware of metaphysics."[15] Scientific knowledge could not have begun with the Schellingian demand for unified knowledge, even properly understood. Progress in philosophy, Hegel argues against irrationalism, depends on and reflects (even while surpassing and culminating) progress in the empirical sciences.

Thus in a few pages, which are expanded more systematically elsewhere in his work,[16] Hegel lays out a sketch of the history of philosophy whose understanding he regarded as intrinsic to the task of contemporary philosophical theory. Beginning with the position of Schelling and others with a similar tendency, Hegel criticizes their negativistic criticism of Enlightenment and scientific empiricism. To clarify his criticism he argues that the modern scientific outlook in turn arose in an analogous rejection of medieval other-worldly thought. The history of philosophy presents itself here as a series of negations in which a position is established through the rejection of its predecessor. No philosophy exists in a vacuum. Each arises in combat with its historical predecessor, and Hegel's own philosophy is no exception. But what is usually misunderstood in this negative treatment of the previous philosophy is the positive character of the relationship, the underlying dependence of the later approach on the one it negates.

A truly self-conscious philosophy ought to recognize this dependence on the historical succession of philosophical systems or tendencies. Recognition of historical dependence on one's predecessor is not merely a matter of courtesy or of informational utility, but also a matter of truth itself. By failing to acknowledge properly its dependence on empiricist pluralism, Schelling's idealist monism is doomed to repeat the real limitations of the theory it scorns. Its inner theoretical structure unwittingly reflects its origins in the negation of empiricism. Thus Schelling, Hegel says, simply alternates between uplifting declamations on the unity of the Absolute and diverting pieces of information drawn from the annals of past "particularistic" science. Schelling's original contribution consists only in bathing the particular bit of knowledge in the light of the Absolute, but the result of so much light in which nothing in particular is clear is a mystical "night in which, as the saying goes, all cows are black."[17]

Granted that the contemporary outlook ought to acknowledge its debt to its immediate predecessors, can the same be said of the negative relation of early modern philosophy to its past? Is not the early modern rejection of medievalism more justifiable? In the course of his argument with Schelling Hegel contrasts the ancient and the modern standpoints in philosophy—in order to make clear the specific nature of modern thought. Ancient philosophy had as its material "the natural consciousness," i.e., forms of consciousness that are bound up with "an immediate, sensuous mode of apprehension," and from this starting point for the first time in human history made ideas in their purity (understood objectively, however, not *as* ideas) a distinct object of thought. This is the real beginning of philosophy. Ancient thought was the period of the formation of theoretical, reflective general concepts—the movement of thought from the concrete world of practical life and imagination to the abstract, reflective conceptions of thought considered for their own sake. Medieval thought dwells for a time in this other-world of ideas created by the ancients, until the emptiness of this mode of consciousness creates the theoretical basis for a return to the world of experience—a thoughtful return, however, quite different from the original thoughtless preoccupation with life of prephilosophical, "natural consciousness."[18]

Thus, Hegel briefly sketches the entire history of philosophy as a presupposition to what has been supposed to be the presuppositionless truth of contemporary philosophy—which he describes as proceeding directly to its target "like a shot from a pistol."[19] The historical links in this succession of philosophies take the form of a series of negations. A chain of negations, and negations of negations, stretches back indeed to Thales, to the origin of philosophy. Hegel's philosophical return to the history of philosophy is not regarded by him as a special "branch" of philosophy, which can be set apart from the pursuit of philosophical truth itself. It is intrinsic to doing philosophy itself. Hegel cannot explain what he is trying to do without distinguishing his own conception of philosophy from that of Schelling. But Schelling's philosophy is tied up with its own negation of empiricism and mechanistic materialism. The early modern scientific outlook arose, in turn, against the background of scholastic speculation, resting on the philosophical products that ancient philosophy wrested from "natural consciousness."[20] Such are the "tensions" that Hegel finds concealed within those concepts of his predecessor or philosophical opponent that the latter takes to be unproblematic and intuitively self-evident.

If Hegel's philosophical practice *exemplifies* a conception of the intrinsic or necessary dependence of philosophy on its history, Hegel also provides an argument to support this conception, an argument that proceeds "internally" from the implicitly contradictory features of would-be nonhistorical philosophical practice.

In this same Preface to the *Phenomenology of Spirit* Hegel criticizes in detail nonhistorically oriented forms of philosophy, in particular that form of philosophical method that he calls "argumentative" philosophy ("*das Rasonnieren*"). Hegel begins the Preface in a characteristically reflective way with the problem of beginnings in philosophy—with the problem of the nature of prefaces. Is it valid to set forth our goals or conclusions, our main concepts, in an anticipatory way in the beginning, and also show how our position is different from others? This is how prefaces are ordinarily written and is a characteristic feature of "argumentative" philosophy.

In such ordinary prefaces, certain contrasting theses or positions are outlined. The various possible theses are presented as more or less directly intelligible or self-evident to intellectual inspection. The author says which one he/she is going to defend and which criticize. The main body of the work consists in the arguments pro and con. The conclusion finally reaffirms what was said in the beginning, with the addition that in the conclusion something that was originally only asserted is supposed to have been proven.

In the conclusion, unlike the preface that outlines the various possible positions, the concept one has defended stands triumphantly alone on the field of philosophical battle. The opposing views do not even have the solidity of corpses. Having been shown to be false, they have vanished into philosophical air. This final result, the solitary concept that is the author's position, is proclaimed to be the truth—until, at least, an opponent again arises with fresh arguments.

Suppose that after reading the preface someone decides to skip the intermediate chapters so as to get to the final result. After all, why should one spend much time on positions that, in the end, turn out to be false? The false is nonexistent, a ghost—it really isn't there. Would not such a reader find it a disappointment to discover, as the final result of a weighty volume, the bare conclusion that, for example, "the will is free"?

This conclusion, of course, contains nothing more than what was in the preface. It is a reiteration of the concept that the author, after duly clarifying what he means by "will," "freedom," "necessity," etc., originally announced would be defended. One who does not want to waste time on shadows should therefore really only read prefaces. We know in the beginning what the end will hold.

Naturally, the problem with reading the final chapter in isolation, no less than with reading only prefaces, is that the heart of the philosophical activity comes in the middle, in the arguments, in the refutations, in the battle against the opposing ideas. This is the real philosophical substance of the work. Yet, from a strictly formal point of view, in the "argumentative" manner of philosophizing, all of this philosophical activity has disappeared from sight when the result has been proclaimed.

We might say that argumentative philosophy has the un-Hegelian form of thesis-antithesis-thesis. The contradiction implicit in this form of philosophical method consists in the fact that although everything depends on the existence of the antithesis, this dependence is not expressed on a conceptual level. The sentiment of truth, won in combat with error, remains just that—a purely internal sentiment. It does not take conceptual form.

Implicitly, the intervening activity and opposition that constitute the philosophical argument are resumed in the final result, in the feeling we have of its truth; yet this is not explicitly present. Here we have the deficiency of this form of philosophy, its incapacity to represent formally, in terms of concepts, the development that brought it from the beginning to the end. This development is not presented as a conceptual development.

Hegel therefore maintains that the main thing in a philosophical work is not the conclusion, but "the result together with the process through which it came about."[21] The philosophical "ladder" should not be thrown away. The inner development of a philosophical argument implicitly contains movement, change, development of thought. Hence, in a broad sense of the term, it is intrinsically "historical." This implicit character of philosophical thought requires a more adequate form of philosophical reasoning, one that makes the historical-developmental character of philosophy conceptually explicit. That means that in the course of the argument the concepts with which we begin should be seen as changing, as developing, as a result of the opposition that motivates the philosophical argument.

Hegel therefore gives arguments based on the inner structure of philosophical thought, its intrinsically antithetical or negative character, for introducing historical method into the core of logical argumentation.

In the spirit of one of the trends of Hegelian interpretation mentioned at the end of Dr. Schmitz's paper, we should like to stress the fact that negation should not be forgotten in considering other Hegelian notions. In his presentation of main elements of Hegel's conception of the history of philosophy, Dr. Schmitz passes briefly over the theory of dialectical negation to dwell more at length on the notions of "Idea," "Spirit," and "development."

Dr. Schmitz defines the unifying "Idea" of Hegel's history of philosophy as a "minimal and quite general expectation" that consists in viewing the diversity of philosophies as constituting a unity of "rational discourse."[22] In one analysis of Stoicism, however, Hegel writes of the Stoic ideal of "reasonableness" as a view that may be "uplifting" but because it is without any definite content its lofty goals "soon become tedious."[23] On the notion of Spirit, Hegel makes an analogous appraisal of the Stoic community of reasonable persons, which he calls the "soul-less community."[24]

The suggestion that the main idea of Hegel's history of philosophy is a minimal standard of rational discourse overlooks Hegel's hostility to establishing initial "positive" principles that are supposed to hold true for the entire work. One must begin with something, and perhaps Stoical "reasonableness" will do. Hegel himself regards this to be a fitting introduction to distinctive philosophical consciousness in his *Phenomenology*. But such beginnings must be negated, left behind, refuted, because of their own abstractness and shallowness (an abstractness that is nevertheless inevitable in any starting point).[25]

Here Hegel cautions against a one-sided interpretation of the notion that the unity of philosophy consists in "rational discourse," for which the differences, the oppositions between philosophers are not significant. On the contrary, it is precisely in these differences—above all, in different conceptions of Reason itself—that the real *development* of the

Philosophical Idea consists. In this *development* it is necessary to find room for the "unreasonable" as well, such as Faust's fatigue with "the shadowy existence of science, laws and principles" and his resolve instead to take "hold of life much as a ripe fruit is plucked."[26] Reason must become practical as well as theoretical, and a purely theoretical view of it, modeled strictly on the existence of the "community of scientific research,"[27] is a one-sided view of the Hegelian Idea, which provokes its antithesis in Faustian reactions. The true "living" community or Spirit, which historical philosophies express, is not the particular community of philosophers, but the broader community of society as a whole, an economic, social, political, and cultural totality.

For Hegel, philosophers do not belong to their own special philosophical community. The historical Aristotle, Aquinas, and Spinoza could not sit together in a philosophical colloquium and exchange ideas, however much *we* can see the dependence of later philosophies on the earlier ones. But such dependence and "sublation" of previous philosophy require negation of aspects that the historical predecessor would not want to give up, aspects reflecting the historically specific character of the "unsublated" position. Historical philosophers belong above all to their own times, to their own historical worlds, whose essential spirit, Hegel thought, was expressed in their concepts. It is in connection with this idea of Spirit as a definite historical world that an answer can be given to the question that forms the title of Dr. Schmitz's paper: Why does philosophy have a history?

The answer proposed by Dr. Schmitz consists in pointing out (1) that thinking takes place in individuals who exist in time and space; (2) that philosophy originates in a transcendence of sensuous immediacy and therefore initially partakes of this to some extent; and (3) that beginnings are inevitably abstract. All this may be quite true, but if it is also true that the philosopher participates in Reason and goes beyond sensuous representations, why does the philosopher not go the whole distance? Why did Thales himself not recognize that what was essential was not the notion that everything is water, but that it is important to view reality as a whole? Then, why could he not continue to develop the entire unfolding of the logical Idea?

Earlier we pointed out the dependence of philosophy on the development of the empirical sciences—clearly a task beyond the capacity of a single individual. We now have an additional reason for the historical existence of philosophy. If philosophy is the expression of a concrete historical period, then we cannot expect more (or much more) from philosophy than its own time has to offer. The beginning of philosophy has an "*abstract* specific nature," Hegel writes, "but this specific nature is also *historical,* i.e., it is a concrete formation of people whose principle has this specific nature, whose principle thus constitutes the consciousness of freedom."[28] It is not an accident that philosophy began with the Greeks, but precisely for this reason Greek philosophy is fundamentally different from that of the modern world. "The necessities of life must have been supplied, the agony of desire must have vanished; the purely finite interests of men must have been worked off, and their minds must have advanced so far as to take an interest in universal matters."[29] Such a condition was, in the nature of things, only possible at a certain stage of human development, and then, for a minority of the people. Hegel writes: "real freedom in Greece is infected by a restriction, because, as we know, slavery still existed there; civil life in free Greek states could not subsist without slaves. Thus freedom was conditioned and restricted, and this is its difference from Germanic freedom." Aristotle could not therefore understand the essential basis of modern thought, that "man as man is free."[30]

If philosophy were the activity of disconnected, unhistorical minds, joining one another on the basis of a special intellectual activity, taking place in a distinctive ideal realm, then it is not possible to say why one individual mind, at any time, could not in principle complete the entire course of Reason—assuming that this course is something that could meaningfully be said to have an end. But if philosophy is an expression of the essential characteristics of a people in history, then to suppose that a single individual could achieve the essential elements of rationality is to suppose that humanity could liberate itself from "the necessities of life" within the lifetime of a single individual.

Dr. Schmitz pictures Hegel's view of the history of philosophy as an "irenic," unitary process, in which the differences between philosophies ultimately drop out, in which behind the negative there appears the positive, the "moment" that can be incorporated into the final system, or at least into the peacemaking ideals of hermeneutical consciousness.

We, on the other hand, have stressed the negativity, the differences, the "martial" conception of the history of philosophy. In the final Hegelian systematic conception, we must acknowledge, the negative tends to give way to the positive, and the historical yields to the logical. Is this not to underestimate the differences that permeate the history of philosophy and contemporary philosophical practices, differences, negations, which for Hegel formed as fundamental a moment as that of reintegration? Each side may tolerantly, and in an enlightened post-Hegelian mode, try to grasp the "positive" in the side it opposes. But the other side never—not so far, at any rate—accepts this opposing view of its essence and is unwilling to allow its cherished ideas to be negated, however pacifically, and relegated to the ash can of prephilosophical, subjective, or contingent "opinions."

In conclusion, we can confidently predict that after this presentation philosophy will continue to be an arena of conflicting ideas. At bottom, such conflict may have as its ultimate source differences in definite historical forms of social life, in the underlying "spirit of a people" that philosophies express. There is progress, however, if we understand that such conflict is not one between light and darkness, between self-evident reasonableness and stupidity, between what is eternally essential and what is historically contingent. It is an essential opposition that is the basis of new ideas, of intellectual and indeed larger historical progress.

NOTES

1. Kenneth Schmitz, "Why Philosophy Must Have a History: Hegel's Proposal," in Doing Philosophy Historically, ed. Peter H. Hare (Buffalo, N.Y., Prometheus Books, 1988), p. 251.

2. Schmitz, ibid.

3. The radically consistent character of Wittgenstein's formulation of the point of view described here consists in its application not just to previous philosophies, but to his own as well: "My propositions serve as elucidations in the following way: anyone who understands me eventually recognizes them as nonsensical, when he has used them—as steps—to climb up beyond them. (He must, so to speak, throw away the ladder after he has climbed up it.)" In Ludwig Wittgenstein, Tractatus Logico-Philosophicus (London: Routledge & Kegan Paul, 1961), p. 74 [#6.54].

4. Philosophy, especially perhaps philosophy of science, has become increasingly "historist" or "sociologist"—to use terminology that Karl Popper used to criticize Hegel and Marx. "Historism," which when applied to morality Popper called "historicism," is the theory that "all knowledge and truth is 'relative' in the sense of being determined by history." K. Popper, The Open Society and Its Enemies, vol. 2 (Princeton, N.J.: Princeton University Press, 1971), p. 214.

5. Hegel's Science of Logic, trans. A. V. Miller (New York: Humanities Press, 1969), p. 50.

6. Schmitz, "Hegel's Proposal," p. 259-60. It was Marx, of course, who attempted to "discover the rational kernel within the mystical shell" of Hegel's idealism. Karl Marx, Capital, vol. 1 (New York: International Publishers, 1967), p. 20.

7. Cf. Richard Rorty, "The Historiography of Philosophy," in *Philosophy in History: Essays in the Historiography of Philosophy,* ed. Richard Rorty, J. B. Schneewind, and Quentin Skinner (Cambridge: Cambridge University Press, 1984). In this article Hegel is classified as belonging to a separate type of history of philosophy, "*geistesgeschichte*" (history of spirit), that results in "canon formation," or the definition of just what of the past shall be regarded as properly philosophical.

8. *Introduction to the Lectures on the History of Philosophy,* trans. T. M. Knox and A. V. Miller (Oxford: Clarendon Press, 1985), p. 22. (Referred to subsequently as "Knox.")

9. Ibid., p. 22; the insert is a clarification of the translator.

10. G. W. F. Hegel, *Phenomenology of Spirit,* trans. A. V. Miller (Oxford: Oxford University Press, 1979), p. 5.

11. "Formerly," Hegel writes, men "had a heaven adorned with a vast wealth of thoughts and imagery. The meaning of all that is, hung on the thread of light by which it was linked to that heaven. Instead of dwelling in this world's presence, men looked beyond it, following this thread to an other-worldly presence, so to speak." Ibid.

12. To get from medieval other-worldliness to the modern empiricist outlook, Hegel writes, "[t]he eye of the Spirit has to be forcibly turned and held fast to the things of this world; and it has taken a long time before the lucidity which only heavenly things used to have could penetrate the dullness and confusion in which the sense of worldly things was enveloped, and to make attention to the here and now as such, attention to what has been called 'experience,' an interesting and valid enterprise." Ibid.

13. "Now we seem to need just the opposite: sense is so fast rooted in earthly things that it requires just as much force to raise it" as must have once have been required to bring it down to earth. Ibid.

14. Hegel describes this contentment with abstractness as a characteristic of the times: "[t]he Spirit shows itself as so impoverished that, like a wanderer in the desert craving for a mere mouthful of water, it seems to crave for its refreshment only the bare feeling of the divine in general. By the little which now satisfies Spirit, we can measure the extent of its loss." Ibid.

Later, in the Preface to the *Science of Logic,* Hegel is more flattering: "it seems that the period of fermentation with which a new creative idea begins is past. In its first manifestation, such an idea usually displays a fanatical hostility toward the entrenched systematization of the older principle; usually too, it is fearful of losing itself in the ramifications of the particular and again it shuns the labor required for a scientific elaboration of the new principle and in its need for such, it grasps to begin with at an empty formalism. The challenge to elaborate and systematize the material now becomes all the more pressing. There is a period in the culture of an epoch as in the culture of the individual, when the primary concern is the acquisition and assertion of the principle in its undeveloped intensity. But the higher demand is that it should become systematized knowledge." Op. cit., p. 27.

15. Cf. *The Logic of Hegel*, trans. William Wallace (Oxford: Oxford University Press, 1968), p. 183 [#98].

16. Cf. the historical introduction to Hegel's "Encyclopedia Logic," ed. Wallace ibid., pp. 1–142.

17. *Phenomenology of Spirit*, p. 9.

18. *Phenomenology of Spirit*, p. 19. A "common sense philosophy," a philosophy that like that of Aristotle more or less deliberately investigates the categories embedded in common thought is in this sense quite different from common sense itself, which lacks such reflectiveness.

19. *Science of Logic*, p. 67.

20. That such natural consciousness too has a history, one that culminates through negations and negations of negations in philosophy, is the subject matter of Hegel's *Phenomenology of Spirit*.

21. *Phenomenology of Spirit*, p. 2.

22. Schmitz, "Hegel's Proposal," p. 256.

23. "To the question," *What* is good and true [Stoicism] again gave for answer the *contentless* thought: the True and the Good shall consist in reasonableness. But this self-identity of thought is again only the pure form in which nothing is determined. The True and the Good, wisdom and virtue, the general terms beyond which Stoicism cannot get, are therefore in a general way no doubt uplifting, but since they cannot in fact produce any expansion of the content, they soon become tedious." *Phenomenology of Spirit*, p. 122.

24. "The universal being thus split up into a mere multiplicity of individuals, this lifeless Spirit is an equality, in which all count the same, i.e., as *persons*." Ibid., p. 290.

25. Thus Hegel writes that "The aim by itself is a lifeless universal . . ." (Ibid., p. 2) and "a so-called basic proposition or principle of philosophy, if true, is also false, just because it is *only* a principle. It is, therefore, easy to refute it. The refutation consists in pointing out its defect; and it is defective because it is only the universal or principle, is only the beginning. . . . The refutation would, therefore, properly consist in the further development of the principle, and in thus remedying the defectiveness." Ibid., p. 13.

26. *Phenomenology of Spirit*, p. 218.

27. Schmitz, "Hegel's Proposal," p. 254. Dr. Schmitz briefly notes, pp. 255–56, the practical and social dimensions of Hegelian thought but does not try to connect this with his concept of the history of philosophy as a community of reasonable thinkers.

28. Knox, *Introduction to Lectures*, p. 166.

29. Knox refers to Aristotle, *Metaphysics* 982b22, ibid., p. 110.

30. Knox, ibid., p. 173.

Part Six

The Scottish
Commonsense Tradition

Motives and Causes in the Scottish Commonsense Tradition

Todd L. Adams

One of the most important and interesting discussions among those concerned with agency theory deals with the status of motives and causes. On the one hand we find that the determinist defends his position precisely because he believes the motive/act relation to be a causal one. On the other hand we find critics of this position attempting to offer criteria that will serve to distinguish motives from causes. However, this question relating to motives and causes is not strictly a modern one. It is an important one in the history of philosophy, and I believe an examination of some of the historical antecedents will help to elucidate the question at hand. There are contemporary philosophers, indebted to the Scottish commonsense philosophy of Thomas Reid, who attempt to show how acting freely is possible by providing criteria that distinguish motives from causes.[1] In light of this I believe we will find it fruitful to examine the position of the Scottish commonsense philosophers concerning motives and causes. Those in the tradition attempted to show that motives are not causes, and some tried to provide criteria that would clearly distinguish between them.

The commonsense philosophers, following the lead of Reid, believed an appeal to consciousness revealed that one does have determination over the will. Since this is the case, we can accept it as a first principle and reject any philosophical theory that denies what is evident. However the commonsense philosopher must still attempt to explain how this freedom is possible and where lies the mistake that led one to deny the first principle. With this goal in mind, Reid presented his agent causality view. The focal point of this theory is that freedom is explained and maintained by showing that the concept of cause is not applicable to human action. It is a theory in which the agent is the cause of his action but is not himself caused to do that particular act. The agent initiates an action. However, if we are to appreciate this position, we have to come to a proper understanding of motives and their relation to actions. Indeed, the heart of the agent causality position is that motives are not causes. The motive/act relationship is different from that of cause and effect. This is precisely the point where the determinist goes astray. He mistakenly believes that motives or reasons are causes, and the agent necessarily acts according to whatever motive is the strongest at any given moment. If the commonsense philosopher is to succeed in the enterprise of explaining freedom, then it is essential to see what further grounds he can give in order to say that motives are not causes.

According to Reid motives or reasons should be viewed in the role of giving advice that may or may not be heeded. With conflicting motives one has several options for actions, and it is then the agent who decides. Reid carefully distinguished between the motives that influence the agent and the determination to act or not to act. The motives are not causes but can influence the agent who is the efficient cause. In his *Essays on the Active Powers of the Human Mind* Reid claimed the motives are not causes and not an agent but rather require an agent or efficient cause. Reid explained:

> We cannot, without absurdity, suppose a motive, either to act, or to be acted upon; it is equally incapable of action and of passion; because it is not a thing that exists, but a thing that is conceived; it is what the schoolmen called an "ens rationis." Motives, therefore, may influence to action, but they do not act. They may be compared to advice or exhortation, which leaves a man still at liberty. For in vain is advice given when there is not a power either to do, or to forbear, what it recommends. In like manner, motives suppose liberty in the agent, otherwise they have no influence at all.[2]

It is clear that Reid believes motives are different from causes, but he did not offer any criteria to distinguish the two. If the two are clearly distinguished, then it should follow that the position of the determinist rests on a mistake. If motives operate in a way significantly different from causes, then perhaps the question of freedom and determinism can be resolved. We will have to look elsewhere in the tradition to find an attempt at offering criteria to distinguish motives and causes.

A colleague of Reid's, James Gregory, supplies a criterion for distinguishing motives and causes by suggesting in his *Essays, Philosophical and Literary,* that there is a uniform connection between a cause and its effect that does not hold for the relation between motive and action. A particular cause, acting on the same object, is always followed by the same effect. However, Gregory claims that this is not the case with motives. The same motives, acting on the same agent, may lead to different actions at different times. Because motives do not lead to the uniform results that causes do, this indicates that the two are different in nature.

Dugald Stewart considers this particular distinction of Gregory's, but finds it lacking.[3] He criticizes it on two accounts. In a cause-and-effect relation one has to consider the cause operating, the state of the object it operates on, and then the effect. Stewart claims that there are cases where the same cause operates in two different instances, but we cannot predict the effect or result because of our ignorance concerning the state of the object. If the state of the object changes, there will be a different effect. There are cases where we would not have knowledge of the change in the state of the object, and thus our predictions would be inaccurate. The second difficulty arises, according to Stewart, because, even though there is some kind of personal identity, the agent changes in very important ways over a period of time. Receiving new information or acquiring new habits will affect one's character. The only grounds we have for accepting Gregory's claim is if we can show "the same motive was followed by different actions *when operating upon the same precise subject.*"[4] Since Stewart believes this is impossible, it follows that Gregory's distinction between the motive/act relation and cause/effect will not hold. Gregory would have to show that the *same* motive acting on the *same* person at two different times can yield different actions if the distinction is to work.

Stewart's critique of Gregory's distinction is not very convincing and deserves further examination to see if it will or will not provide a criterion to distinguish motives and causes. Stewart's first point has nothing whatever to do with Gregory's argument. It is of course true that uniform results will not be forthcoming if the state of the object in question changes. Gregory maintains that when the circumstances are the same—when the cause and state of the object it is operating on are the same—then the effect will be uniform in all such cases. We can only make accurate predictions when the situations are the same. This part of Gregory's argument has not been affected by Stewart.

Stewart's second criticism is a little more difficult to answer. It looks as if he may be a bit of a necessitarian himself, since he appears to believe that we could predict what an agent would do if we were aware of how the agent had changed. If the same cause is operating, and we know what the difference is between the agent now and when the cause previously operated, then we could predict what the result would be. However if there is such a thing as personal identity, as Stewart believes, then we may be able to claim that in an essential way the same motive acting on the same individual at two different times may produce different results. If this is the case, then Gregory's distinction deserves to be considered as one that will differentiate motives and causes.

What is curious about this discussion by Stewart is that after considering and rejecting Gregory's criteria, he made no attempt of his own to distinguish motives and causes. Stewart recognizes Gregory as an ally, and his attempt is a laudable one, but it is ultimately rejected. However, it does seem that Gregory is on the right track, and Stewart does not follow up. He definitely believes the two are different and writes: "[W]hatever may be the nature of the relation between a *motive* and an *action,* there is no reason for concluding it to be at all analogous to that between a *cause* and its *effect.*"[5] We might very well expect that Stewart would then take up where Gregory left off and try to provide us with criteria to distinguish motives from causes. However, this attempt does not materialize. It is in this area that the work of Henry Tappan is so instructive. Although the American commonsense philosophers follow Reid closely on many points, they are also important philosophers in their own right, with their own contributions to make. Tappan is able to contribute greatly to the tradition with his discussion of motives and showing how they differ from causes.

In attempting to show that motives do not cause an agent to act in a given way, Tappan carefully distinguishes between three distinct faculties—the intelligence, the sensitivity, and the will. This faculty psychology is not unique to Tappan, but he does emphasize it in order to distinguish between motives and causes. The will turns out to be the essential aspect of the agent. The will as a distinct faculty refers to the ability to choose between motives. The agent may then act rationally or sensitively, but what he does is up to the will or agent himself.

The chief criterion that distinguishes the sensitivity and the intelligence on the one hand, and the will on the other, is that the will is contingent whereas the other two are necessary. Regarding the sensitivity and intelligence, Tappan claims we are aware of no conscious choice concerning whether they shall exist or not. To will or to do is something entirely different from to know or to feel. The first arises contingently, that is, it may be but might not have been, and the other two arise necessarily. This serves to distinguish the volition from the motives associated with it.

The chief characteristic of the will, as mentioned above, is that it is contingent. When I will to do something I am conscious that I can either make the volition or refrain from doing so. The will has the ability to create or originate. Tappan claims that when a person makes a volition at a given time, it originates at that moment.

> Now it cannot be said that the volition had an existence previously in the potentiality of that person's will, because the very opposite volition lay equally in the same potentiality. The volition as it actually appeared, had no being whatever until it appeared, inasmuch as it appeared under the equal possibility of the very opposite volition.[6]

Since the opposite volition is possible up to the moment of decision, the conclusion reached is that the will is contingent.

Tappan claims the act of knowing is different—it is a necessary development. The judgment that takes place must take place with no possibility of the opposite doing so. Tappan explains:

> We have seen that upon sensation as the conditions of intelligence, certain judgments appear, as those of time and space, cause and effect, substance and attribute, the finite and the infinite, right and wrong, the beautiful and the ugly, &c., and that these cannot but appear. There is no potentiality in the intelligence for opposite judgments, under the given conditions.[7]

These considerations lead to the conclusion that the intelligence and will are two distinct faculties. That which arises from the intelligence does so necessarily, whereas what arises from the will does so contingently.

Regarding the sensitivity, which includes sensations, emotions, desires, and passions, Tappan claims that we are aware of no conscious choice concerning whether those things that arise from the sensitivity shall exist or not. "Let any appropriate object be presented to the sensitivity, and we are conscious of no choice, whether the sensation shall exist or not; on the contrary, its existence is inevitable."[8] The will does not have the ability to create a passion or emotion. These arise necessarily from the presence of some object. The will can focus the attention on the object or not as it chooses. This serves to distinguish the volition from the motives associated with it. To illustrate this point, Tappan says that walking among beautiful trees and flowers is an act of will that is different from the sensations of color and fragrance. There is no confusion between the two operations involved. I am active in the one and passive in the other.[9]

In the following example, Tappan stresses the distinction between desires and the will. It is one often used by the commonsense philosophers, and in fact Stewart mentions it and refers to Locke's making the same distinction. Tappan says that in a case of taking a piece of fruit from a bowl, the desire for the fruit is not the same as the volition that results in the taking of the fruit. After the desire is created in me for the fruit, I am conscious of making an effort, what Tappan calls a "nisus," to either obtain the object of desire or to resist that object. This "nisus" is something entirely different from the desire. Employing a distinction made earlier, Tappan says that the desire for the fruit results necessarily from my perception of it. There is no effort on my part one way or another concerning the desire. However, the nisus or effort to get the fruit or resist the desire for it is the result of deliberation and is something within my power, unlike the desire itself. The volition is contingent whereas the desire arises necessarily. By appealing to consciousness it is possible, then, to distinguish clearly between the sensitivity, the will, and the intelligence.

The sensitivity and the intelligence provide reasons for acting, but it is the will as a distinct faculty that is responsible for choosing or for directing its attention in a certain direction. But whereas these motives arise necessarily, the will remains contingent. The motives do not cause the will to choose one over another. Thus Tappan concludes about motives:

> The phenomena of the reason and the sensitivity supply the will with objects, laws, rules, and aims of action. Without these, action would be impossible, not for the want of a *cause* of action, but for the want of *something* to do: just as perception would be impossible without objects, not for the want of a *perceiving faculty*, but for the want of *something* to perceive.[10]

Finally, then, we can say that the intelligence and sensitivity, although of vital importance, do not cause or necessitate any particular action. That which arises from the intelligence and sensitivity does so necessarily, but the volition is not compelled by the motives that are provided. When the agent does will to do something, Tappan claims he is not aware of anything that requires him to do so. The agent can will in various different directions. Regardless of which motives are present, it is up to the agent to decide which one to pursue. Thus, we should not commit the error of the determinist who believes that it is a cause/effect relation—motives are not causes. The agent is the cause of his volitions, and motives or reasons do not have this power. They serve only to guide the agent, or to provide him with something to do; but they do not dictate what has to be done.

This distinction of Tappan's further illustrates another criterion that is functioning in his work. We have seen that motives arise necessarily, but the will functions contingently. Given the motives it is the will that decides which one to be guided by. This distinction can be applied further to the way the world operates and the way humans act. Regarding the notion of cause, Tappan claims that what distinguishes agent causality from causality in the physical world is that given the nature of the cause and the object we obtain uniform results. When the fire is placed among combustibles it necessarily burns each time it is so placed. But because of the contingent nature of agent causality, arising from the contingent nature of the will, the same motive may result in different actions at two different times. We see that the position of Tappan is very close to that of James Gregory. Stewart attempts to show that Gregory's distinction would not work, but the tools are present in Tappan to resurrect Gregory's criterion. Tappan's formal distinction contrasting the necessity involved with the sensitivity and intelligence, and contingency involved with the will, entails the kind of distinction Gregory provides. Whereas a cause in the physical world provides uniform results because of the necessity involved, the will being contingent does not provide uniform results from the antecedent motives. By focusing on the faculty psychology and distinguishing the will as a separate faculty, Tappan has further explained why it is that whereas causes in the physical world do operate uniformly, this is not the case with human action. The conclusion drawn is that since motives do not necessitate as causes in the physical world do, motives are not causes. The agent is the cause of his actions but is not himself caused.

I believe Tappan's work on this question is first-rate. Following Reid, Tappan believes that differentiating between motives and causes is the crucial point in the freedom/determinism question. If it can be shown that motives are not causes, then it is possible to claim that determinism rests on a mistake. Tappan has, I believe, presented a very credible theory in that regard.

However I believe one further point is essential, and this goes back to Stewart's position. You will recall that after rejecting Gregory's criteria, Stewart made no attempt of his own to provide any. Why Stewart offers no criteria is left unanswered. He simply sees no need of pursuing the question any further.[11] Without going into the commonsense metaphilosophy, we can say that Stewart believes it is evident that motives do not operate as causes do. What is evident needs no further justification or criteria to establish it. One need only rebut criticism that might arise. We are aware, as agents, that we can initiate an action or refrain from doing it. We do not need to provide criteria to show this is different from causation in the physical world.

The important point that is made by all of the commonsense philosophers is that we must understand what it is to be an agent. The agent not only causes a particular action but also initiates that action. Insofar as we can do this, agent causality operates in a manner different from causality in the physical world. The two following quotations, one from Stewart and one from Tappan, illustrate this difference. When considering the maxim "that every change requires a cause," which Stewart claims is the main argument of the determinist, he writes: "But this maxim, although true with respect to inanimate matter, does not apply to intelligent agents, which cannot be conceived without the power of self-determination."[12] Tappan says the following:

> So decisive are our conceptions on this subject, that the moment we suppose mind as cause to be necessitated in the exercise of its causality, we seem to destroy mind itself, and to bring it down to the mere conditions of physical causes. These physical causes cannot but act under their appropriate circumstances, and cannot but act uniformly.[13]

In the final analysis the positions of Stewart and Tappan are not very far apart. Tappan attempts to offer criteria to distinguish causes and motives. Stewart believes the two are in fact quite different but believes it is not necessary to provide criteria for that which is evident.

NOTES

1. Richard Taylor is an example of one.

2. Thomas Reid, *Essays on the Active Powers of the Human Mind*, ed. B. Brody (Cambridge: M.I.T. Press, 1969), pp. 283–86.

3. Dugald Stewart, *The Collected Works of Dugald Stewart*, ed. Sir William Hamilton (Edinburgh: Thomas Constable, 1854-60), 6: 352–53n.

4. Ibid., p. 353n.

5. Ibid., p. 352n.

6. Henry P. Tappan, *The Doctrine of the Will: Determined by an Appeal to Consciousness* (New York: Wiley and Putnam, 1840), pp. 285–86.

7. Ibid., p. 286.

8. Ibid., p. 151.

9. Ibid., p. 152.

10. Ibid., p. 297.

11. See E. H. Madden, "Stewart's Enrichment of the Commonsense Tradition," *History of Philosophy Quarterly* 3, no. 1 (1986): 57–58.

12. Stewart, *Collected Works*, p. 352.

13. Tappan, *Doctrine of Will*, pp. 66–67.

Commentary—
Among the Indeterminists

Phillip Cummins

If to articulate and endorse the work of a past philosopher is to do philosophy historically, then Todd Adams is doing philosophy historically. He presents an argument for indeterminism by Henry P. Tappan, a nineteenth-century American philosopher, and goes on to say,

> I believe Tappan's work on this question is first-rate. Following Reid, Tappan believes that differentiating between motives and causes is the crucial point in the freedom/determinism question. If it can be shown that motives are not causes, then it is possible to claim that determinism rests on a mistake. Tappan has, I believe, presented a very credible theory in that regard. (Adams, p. 289)

I have doubts about how historical my contribution is, since in writing it I had access to neither Gregory's nor Tappan's book. Whether I manage to do any philosophy remains to be seen.

For the sake of this discussion, assume provisionally the intelligibility and appropriateness of the following terminology. An *action* is a state of an agent that results from an act of willing. The state may be purely mental, purely physical, or a combination of both. An *act of willing* is a mental act that not only has as part or all of its intentional object a state of the agent whose mental act it is, but also involves *nisus*, an effort to bring about that state. By *will* I mean the power to have such acts of willing. A *motive* is either (a) a mental act antecedent to an act of willing that contributes in some way to the occurrence of the latter, or (b) an intentional object of such a mental act. A motive in the intentional object sense can be considered a reason for acting. It might be an object of desire, a norm, or a causal proposition such as "cashing this check as my own will make me rich." Adams's defenders of indeterminism probably thought of motives, volitions, the will, and actions along roughly these lines, so employing my definitions in examining their arguments does not seem unfair or inappropriate.

Adams does not define indeterminism. For purposes of discussion let it be understood as U: *Acts of willing are uncaused.* Adams presents three arguments for indeterminism, one by Thomas Reid, one by Dr. James Gregory, and one by Tappan. I shall interpret them as arguments for U. The key element in Reid's argument is the following passage:

> We cannot, without absurdity, suppose a motive, either to act, or to be acted upon; it is equally incapable of action and of passion; because it is not a thing that exists, but a thing that is conceived; it is what the schoolmen call an "ens rationis."

My interpretation of Reid's argument as an argument for U is: (1) If acts of willing were caused, then motives would be their causes. (2) Motives are intentional objects. (3) A mental act's having a given intentional object does not imply the existence of the object intended, that is, intentional objects are not existents. (4) Only existents are causes. First conclusion: Motives are not existents. Second conclusion: Motives are not causes. Third conclusion: U: Acts of willing are uncaused. This argument is unsound. Motives in one sense of that term are intentional objects; their being thought does not imply their existence. Motives in this sense cannot be causes. It is equally true, however, that the acts whose intentional objects are motives in the first sense are themselves motives in a second sense. They exist and so can be causes. Consider an example. It was my belief that I would learn something worthwhile here that was my motive for and may or may not be a cause of my attending this conference; what was believed, the intentional object, matters only because the belief occurred. Motives, in the occurrent sense or dispositional sense, are what determinists consider to be causes of actions. Hence, Reid's argument is irrelevant.

Here is James Gregory's argument as presented by Adams.

> There is a uniform connection between a cause and its effect that does not hold for the relation between motive and action. A particular cause, acting on the same object, is always followed by the same effect. . . . This is not the case with motives. The same motives, acting on the same agent, may lead to different actions at different times. Because motives do not lead to the uniform results that causes do, this indicates that the two are different in nature. (Adams, pp. 284–85)

Taking this to be part of an argument for U, I formulate the full argument as: (1) If acts of willing were caused, then motives would be their causes. (2) Causes are uniformly conjoined to their effects, that is, a particular cause, acting on the same object, is always followed by the same effect. (3) Acts of willing are uniformly conjoined to the actions they cause. (4) Motives are not uniformly conjoined to the actions caused by acts of willing. First conclusion: Motives are not uniformly conjoined to acts of willing. Second conclusion: Motives do not cause acts of willing. Third conclusion: *U:* Acts of willing are uncaused. Dugald Stewart, Reid's disciple, rejected Gregory's argument. He noticed the ambiguity of the expression, "a particular cause, acting on the same object, is always followed by the same effect." It is ambiguous because "same object" might mean either the same individual or the same individual in the same condition. Motives may be causes, a determinist might argue, even though the same motive may cause the same agent on two occasions to have different acts of willing and so do different actions. Provided the agent's character or state of mind has changed, that difference in outcome is as it should be. Just as rubbing the same chalk on the same blackboard yields different results when the blackboard is wet instead of dry, so the same motive yields different acts of willing by the same subject when he is manic instead of depressed. To make his case, Gregory must show that even when an agent's character traits and mental states are held constant, the same motives result in different acts of willing. That he has not done so is, I take it, the heart of Stewart's criticism.[1]

It is worth noting here that I have construed Gregory's argument as an argument that motives are not causes of acts of willing and thus as an argument for *U*. Recall, however, how Adams presents Gregory's conclusion. He said, "Because motives do not lead to the uniform results that causes do this indicates that the two are different in nature" (Adams, p. 285). On this reading, Gregory's is an argument that motives and causes differ in nature. To me that does not require argument. Even if motives cause acts of willing and so are causes in one sense of "are causes," it does not follow that motives and causes are the same in nature. To be a motive is not to be a cause. To be a cause is not to be a motive. Consequently, even though motives are different in nature from causes, motives may be causes. One need only recall G. E. Moore's distinction between pleasure is good and pleasure is a good to grasp this point.

It seems to me that Tappan's argument for *U* has very little to do with the other two arguments. They argue directly that motives do not cause acts of willing and indirectly for *U*. Tappan argues for *U* directly. I reconstruct his argument as: (1) If something is an effect, then it is necessitated (by its cause). (2) What is not necessary is not necessitated. (3) Acts of willing are not necessary. (4) Whatever is not an effect is uncaused. First conclusion: Acts of willing are not necessitated. Second conclusion: Acts of willing are not effects. Third conclusion: *U:* Acts of willing are uncaused. Am I alone in finding premise 2 baffling? Are not a state of affairs being necessary and its being necessitated or determined by some cause two different things? If so, how can the contingency of the will or some act of willing prove that it is unnecessitated and thus causally undetermined? Let us next consider the two arguments offered for premise 3. The second is that the will, unlike sensitivity and intelligence, is contingent; this implies, supposedly, that acts of willing are contingent. I do not understand this argument. I feel hardly more confident regarding the first argument, which Tappan expresses as follows:

> Now it cannot be said that the volition had an existence previously in the potentiality of the[2] person's will, because the very opposite volition lay equally in the same potentiality. The volition as it actually appeared, had no being whatever until it appeared, inasmuch as it appeared under the equal possibility of the very opposite volition.

The argument seems to turn on the point that we speak of acts of willing (volitions) only when there are alternative actions available to the agent and thus alternative acts of willing. Tappan's thesis seems to be that the act of willing that actually occurs is radically contingent because it does not exist in potentiality prior to existing. It does not exist in potentiality prior to existing because the opposite (alternative) act of willing is equally possible until the very moment the act of willing occurs. If I understand this argument, either it proves too much, for the same argument could be given for every change and the alternatives to it, or it begs the question by supposing that acts of willing and only such acts cannot be determined by anything besides the potentialities of the agent.

I turn next to Adams's claim that Tappan has supported Gregory's argument by showing that motives are not causes. On pages 288–89 Adams says,

> Tappan's formal distinction contrasting the necessity involved with the sensitivity and intelligence, and contingency involved with the will, entails the kind of distinction Gregory provides. Whereas a cause in the physical world provides uniform results because of the necessity involved, the will being contingent does not provide uniform results from the antecedent motives.

He adds,

> The conclusion drawn is that since motives do not necessitate as causes in the physical world do, motives are not causes. The agent is the cause of his actions but is not himself caused.

Do these connections really hold? Clearly, Tappan wants to prove that acts of willing are uncaused. Clearly, too, this conclusion implies that acts of willing are not caused by motives. However, neither of these conclusions implies that motives are not uniformly connected to actions or that motives are not causes. The latter does not follow because a motive's not causing one thing does not logically preclude its causing something else. The first point is less trivial. Suppose an agent is virtuous, knowledgeable, and consistent. Suppose indeterminism is true. It is possible the agent, believing "My duty is to do X," always does X in appropriate circumstances, even though his acts of willing X are uncaused. This seems to show that indeterminism is compatible with a completely uniform correlation between an agent's motives, acts of willing, and actions. Indeterminism, therefore, does not entail nonuniformity, even if nonuniformity entails indeterminism. Even if successful, Tappan's argument does not help Gregory.

One final solution: Is determinism discredited if motives are not causes? Assume causation implies uniform connection and that conscious motives are not uniformly connected to acts of willing. Suppose, in short, that neither acts of willing nor actions are caused by motives. Could not a determinist nevertheless hold that acts of willing and actions are causally determined by something else, unconscious motives or even, God forbid, brain states?

NOTES

1. It seems to me that Stewart does not offer two criticisms of Gregory. Instead, his comments about personal identity illustrate somewhat awkwardly the ambiguity of "the same object" and "the same agent."

2. "The" replaces "that" for ease of exposition.

Part Seven

Recent American and European Philosophy

Myers and James
A Philosophical Dialogue
Edward H. Madden

1

The history of philosophy is related quite differently to philosophy than, say, the history of physics is to physics. The history of philosophy is relevant to contemporary philosophy in a way that the history of physics is not relevant to contemporary physics. Philosophers argue the truth or falsity of historical positions because their truth values often have significance for contemporary issues, either because the issues are perennial ones or isomorphic with them. The historian of science does not argue the truth values of past theories; rather, he tries to clarify them, relate them, show continuities or discontinuities with earlier or later theories, show how changes in scientific institutions have determined the directions science has taken, and so on.

To be sure, the historian of philosophy is also deeply interested in the meanings of past philosophical claims and systems. He needs to clarify them by drawing them out dialectically as a check on consistency, to explicate archaic terminology, and, in cases of translated texts, to point out misinterpretations and clarify overly literal renditions. But the point of clarification and explication is, again, to be in a position to argue the.truth values of claims and systems because they have significance for contemporary issues. This way of viewing the history of philosophy is what I shall mean by doing philosophy historically. The one great error to avoid in treating the history of philosophy in this manner is projecting current concepts anachronistically backwards in time and interpreting earlier philosophers either wittingly or unwittingly along lines designed to gain a usable past. One unfortunate example along these lines is the characterization of Thomas Reid as a pragmatist.

There is another approach to the history of philosophy that seems to me also of great significance and not competitive or incompatible with the view sketched above. On this view the clarification of meaning is central: inquiring into consistency, explicating archaic terminology, providing an interpretive milieu, and evaluating or producing translations that catch the sense and not simply the literal meaning. The truth or falsity of past claims and systems is never at issue. This sort of historian of philosophy, in addition to clarifying dialectically individual philosophers, also classifies and categorizes the many philosophers into manageable groups, thereby reducing what appears to be babble into traceable trends and family resemblances. This sort of philosopher not only discovers trends but also points out how past philosophers have prefigured—not stated—subsequent development. The pitfall to avoid here is reducing philosophies to a series of pointless summaries and antiquarian details.

I have a high regard for both ways of doing the history of philosophy and suspect that the best history of philosophy is a subtle blend of both modes. A splendid example of this blend is Gerald Myers's recent book *William James, His Life and Thought*. There is much evidence that Myers conceived his job, in large part, to be doing philosophy historically as well as clarifying texts. He writes: "James's theorizing on time is a valuable starting point for modern dialogues between philosophers and psychologists." "Even where the original philosophical suggestion may lead to an absolute dead-end, James's writings can be a stimulating occasion for our own philosophizing." "[H]e is often responsible for suggesting the questions that get us started."[1] James's discussion of the overlap between will and attention "has been permanently stimulating," and his philosophical psychology has provided professionals and nonprofessionals alike "a fund of practical insights for their own lives."[2] Myers constantly argues with James; the whole book is a fascinating philosophical dialogue. It is exciting reading since one never knows on a given issue whether James will turn out right or hopelessly wrong. Myers raises objections, shows resources in James's philosophy to meet the objections, and concludes that James has made permanently relevant contributions to philosophy. Other times the objections are devastating, and the resources of James's philosophy are found scanty indeed to rebut them. But ahead of time the reader does not know how it will turn out, so truly there is never a dull moment in reading Myers's fine book. Usually he argues and counterargues from Jamesian texts, but occasionally he will extrapolate and write, "I think [James] would have answered";[3] and usually the extrapolation seems justifiable. Myers also sees his work as clarifying James's texts.

Myers's knowledge of psychology and physiology, as well as philosophy, is prodigious, and he shows conclusively that James significantly influenced recent and contemporary psychologists as well as physiologists. His interpretations and judgments of James's philosophy are the most comprehensive and important yet to appear. If they are not definitive, that is because a definitive analysis of James will never be written. Myers states the reason with his usual charm and insight: "Indeed, James the psychologist and James the philosopher slip often into James the artist, leaving his critic to follow a chameleonic trail."[4]

Myers's achievement cannot be overestimated; it is a brilliant book. It is intellectually rewarding and stimulating; it is also morally refreshing. I have never read a less dogmatic book, one more dedicated to seeking truth than to stating it, one more sympathetic and yet critical and deep probing. Academic books are rarely like this. Reading this book is an intellectual adventure but a lesson in morals as well. It is a good book written by a good man.

The scope of James's work is overwhelming. Most writers confine themselves to some aspect of it. Intending to do the same thing, Myers was drawn into the whole of James's philosophy. Not all of it could be considered with the same thoroughness and certainty of touch that most of Myers's book exhibits. So in what follows I shall raise some questions the point of which is not to prove Myers wrong but to stimulate further profitable dialogue between him and James.

2

I want to consider more than a few issues in order to give a representative view of Myers's book. To achieve this goal, I will deal with various issues in broad strokes and, in subsequent sections, discuss other issues in greater detail. In this way we can hope to get a proper appreciation of both the breadth and depth of Myers's work.

A. Myers's attitude toward psychobiography and psychohistory is not clear-cut. He rejects Leon Edel's account of the relationship between William and his brother Henry and, as he puts it, tones down Jean Strouse's portrayal of William's treatment of his sister Alice. Yet it is difficult to ascertain his attitude toward the propriety of psychoanalyzing James at all.

Edel ascribes a Jacob-Esau relationship between Henry, Jr., and William, the latter having the role of Esau, and sees William's hidden animus finally surfacing in 1905. In declining membership in the American Academy of Arts and Letters, William wrote in a letter to the secretary of the organization, "And I am the more encouraged to this course by the fact that my younger and shallower and vainer brother is already in the Academy."[5] It is the final evidence for the Jacob-Esau theory, says Edel. Myers disagrees; the whole letter was a bit of literary jollity. James knew that Henry himself took his election lightly. Election to the academy was not a genuine honor, but old cronies bringing other friends in for personal glorification, something that Henry could laugh at but William could not tolerate. As Myers says, "one looks in vain for a display of animus toward Henry in William's most confidential correspondence."[6]

In her biography of Alice James, Jean Strouse portrays William as unsympathetic, arrogant, and dominating, thereby wounding his sister. His domination was sexual and flirtatious and endured into adulthood. She argues that William's marriage precipitated Alice's 1878 breakdown. Myers's "toned-down" version of Strouse is this: "A person need not be vain, unsympathetic, or arrogant to unsettle another's sensibilities; it is sometimes enough to be intensely self-preoccupied."[7] William's banter with his sister tended to be "smarty" rather than sexual in nature. Moreover, Alice's physical condition may have deteriorated at the time of William's marriage, and hence her depression required no psychoanalytic explanation.

I agree entirely with Myers's criticism of Edel and Strouse, though God between us and all harm when William was being jolly! Was the secretary of the academy in a position to know it was banter? In any case, the letter showed at worst William's bad judgment, not brother Esau bursting forth. In the case of Strouse, it should be pointed out, Myers does not give a toned-down version of her views but gives an entirely different, nonanalytic explanation.

In any case, the serious problem is that Myers simply rebuts several psychobiographical accounts; but there are innumerable others that have been offered, and refuting them all would be an endless task. What we need is an explanation of why a psychoanalytic approach to James is on the whole pointless, or why psychobiography in general is pointless. James himself believed that psychological problems are largely physical in nature and must be dealt with medically and by careful retraining of bad habits and inappropriate behavior. Later events seem to prove that he was on the right track. There is a current psychiatric trend away from psychoanalysis: lithium, drug therapy, and retraining rather than dream analysis seem to be the order of the day. More specifically, what is the point in psychoanalyzing a corpse? A patient's response to an analyst's interpretation is itself a crucial element in retaining or rejecting the interpretation. We can imagine James's humor, were he alive, in replying to Edel's and Strouse's interpretations. Myers, however, does not consider these general issues. He is content to say merely that he questions the confidence with which psychohistorians present their hypotheses.[8] To be sure, any discussion of the legitimacy of psychobiography or history is a large topic indeed and no one expects Myers to go into it thoroughly. We do need to know, however, if he thinks that only Edel and Strouse are wrong but, at the same time, that some other psychoanalysis of James might be in order and correct.

B. Myers believes that James was inconsistent in holding Locke's strict separation of a priori and empirical propositions and yet blurring that distinction. We need to raise the question whether or not this inconsistency is only part of a nest of related inconsistencies.

James, Myers tells us, followed Locke and Hume in making a sharp distinction between demonstrative and factual knowledge, the former being necessary, a priori, and nativistic, the latter contingent and a matter of inquiry. According to James, demonstrative knowledge follows from the very meaning of terms. "*What we mean* by one plus one *is* two; we make *two* out of it; and it would mean two still even in a world where *physically* (according to a conceit of Mill's) a third thing was engendered every time one thing came together with another. We are masters of our meanings."[9] James was committed to this viewpoint throughout his life. On the other hand, however, James did not acknowledge a clear-cut division between a priori and empirical propositions since he acknowledged the a priori character of some scientific truths. This view clearly destroys the distinctness of the two types of propositions contrary to James's professed Lockean commitment.[10]

I wonder if there is another inconsistency lurking in the vicinity. It can be convincingly argued that James also blurred the distinction in the direction opposite to the one described by Myers. In *A Pluralistic Universe* James was converted to the compounding of consciousness which, he believed, implies that two or more distinguishable things are a single thing and hence require the rejection of the logic of identity.[11] James here blurs the distinction in the opposite direction since logical truths have no intrinsically different status than empirical propositions. They can be rejected, as James rejected the law of identity for nonformal reasons. However, the two blurrings in opposite directions seem incompatible because the one implies that some propositions are necessary and incorrigible, while the other implies that no propositions, even the laws of thought, are incorrigible.

Morton White has ably argued that James blurred the distinction in the second way.[12] James's "subjective pragmatism"—his notion that all concepts are cut out of the flux of experience and always reflect human motives and interests, thereby having subjective import only—White argues, shows that all concepts, including those of logic, are at the mercy of life and concrete experience. Thus there appears to be an inconsistency between James's "subjective pragmatism" and his ascription of a priori elements to science.

Yet another difficulty arises. Myers shows conclusively that James in *The Meaning of Truth, A Pluralistic Universe,* and *Some Problems of Philosophy* officially embraced logical realism. He now rejected his idea that percepts are the only realm of reality and treated concepts, or meanings, as a coordinate realm. In this case there appears to be an inconsistency between "subjective pragmatism" and logical realism, on the one hand, and between logical realism and the corrigibility of logical truths, on the other. Does Gerald Myers accept these prima facie inconsistencies as real ones, as he does the inconsistency he first pointed out?

C. Myers consistently describes James as a Berkeleyan. This description, it seems to me, is true in one sense and false in another, more fundamental one. He was a Berkeleyan in the sense that he viewed a physical object as nothing more than it is experienced to be; he rejected the concept of a physical substance in which experienced qualities inhere. He long adhered to this view but formalized it in one of his uses of the pragmatic maxim, albeit an atypical use. "Berkeley's criticism of 'matter' was . . . absolutely pragmatistic. Matter is known as our sensations of color, figure, hardness, and the like. They are the cash-value of the term. . . . These sensations then are its sole meaning."[13] Berkeley's position, of course, went much further than this. He insisted that sensations cannot exist independently of a knowing mind. It is this aspect of Berkeley that James denied in his epistemic realism and natural realism, terms he explicitly used on various occasions in fending off subjective idealism. He wrote to C. A. Strong, "Schiller, Dewey, and I are all (I, at any rate!) epistemological realists,—the reality known exists independently of the knower's idea, and *as* conceived, if the conception be a true one. . . . [E]pistemological realism [is] at the very permanent *heart and center* of *all* my thinking."[14] James was here explicitly rejecting the second dimension of Berkeley's view and hence can be called a Berkeleyan only in the first, weaker sense. These considerations suggest that Myers's characterization of James as a Berkeleyan in what amounts to the strong sense requires further justification. Myers, fair-minded as always, acknowledges that James never rejected his natural realism, so either James is inconsistent again or else he was not a Berkeleyan in the strong sense.

It must not be supposed that James only once rejected Berkeley in the strong sense; he did so in a number of other contexts. He wrote, "Radical empiricism has, in fact, more affinities with natural realism than with the views of Berkeley or of Mill, and this is easily shown." On Berkeley's view, James held, we have no grounds for saying that two people perceive the same object. "The incredibility of such a philosophy is flagrant."[15] In addition, as Myers himself stresses, James acknowledged that his pragmatic view of truth presupposed an antecedent reality of some sort, which was not called into question during the debate. As Myers sagely remarks, "Since he, like his critics, had always wanted the usual, commonsense constraints on truth, there is little doubt the debate was largely over terminology."[16] Moreover, it must be kept in mind, that James not only never renounced his commitment to natural realism but also defended it at the very time he was composing his Hibbert Lectures, soon to be published as *A Pluralistic Universe*.

James's relation to Berkeley is a crucial one since Myers views it as a bridge from radical empiricism to the alleged panpsychism of *A Pluralistic Universe*. "Pure experience" was interpreted as a neutral monism or phenomenalism by many of James's contemporaries as well as by recent and current commentators. Myers, however, sees "pure experience" via the overtones and implications of "experience" as opening the gates for the onrush of idealistic and panpsychistic consequences.[17] Whether or not James was panpsychistic—which I doubt, since James construed "panpsychism" in Pickwickian ways—I am claiming that he did not reach this curious position by virtue of being a Berkeleyan in the strong sense.

However, Myers is extremely careful and cautious in his discussion of James's metaphysics. He does not claim that James ever announced, or even agreed, that he was a panpsychist, far from it; he limits himself, on the whole, to the claim that James appears logically committed to it in *A Pluralistic Universe*. In a long and thoughtful footnote Myers further qualifies his thesis. For James panpsychism was an ambiguous concept. "James called Fechner's system panpsychic even though it was clearly dualistic in holding that vaster psychical systems attach to vaster physical systems." "James found his own attempts to identify panpsychism almost as obscure as we find them; given the absence of any evidence that he resolved such obscurities, we must infer that he dropped the question." If "panpsychism" meant what others meant by it, "he was at least uncertain if not against it."[18]

On the other hand, in the same or adjacent contexts, Myers states a stronger thesis. "I believe that Jamesian metaphysics was well on its way to panpsychism, propelled to it by Berkeley's view of physical things." "If panpsychism meant nothing more than what he called pure experience, he would probably have called himself a panpsychist."[19] Unfortunately, "propelled by Berkeley's view" is ambiguous; Myers easily shows that James accepted Berkeley's weak thesis but never argues that he accepted the strong one. And, to say that if "panpsychism" is the same as "pure experience" then James was a panpsychist is not helpful since the main issue is what James meant by "pure experience." Was it equivalent to neutral monism, phenomenalism, or was it Berkeleyan in the strong sense? Are mental and physical distinctions functional or metaphysical?

Panpsychism is not only incompatible with James's epistemic realism but also with his logical realism. Concepts are a distinct type of reality, different from sensations. Meanings are abstract and fixed and can scarcely be construed as levels of consciousness. Moreover, subjective pragmatism is inconsistent with panpsychism since the former claims that all classification reflects subjective motivation. Phenomenalism is also incompatible with panpsychism since it reinforces the neutral monism interpretation of pure experience. Myers constantly labels James a phenomenalist in spite of the fact that it conflicts with his panpsychism thesis. In any case, the ascription also seems false since phenomenalism is essentially a foundationalist epistemology, and foundationalism is incompatible with James's view that empirical propositions, and apparently logical expressions as well, are never incorrigible. Some of James's views that are incompatible with panpsychism are also incompatible with each other, as is the case with subjective pragmatism and logical realism. In Dickinson Miller's words, "The truth was that the man's mind was so big, there were so many elements present in it, that it was almost riven asunder."[20] In his metaphysical views, more than elsewhere, one must agree with Myers that James was chameleonic, leading his critics a merry chase.

3

The three issues that I will consider in detail are James's dilemma of determinism, his moral philosophy, and his social views. In each case I will first give Myers's exposition and criticism of James's views and then follow with my own response.

Affected as he was by a skeptical strain himself, Myers writes, James was unconvinced by theoretical proofs of freedom. "The utmost that a believer in free-will can ever do will be to show that the deterministic arguments are not coercive."[21] James here relies on another sense of "subjective pragmatism." A person can compare the doctrines of freedom and determinism by tracing out and contrasting their consequences, see which set of consequences he prefers, and deliberately opt for the view with his preferential consequences. "This technique cannot objectively settle philosophical debates, but it can help us find a rationale for making up our mind when objective guidelines fail."[22]

Deterministic consequences, James believed, lead to a devastating dilemma, one horn of which is universal pessimism, the other subjectivism, either one being difficult to accept. How can a determinist judge the Brockton murder? He cannot judge the individual event as evil since it could not have been otherwise. All he can do is regret the whole universe in which such an event is necessary. "To avoid this horn of the dilemma," Myers writes, "one must adopt subjectivism, the attitude that what really counts is less the objective world, where murders take place, than our subjective responses to that world. Subjectivists are tempted to excuse the murder and its inevitability because it awakens noble and exquisite sensitivities in us."[23] However, James thought such a view transforms life from a tragic reality into an insincere melodrama. The consequences of indeterminism, on the other hand, with its concept of an open future the configurations of which are at least partially filled in by human choices and actions, if not optimistic are at least melioristic—human beings would have the opportunity to fight evil heroically and make the world a somewhat better, if far from perfect, place to live.[24]

It should be noted that determinism, in trying to make sense of the concept of regret, leads to inconsistent consequences. We condemn the Brockton murder by regretting its occurrence but such regret, according to the determinist, is pointless since its occurrence was necessary. Yet the feeling of regret is itself determined; hence the determinist is committed to the view that what ought to be is impossible. Like Aristotle, James believed that the existence of any feeling proves that it has a function, so that the very occurrence of feeling regret is prima facie evidence that the act need not have been chosen.[25]

According to James, philosophers think they reach their conclusions by objective facts and arguments. In reality their choices in ethics and metaphysics reflect and serve their personalities, and their reasons come trailing after. There is a sentiment of rationality that is not discursive but reflects what a personality counts as a sane universe. The determinists see a block universe as rational while indeterminists see a pluralistic one as rational, and each one supports his own concept of what counts as a sane world by seeking supportive, discursive arguments.

While appreciating James's views, Myers is strongly critical of them. James was unduly eager to make the freedom-determinism issue a metaphysical one and hence ignored the many commonsense ways we have of ascribing responsibility and inflicting penalties. Commonsense does not suggest that we can always make the right judgments, "but there are times when we have overwhelming evidence that a person decided freely . . . to act as he did." Despite the existence of borderline cases of acting freely, "we should not jettison the methods we use in daily life to sort out free from unfree choices and actions. We suppose in our routine existence that hard determinism is not only testable but is also false; we should not scrap the evidence to which we commonly appeal in calling a choice free merely because someone suggests, without relevant evidence, that perhaps no choice is ever free."[26]

Moreover, James did poor service in embracing "the personal approach" and saying in effect not to be too concerned about particular arguments since we are already either determinists or indeterminists by temperament, the supporting arguments largely being rationalizations. However, "this rationale buckles under the charge that James's advocacy of indeterminism was merely the expression of his own temperament, that even he did not freely choose his arguments since they were determined by the kind of person he was."

Further, James did not sufficiently realize that temperaments can be altered, perhaps obliquely, through dialogue and debate: he "does not seem to have recognized fully that an argument or an insight can have the force that he reserved for temperament or personality alone; the force of an argument by itself may not activate a decision, but it can liberate us from our prejudices so that we can make more enlightened (and therefore freer) choices about the beliefs and norms by which to guide our lives."[27]

Myers's statement of James's view is precise and well stated, and his criticism of it is devastating. James did indeed ignore commonsense (and legal and medical) criteria by which we distinguish agents from automata, responsible and nonresponsible agents, degrees of responsibility and corresponding liabilities, including impaired, strict, mitigated, imputed, and transferred liability.

However, I am not wholly convinced by Myers's explanation that James ignored ordinary criteria because he was unduly eager to make freedom-determinism a metaphysical issue. It seems to me that James legitimately wanted to make the issue a metaphysical one since he felt that as long as the debate concerned only agency theory, the soft determinist appeared not only distinct from the hard determinist but also superior to him. This distinction and superiority were illusions, James felt, since the soft determinist, in replacing external causes by reasons and motives conceived as causes, forecloses all future truth values and wipes out the possibility of a pluralistic universe as thoroughly as the hard determinist does. The trouble with soft determinists like Hodgson, Bradley, and Howison was that they wanted both a foreclosed future and human freedom; and the two concepts are incompatible. James, it seems to me, is on quite sound ground in emphasizing the metaphysical desideratum of freedom and thereby rejecting the privileged position the soft determinist has when only agency theory is discussed. Unfortunately, James never got around to formulating any adequate agency theory himself—and it was this neglect that led him to do less than justice to ordinary criteria of responsibility. In his chapters on attention and will he makes a decent beginning in discussing agency theory. Attending to the book in front of me is free either if it is a spontaneous event "or, somewhat differently if the cause of the attending is simply our willing to do it." But he neither developed the latter into a case of immanent (as distinct from transeunt) causation nor parlayed his discussion of deliberation in his chapter on thought into anything resembling an agency theory.

I am puzzled by Myers's claim that in routine experience hard determinism is not only testable but also false. No doubt many scientific renditions of it can be shown to be false (the psychoanalyst's formulation being one of them) but conceptual renditions of the problem cannot be so disposed of in routine experience. If conceptually "x causes y" implies that nothing else than y could occur, then, whether x be genetic, physiological, or rational in nature, the outcome could not have been otherwise. The historical alternative has been to deny that human actions are caused, thereby inviting the criticism of moral chaos. Thomas Reid, and those recent philosophers who have followed his lead, claim that the concept of cause is not *applicable* to human agency, that motives are inappropriately construed as causes. The issue, then, is to find a criterion that distinguishes the cause-effect and motive-action models of explanation. But this conceptual issue and dialectic is strictly a philosophical issue, and not one that can be settled by ordinary experience or matters of fact of any kind.

Myers does well to criticize James's claim that we are either determinists or indeterminists by temperament and that reasons for either view are rationalizations. I applaud his emphasizing that James undercuts his own indeterminism by this claim, as well as his criticizing James for not appreciating that temperaments can be altered by rational considerations. Though I genuinely appreciate such criticisms, I do not see how they square with Myers's characterization of James as an existentialist beginning with his 1869–70 crisis over the determinism issue. Under the influence of Renouvier, James decided that his first act of free will would be a voluntary belief in the freedom of will. Myers describes this claim and subsequent variations of it as equivalent to certain existentialist claims. By his choice freely made a man not only acts in a certain way but is himself also deciding what kind of a human being he is going to become. By freely acting one way rather than another we are choosing between one of several equally possible future characters. However, this view of James seems to flatly contradict the view that personalities and characters, presumably antecedent in nature, cause us to be determinists or indeterminists. James's subjective sentiment of rationality reinforces the view that antecedent temperaments determine philosophical position. Thus the sentiment of rationality and the existentialist motif come into conflict. Is there any way to avoid this apparent inconsistent set of propositions or is the conflict unresolvable? If James held the existentialist view he would also have held that temperament can be altered, thereby avoiding one of Myers's criticisms. But in thus avoiding it James would be committed to abandoning his view that temperaments and characters determine philosophical views and that reasons are rationalizations on ethical and metaphysical issues.

4

As an introduction to moral philosophy Myers quotes from James's 1879 review of W. K. Clifford's essays, "The miraculous achievement . . . must be a metaphysical achievement, the greatest of all time—the demonstration, namely, that all our different motives, rightly interpreted, pull one way. . . . Can the synthesis and reconciliation come?"[28] Making this idea credible was a dominant motive in "The Moral Philosopher and the Moral Life," though, whatever else he achieved, making this idea credible was a failure.

In this essay, which he thought one of his best, James distinguished three types of ethical questions: (1) How do moral ideas originate? (the psychological question); (2) What do moral terms mean? (the metaphysical question); and (3) How can the immense variety of values be sorted out and measured? (the casuistic question). Myers discusses them in the order (1), (3), (2).

According to James, not all moral ideas originate from associations, as Mill claimed, "but some moral judgments are based on intuition grounded in cerebral rather than environmental structures." " 'Experience' of consequences may truly teach us what things are *wicked,* but what have consequences to do with what is *mean* and *vulgar*?" "The nobler thing *tastes* better and that is all we can say."[29]

However, since intuitions jostle and compete with each other, how do we choose between incompatible ones? The more exclusive ones must be butchered in order to reach the most cohesive and inclusive moral whole. James described the goal of "the great experiment" as maximizing the greatest number of morally satisfied people, a utilitarian goal superior to the hedonistic one that defines satisfaction in terms of pleasure or happiness. Unfortunately, Myers writes, James's union of intuitionism and utilitarianism encounters grave problems. How can James at one and the same time make his own maximizing intuition immune from butchering and yet insist on the butchering of other intuitions and ideals in the maximizing process? Nothing justified James's confidence in this process except his own intuition that such a good ought to be—period. This ineliminable reliance on intuition by the objective philosopher and partisan alike undermines James's notion that maximizing good is an impartial task. Moreover, James failed "to provide even a hint of how the moral philosopher ought to select which part of the ideal to save and which to butcher."[30] The tepid response of his audience, which disappointed James, may have resulted from this failure.

At the end of his discussion Myers returns to the metaphysical question about the meaning of moral and value terms. James argued that value terms have no meaning apart from feelings or desires. "So far as [a person] feels anything to be good, he *makes* it good." Apparently, Myers writes, James thought that "feeling something to be good" provides the meaning of "good." However, the first phrase scarcely provides the meaning of "good" since it provides no explication of the term. In fact,

James nowhere proposed straightforward definitions of "good," "right," or "ought." "[I]f we are already puzzled by what *good* means, James's remark that it refers to an object of desire is not very helpful, leaving us to ponder which object of desire he meant."[31] Though he never acknowledged the fact, James concluded that "good"and "ought" are undefinable; they cannot be expressed in other words and thus deserve to be called "primitive terms" in the language of morals. Apparently one can understand such words only through directly experiencing desires or imperatives. While James was not interested in formally relating moral terms, Myers thinks he might have agreed that *right action* is definable as *what one ought to do.* Since he thought good and ought are available only within experience, we might in the interest of economy define *good* as *what ought to be,* retaining obligation as the only primitive concept that must be experienced to be understood.[32]

Myers's discussion here, as elsewhere, is clear and instructive, and his criticisms of James appear convincing. I heartily agree that in this essay James failed to produce the greatest metaphysical achievement of all time—the demonstration that all our different motives, rightly interpreted, pull one way—which had been his ideal in the Clifford review. It is difficult to believe that the ideal was still alive in this essay, though there are echoes of it in his belief that even in the moment of triumph the inclusive side will do some degree of justice to the vanquished party's interest. But he gives no hint how this result is possible if, as is usually the case, the two are incompatible. He had no Hegelian synthesis.

I have one reservation about Myers's discussion here; I am not quite convinced that James was the intuitionist he is portrayed to be and hence that his intuitionism and utilitarianism come into conflict. And I have one worry: I wonder whether his utilitarianism has been convincingly stated. To begin with, in answering the psychological question James was by no means endorsing intuitionism as a general moral philosophy. Intuitionists are right in the psychological context, to be sure, because they insist that some values and ideals at least are basic and underivable— "brain born," a priori, nativisitic imperatives (whether demands for the satisfaction of desires or demands for realizing some ideal)—and hence these values and ideals cannot arise from experience. James applauded the intuitionists for fending off genetic accounts—be they psychological (Mill), sociological (Comte), or evolutionary (Spencer)—designed to undercut these nativistic views, and, indeed, to dispose of metaphysical claims in general by generating them out of individual, social, or "racial" experience.

While intuitionists are on the side of the angels on the psychological question, James seems to suggest that they fare poorly elsewhere.[33] He did not spell out how they failed but no doubt thought it too obvious to dwell upon. The trouble with intuitionism is that its judgments are absolute, inflexible, and completely lack the plastic quality required of an ethics James could accept. For the intuitionists morality is made up in advance, while for James morality is ever and always in the making, a forward-looking process that will never be complete "until the last man has had his experience and said his say."

Moreover, in sections (2) and (3) James's references to intuitions tend to disappear for the most part. He speaks increasingly often of satisfying demands, whether they be earthy and specific or ideal. But ideals must not be confused with intuitions for the former are forward looking and dynamic while the latter are timeless and irrelevant to the movement of morality. In a perfect world every one of the demands would be satisfied, but that is not the world we have in fact. Specific demands and ideals must take their chances among the many contending wants, desires, and ideals. Intuitions, like other demands, must be unstiffened and take their chances with all the rest. Since not all the contending demands can be satisfied or accepted, some of them must be butchered. But they cannot be butchered according to *any* of the contenders, including intuitions; there must be some impartial way of resolving the conflicting claims. Section (3) contains the alleged principle of impartial butchery. It amounts to what has been felicitously called negative utilitarianism. According to James,

> That act must be the best act, accordingly, which makes for the *best whole,* in the sense of awakening the least sum of dissatisfactions. In the casuistic scale, therefore, those ideals must be written highest which *prevail at the least cost,* or by whose realization the least possible number of other ideals are destroyed. Since victory and defeat there must be, the victory to be philosophically prayed for is that of the more inclusive side—of the side which even in the hour of triumph will to some degree do justice to the ideals in which the vanquished party's interests lay.[34]

There is no indication that James saw his principle of negative utilitarianism as intuitive in nature. On the contrary, he explicitly rejected this notion. The philosopher is rightly confident, he wrote, that his own intuitive preferences would be certain to end in the mutilation of the fullness of the truth. They must become part of "that howling mob of desires, each struggling to get breathing-room for the ideal to which it clings."[35] The fate of the philosopher's intuitions and ideals, like any other, will be decided by the maximizing process. Indeed, James seemed never to construe his maximizing principle as intuitive. This principle, he thought, captured the required senses of impartiality and fairness needed to resolve value conflict but was a principle not in itself needing justification either by intuition or by J. S. Mill's claptrap psychological methods. What, after all, could you say to a person who asks why he should be fair? James would simply say that such a person had no aptitude for morality. Hence, if James is not himself an intuitionist this view and his utilitarianism can scarcely come into conflict.

Myers's construal of James's utilitarianism, in turn, raises questions. That James would have agreed that "right action" is definable as "what one ought to do" is doubtful but in any case difficult to assess because of its subjunctive character. The crucial point is that he should not have agreed since, as G. E. Moore pointed out, on utilitarian grounds of any sort two actions may be right if an equal amount of good is produced by each, in which case there is one right act that is not our duty. Even more seriously, if James were to define "good" as "what ought to be," retaining obligation as the only primitive concept, it is difficult to see how he would be a utilitarian at all. Any teleological position derives the concept of ought and makes good (however it is interpreted) basic. However he construes "good," the teleologist discovers through experience what act will produce the most good and hence constitutes his duty. Thus he derives obligation from value considerations. James, it would seem, was a teleologist since he wrote that experience can tell us what is wicked but not what is mean or vulgar. Indeed, his maximizing principle commits him specifically to the utilitarian form of teleology.

Moreover, a wise teleologist, or utilitarian, refrains from defining "ought" as "maximizing the good" because such a procedure confuses reasons and synonyms. By not asserting a definitional equivalence the teleologist is able to look upon the maximizing of good as a *reason* why some act counts as a duty. James did not offer any definition of "ought" as "maximizing good," and that is all to the good. Unfortunately he was on the right side of the fence here by default; he never offered a definition of any term.

It must not be assumed that I think James's position was unassailable—far from it. Myers offers numerous trenchant criticisms with which I agree, including the one that James failed to offer even a hint of how the moral philosopher ought to select which part of the ideal to save and which to butcher. Myers's whole discussion of the relation between James's moral and religious views, which I have no time to discuss, is a brilliant one, a model of clarity and close-knit argument.

5

According to Myers, James was publicly concerned about disadvantaged groups, including American blacks. In a speech delivered at the Boston Music Hall in 1897 James eulogized the abolitionists and the Fifty-fourth Massachusetts Regiment, largely black, and wrote: "A land of freedom,

boastfully so-called, with human slavery enthroned at the heart of it
. . . what was it but a thing of falsehood and horrible self-contradiction?"[36]
It is also possible, Myers adds, that James might have given W. E. B.
DuBois a check to aid the Tuskegee Institute.[37] Indeed, "that he had the
energy to be concerned with the position of blacks, women, immigrants,
minorities in other countries, the care of the insane, vivisection, medical
legislation, educational policy, the temperance movement, the imperialism
and militarism of the Spanish-American War, the annexation of the
Philippines, and the Monroe Doctrine is a remarkable feature of his life
and thought."[38] One may fault James for not being more aggressively
against American racism, yet for a college professor he was singularly
ahead of his time in his attitude toward blacks.[39]

James was likewise publicly concerned about a larger disadvantaged
group, women. In reviewing *Subjection of Women* James regretted Mill's
emotional involvement and resisted his equation of love with friendship
and shared interests. The astronomer's wife, he felt, need not feel
passionate about astronomy. Mill also failed to deal with the implications
of divorce at will for the family. Yet James detected in this book the
ultimate tendencies of the democratic flood. The merits of Mill's case,
indeed, had to be recognized. "The question was largely how the forces
for change . . . could most effectively modify the forces for tradition."[40]
Moreover, James was deferential to women's judgments and believed that
they had the right to determine what was in their own best interests.
He was not offended by active suffragettes and held Jane Addams in
high esteem. He even applauded women hiking in knickerbockers. Such
anecdotes, Myers acknowledges, hardly show James to be a committed
activist, but for a Harvard professor he was singularly ahead of his time
in his attitude toward women as well as blacks.

James's social commitment is further exhibited in his testifying at
the Massachusetts State House against a proposed bill to require the
examination and licensing of medical practitioners, a bill aimed at
eliminating "moral medicine" in general and faith healers and Christian
Scientists in particular. His work on behalf of the insane was far from
superficial. He was unimpressed with both sides of the vivisection issue,
but he did heartily insist that careful moral monitoring of animal
experimentation was necessary.

In politics James wrote vehemently against American imperialism
in the Spanish-American War and the annexation of the Philippines. James
was, in fact, deeply upset by these events. Why? Santayana suggested
he felt that America had betrayed him; how could *my* country do this!
Recently R. L. Beisner explains it by James's naiveté about America's
past. "To think that war and the suppression of insurrection in the
Philippines had revealed for the first time that the American people shared
the universal human condition was to overlook a history which included

religious conflict and witch-hangings, slavery and lynchings, corruption and industrial warfare, and the near-extermination of the American Indian."[41] Myers concludes that this answer is "arguably" the right one.

Myers's discussion is impressive since he neither oversells nor undersells James's social commitments and activity. In my opinion his discussion is by far the best account we have on these topics. However, each virtue has a related (minor) vice. In being fair-minded we often tend to vacillate, if ever so slightly. Has Myers done so? Perhaps slightly. But let me emphasize that this issue is a difficult one to deal with since any differences between Myers and myself are subtle ones of emphasis rather than substance.

The evidence that Myers gives for saying that James was concerned about disadvantaged American blacks is his oration delivered at the Boston Music Hall and the possibility that in 1909 he might have given W. E. B. DuBois a check to aid the Tuskegee Institute. No doubt this evidence does establish the minimum claim that James was publicly concerned about American blacks. However, Myers suggests more than this minimal claim. He writes that James was concerned about the position of blacks, women, immigrants, and the insane, vivisection, medical legislation, temperance, the Spanish-American War, and the annexation of the Philippines, and that this concern "is a remarkable feature of his life and thought." Much of this series of concerns did constitute a remarkable feature of his life, but to include his care for the blacks as part of the series seems to me to constitute credit by association. It does not seem to me, that James deserves credit in this context. It is arguable that James was sufficiently ill in 1860 to prevent his enlisting in the Civil War, but he was not ill enough to be unable to help in other ways. Through the years William showed no sensitivity to the needs of the blacks. He wrote or did nothing during the Reconstruction years. He neither wrote nor did anything to support the Civil Rights Act of 1875; he did not protest the Supreme Court decision (1883) declaring the 1875 bill unconstitutional; he was silent about the Berlin Conference (1885) where European powers met to partition Africa for colonization; he was silent about the Pressy-Ferguson decision (1896); he was never active in the Niagara Movement or the NAACP. Indeed, whatever feeling James had for blacks, he did nothing significant to improve their lot. To compare him favorably with other college professors scarcely shows James in a good light, but the others in a bad one.

The evidence that Myers gives is no doubt sufficient to show that James was publicly concerned about women. However he again suggests more than this minimal claim by associating James's views on women with his significant reforms. Again, this credit by association seems unwarranted. I can find no place in James's review of Mill where he *endorses* Mill's view, whatever he might have said about the likelihood of the acceptance of Mill's view in the future. I find no subsequent endorsement or any contribution to the women's suffrage campaign. To be told he was not offended by the suffragettes is cold comfort. I heartily agree with Myers that the knickerbocker anecdote hardly identifies James as a committed activist. Still Myers takes the sting out of this by saying that, for a Harvard professor, he was singularly ahead of his time in his attitude toward women. The contrast, however, can go the other way. Instead of comparing him with Harvard academicians, let us compare him with his friend Chauncey Wright, who did teach briefly at Harvard and who, in fact, said the sorts of things we might expect James, as a champion of the underdog, to have said. Wright defended women's right to vote and their right to legal equality; charged that men have so arranged the affairs of life that they have the best opportunities for acquiring power; and rejected the claim, advanced by James, that American women were not in jeopardy. The fact remains, Wright averred, that most American men not only think women are in subjection but also think they should be. "That their subjection, however, is not in the nature of servitude, but rather of religious obligation, is a part of the arrogant opinion, which springs from a sentimental estimate of 'the fact of sex,' and blinds men to the truth that personality is a still greater fact."[42]

I certainly agree with Beisner, and apparently with Myers also, that James's dramatic response to the annexation of the Philippines was naive. It is just such naiveté about political events that marks his response to the Irish fight for home rule and eventually independence from England. The point is not so much, as Myers writes, that James can be faulted "for not sympathizing more with his sister Alice's siding with the Irish against England,"[43] but that he was not even competent to make a judgment. He was simply not knowledgeable about Irish history and Parnell's role in English Parliamentary life. To be in favor of the underdog is not enough; one has to know enough to identify him. The further away James got from his professional interests, the less intense and less knowledgeable were his defenses of the underdog.

My own estimate of James's humanity and social consciousness— not so far different from Myers's fine portrayal, I trust—is this: he was a compassionate, warm, and helpful person. He had a way of inspiring in his students and colleagues the best of which they were capable. People related more humanely toward each other in his presence. He was genuinely helpful in social causes close to his professional interests. Outside of these interests he was sometimes helpful and at other times lacking in insight. It must be said of him that his disappointing performances always resulted from ignorance, but never from prejudice. Yet a person has a duty to be informed on moral and social issues on which he takes a stand. In the case of a complex person like James we need to attend to his occasional warts as well as his beauty marks. I do not wish to detract from the man's reputation. On the contrary, I am so fond of him that I cannot bear to have his occasional wart and wen go unnoticed. It is one mark of the greatness of James that he would be the last one to want it otherwise.

NOTES

1. Gerald E. Myers, *William James, His Life and Thought* (New Haven: Yale University Press, 1986), p. 160.

2. Ibid., p. 209.

3. Ibid., p. 210.

4. Ibid., p. 415.

5. Ibid., p. 24.

6. Ibid., p. 28.

7. Ibid., p. 33.

8. Ibid., p. 492. That Myers is not in principle antagonistic to psychobiography is suggested by his reference to Crouse's biography of Alice James as definitive and a qualification of his criticism of Edel. Even if Edel overworks the Jacob-Esau theme, "we may gradually accept the conjecture of a sub-conscious struggle for primacy as the purported evidence accumulates" (p. 23). The nature of James's problem, let alone its explanation, is never clear. Myers refers to James's depression (pp. 20, 47), deep depression (p. 46), chronic depression (pp. 20, 21), psychosomatic illness (p. 47), so-called psychosomatic illness (p. 49), neurosis (p. 33), neurasthenia (pp. 31, 39, 214), nervousness (pp. 20, 21), nervous breakdown (p. 34), despondency (p. 51), and pessimistic crisis (p. 51).

9. Myers, *William James*, p. 284.

10. Ibid., p. 289.

11. Ibid., p. 358.

12. Morton White, *Science and Sentiment in America* (New York: Oxford University Press, 1972), pp. 204-16. Specifically White construes Appendix C of *A Pluralistic Universe* as a departure from a sharp distinction between a priori and empirical propositions. In this appendix James wrote that the dictum *de omni et nullo* cannot be applied in many concrete situations. White interprets James here as admitting that even logical truths are plastic. White acknowledges that James does not reject the *dicta* in mathematics and logic which deal with abstract concepts and hence are exact and not plastic. However, White points out, "the whole thrust of his argument is that such exactness is 'fake,' as Whitehead might have put it later, simply because the concepts have been made or devised in such a way as not to be adequate to 'reality, life, experience, concreteness, and immediacy.' One cannot avoid the conclusion that James *did* think that experience could conceivably overturn the beliefs of logic and mathematics" (*Science and Sentiment*, p. 216).

13. William James, *Pragmatism* (Cambridge: Harvard University Press, 1975), p. 47.

14. R. B. Perry, *The Thought and Character of William James*, 2 vols. (Boston: Little, Brown and Co., 1935), 2: 536, 549.

15. *The Writings of William James,* ed. John J. McDermott (Chicago: University of Chicago Press, 1977), pp. 208-209.

16. Myers, *William James,* p. 303.

17. Ibid., p. 574. For James as a Berkeleyan see the whole of chaps. 11 and 12.

18. Myers, *William James,* pp. 612, 613.

19. Ibid., pp. 574, 613.

20. Ibid., p. 606.

21. Ibid., p. 207. (James quoted by Myers.) James was not always as close to skepticism as he intimated. It was not only James's "will power" that sustained his indeterminism. A crucial reason for his adopting indeterminism was his belief that science had finally succeeded in undermining the automaton theory, to which he had previously been committed. His respect for scientific evidence had to be met and it was. In some contexts it is easy to think of James as credulous. Where metaphysical issues are concerned he was the essence of incredulity. As in his life, so in his metaphysics he found it very difficult to decide conclusively on anything.

22. Myers, *William James,* p. 197.

23. Ibid., p. 208.

24. Ibid., p. 305.

25. Ibid., p. 392.

26. Ibid., p. 208, 394.

27. Ibid., p. 393. This quotation and previous one.

28. Ibid., p. 396. (James quoted by Myers.)

29. Ibid., p. 397. (James quoted by Myers.)

30. Ibid., p. 400.

31. Ibid., p. 402.

32. Ibid., p. 403.

33. *The Will to Believe and Other Essays in Popular Philosophy* (Cambridge: Harvard University Press, 1979), pp. 144-45.

34. Ibid., p. 155.

35. Ibid., p. 154.

36. Myers, *William James,* pp. 423-44. (James quoted by Myers.)

37. Ibid., p. 596 n. 99.

38. Ibid., p. 429.

39. Ibid., p. 424, 429.

40. Ibid., p. 427

41. Ibid., p. 440. James's naiveté or lack of judgment, even good taste, surfaces more than once. In his correspondence he not only refers to "darkies" (Perry, *Thought and Character* 2:544) but also writes that he had been working "like a whole gang of niggers" (Perry, *Thought and Character* 1:418.) Myers excuses the first reference. "Using *darky* was James's way of trying not to be stilted, artificial, or sentimental, but to indicate that he was himself relating with respect and admiration to a person whom many described, whether endearingly or otherwise, as a 'darky'" (p. 596). Whether or not one is satisfied with this explanation, does it extend to "nigger"? I hardly see how. There are limits to how one avoids being stilted and artificial. The same sort of thing occurred in

other contexts. In "Remarks at the Peace Banquet," he wrote, "Let the general possibility of war be left open, in Heaven's name, for the imagination to dally with. Let the soldiers dream of killing, as the old maids dream of marrying" (quoted by Myers, p. 442). James referred to the Haymarket riot as "the work of a lot of pathological Germans and Poles" (F. O. Matthiessen, *The James Family* [New York: Knopf, 1961], p. 622). I do not want to accuse James of racism and sexism—far from it. I do want to suggest that amid much good judgment and taste James sometimes exhibited odd bad judgments and taste.

42. *The Letters of Chauncey Wright*, ed. J. B. Thayer (Cambridge: John Wilson and Son, 1878), p. 162.

43. Myers, *William James*, p. 430.

On Interpreting William James with Edward Madden

Gerald E. Myers

Edward Madden's review of my book on James is as generous as it is perceptive. Continuing his support of my Jamesian inquiries, Madden treats me very kindly in the course of providing a remarkably succinct yet broad report of the book's contents. The pleasure felt upon reading the review by this astute critic, himself a noted Jamesian scholar and distinguished contributor to a related literature, a critic formidably equipped for espying any rust under the polish, that pleasure was, I confess, saturated with relief.

Madden presents us with an adroitly compacted package of issues, and, selecting from it as time allows and the occasion encourages, I begin with his persuasive observations about the two ways of doing philosophy historically and how these may be blended. It would have been disappointing if he had interpreted my effort differently, having construed it myself as not unlike Warnock's way with Berkeley, Peters's with Hobbes, or Wollheim's with Bradley. These studies combine textual exegesis with fresh philosophizing that, when successful, illuminate both past and present thinking. Or, as investigating Descartes's intentions, for instance, can simultaneously consolidate one's own conception of *cogito* as being noninferentially rather than inferentially evident, so in the process of examining James's arguments, say, on determinism, one may solidify one's own views of human freedom.

What I've written about James is aptly called a dialogue by Madden. Conversing with a historical figure through a book has advantages over journal joustings with contemporaries (including of course the right to construct both sides of the dialogue!). The historical context often suggests interpretations of particular arguments that would not occur if those arguments were mulled in isolation. Because the context indicates, I think, that James typically transformed philosophical questions into metaphysical ones, I interpreted his treatment of determinism as a slight case of overkill, leading Edward Madden to wonder justifiably whether here I cut James too abruptly out of the dialogue.

James was right in holding that not soft but hard determinism is freedom's real enemy, and he was also right in applying his subjective pragmatism to metaphysical debates about hard determinism. Madden sympathizes with my worry, however, that James moved to metaphysical debating before consulting commonsense criteria for distinguishing free from forced behavior, hypothesizing that this neglect resulted from James's failure to develop an adequate agency theory. But, apart from details of Jamesian interpretations, Madden is understandably puzzled by my unelaborated endorsement of commonsense in questioning James's position.

James developed the habit, I believe, after transferring much of psychology to metaphysics in *The Principles of Psychology,* of keeping philosophical issues permanently unsettled by transferring them to metaphysics. Given his interest in the motivations to philosophize in particular ways, I wondered why he didn't more eagerly commend commonsense motives on the issue of determinism. So I spoke for them, asserting that routine experience shows hard determinism to be false, believing that from James's perspective this is as good as any metaphysical reply to a hard determinist, who will not be converted in either case. Why surrender commonsense criteria for distinguishing free from forced deeds? There is no need to do so simply because the *suspicion* defined as hard determinism exists.

Since James's opponents entertained a wholesale suspicion that excluded any felt need for experimental refutations of commonsense criteria, I think that James could have insisted, short of taking the metaphysical route, that commonsense criteria are innocent until experimentally proven guilty. Suppose, for instance, that at t_{10} I fail to high-jump six feet, and whereas my coach says I could have succeeded or done otherwise, the hard determinist says I could not. My coach bases his assertion on the fact that I jumped six feet at all prior times t_1 through t_9, but the determinist bases his on a metaphysical picture of human action lodged in causal chains. The coach's claim, unless countered by evidence that I was sick, etc., at t_{10}, is experimentally confirmed, and it is not contradicted but bypassed by the determinist's suspicion.

Because it appears that quotidian experience displays empirically confirmed claims that persons could have done other than what they did, that hard determinism is therefore a suspicion without empirical credentials, I thought that James could be cited for failing to ask the determinist for such credentials. Yet, having said this to fill the vacuum that Madden noted, I quickly add, especially in light of Madden's helpful observations about the arguments of James's opponents like Hodgson, Howison, and Bradley, that, to be sure, James was at some point duty bound to confront the determinist on his own ground, i.e., at the metaphysical level.

It is in this same context that Madden's sharp eye detects another problem. How can an interpreter like myself characterize James as an existentialist who simply chooses indeterminism (as James said he did during a personal crisis in 1869-70), at the same time remembering his recurrent claim that philosophical beliefs, including those expressed in determinism and indeterminism, are but manifestations of different temperaments? James was not unaware of the problem or some of its aspects anyway,[1] but he never troubled, it appears, to set out its resolution. My impressions follow Madden's suggestion that, if pressed, James would have opted for the existentialist side of the dilemma, holding that temperaments are alterable by philosophies, but having thereby to qualify, if not abandon, the converse of this that he had so often asserted. Philosophies, he and we could then argue, are the expressions of the temperaments that they themselves help to mold and remold. To suggest that conservatism and liberalism, for example, are largely philosophical manifestations of two distinct personality types need not imply helplessness anywhere.

The connections between philosophy and personality are among the attractions of doing philosophy historically, and they figure prominently in this exchange between Edward Madden and myself. They excited my interest in James to the extent that I miss the Jamesian spirit in current philosophy. I naturally welcome Morton White's recent testimony to James's greatness and his locating some of that greatness in James's having shown philosophers how personality may legitimately decide between conflicting beliefs, including those on determinism, when logic and experience are insufficient for doing so. White lauds James for having driven home the lesson that the "whole" man and nothing less deserves to participate in certain kinds of philosophical decisions.[2]

The attractiveness of doing philosophy historically obviously does not depend upon any particular theme or claim such as James's. It stems from the opportunity provided not only to scrutinize the logic of a philosopher's arguments, but also to elicit their *significance* as well. Significance is always significance for someone, and it is revealed in the context of what someone wants to believe, of what else he is inclined to believe, and of what he believes to be at stake in the fate of his beliefs.

Philosophizing with contemporaries tends to sacrifice significance to the analysis of problems that are defined as publicly and impersonally as possible. This is largely due to the circumstance that unless one is exceptionally privileged, to plead significance in one's own case is unseemly or unconvincing or both. Consequently, one who would extend the logical analysis of arguments into an interpretation of their significance finds that opportunity in dialoguing with distinguished thinkers whose lives and ideas supply an appropriate interpretive setting. Discovering the connections between philosophy and personality becomes a legitimate part of the search for significance.

Personality looms so conspicuously in James's career and work that we inevitably confront Madden's queries about the methodology employed in more intimately identifying the Jamesian personality. In trying to approach that personality, I was quite astonished by the numbers who have made or are making their own approach. Interest in William James and the entire James family, especially brother Henry, the novelist, is ever increasing, much of it coming from representatives of psychobiographical and psychoanalytic persuasions. Madden agrees in the main with my dissenting opinions and appreciates the complications involved if I had sought to assess the credits and debits of psychohistory in general. But by the nature of my enterprise, he urges, a better light deserves to be cast on the methodological seat wherein I sit.

I do not believe in psychoanalyzing corpses or applying rigid psychoanalytic theories as a part of psychobiography or psychohistory. Such theories, as Madden notes, are under constant challenge; moreover, without the patient live and freely associating, a necessary condition for successful application is missing. For such reasons plus what my own biographical research discloses, I hold no hope for future psychoanalytic determinations of the Jamesian personality. But if conjectures, not excluding psychoanalytic types, about motivation and complexes constituting personality are suggested by the evidence and are employed fragmentarily and more like possible camera angles than actual photographs, they can fruitfully expand our ways of viewing historical persons and events. Incidentally, a stimulating paper on the personality of William James by Edward and Marian Madden is an example of what I have in mind.[3]

Personality connects visibly with social and political convictions, and in discussing James's convictions I had a better sense, because of Madden's writings, of what needed to be looked for and thought about. His approving words in this area are therefore all the more appreciated. Although still persuaded that, as academics go, James exhibited a vigorous social conscience and gave considerably to nonacademic projects (even when unwell and involved in personal crises), I am the first to admit that what Madden says on this score is essential for a balanced judgment. Compared to Chauncey Wright, yes, James presents a different profile. In turning my ponderings to such things as the *Plessy* v. *Ferguson* decision, the Niagara Movement, and the NAACP, Madden shows why, by these instances alone, no truly definitive study of James should be expected.

Madden fires up one's research interests again, and, given the chance, I'd like to clarify, say, James's relationship to the events leading to the formation of the NAACP in May 1910, only a couple of months before

James died. A founder of the organization, W. E. B. DuBois, had been a student and lifelong friend of James's, and I seem to recall, from investigating DuBois's friendship with James, that James was concerned about the quarrels, including those between DuBois and Booker T. Washington, that attended creation of the NAACP. I'd like to clarify James's role because others like John J. McDermott share Madden's reservations, and because I tend to believe, with respect to blacks, that one can do somewhat better by James than I've done thus far. But whatever the supplemental accounts of James's social and political philosophies turn up, they will not altogether eliminate the warts that Madden has identified for us. As Madden wisely notes, to want to do that would be to offend truth and James as well.

In researching the significance and the logic of James's moral arguments, I benefited from Edward Madden's excellent introduction to the Harvard edition of *The Will to Believe,* although, as his review under discussion shows, my reading of James in this area can be benefited further. If we shade our interpretations of James's ethics somewhat differently, it may be due partly to the perennial problem of relating individual and community in James's philosophy. Some Jamesian passages suggest Abraham Edel's interpretation of the "lone individual on the frontier of decision as the moral situation,"[4] whereas others bear out Madden's emphasis on the communal, maximizing process. I see both tendencies in James's moral theory, but in an uneasy relationship.

Madden and I apparently agree that in "The Moral Philosopher and the Moral Life" James applauds intuition as a source of ideals while warning against our hiding within our intuitive preferences. Intuitions taken as absolute and immune to communal testing are rejected, but belief in the possibility of intuitions that survive such testing, including the intuition that grounds the principle of negative utilitarianism itself, struck me as being essential to James's ethics. I was struck, among other things, by James's concept of the "moral revolutionary" bolstered by "Abstract rules indeed help; but they help less in proportion as our intuitions are the more piercing, and our vocation is the stronger for the moral life."[5] But textual citations are unlikely to remove Madden's "one reservation" about my alluding to James's intuitionism, because the trouble arises, I take it, from my thinking that James saw his principle of negative utilitarianism as intuitive in nature.

Because of what James said in favor of undogmatic intuitions as the source of moral insight, I did suppose that, if asked how he himself came by the principle of negative utilitarianism, he would have replied, "By intuition." But on Madden's reading, James, instead of appealing to intuition, would simply have lamented the questioner's inaptitude for morality. What I wonder now is whether, if a sweeping distinction between ideals and intuitions is modified such that dynamic, forward-looking intuitions are admitted, a serious objection remains for supposing that, for James, the fount of the utilitarian principle is one such dynamic intuition?

Madden's demurrers about a possible way of construing James's utilitarianism, which I suggested rather in passing, are well taken. I would amend or revise that now in the light of those demurrers. Whether one worry I had about James's utilitarianism lives or not, as a result of this exchange with Madden, is unclear because of the complexities involved. I worried in my book that, while James rejected traditional utilitarianism because the general happiness is illegitimately bought through the torture of a single individual, he nevertheless held that the communal moral ideal is legitimately bought through the "butchering" of an individual's moral ideal. Although I connected the apparent dilemma with intuitionism, it seems to me that, independently of that issue, my release from worrying about James's utilitarianism in this regard is still pending.

Another feature of James's ethics is its explicit conservatism. "The presumption in cases of conflict must always be in favor of the conventionally recognized good."[6] This conservatism reappears in *Pragmatism,* and the manner of its appearance there is noticed by Edward Madden and Morton White, both of whom recommend my heeding more closely its implications for James's treatment of a priori and empirical knowledge. James speaks in *Pragmatism* of our bringing to each new experience a stock of established beliefs that we should treat conservatively or protectively by modifying it only to the extent that the surprise of some new experience requires. What is important for Madden and White is that the stock is "plastic," and, interpreting the stock as they do as probably including mathematics and logic (in James's later thinking), my story of James's view of a priori and empirical knowledge can stand some emendations.

James does not explicitly include logical and mathematical propositions among the modifiable stock, but one can appreciate why White, for instance, thinks we are perhaps entitled to infer such.[7] If so, presenting James as a forerunner of Quine's and White's dismantling of the analytic-synthetic distinction becomes plausible. Further, as Madden notes, besides the inconsistency in James that I mention, that he sometimes permitted scientific knowledge to be a priori while never seeming to relinquish the positivist demarcation between truths of reason and truths of fact, there is now a second inconsistency, going the other way, of surrendering the incorrigibility of propositions of logic and mathematics while never officially renouncing the positivist demarcation as described. Without question, in abandoning the logic of identity as he did in *A Pluralistic Universe,* James was implicated in surrendering incorrigibility, although his purpose there was not to sabotage the analytic-synthetic distinction, but to make all empirical claims to knowledge, with whatever a priori elements that might be involved, collapse into a distorted rendition of reality.

James is at his most elusive when theorizing about the nature of concepts, and, when Madden asks if I find the prima facie inconsistencies real, I have unfortunately to say I do. In the book I hope that, although the inconsistencies remain unreconciled, I shed some light on the reasons for James's difficulties in maintaining logical realism while often sounding like a nominalist, or, more seriously, while defending a very subjective brand of pragmatism. I see him torn between the competing claims of traditional rationalism and empiricism, between the abstract demands of logic and the concrete ones of psychology, admitting at the end of his life that *Some Problems of Philosophy* was "somewhat eccentric in its attempt to combine logical realism with an otherwise empiricist mode of thought."[8] I think, too, that working out a theory of concepts was a major goal of his *Some Problems of Philosophy,* a goal that might have been achieved to a degree such that some of the apparent inconsistencies could have been resolved, but he did not live long enough for that to occur. *Some Problems of Philosophy,* a very unfinished study, was published posthumously and in some respects only adds to the confusion. Hence, for now anyway, I have nothing better for interpretation than what was presented, especially in chapters 9 and 10, in my book.

Another item of interpretation, James's relation to Berkeley, does not escape Madden's expert eye. I puzzled for some time over this issue and for reasons mentioned by Madden in his review. James agreed with Berkeley, in what Madden calls the weak sense, that matter is known as simply a complex of sensations. But I owe an explanation of my consistently describing James as a Berkeleyan since I never claim that James agreed with Berkeley, in what Madden calls the strong sense, that sensations depend for their existence upon a knowing mind or experiencer. The doctrine of natural realism (known objects exist independently) that James defended is inconsistent with Berkeley's view in the strong sense, so either James is again inconsistent or I need to revise my description of him as Berkeleyan. Moreover, as Madden proves, the Berkeleyan interpretation does seem to run afoul of James's own denials of Berkeleyan doctrine.

Briefly put, my reasoning started from the fact that James's radical empiricism (as had his psychology earlier, I believe) insisted on the truth of Berkeley's *esse est percipi.*[9] Our sensations *are* the things themselves, he wrote explicitly, the content of the physical is none other than the psychical, thus suggesting a leaning towards panpsychism. For me, *this* was a strong sense of Berkeley's view, since it left James with the horrendous problem of explaining how this is possible and how a world of sensations can exist independently of being experienced, as his natural realism requires. Besides, one had to account for James's seeming misreading of Berkeley in claiming that the latter's position prohibits two of us from ever perceiving the same object. James certainly knew that Berkeley disavowed any such prohibition, yet no explanation is given for his ignoring Berkeley's insistence that we do indeed perceive a common world because the knowing mind upon which objects-as-sensations depend is, luckily, God's and not ours. I called James Berkeleyan because his reality, like Berkeley's, comes down to sensations (and sometimes also concepts but those that are said to be of the "same stuff" as sensations), and his only difference with Berkeley (other than attributing to him a view that Berkeley had always vehemently denied) would seem to be a difference in explaining how sensations can exist on their own.

In fact, James never explained this satisfactorily, even to himself, but so long as he made the effort he remained officially consistent with his theory of natural realism. Yet one is left wondering why, when he was so close to Berkeley's view, James spoke against it and as he did. That was the enigma. If his objection was simply that Berkeley's God was an intolerable *deus ex machina*, why not just say so? I felt that there must be more to it, and subsequently an interpretation occurred that seemed promising. It suggests that James objected to Berkeley's failure, in one sense, to go far enough in reducing objects to sensations; Berkeley failed to reduce the "entitative" character of physical objects, as commonsense conceives them, to *unboundaried* complexes of sensations. The effect of this failure is to introduce a metaphysical "discontinuity" between things, of the sort that James's metaphysics of radical and pluralistic empiricism always sought to repair. This interpretation, suitably developed, may elicit the significance of James's various statements on Berkeley. A fuller formulation can be found in my book's chapter 11 "Reality" (pp. 319-24).

This kind of inquiry, I should add, is atypical of the book's approach. The book mostly concentrates on Jamesian texts to the exclusion of historical influences, which, if included, would have demanded another volume or two. Locating James's relation to historical themes and thinkers is a scholarly challenge that I hope my own efforts, while meager in this regard, will nevertheless help to stimulate.

Doing philosophy historically is often rewarding by putting one on the track of a special concept. In my case, it is the notion of introspection, and much of my James book, in its concern with James's psychology and theorizing about consciousness, self, space, time, emotion, memory, and the like, turns on this concept. Now at work on a full-length study of introspection, both historically and currently in both philosophy and psychology, I am profoundly indebted to James for having this project to pursue.

I am of course deeply indebted to Edward Madden for his sensitive, penetrating, and corrective review. I appreciate the gentle touch of his critique, but I also appreciate his fondness and respect for William James, which plainly sustained him through the interpretive labors represented by his critique. Those labors, he can be sure, are permanent contributions to my dialogue with James, and they are clearly essential for anyone's assessment of that dialogue as found in my book.

NOTES

1. See Gerald Myers, *William James; His Life* and *Thought* (New Haven and London: Yale University Press, 1986), pp. 341-42.

2. See Morton White's review article of my book on James, "Good in the Way of Belief," *The New Republic* 195 (1986): 25-30.

3. Edward H. Madden and Marian C. Madden, "The Psychosomatic Illnesses of William James," *Thought* 54, no. 215 (1979): 376-92.

4. Abraham Edel, "Notes on the Search for a Moral Philosophy in William James" in *The Philosophy of William James,* ed. Walter Robert Corti (Hamburg: Felix Meiner Vorlag, 1976), p. 253.

5. "The Moral Philosopher and the Moral Life," in *The Will to Believe* (Cambridge: Harvard University Press, 1979), p. 158.

6. James, oc. cit.

7. White, "Good in the Way of Belief," pp. 376-92; and see White, *Science and Sentiment in America* (New York: Oxford University Press, 1972), pp. 204-13.

8. William James, *Some Problems of Philosophy* (New York: Longmans, Green & Co., 1911), p. 106.

9. See Myers, *William James,* p. 320.

Historical Philosophy in Search of "Frames of Articulation"

Frithjof Rodi

When H.-G. Gadamer sought to delineate the philosophical dimension of the history of concepts (*Begriffsgeschichte*), he emphasized the fact that philosophy, in its endeavor to create new expressions, often experiences what he called "*Sprachnot*" (being in need of language). "Anyone who thinks philosophically is dissatisfied with the existing possibilities of verbal expression, and he shares in thinking only when he also shares this being in need of language as it is experienced by everyone who dares to express his thought through concepts which still have to prove their own strength."[1] That philosophizing means thinking in a state of *Sprachnot* has to do with the fact that everyday langauge, through which we express our ordinary life relations, provides no means to express the stages of calling these relations themselves into question. Also vis-à-vis the language of philosophical texts we always have to take into account the inadequacy of verbal expression to philosophical thought. Sharing the thoughts of the tradition can also mean sharing that *Sprachnot* that came to expression in the text we are trying to understand.[2]

It is in this connection that the history of concepts (*Begriffsgeschichte*) has an important role to play. The title of Gadamer's essay "Begriffs-geschichte als Philosophie" ("History of Concepts as Philosophy") expresses the conviction that it is not with a purely historical interest that we see a philosophical term over against its historical background. On the contrary, the history of concepts endeavors to regenerate the tension of thought that can be felt in the fissures of philosophical language where the *Anstrengung des Begriffs* develops a kind of "dislocating" force. Taken in this sense, the history of concepts has to follow a movement of thought "which always tends to transcend the limits of familiar words and strives to dislocate their original meaning." Therefore the relationship between the words of everyday language and philosophical terminology is of particular interest here. By metaphors such as "dislocation" or "fissures of philosophical language" Gadamer points to the region where shifts from the everyday to unusual use of language take place, and these fissures or turning points have to be marked by the history of concepts. Its task of seeing the philosophical term against its historical background includes finding its roots within the potentialities of living speech.[3]

If we slightly change the perspective by which Gadamer visualizes these phenomena, it is possible to replace the word *Sprachnot* (being in need of language) by the term "articulative tension." This change of perspective consists of a stronger emphasis on the historical "systems of influences" (*Wirkungszusammenhänge*) that generate the necessities or tendencies to coin new philosophical terms or to modify existing terminology. Taken generally, this kind of articulative tension is by no means restricted to philosophy. The urge to go beyond existing verbal or nonverbal means of expression in order to make newly seen phenomena visible might be called the most universal law of creativity. When we disregard some non-Western civilizations whose cultural traditions seem to be more static than dynamic, the implications of our concept of culture already point to this law of creativity. Cultural achievements are stages rather than terminals. Whatever the motivating factors may be, they result in a continual pressure for innovation.

Naturally, we have to distinguish between the kind of innovation pressure generated by extrinsic factors, such as boredom, vanity, and, above all, commercial interests and the intrinsic articulative tension that, independently of external motives, leads to modifications and reformulations of past achievements. Thus our concept of "avant garde" presupposes the notion that movements, developments, and trends within society can be anticipated and advanced by a few, and that these anticipations follow the articulative tensions inherent in certain areas of cultural life.

In philosophy, too, articulative tension creates ever-renewed dialogues, discussions, even confrontations with tradition. I am not referring to the high level of great scientific revolutions where changes of paradigms and the origin of new theories together with scientific research introduce new epochs of intellectual history. I am rather interested in the lower level of innovative achievements to which the term "articulation" can be applied in a more appropriate way. As Gadamer has pointed out, philosophical terminology, like language in general, is always in some sense "pre-judicial" as it prejudges subsequent concepts and questions. It has to be reconsidered again and again—"broken up," as it were, by critical reflection. Articulative tension in philosophy therefore means in the first place that questions have to be put in new ways, as problems appear within new horizons and require new concepts and verbalizations. Or we encounter new elements of everyday language such as metaphors, intracultural allusions, and analogies, etc., that exercise some influence on philosophical language. Furthermore philosophy is continually challenged by scientific innovations and takes over new concepts (as is illustrated by the career of the term "structure"). In many such cases articulative tension does not yet mean that a problem has to be reformulated explicitly or a theory reconsidered. There are cases where a new concept leads to a gradual restructuring of a semantic field within a theoretical context that as a whole is not overtly affected.

To give one example: the reader of Max Scheler's book *Der Formalismus in der Ethik und die materiale Wertethik* can follow up the gradual replacement of the term "milieu" by the term *"Umwelt,"* which was then coming into parlance. Scheler seems to treat the two terms as synonyms, not realizing that a whole set of connotations in each tends in different directions and therefore affects the theoretical context from below, so to speak.

Finally, articulative tension is also at work where complex phenomena are being discussed within a broad interdisciplinary field on the basis of undefined terms. This can be illustrated by the discussion of "postmodernism" that has been going on for years more or less outside philosophy but has finally become a major topic of philosophy, too. The vagueness of the term "postmodern" is largely due to the fact that the range of meaning implied by the word "modern" creates a kind of complexity that remains, so to speak, behind the speaker's back. When we apply Eugen Fink's[4] distinction between "operative" and "thematic" concepts, we find that the word "modern," with all its implications, is an "operative" concept, i.e., its use as a term is a prerequisite to making something else "thematic." Operative concepts are normally not defined. They are used as tools or as a basis on which a thematization can take place. In the case of "postmodern" the thematic function of the term as a whole is overshadowed by the operative component "modern."

Such "operative overshadowing" (*Operative Verschattung*) plays an important role in the process of philosophical articulation. Eugen Fink has shown that in Husserl's writings, even fundamental concepts such as "phenomenon," "epoché," "Leistung," etc., that one would have expected to be fully thematic, remain within the operative "shadow," i.e., they are the means of reflection, rather than its object. According to Fink even the great philosophers are prone to a certain "operative bias." Of course this applies to a much greater extent to a situation where an interdisciplinary discussion has to deal with undefined terms and concepts. Anyone who has tried to come to grips with the basic concepts of the postmodernism debate might have felt the articulative tension inherent in these discussions.

We have now to ask what the discussion of the problem of articulative tension can contribute to a theory of historical philosophy. So far we have seen that one particular section of history of philosophy, namely, the history of concepts, is given the task of following up the movement of thought, which results in a productive "need of language" that we call articulative tension. The history of concepts—taken as genuine philosophy and not just as history—has to reestablish the tension inherent in certain situations or stages of intellectual history. This leads us on to a second task of historical philosophy: articulative tension does not take place in empty space. It requires a *frame of conditions,* such as a concrete historical situation with inherent tendencies. We call this a *frame of articulation.*

FRAMES OF ARTICULATION

In a paper dealing with the functions of the history of philosophy Hans Krämer has studied the relationship between the formative processes of a philosophical theory and the philosophical positions.[5] He makes a distinction between the *phases* through which a theory unfolds on the basis of traditional elements, on the one hand, and the *functions* of the historical orientation of philosophy on the other. In both cases there is a direct bearing on the problems I discuss in this paper. First, it is of interest to see how Krämer singles out a special *phase* within the development of a theory (the second phase of five phases in all). In this phase the philosopher articulates his basic ideas at the level of existing systems or theories (normally those of his contemporaries). He adopts their concepts and categories, as can be illustrated by Plato's involvement in the Sophistic discussions of politics and ethics; by hellenistic philosophy's use of early issues of Socratic ethics in dealing with problems of security and autarky; by Plotinus's articulation of the problem of the individual soul with the help of concepts taken from Platonism, etc., etc.

After discussing the *phases* within the development of philosophical theories where the historical orientation plays an important role, Krämer turns to the *functions* of historical philosophy. He singles out a direct equivalent to the second phase just mentioned. Here, historical orientation within the process of systematic philosophy can function as "the hermeneutic assimilation of tradition in view of an already existing or emerging position." The term "assimilation" is of particular importance as it involves the fact that tradition here is not the stable and unchanging basis for our philosophical adventure, but something that has to be transformed and incorporated within our own thought (as Nietzsche has shown in his second "Unzeitgemaesse Betrachtung"). Krämer distinguishes between various forms of such an assimilation that take place through interpretations. There is, for example, the seemingly orthodox exegesis of a major philosopher within his own school of thought. Krämer calls it "seemingly" orthodox because what happens in many cases is an articulation of the interpreter's own systematic ideas, and the results of his interpretrations could be called "pseudomorphosis of unacknowledged systematic intentions." This phase of seemingly objective treatment of tradition can also be called the "incubation-period" of a systematic position that later on becomes explicit, as famous examples of first books (from Marx to Nietzsche and Heidegger) show. Krämer adds: "This transitional stage of exegesis has so to speak a mëeutic[6] function for the self-discovery of the systematic philosopher" (p. 71).

Krämer's considerations are not directly applicable to our problem of articulative tension, as they deal in the first instance with the relationship between systematic philosophy and assimilated tradition. There is, however, good reason to presume that every hermeneutic assimilation of tradition takes place under certain conditions that can be interpreted as tension within a certain frame of articulation. As we have seen, tradition is not something like a ladder on whose topmost rung we stand in order to add, through our own thinking, a further position for someone else to stand upon in turn. On the other hand, tradition is not (or should not be) merely an object for our historical research guided by whatever interest or curiosity we happen to have. In both cases we would lack the twofold relationship with tradition through which productive tension is created: the ambivalent relation of being supported and hindered at the same time. Tradition gives our thinking support and stands in its way. It supports us by providing the conceptual basis for our own thought, by giving answers that enable us to put new questions, by yielding horizons for our orientation.[7] It hinders us by the fixation of certain questions and the conclusive character of their answers. It narrows our outlook by the one-sidedness of its concepts, by its interests and tendencies that are not congruent with our own motives. Taken in this sense of ambivalence, tradition is both a challenge to our own thinking and the channel for our response. It is part of our historical situation, a kind of frame within which we move about and to which we belong in various ways.

There are two forms of belonging to tradition where the ambivalent relationship is reduced to a one-sided dependency. I call them the "pastiche involontaire" and the "jurare in verba magistri" attitude. By "pastiche involontaire" I mean the involuntary imitation of a classic by an epigonous descendant. Within certain limits this dependency belongs to the most natural traits of any cultural continuity. Just as the young Beethoven composed à la Mozart, as Raphael started off by painting à la Perugino, as the young Marx wrote like Hegel, the young Nietzsche like Schopenhauer, every achievement, however original it may be, needs some historical basis as a starting point or a mark of orientation. The pastiche involontaire when restricted to an initial stage of productive activity denotes the "incubation-period" on a very elementary level.

The second form of a one-sided dependency I call the "*jurare in verba magistri*" attitude. Here the work of the great master is not imitated but fully accepted as the only true philosophy that is fostered within the inner circle of believers or with missionary zeal. H.-M. Sass distinguishes two functions of such a close relationship with the classical author: the historical interest either serves the purpose of making the classic even more classical by didactic mediations; or the orthodox exegesis tries to modernize the author by drawing consequences from his work that he himself could not have drawn for historical reasons.[8]

There is little articulative tension at work in either case; yet even these forms of dependency on historical concepts display various ways of being "framed" by tradition. This is even more visible in cases where historically oriented philosophy is tied up with tradition in the ambivalent way mentioned before. Especially in cases of "hermeneutic assimilation" we can speak of a "frame of articulation" within which this assimilation takes place.

I understand by "frame of articulation" the totality of those conditions that exercise a guiding influence on the processes of philosophical articulation. To be sure, a frame of articulation is not just the operative platform for a new theory that we can derive through the history of concepts from former positions. It is a complex network of influences, orientations, and mediations focused on the development of an individual theory or system. A frame of articulation is more than the mere point of contact with former positions, but less than the complete historical situation. It is a frame in the sense that the philosopher is engulfed by these conditions that he cannot deliberately objectify. They remain in many respects a *vis a tergo* to him, that is to say, they direct influences behind his back which only the later historian can reconstruct. Such a frame is composed of elements of common language as well as technical terms; notions and definitions by individual authors; their integration and interpretation by subsequent philosophers; reflections on such mediations that in turn become new theories and systematic positions; and also determining factors from outside philosophy, such as general issues of the time, political and social trends, cross-cultural relations with literature, arts and sciences, etc., etc.

As already pointed out, the impact of such a frame of conditions on an individual theory in its early phases of articulation remains largely below the surface and cannot be thematized deliberately by the philosopher who is influenced by them. We should not be misled by the fact that philosophers explicitly take up a forerunner's terminology, issues, and solutions. This is the part of their articulation frame of which they are directly aware. But they are normally far from being able to account for the ways in which an articulative tension got hold of them within this frame. Only later historical research can reconstruct such frames. The "hermeneutic assimilation of tradition" especially should not be mixed up with the reconstruction of the frame of conditions under which such an assimilation takes place.

Thus we have to distinguish between two totally different relations with tradition, both of which have to do with frames of articulation. First, there is the productive assimilation of tradition taking place under certain sociohistorical conditions within a frame that cannot be changed arbitrarily. Second, there is the historical reconstruction of such frames of articulation. The philosopher who seeks guidance from tradition cannot investigate his frame of articulation from outside without losing the articulative tension he is depending on. The "purely" historical philosopher, on the other hand, has to put up with this loss. He delivers himself from the articulative tension by investigating its historical conditions.

In this juxtaposition of two ideal types, I am not maintaining that combinations of the two approaches are not possible. On the contrary I consider it a central task of any theory of historical philosophy to delineate possibilities of historical research where the reconstruction of frames of articulation permits us to share the inherent articulative tension. The analysis of a frame of historical conditions could follow the same pattern Gadamer has shown for the reenactment of *Sprachnot*. In this case, however, we could not call this approach a history of concepts. The historical investigation would not "vertically" follow the life of single concepts but rather would "horizontally" analyze the sources of articulative tension prevalent within a certain situation of intellectual history. In order to characterize this approach, I am adopting a term that Wilhelm Dilthey has occasionally used in a purely operative way: the term "synergetic analysis." It was a way of describing his approach that he also called "historical research with philosophical intentions."

SYNERGETIC ANALYSIS OF FRAMES OF
ARTICULATION: DILTHEY AS EXAMPLE

Dilthey used the word "synergetic analysis" in a marginal note added to a letter he had received from his friend Paul Yorck von Wartenburg. His student Georg Misch took up the term, giving it a certain prominence in his book *Lebensphilosophie und Phänomenologie.*[9] Misch himself preferred the term "structural analysis," by which he meant the procedure of the human sciences for demonstrating how the "working together" (synergy) of heterogeneous elements make up a new, meaningful unity. In such an analysis Misch wanted to show "how the merging of the heterogeneous elements, the impact of alien forces on the subjective *Innerlichkeit* plays a decisive role within historical processes of formation and how even the accidental confrontation can come to be a productive encounter." The historical reconstruction of the frame of conditions for a newly emerging thought is here not satisfied with localizing the determining factors. It tries to share the articulative tension created by the merging of the heterogeneous elements. For this kind of unification means to generate new meaning that is seeking expression and therefore creates new forms of *Sprachnot.*

As an example of such a synergetic analysis, I choose Dilthey's biography of Schleiermacher. To put it in our own terminology: Dilthey here attempted to make visible the wide frame of articulation within which Schleiermacher gradually developed his ideas. Dilthey considered it his task to understand and to show "how quite separate elements of culture, given as general states of affairs, social and moral presuppositions, influences by forerunners and contemporaries are worked up in the workshop of an individual mind and molded into a new, original whole which in turn exerted a creative impact on the life of the community."[10]

Dilthey carried this program through in the first volume of his *Life of Schleiermacher.* He drew lines from various points, leading from all sides to the individual personality and its development: childhood with the Moravian brethren; contact with that branch of the German enlightenment that resulted in a moral and religious *Weltanschauung;* struggling with Kant's philosophy; influence of Shaftesbury and Spinoza; the great experience of the rise of German literature during the eighteenth century from Lessing and Herder to Goethe, Schiller, and the Romantic poets.

Through this broad foundation of his approach Dilthey sought to avoid the Hegelian pattern of history of philosophy that he characterized as a procedure of "letting emerge a new philosopher's position out of the understanding and immanent criticism of a previous standpoint."[11] Over against this approach Dilthey maintains that again and again we find in the history of philosophy a high tension, consisting of both most intensive studies and strongest antipathy between one thinker and his forerunner. This tension is exemplified by the relationship between Aristotle and Plato, Leibniz and Spinoza, Herbart and Kant. Dilthey finds in some of the great philosophers a special attitude toward the world that makes them refuse immediately as something alien the conceptual frame offered by the intellectual achievement of the age. He sees this relationship particularly well illustrated by Schleiermacher's attitude toward Kant and finds that there was "hardly a second case where this relationship is made so transparent."

It is characteristic of Dilthey's anthropological approach grounded on the "totality of human nature" that his method is not to construct chains of intellectual problem solutions but to take into account, too, irrational factors such as moods and purely emotional attitudes toward the world. In his synergetic analysis he emphasizes the role played by the emotional content of the older German enlightenment that Schleiermacher imbibed after having freed himself from pietism. "For him, there always remained something of the affirmative mood of this Weltanschauung which lies in the idea of harmony of the whole universe, of the value of each single individual and the continuity of its development, and this mood intensified the active force of his existence." Out of this mood there arose the power to contradict Kant's moral theory, although Schleiermacher acknowledged the superiority of Kant's critical foundation through most intensive studies and accepted the basic pattern of his system.

In a similarly differentiating way Dilthey analyzed the network of personal relations in which Schleiermacher was entangled through his friendship with Friedrich Schlegel. As parts of his frame of articulation Dilthey took into account not only the peculiarity of Romantic poetry ("A stream of moods, fading away like music in rhythms, rhymes and passing images, formless, orderless, shapes whose law is phantasy in its frolicsome play"), but also the poetical presuppositions of Romantic hermeneutics. "From all sides, poetry and scholarly research were busy to re-experience and re-awaken the innermost life of feelings and imagination of bygone times. Within this circle Schleiermacher consciously developed his method to understand the individuality of a work of literature, and he conceived the idea that imagination was the organ of all understanding and that it is through imagination only that we can grasp individuality."[13]

In a short characterization of his first book Dilthey once mentioned that he had sought "to explain a philosopher by an essential trend of a cultural epoch and through an exact investigation of a series of developmental factors."[14] We should, however, not take these words too literally. Dilthey's approach was more complex than this characterization sounds. He repudiates, for instance, the presupposition that there is a steady handing down of concepts from one philosopher to another; yet he discarded the idea of a merely accidental chain of extrinsic factors for any analysis to investigate. He emphasized the unfathomableness of the nexus that exists between external conditions and the "unconscious, unguarded, secret life of the mind."[15] In this unfathomableness, however, he saw no reason for resignation as a researcher, but rather a challenge to go to the very limits of a historical reconstruction.

I cannot follow up the details of the reconstruction of this frame within which Schleiermacher reached his own philosophical position. Dilthey was aware of the articulative tension inherent in his synergetic analysis. He didn't want just to "bury" Schleiermacher with a kind of biographical state funeral but to gain a reunderstanding of him within his epoch. He went as far as saying that "the continuity of our own intellectual existence depends on the degree by which we are able to combine the achievements of that great epoch with the tasks of our own time and to give them in their lasting results a renewed impact on us." That is why he didn't want just to narrate, but to convince. "It is my intention to make the reader have before his inner eye the image of this great existence, but at the same time visualize the network of lasting ideas as they influence—on the basis of sound research—both the scholarly work and active life of our present time."[16]

We know how intensely Dilthey felt himself tied up with this program. The synergetic analysis of his *Life of Schleiermacher* was for himself the medium within which his own ideas could grow. The main argument of this paper, that historical research in philosophy can share the articulative tension within the frame we reconstruct, is based on the observation of Dilthey's procedure. But we have to ask: in which direction has this shared articulative tension led him?

The answer one should expect is it was Schleiermacher's hermeneutical theory from which Dilthey received his decisive impulse. This answer would not really be sufficient. To be sure, there can be no doubt as to the extent of Dilthey's assimilation of Schleiermacher's hermeneutics, especially through his early prize-winning thesis on this topic. But making him just Schleiermacher's descendant within this scope of scholarly ideas would mean narrowing the frame within which the encounter took place. The relationship entailed the totality of Schleiermacher's existence, rather than a particular aspect of his thinking. This "existential" relationship, as one might call it, is characterized in a short fragment belonging to the bulk of manuscripts of Dilthey's *Introduction to the Human Sciences*. Here Dilthey gives Schleiermacher a special place in the history of modern philosophy because "this full and great personality had an attitude toward abstract concepts and truths which was totally different from any other modern philosopher." By this he means "He didn't leave the totality of his human existence behind as something not to be taken care of, but rather saw his intelligence being deeply involved in it." In this attitude, Dilthey continued, Schleiermacher was only comparable to some poets, to Wilhelm von Humboldt, and to the Historical School.[17]

But Dilthey also did see the negative sides of his intellectual existence, underlining the fact that Schleiermacher hardly ever reached a conclusive stage of his ever-renewed thinking, and that what he saw before him materialized only "through aperçus and bits and pieces." Dilthey tells us that only when his own approach had become clear to himself was he able to make Schleiermacher's position fully transparent to him. "That is why I thought that the reader who hopes to find more than just a biography should in the first place be able to share the standpoint from which I believe to have understood Schleiermacher historically. This is the reason for publishing a book which otherwise would have rested in peace for some more years and would then have appeared in a more elaborate shape."[18]

The book mentioned here is not the biography but nothing less than Dilthey's systematic chef d'oeuvre, the *Introduction to the Human Sciences* whose first volume appeared in 1883. We know that Dilthey, after concluding the first volume of his *Life of Schleiermacher*, got more and more involved in the development of his own systematic ideas. After an interval of thirteen years, during which he had published only two essays of some systematic relevance besides hundreds of reviews, he decided to publish the first volume of the *Introduction* before completing the biography. The reason he gave in the Preface was that with continued work on Schleiermacher he would everywhere have to presuppose last questions of philosophy with which he didn't want to overburden the biography. This the more so as some critics had already reproached Dilthey for having written a philosophical rather than a biographical study.

It is a well-known fact that in the end the huge project of the *Introduction* was in turn never completed during Dilthey's lifetime and therefore stood in the way of the book on Schleiermacher for the rest of Dilthey's life. It thus gives us an example, perhaps unique in the history of philosophy, where the articulative tension shared through historical investigations exercises not only an enhancing influence, but also at the same time impedes the further analysis since it carries away, so to speak, the historian as a philosopher. For when Dilthey sought to reconstruct the frame of conditions under which Schleiermacher had developed his ideas, he made this reconstruction the frame of articulation for his own thought.

[Translated by K. L. Heiges]

NOTES

1. H.-G. *Gadamer*: Begriffsgeschichte als Philosophie. In: Kleine Schriften III. Tübingen 1972, p. 245.

2. H.-G. *Gadamer*: Die Begriffsgeschichte und die Sprache der Philosophie. In: Kleine Schriften IV. Tübingen 1977, p. 7ff.

3. Cf. Gadamer, Kl. Schr. III, p. 248f.

4. E. *Fink*: Operative Begriffe in Husserls Phänomenologie. In: Nähe und Distanz. Phänomenologische Vorträge und Aufsätze. Freiburg/München 1976, p. 180 ff.

5. H. *Krämer*: Funktions- und Reflexionsmöglichkeiten der Philosophie-historie. Vorschläge zu ihrer wissenschaftstheoretischen Ortsbestimmung. In: Zeitschrift für allgemeine Wissenschaftstheorie XVI/1 (1985), p. 67ff.

6. "Mëeutic": Greek word for obstetric (Socrates, son of a midwife, called his philosophizing mëeutic).

7. Cf. R. A. *Makkreel*: Tradition and Orientation in Hermeneutics. In: Research in Phenomenology, XVI (1986), p. 73 ff.

8. H.-M. *Sass*: Philosophische Positionen in der Philosophiegeschichtssch-

reibung. In: Deutsche Vierteljahresschrift f. Literaturwissenschaft und Geistesgeschichte Jg. 46 (1972) H 3. p. 552.

9. *G. Misch*: Lebensphilosophie und Phänomenologie. Eine Auseinandersetzung der Dilthey'schen Richtung mit Heidegger und Husserl. Darmstadt 1967, pp. 65, 95, 142. — Cf. *F. Rodi*: Morphologie und Hermeneutik. Zur Methode von Diltheys Aesthetik. Stuttgart 1969, p. 109 ff.

10. *W. Dilthey*: Gesammelte Schriften, vol. XIII/1, p. xxxiii.

11. Dilthey, p. 133.

12. Dilthey, p. 157.

13. Dilthey, p. 284 f.

14. *Cl. Misch (ed.)*: Der junge Dilthey. Ein Lebensbild in Briefen und Tagebüchern 1852–1870. Stuttgart/Göttingen (Teubner/Vandenhoeck & Ruprecht) 1960, p. 286.

15. Dilthey, p. 166.

16. Dilthey, p. xxxv f.

17. Dilthey, Ges. Schr. vol. XIV, p. 32.

18. Ibid.

Assimilation and Reconstruction in Historical Philosophy

A Skeptical View

Rudolf Lüthe

SKEPTICISM WITH REGARD TO HISTORICAL PHILOSOPHY

After more than two thousand years philosophy is still pondering the same questions as those that first gave birth to it—to the extent that it does not seem to be able or even interested in solving these problems. Still, as far as I can see, philosophers seem to think that what they do is trying to solve them. This is indeed somewhat peculiar. In order to understand what is going on here one can try to answer the question: "What does it mean to do philosophy historically?" In order to answer this question we will first have to come to a conception of the sort of problems that philosophers deal with.

I propose to say that philosophy deals with questions of the sort formulated by the German philosopher Immanuel Kant: "What can I know? What am I to do? What may I hope for?"

In the history of philosophy we find these questions and a large number of variations on them—and also a lot of different answers. Very often the answers contradict each other.

What, then, can we learn by doing philosophy historically? Here a special sort of skepticism can be of help in sharpening our ideas. The skeptic asks: Why do you waste your time with a history of philosophers contradicting one another instead of solving your own problems quite independently of what others have thought? We might answer this question by quoting Rodi's assertion that in philosophy we have to find a language that adequately expresses our problems and solutions, and that we can only find this language by doing philosophy historically, that is to say, in a process of articulation inaugurated by critically discussing the ideas of our ancestors. Philosophical questions, according to Rodi, are of such a kind that language does not easily express them adequately. Therefore, philosophy is always occupied with looking for its own language (*Sprachfindung*). It is always *in need* of such a language (*Sprachnot*), as Gadamer puts it.

The significance of historical philosophy on this view lies in the capacity of our conversation with the past to satisfy our need for a special philosophical language—a language we need to solve our own problems.

In order to clarify the ideas on which this conception of historical philosophy is founded, I direct against it another skeptical question. The skeptic now asks: How do you know that such a "conversation with the past" is possible at all? He gives a reason for doubting that it is, namely, the philosophy of the past is "radically different from present-day philosophy."[1] Therefore, we have to face the dangers that either (1) we do not really understand past philosophy, or (2) understanding it will not help us very much in coping with our problems because it is so different from our own philosophy. The skeptic here argues with the concept of the radically new. Indeed, there seems to be a fatal dilemma for historical philosophy: we have to treat our ancestors either "as if they were contemporaries,"[2] or we unwittingly turn them into "museum pieces."[3]

This is a dilemma, because none of the alternatives is convincing. If we treat the dead philosophers (and their writings) as museum pieces, then we are doing history, not philosophy; if, however, we treat them as our contemporaries, we seem to commit a scholarly sin: we misrepresent the ideas of our ancestors in our own thought by "minimizing or ignoring . . . that which refuses such transmutation."[4] The gap opened by the notion of the radically new does not allow us to treat Aristotle, Hume, Kant, and Hegel as our contemporaries.

It is obvious that Rodi's conception of historical philosophy implies a conflict with such a skeptical position. I will, therefore, try to disarm this sort of skeptic with arguments that I can take from Rodi's paper. My general aim in doing this is the attempt to refute the application of the idea of the radically new to the history of philosophy, i.e., the establishing of the idea that there is no *radical* difference between past and present philosophy. If I succeed, then it would follow that we are allowed to treat our ancestors as contemporaries, that we can understand them at least to such an extent that they may help us cope with our own problems. They do this (among other ways) by providing us with the language that we need: the frames of articulation, as Rodi puts it.

FAMILY RESEMBLANCES WITHIN THE HISTORY OF PHILOSOPHY

"The sun shone, having no alternative, on the nothing new." I want to apply this first sentence of Samuel Beckett's novel *Murphy* to the problem of doing philosophy historically. I shall take Beckett's line as a frame of my own articulation. The question I want to answer is how it is possible to explain a fact that Ian Hacking describes in his contribution to *Philosophy in History*. Talking about his students, he writes: "Descartes speaks directly to these young people. . . . The value of Descartes to these students is completely anachronistic, out of time. Half of them will have begun with the idea Descartes and Sartre were contemporaries, both being French. Descartes, even more than Sartre, can speak directly to them across the seas of time. Historicism, even Rorty's, forgets that."[5] I doubt that Rorty forgot this, but I think that the above-mentioned skeptic did. Here, then, seems to be a chance of refuting this kind of skepticism.

In Rodi's terms the intellectual situation of Hacking's students may be reconstructed in the following way. They feel a specific "pressure towards articulation," i.e., their minds are filled with definite questions and a rather vague but directed tendency toward a certain kind of answer to them.

Reading Descartes, the students find that he provides this tendency with a special *frame* consisting of terms, concepts, questions, and arguments—a language in which they are able to articulate adequate solutions to their own problems.

It is not necessary for them to reconstruct the frame and the pressure that determined Descartes's own philosophical thinking; all they need for a *productive assimilation* of Descartes's philosophy is a sort of intuitive insight into the "family resemblances" between the language game that *they* play, and the one that Descartes played some centuries ago.

I think this is a convincing description of a productive assimilation of the philosophical past. It is, therefore, also an explanation of what happened in Hacking's philosophy class, but it is not a conclusive argument against the historical skeptic whom I introduced as a counter to both Hacking and Rodi. The skeptic's question is still valid: How do we know that Hacking's students are *right* in supposing there is such a family likeness between their thought and that of Descartes? They might be misrepresenting his philosophy *fundamentally*, getting it *completely* wrong. In order to solve this problem we have to introduce a difference that is also to be found in Rodi's paper.

Rodi's concept of historical philosophy as providing the philosopher with a frame of articulation is a theory of the *subjective* use we can make of our ancestors and their ideas. In a way, it may be regarded as an explanation of what it means to treat Descartes as a contemporary. But a satisfying answer to the skeptic requires a second step, a step toward a *justification* of this subjective use we make of history. Now, I think that a theory of this sort would have to give a reason why there *must* be some kind of family likeness between all the philosophical theories of our tradition, however young they might be. It is exactly in this sense that Descartes's value to the students can be "completely anachronistic," or "out of time." Certainly all family resemblance is quite different from any sort of identity. We have to establish the *degree* of resemblance between Descartes and the students as far as their respective philosophies are concerned. Obviously, we ourselves can establish this only when we compare *our* specific interpretations of these two respective philosophies; and, influenced by the skeptic now, *we* are led to doubting whether we could ever be sure of the degree of resemblance between our own reconstructions and the philosophies reconstructed.

I think I need not go on in this line in order to make clear why I find it hard to articulate a conclusive argument against this kind of skepticism. All we can say is that our experience in doing philosophy historically seems to show evidence of some productive assimilation— and that this gives us a reason for believing in family resemblances among the different kinds of philosophy done in our tradition. An argument of this sort, by way of "productive assimilation," cannot prove that such resemblances across time really do exist, that the notion of the radically new is less ferocious than we think. We simply *feel* that Beckett's sentence gets at some kind of truth about historical philosophy: we think, having no alternative, on the nothing new.

"Doing philosophy historically" might however mean something quite different from the productive assimilation of old ideas in our present work. It might refer to the attempt to understand the old ideas themselves and for their own sake, to reconstruct objectively a philosophy of the past. In Rodi's terms this reconstruction could have as its objects both the pressure and the frame that determined the process of articulation that led to the philosophy to be reconstructed.

Even this objective sort of historical philosophy has to include a reflection on the historical presuppositions of its *own* acts of reconstruction, i.e., a reflection on the pressure and frame of articulation that shapes the reconstructions in question. Still it does not aim at a merely subjective *productive assimilation*, but at an *objective reconstruction* of the past. Rodi's example of Dilthey's treatment of Schleiermacher shows how such an objective reconstruction might work. I doubt that our skeptic would be satisfied with this account.

The skeptic has bothered us enough, however. I am going to shoo him off with a sentence taken from Hume's first *Enquiry*: Your arguments "*admit of no answer and produce no conviction.*"[6]

In the same way that Hacking's students are *sure* that there is a family likeness between their thought and that of Descartes, so Rodi's Dilthey can be sure that *his* reconstruction of Schleiermacher's philosophy is objective. Both productive assimilation and objective reconstruction enjoy the same intuitive security. Obviously, this intuitive security is enough to keep both kinds of historical philosophy alive. They are indeed still going strong.

PRODUCTIVE VERSUS HISTORICAL PHILOSOPHY

There is a final opportunity for the skeptic to annoy us: the mere existence of the two kinds of historical philosophy may be turned into a skeptical argument against the right to exist of either. The idea here is the following. Productive assimilation without objective reconstruction, we might say, is *empty* (we do not have in our hands what we wanted to have). Objective reconstruction without productive assimilation is *blind* (it does not help us *do* philosophy). Historical philosophy, we might suppose, must be an integration of both in order to become a justifiable intellectual enterprise, and such an integration, the skeptic tells us, cannot be achieved. There are a number of things that can be said to this even leaving aside the healthy reaction we get from Hume that the argument "produces no conviction." For example, it is surely clear that productive assimilation of the richest sort can be achieved even on the basis of a misunderstanding of ideas of the past. We do not, in such circumstances, have in our hands what we think we have, but our hands are far from being empty.

It is also obvious that an objective reconstruction of past theories can even be achieved by someone who harbors no goal of "assimilating" them in his own work, perhaps because he thinks they are false. He is not blind at all. On the contrary, he has means of finding his way around one of the most rugged intellectual terrains that there is—the terrain of philosophy, in its development from Thales to the present day.

NOTES

1. Alasdair MacIntyre, "The Relationship of Philosophy to Its Past," *Philosophy in History,* ed. by R. Rorty, J. B. Schneewind, Q. Skinner (Cambridge: Cambridge University Press, 1984), p. 31.

2. Charles Taylor, "Philosophy and Its History," *Philosophy in History,* p. 17.

3. Alasdair MacIntyre, *op. cit.,* p. 31.

4. Ibid., p. 31.

5. Ian Hacking, "Five Parables," *Philosophy in History,* p. 106.

6. David Hume, *Enquiries concerning Human Understanding and concerning the Principles of Morals,* ed. by L. A. Selby-Bigge, 3d ed. (Oxford: Clarendon Press, 1975), p. 155, n.1.

Index